Being and Becoming Indian

Biographical Studies of North American Frontiers

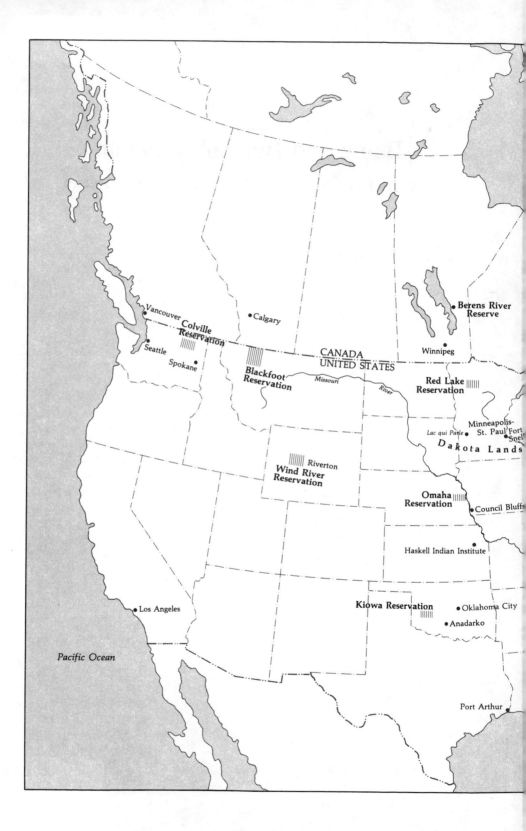

Vancouver

Colville
Reservation

Calgary

Berens River
Reserve

Seattle

Winnipeg

Spokane

CANADA
UNITED STATES

Blackfoot
Reservation

Missouri

River

Red Lake
Reservation

Minneapolis-
St. Paul Fort
Snel

Lac qui Parle

D a k o t a   L a n d s

Riverton

Wind River
Reservation

Omaha
Reservation

Council Bluffs

Haskell Indian Institute

Los Angeles

Kiowa Reservation

Oklahoma City

Anadarko

Pacific Ocean

Port Arthur

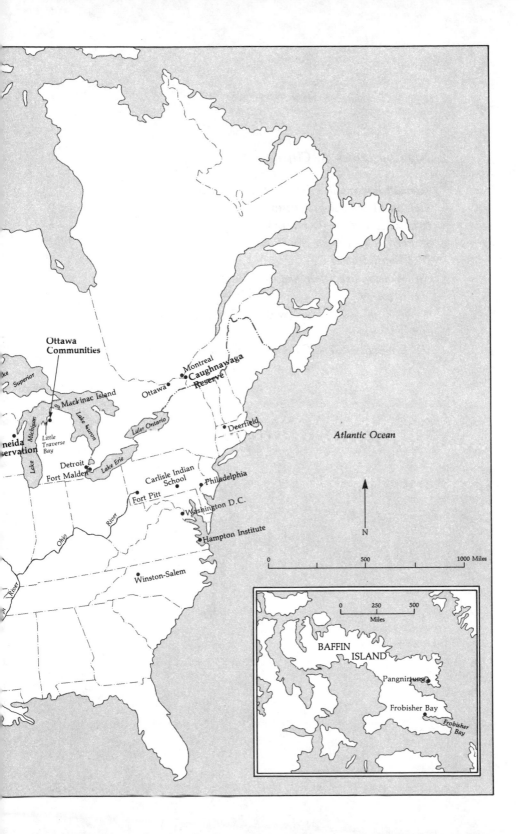

Ottawa
Communities

Montreal
Caughnawaga
Reserve

Ottawa

Mackinac Island

Lake Superior

Lake Michigan

Lake Huron

Lake Ontario

Lake Erie

Little
Traverse
Bay

neida
servation

Detroit
Fort Malden

Deerfield

Atlantic Ocean

Carlisle Indian
School

Philadelphia

Fort Pitt

Washington D.C.

Ohio River

Hampton Institute

N

Winston-Salem

River

0   500   1000 Miles

BAFFIN
ISLAND

0   250   500
Miles

Pangnirtung

Frobisher Bay

Frobisher
Bay

Also by James A. Clifton

Klamath Personalities (with David Levine)
Cultural Anthropology (editor)
Applied Anthropology (editor)
A Place of Refuge For All Time
The Prairie People
Star Woman and Other Shawnee Tales
The Pokagons
People of the Three Fires (with G. L. Cornell & J. M. McClurken)
The Potawatomi
The Invented Indian: Cultural Fictions and Government Policies

Being and Becoming Indian
Biographical Studies of
North American Frontiers

Edited by
James A. Clifton
Western Michigan University

WAVELAND

PRESS, INC.

Prospect Heights, Illinois

For information about this book, write or call:

Waveland Press, Inc.
P.O. Box 400
Prospect Heights, Illinois 60070
(708) 634-0081

To Homer G. Barnett
(1906–1985)
An Anthropologist Who Never
Lost Sight of the Individual

Preface

Several summers ago, in the space of a single week, two young historians contacted me about their current research efforts. Both essentially asked the same question: "Do you know anyone else working on individuals like this?" The "like this" expression referred to individuals whom some years earlier I had characterized as culturally marginal in essays about one such frontier personality, Captain Billy Caldwell. Knowing of my attempts to interpret the significance of the careers of Caldwell and others like him, the two historians had turned to me, seeking intellectual company and, perhaps, stimulation.

In turn, these unexpected queries excited me; they provided the first impetus for this book, for it occurred to me that if there were three of us asking the same kinds of questions there might be more. A few weeks of letter writing and telephone calls confirmed this hunch. Soon, I had identified more than forty anthropologists and historians who had collected information about many culturally marginal personages, mainly historical figures but some contemporary, in both Canada and the United States. Moreover, I doubt that I have exhausted the list of scholars interested in such individuals. However, the strong interest displayed by many persons I contacted in joining forces to publish the results of their studies gave an additional push, and the design of this book emerged.

Although, on the surface, the essays in this book explicitly concern the lives and experiences of fourteen individuals, our interests and aims are different and broader. In this book, we use biography not as an end in itself but as a method. Our aim is to improve and to intensify understanding of a variety of social and cultural processes, significant phenomena in the long history of changing relationships between the diverse peoples of North America, both long-time residents and more recent immigrants. Using biography as a magnifying glass, peering closely at the experiences of particular individuals, we aim at revealing more texture and intricacy than what emerges from other types of anthropological and historical studies, and at generating some new insights.

To accomplish this purpose, we have viewed the lives of our subjects in fresh ways. The uncritical use of standard American rubrics such as "Indian," "white," and"mixed blood," for instance, does not serve our purposes. These words are no more than everyday English language idioms, the conventional labels for American and Canadian ideas about social races, not the technical concepts of the social sciences. Indeed, such words and the associated culturally specific thinking are part of the phenomena we are examining. How was it that North Americans came to believe that a biologically and culturally intermixed population numbering in the hundreds of millions could be neatly divided into such arbitrary categories as White, Red, and Black people? When and how did labels such as Half-Breed and Mixed Blood, standing for interstitial individuals and groups, get invented? And why, in recent years, have such intervening categorizations fallen out of favor, so that today an individual with one great-great-great-great-great grandparent identified as a member of some native tribe may claim an Indian identity and be unquestioningly accepted as such?

The phenomena revealed in the lives of our fourteen subjects are of several different types, but they are related to one another. To approach a fuller appreciation of their experiences, we start with the notions expressed in the title of this book. These essays are about the experience of being and becoming Indian on different cultural frontiers, in various periods. To be precise, a particular essay may be about the experience of being a Salish woman in the early years of the twentieth century, one who struggled to carve out a special expressive niche for herself as an author writing in English; or about an eighteenth century Anglo-Mohawk lad who wanted to be accepted as a Congregational minister in a Massachusetts pulpit, but when rebuffed turned to several other professional and ethnic identities; or about an eighteenth century Pennsylvania Irish-American who, taken captive, for years lived as a Shawnee before assuming an occupational role as an interpreter and diplomatic intermediary.

Cultural, ethnic, and personal identity form the central core of these essays. We can see in the lives of our subjects many of the processes and consequences of a great social transformation that occurred in the recent history of North America. Out of the increasing contacts of persons with European and African ancestry with persons of native American heritage on the same continent, what was once a landscape inhabited by many politically independent, culturally distinctive peoples became two nation-states, the United States and Canada. As this social-political transformation proceeded, the surviving identity groups were incorporated into a few, larger, all-encompassing social systems divided vertically into ethnic groups. The lives of our subjects illustrate some of the specific ways in which this great transformation came about.

Of the technical ideas used by social scientists to analyze the details of such developments, we use and stress but a few. Two of these, as suggested, are ethnic group and ethnic identity, whether social or personal. As readers will discover, some of our subjects adopted two or more such identities, either in sequence over their lives or at one time, according to what context they were in at the moment. The notion of biculturism often applies to such personalities, meaning that they had somehow acquired the knowledge and skills needed to exist in several distinct cultural settings. Similarly, social and ethnic mobility are ideas needed to ask about the efforts of some persons to move from one ethnic identity to another. For people to make such moves successfully, they had to experience considerable reeducation or resocialization, but they also had to contend with ethnic boundaries, whether defined restrictively or openly. The element of personal choice, of making decisions about what part the person would play, about which identity might be assumed, in addition, is evident in nearly all lives depicted in these essays, as are several types of constraints hampering such choices and ethnic mobility.

Our readers should understand that, with a few exceptions, not all authors of these essays intentionally collected information on their subjects with the thought of writing biographic studies about them. For the most part, these scholars came across information about their subjects when engaged in other research tasks, while as Robert J. Stahl will explain, one individual literally walked in his door to begin an encounter that called forth the anthropologist's skills to achieve understanding. In this sense, most of the essays are by-products of other scholarly activities. Nonetheless, during their research-for-other-purposes, each author became fascinated with the subject whose life is described in these pages.

Similarly, readers must appreciate that the authors of the essays do not speak with the same voice. Their approaches to converting the raw materials of their observations into meaningful exposition are different. Saying that the main distinction lies in the different styles of the historian and the anthropologist, between essays that depend on written documents salvaged from the past against writings from personal observation of living persons, however, is too simple. In the first place, most of the authors are involved in an interdisciplinary enterprise called *ethnohistory*, where anthropologists, historians, and representatives of other disciplines embrace a common scholarly enterprise, combining the perspectives of several fields to create improved knowledge of the past and the present. Indeed, this book represents an interdisciplinary, ethnohistorical enterprise.

The authors, like their subjects, have all experienced some professional identity transformation during their careers. Gary C. Anderson, for example, trained and experienced as a historian, is as knowledgeable of the workings of the Dakota ethos and kinship system as any experienced anthropologist, while Jennifer S. H. Brown, trained as an anthropologist, is employed as a professor of history.

Furthermore, broad contrasts between the styles of history and anthropology tend to be stereotypic. In truth, there are many styles in both subjects. In this book, for instance, while one trained anthropologist, Professor Brown, spends most of her time applying the ideas of social anthropology to historical questions, another, Mary Black-Rogers, works in an essentially ahistorical frame. Her manner of understanding her subject is that of a sociolinguist, closely analyzing an individual's verbalizations and behaviors as revealing texts and performances. On the other hand, Ann McElroy's methods of research are psychological and ethnographic. That the authors speak with different voices, instead of being a handicap, is an advantage. To the degree that their interpretations and conclusions converge, we are better assured that their ideas are meritorious and valid, not just the repetitions of a dozen scholars narrowly trained to think alike.

Nevertheless, when more than a dozen scholars approach particular issues from many vantage points, there is always some danger of producing babel. As the elder member of the crew, and as editor, I have tried to reduce the discordant noise produced, for instance, when several different scholars use different names for the same idea, or the same type of phenomena. Thus, one point I have pressed on my colleagues is the selection and consistent use of a common technical vocabulary. Similarly, I have repeatedly pressed the authors to avoid casual use of what anthropologists call *folk constructs*, the common sense vocabulary of our every day lives. This is especially important, as readers will discover, in avoiding uncritical use of such phrasings as Indian, white, and mixed-blood. The history of their meanings and the social and cultural significance of their modern use is one issue that the essays in this book clarify.

In saying that the materials for these biographic studies were collected for other purposes, I do not imply any original disinterest by the authors in either their subjects or the close study of individual lives. On the contrary, the concern displayed by the two historians three years ago, and the expressed interest of many others represents a trend. Recent years have seen the start of a movement in anthropology, for example, toward what is sometimes called *person-centered studies* of other cultures. Similarly, in history, there has been a resurgence of interest in writing biography. Individual centered studies in anthropology represent efforts to portray the lives of ordinary people, not notables or celebrities, and most often these reports concern contemporary personalities in cultural contexts distant from our own. The object of such person-centered research is to transform unknown strangers into intelligible human beings.

Our book applies this approach in an historical dimension. The persons whose lives are described and interpreted may be seen as culturally alien, not only because of social and cultural differences, but because by-and-large they represent facets from the past of our own developing institutions. It is too easy to treat our past judgmentally, applying the values and standards of our historic time and cultural place to events and practices that are made both exotic and problematic by a combination of chronological distance and closeness in heritage. That their careers represent elements and features of our social history makes them no less strange; instead, this poses distinctive difficulties in interpreting and appreciating their experiences. This is because their lives were spent on cultural margins, on the frontiers between the predecessors of ethnic groups familiar to us today; conflict, discrimination, and repression were commonly their lot. Our subjects coped with their frustrations and stresses in turbulent eras and contexts. How they did so provides useful lessons for today. To master these lessons, however, requires suspending value judgments and developing compassionate understanding of our subjects and of others with whom they interacted.

Several of them achieved a certain amount of notoriety during their lifetimes, becoming at least locally or regionally famous—or infamous. But they were not selected for inclusion in this volume for that reason. So far as we are concerned, whether Simon Girty's contemporaries hated him as a renegade or that Christine Quintasket became known as the first American Indian woman novelist is not relevant to our purposes. None of them were born celebrities; they achieved whatever distinctions characterized their reputations. However, we are concerned with the mundane features of their lives, how they coped with the experience of living on ethnic frontiers, not with touting them as notables or exemplars, or celebrating them as movers and shakers. These biographic studies are about the ordinary aspects of our subjects' existence, they are not stories about heroes and villains. Each is viewed not merely as an uncommon individual, but as a human sample of others like themselves. In the recurrent styles of their coping with adversity and opportunity are the lessons that readers may discern in these essays.

The plan of the book is straightforward. Chapter 1 is designed as a conceptual introduction to the twelve substantive essays that follow. Any reader with an aversion to what some disparage as social science jargon may avoid the first chapter and start with the next, with the author's best wishes. The biographic studies are arranged roughly in chronological order, starting in the late eighteenth century and ending in the present. As editor, I have selected subjects whose lives provide a broad sampling: their careers span several centuries; they lived in many parts of North America; and they are of diverse cultural, linguistic, and ethnic backgrounds. However, in no sense are these essays a representative sampling of the millions of people who, over the past five centuries, have come together on this continent creating new social contexts for conflict, coordination, cooperation, and change, out of which came what we call *cultural marginality* and new ethnic identities and relationships, processes that are ongoing and that will never end.

JAMES A. CLIFTON

Acknowledgments

To Geoffrey E. Buerger and Donald B. Smith, with their inquiries about biographic studies of culturally marginal individuals, goes the credit (but not the blame) for stirring me into motion for organizing this book. Along the way, many distant colleagues provided leads, advice, and succor. Among them, most notable are Nancy O. Lurie, L. L. Langness, Robert Edgerton, Thomas Biolsi, Phillip Bock, Roy G. D'Andrade, Beth Dillingham, Loretta Fowler, Nancy P. Hickerson, Alice Kehoe, J. Anthony Parades, Glenda Riley, William Sturtevant, Robert Surtees, Robert M. Kvasnicka, Victor Barnouw, James Ronda and Oswald Werner, who reviewed early samples of the manuscript for the Dorsey Press; each provided helpful and encouraging critiques. As always, Michael Green provided sound advice, and I particularly regret that his research on Mary Muskgrove, an early eighteenth century Anglo-Creek woman, was not complete in time for inclusion of an essay about that fascinating, frontier diplomat-entrepreneur in this book.

I am also grateful to the participants in the Roundtable on Biographic Studies of Cultural Marginals at the 1986 Annual Meetings of the American Anthropology Association. Any two dozen professionals who voluntarily devote their lunch hour to intellectual interchange aimed at improving ideas is worthy of special mention. Several of the thoughts and suggestions raised by this seminar group found their way into these pages. Moreover, for two years I have been telling my students about the individuals described herein, and their comments were useful. A special debt goes to a half dozen of them—Beth Hull, Patricia Jo Cook, Jean F. Jagla, Lori Kidder, Joann Knierim, Nichole M. Neuman, Laura L. Parkinson, and Annette R. Zaboj—for reading and providing critical commentaries on early drafts of these essays. The help of David Griggs, my trusty project assistant, was indispensible.

As editor, I remain indebted to the thirteen anthropologists and historians who elected to take time away from their other obligations to write essays for this volume. Scattered across Canada and the United States, they were a remarkably diligent crew, in addition to their creative efforts especially noteworthy for delivering manuscripts, maps, and plates in a timely manner. I appreciate the great patience they have displayed in dealing with a sometimes taxing commentator. Operating on the frontiers between several distinct schools of thought in two scholarly disciplines as middleman, broker, interpreter, and traffic manager, I have often identified with the fourteen subjects whose careers are examined in the following pages.

My thanks also to the understaffed and hard-pressed crews of the Iconographic Department of the State Historical Society of Wisconsin—especially Michael Doyle and Myrna Williamson, and the Reference Branch of the Minnesota State Historical Society—especially Bonny Wilson, for their invaluable help in locating and delivering illustrations. John Aubrey, of the Newberry Library, performed similar noble service.

Over the years, my ethnographic and ethnohistorical research among various groups of Indians has been supported by the Social Science Research Council, the National Institute of Mental Health, the National Science Foundation, the Wenner-Gren Foundation, and—most recently—the National Endowment for the Humanities. Much of what I have learned under the auspices of these organizations is fed into this book.

For permission to reproduce or use materials for plates and maps, my thanks go to the Minnesota Historical Society for Mary Riggs' sketch of the Renville community, for the photograph of Gabriel Renville, and for providing a copy of the sketch of Michael Renville; to the Newberry Library for use of the sketch of Michael Renville from the Edward E. Ayer Collection; to the Nebraska State Historical Society for the photographs of Susette and Susan Laflesche; to the Grand Rapids Public Library for providing a copy of the plate of Augustin Hamlin from *The McKenney-Hall Portrait Gallery of American Indians*; to the State Historical Society of Wisconsin for George Catlin's painting of Eleazer Williams; to the National Portrait Gallery, Smithsonian Institution, for Guiseppe Fagnini's painting of Eleazer Williams; to Jay Miller for the photograph of Mourning Dove; to the Glenbow Archives for the Newman Dalton photograph of Sylvester Smith, for the photograph of Sylvester Chahuska Long-Lance, for the photograph of Chief Buffalo Child at the Calgary Stampede, and for the drawing of Buffalo Child on Broadway; to Jennifer S. H. Brown for the photograph of Chief Jacob Berens and his wife, Mary McKay; to Maurice Berens for the photograph of Chief William Berens; to Christine Tikivik for her photograph of Ann McElroy; and to Helen Hornbeck Tanner for the use of a base map from her *Atlas of Great Lakes Indian History* project.

My special thanks go to Kent Brown and his associates at Design Software, Chicago, Illinois, and to Tom and Chris Snider of Computer Edge Technology, Green Bay, Wisconsin, for their creative help with my computer and word-processing perplexities. The manuscript for this book was prepared on a KayPro PC/30 computer and a NEC P6 Pinwriter printer, using Micro-Pro's *Word Star 4.0*, Digital Marketing's *Bibliography* and *Footnote*, and Oasis Systems' *Punctuation and Style*, backed up nicely by Design Software's *Hard Disk Survival Kit*.

I have dedicated this book to the late Homer G. Barnett, scholar, mentor, and friend. Throughout his long, productive career as a truly interdisciplinary anthropologist, Homer constantly stressed the vital importance of always keeping individual humans clearly in mind, of never allowing them to be lost or obscured in anthropological theorizing about abstracted, anonymous collectivities. For Mr. B, as his students addressed him, taught and practiced the principle that only through understanding the activities, coping styles, and innovative contributions of individuals in groups could we fully understand the dynamics of cultural persistence and change, both past and present. My hope is that he might have found this book to be his sort of approach to understanding people.

J.A.C.

Contents

LIST OF ILLUSTRATIONS

LIST OF MAPS

CHAPTER 1

Alternate Identities and Cultural Frontiers

James A. Clifton

Canadians and Americans know what to think about Indians but they do not know how to do so critically and analytically. What they think about Indians forms a large part of generic North American culture, defined by anthropologists as a historically derived, socially transmitted, and patterned construction of reality. This learned and shared knowledge about Indians is used automatically and credulously to organize behavior and to explain the behavior of others. Thinking clearly and critically about Indians, on the other hand, requires special intellectual discipline and technical ideas. This introductory essay provides a guide to that end, a discussion of basic concepts with some illustrations showing how sharper insights and deeper understanding are achieved by disciplined analysis.

We can begin by clarifying the key phrases already used. That ideas about Indians are historically derived, for instance, requires us to appreciate change in the content of such cultural knowledge and in behavior toward Indians. Some elements of this knowledge are persistent, others have disappeared or were greatly transformed, and more have been added. One tenacious element is a We-versus-They theme, and associated with this polarized duality is the lasting conviction that They are significantly different in various ways. However, no Canadian today thinks about Indians in the same way as did the Jesuits organizing early missions among the Hurons in the first half of the seventeenth century. Nor could anyone behave toward the Miwok or Maidu of Northern California as did American gold miners in the 1850s. Equally true is the reverse, viewing matters from the other side of the artificial We-They divide. No contemporary Canadian Mohawk can think about others in Quebec or Ontario in the same fashion as those originally known by this name. Nor do modern Citizens Band Potawatomi interact with others as did the minority of their ancestors who were Potawatomi.

In the past forty years, there has been a radical transformation in thinking about Indians, and about the proper relations between Indians and others. Until the 1920s, the dominant idea was that they could not and should not persist as distinctive peoples, and the policy, especially of the United States, was one of incorporation or assimilation. Since then, with the ascendancy of minority rights and acceptance of ethnic distinctiveness as a popular ethic, Indians have been significant beneficiaries of increased tolerance and many

1

programs promoting cultural persistence, political separatism, and—supposedly—the enhancement of their situation. By the late 1960s, this reform movement had progressed so far that some of its strongest supporters spoke of an "Indian Renaissance."[1]

Cultural knowledge about Indians transmitted over time, therefore, has been in flux, and there is no reason to suppose that what North Americans know about Indians will not metamorphose in the future.[2] Also, the means of social transmission of this knowledge have enlarged. To informal means of communication are now added the weight of visual mass media, popular literature, the pronouncements of powerful political and religious institutions, and the teaching of college professors. Since the 1950s, for instance, movies and television productions have no longer portrayed Indians as vicious, horse-riding Plains nomads menacing unwary settlers, substituting instead more sympathetic images that display Indians as innocents, as despoiled underdogs.[3] Simultaneously, a whole new genre of pulp literature has emerged, some in admittedly fictional form but other volumes written by authors with allegedly expert inside understanding of particular groups of Indians. The multimillion dollar sales success of Carlos Castenada's Don Juan series, for example, moved Oxford University anthropologist Rodney Needham to coin the phrase *orectic ethnography* to identify such spurious representations, meaning that they are designed to sway the emotions, not to inform the intellect.[4]

Our most powerful political institutions contribute to popular beliefs about Indians. In the fall of 1987, for example, the U.S. Congress passed a concurrent resolution declaring that the Articles of Confederation and the U.S. Constitution were modeled on the principles of the League of the Iroquois. This bizarre revision of constitutional history was issued in response to a skillful pressure campaign by the national Indian rights lobby, and it was staged to coincide with the bicentennial of the Constitution. That there is not a whit of objective evidence to support this political myth caused no apparent hesitation among the senators and representatives.[5] Not to be outdone in the invention of politically useful fables, major religious organizations make their own contributions. A case in point is the now famous "speech" of Chief Seattle, which has been accepted as the "fifth gospel" by environmentalists, and is regularly declaimed before gullible audiences in North America and Europe. Unfortunately, this document has a skimpy history, written more than a century following the death of the Puget Sound leader to whom it is attributed. The author of the first 1972 draft, in truth, was a Professor of English at the University of Texas, but the popularized version was rewritten and disseminated by the Southern Baptist Conference as a press release.[6]

Although their views are often overwhelmed by messages spread by the mass media and other institutional forces, scholars and academics make their distinctive offerings to what North Americans know of Indians. Until the 1950s, the scholarly study of Indians was dominated by anthropologists. Indeed, until the World War II years, American and Canadian anthropology was concerned with little other than Indians. Since then, droves of historians and smaller numbers of geographers, literary specialists, and political scientists have joined in, establishing Native American Studies as separate programs in most universities and colleges and many research institutes throughout the continent. Collectively, the details of what these academics report to students and readers about Indians, as Edward M. Bruner has pointed out, is organized by a single coherent narrative structure, a dominant plot.[7] Yes, there have been and are dissenters arguing alternative interpretations, but these are little heeded.

Bruner observes that until the 1950s, the paramount storyline about Indians used by anthropologists stressed the Indian past, which was presented as a time of stable cultures strongly contrasted with a maladapted, disorganized present. The connecting link between a well-adapted past and a culturally disintegrated present was through the consequences of contact with and domination by Europeans, those social and cultural processes known by the rubric *forced acculturation*. Moreover, Bruner argues, anthropologists commonly stressed only one possible outcome of culture contact for the future of Indians. This was to be a time when Indians—politically, linguistically, and culturally—would become indistinguishable from other Americans and Canadians. They were destined to move into the mainstream of North American national life, becoming—again in a specialized meaning—assimilated.[8] These accounts and forecasts, moreover, were communicated in a dispassionate, neutral, objective style. In this period, which ended anthropology's first century as a profession, some occasionally acted as advocates of Indians, calling for tolerance of the remnants of cultural distinctiveness or protesting particular injustices, but mainly working to smooth the transition toward final assimilation.

The 1960s, however, witnessed a sharp, sudden break from the earlier narrative structure, Bruner notes. In its place was a radically different plot, one followed by anthropologists and increasingly followed by many historians and other scholars who work among and study Indians. Rather than stressing cultural loss and disorganization among Indians, the new narrative structure emphasizes continuity and persistence. No longer was there a need to reconstruct the Golden Age of the Indian's prehistoric past because a new one was emerging. Instead of fast disappearing, Indian cultures were again beginning to flourish.

The code words in these new accounts are exploitation, oppression, colonialism, liberation, self-determination, victimization, sovereignty, cultural pluralism, resistance, and nationhood. The new task for scholars was to document how Indians had been exploited, to show how they had overcome injustice, to stress how they had perpetuated old ways and their identities, and to forecast a more beneficent, independent future. This shift, as Bruner observes, creates a distinctive role for students of Indian culture and history, an expectation that they should participate actively in such developments either as helpful commentators or as involved advocates.[9] This dominant story line, and the associated role obligations assumed by scholars, are apparent in the growing number of anthologies and separate volumes of Indian biographies. Characteristically, sometimes admittedly, these works consist of glamorized accounts of great heroes, celebrities, leaders, and other distinguished notables. Their authors apparently have elected to play the part of a Parson Mason Locke Weems, constructing suitable moralizing stories about the contributions of larger-than-life heroic figures to serve, in the phrasing of modern pop-sociology, as role models.[10]

How can this transformation—the leap from one to another dominant narrative structure used by scholars to fashion their portrayals of Indians—be understood and explained? And, of greater importance, what might be done to avoid the strong biases inherent in such stereotyped assumptions, styles, and images? The sudden break with the narrative form preferred earlier coincided with other sweeping political and economic developments in North America and elsewhere. The decline of colonialism and the rise of new nation states throughout the world were among these, as were the rise of ethnic awareness and civil and minority rights movements in the old nations. In particular, in both the United States and Canada, Indian communities long recognized by central governments achieved positions of power and a level of funding never before enjoyed. Developing many regional, national, and international special-interest organizations, contemporary Indians have effectively lobbied for a larger share of public attention, government budgets, and special political status based on their distinctive histories (see Chapters 11 and 13). Moreover, several hundred local groups, small or large in population, of composite ancestry, all claiming distinctive Indian heritage and rights, have petitioned for recognition and acceptance as official Indian tribes, some successfully.[11]

The new style of reporting about Indian culture and history developed in tandem with the larger political movements and both reflects and contributes to them. As North American Indians achieved greater power over their affairs and increased influence in private and public institutions, for instance, they acquired the ability to impose on researchers their standards and expectations, demanding some conformity to their wishes. Tribal governments can control admission to Indian communities and archives, thereby limiting access to the information scholars need to complete their studies. Similarly, the influence of regional and national Indian organizations touches the decisions of private foundations, government institutions, and university presses, affecting other resources needed to research and publish. Increasingly, historians and anthropologists deliver their manuscripts to tribal governments for commentary, criticism, and correction before publication.[12] This clearly reflects the new style of behavior implicit in the dominant narrative structure used in reporting about Indians as much as it does overt pressure applied by any tribal government. Usually, American and Canadian students of Indians voluntarily strive to present themselves as cooperative, sympathetic, equal partners, and to avoid being labeled as exploiters. In contrast, European anthropologists and historians writing about Indians are much less prone to such displays of deference. Possibly the breadth of the Atlantic gives them the distance needed for greater objectivity, balance, and good humor.[13]

As Bruner suggests, these preferred narrative structures have a coercive element. In unrecognized ways, they bend thoughts along certain paths toward a limited array of interpretations. How, then, to avoid their biasing effects? Historians frequently judge the merits of leading figures of the past as to whether they did or did not rise above the dominant passions and ethos of their times. To see around the blinders of the current popular story line about Indians, it is necessary to do precisely this. The example of European scholars writing about Indians provides a guide for this purpose: some distance is required, as are the use of alternative styles of interpretation, and open-mindedness about representations that depart from the standard. One large step is to recognize that the current most-favored image of Indians past and present is a human invention, one construction of a complex social and historical reality. There are alternatives. What has been fabricated by some can be reconstructed by others. The biographical essays in this book represent an alternative way of viewing the experience of being and becoming Indian through history.

The now acceptable fashion of depicting Indians, combined with the advocacy role assumed by many, creates more than its share of exaggerations and excesses. An example is the highly inflated estimates of pre-Columbian native populations presented in recent years, which have been based on shaky data, the careful selection of only historical sources that support a preconceived "High Count," and questionable methods of interpretation and analysis.[14] Such exaggerated population estimates are compared with later, much smaller, Indian population enumerations to support an often repeated interpretation, that the "White man" committed genocide against "the Indian" in the densely populated Americas. Even with population estimates, what would seem an objective task is marred by politically driven moralizing.

The terms used in these portrayals commonly use such stark contrasts as White versus Indian, assuming a monolithic unity of behavior and equivalence of motives for both populations, making the former uniformly the victimizer and the latter the victim. Phrased in this manner, the assumption involves a racial confrontation and the stereotyped interpretations are often racist in style, except that it is persons of European extraction who are derogated. A much-favored moral position associated with this stereotyping is the doctrine of collective guilt, with modern White Americans and Canadians held responsible for the unconscionable sins of their ancestors, obligated thereby to make perpetual recompense.

Other similarly contrived opposites and a select, emotionally laden vocabulary are regularly used to reinforce the presumptions of the dominant narrative style. Frequently, we can also see a double standard of interpretation and judgment applied, one for the "White man," the other for "the Indian." Thus, the White man is described as invading America, despoiling and dispossessing Indians, while Indians expand their territories peacefully by migration, or defend their "sacred holy lands" patriotically. The White man is motivated by greed, especially land hunger, but thoughtlessly desecrates the landscape, whereas the Indian worships and lives in perfect harmony with Mother Earth. The Indian enjoys a perfectly democratic and egalitarian social life, and the White man exercises centralized power ruth-lessly, exploiting the weak and defenseless. Although the Indian is content with the minimum of material goods, the White man lusts for an ever-increasing abundance. A crass materialism and disregard for the rights of others marks the White man but not the Indian, who is eminently spiritual and considerate of friend and stranger, young and old. Some of these stereotyped contrasts are not new, nor is the literary device of using a counterfeit image of the Indian as a foil to express the vexation or alienation some disgruntled authors feel about their own lives and times. Sham images of the Indian have been used regularly for such purposes since the seven-teenth century. The best defense against being taken by such phrasings is a decent amount of skepticism, and the ability to recognize them as highly politicized rhetoric.[15]

This discussion of the images many academics press on students and readers should clarify some other key terms in the opening paragraph. Americans and Canadians do not simply come to know of Indians passively; they are made to believe in certain things actively. In this sense, cultural knowledge about Indians is more-or-less deliberately constructed. Moreover, once people are persuaded of the validity of such interpretations, their behavior is affected, for there is a moral injunction implicit in the teachings. Annually, in many colleges and universities, students in courses titled "American Minorities" or the like are presented with a multiple choice question reading as follows:

Through the nineteenth century, American policy toward Indians consisted of:
     A. Assimilation
     B. Acculturation
     C. Genocide
     D. Socialization

To obtain a passing grade, students must mark "C" as the "correct" answer. In truth, the only proper answer to such a question is none of the above, since the complexities and varieties of American policies respecting Indians in the last century cannot be captured with any one word drawn from the lexicons of sociology and anthropology. The "correct" answer is, moreover, a complete falsehood. In the over 200 years it has existed as a nation, no U.S. administration from George Washington to Ronald Reagan has ever ap-proved, tolerated, or abetted a policy aimed at the deliberate, systematic extermination of Indians.

North Americans begin acquiring culturally patterned knowledge about Indians soon after birth. By the age of seven or so they have a well-developed mental image of what Indians look like, and when asked to do so, they will happily render their image as an icon on paper. If colored pencils are

AMERICAN CHILDREN'S IMAGES OF THE INDIAN. By the age of six or so, American children have formed lasting images of the Indian. Their impressions depict a distinctive physiognomy, cultural features, and place the Indian in a wilderness setting close to rugged nature. (Courtesy of Keith and Kyle Wyman.)

available, so much the better, for then youngsters can indicate that Indians have a reddish-brown skin tone, and they will typically embellish faces and arms with garishly colored war paint. The figure of the Indian is set into a rugged natural environment, marked by high mountains or tall trees, suggesting the better defined verbalizations of later years that the Indian "lives close to nature." Ordinarily, suitable animals populate the environment in representations such as buffalo, bears, wolves, or horses. Lastly, the Indian figure is dressed appropriately in breech-clout, headband with feathers (or a full warbonnet), moccasins, leggings, or jackets (with fringe). If the figure represented is male, then it clutches bow and arrows or a spear, less commonly a rifle; if female, an effort is made to draw a child in a cradle-board. Given the opportunity in dress-up role play, youngsters will create and don such costumes and mock weapons and behave in a manner they know as appropriate for an Indian. Children who identify themselves as Indian are little different, except they sometimes have access to more information and better wardrobes.[16]

Children approach adulthood with powerful visual images firmly embedded in their minds. Unless they spend much time in the Girl Scouts or Boy Scouts, which teach their own versions of Indian ways, their cultural knowledge of the Indian becomes more extensive but mainly in adding fragments that are poorly articulated. At an early age, children start acquiring attitudes—emotionalized position statements—about Indians. In the United States, one regularly used institutional means of inculcating a positive attitude—gratitude for what the Indian has given—is the annual Thanksgiving school pageant, when the legend of Squanto teaching the Pilgrims how to plant corn "Indian-style" is enacted. From this dramatized legend, children absorb as compelling fact the fiction that the first English settlers in America depended on Indian teachings and technology for their survival. No one bothers to inform them that the real Squanto learned how to fertilize crops with fish when living in Europe, or that at the time he was an employee of and acting under the instructions of the British Governor of Nova Scotia.[17]

In their adult years, North Americans' knowledge of the Indian emerges full blown. It contains a special vocabulary—reservation, warpath, smoke signals, powwow, and the like. Included in this special lexicon are words and phrases of special interest to the essays in this volume, such as *mixed blood*, *Indian blood*, *half-breed*, and—it may not be obvious—the word *Indian*, with all its connotations. Some of these terms are combined into regularly used metaphors, like *Indian summer*, *Indian giver*, *Indian file*, and *forked tongue*. Also included in this knowledge are firmly held beliefs about the Indian past and present, which are tied to powerful sentiments. The legend that "the White man taught the Indian how to scalp" is one belief, implying that Indians have fallen from grace and acquired such customs through the influence of corrupt Europeans.[18] Various values and symbols are also part of this cultural knowledge. Ideals about proper ways of dealing with the weak, powerless, and dispossessed are an example, for the Indian is generally characterized as such. Similarly, the Indian, along with others like the sturdy frontier sodbuster, the hardy voyageur, and the cowboy, have long served as major expressive symbols of core images for the continent's past. Associated with the Indian as key symbol is the idea that they were the original owners of the North American landscape, which was stolen from them. Such images, sentiments, legends, sayings, metaphors, beliefs, and symbols form the content of cultural knowledge about Indians.

Adult North Americans are usually conscious of this traditional cultural content. In appropriate contexts, when called on to do so, they will express such material in the ways they think, speak, write, and otherwise organize their behavior. Newspaper editors, for example, regularly send reporters and feature writers off to "do an Indian piece." These reporters have no special qualifications or training for such assignments, so they approach the task with the same body of folk knowledge known and used by ordinary citizens. In early September 1987, the editor of the *Christian Science Monitor* dispatched J. Denis Glover to cover an Indian happening in Concord, Massachusetts, reported on the seventeenth of September under the title, "How the Founding Fathers took a page from the Iroquois book." The piece opens with melodramatic phrases, "The pines and the hemlocks murmur in the breeze . . . as Slow Turtle and Medicine Story quietly walk side by side . . ." In this fashion, the Indian—here a duo with Indian-sounding names—is placed squarely in rustic nature. The phrasing, however, is borrowed from James Wadsworth Longfellow's *Evangeline*, suggesting that the writer had the Indian confused with the Acadians tragically deported from Nova Scotia in 1755, or else wanted unwary readers to make this association.

This "news story" identifies Slow Turtle as the "Supreme medicine man of the Wampanoag nation." An accompanying photo shows Slow Turtle as a long-haired, elderly gentleman of rugged countenance, obviously of mixed biological antecedents, dressed in a western shirt and wearing a Plains Indian-style choker. The story quotes Slow Turtle, and his partner Medicine Story, as they recount how Benjamin Franklin and "others of the Founding Fathers" copied the U.S. Constitution and the fundamental principles of American democracy after "the book" of the New York Iroquois League. The news writer presented this account as if the tale were handed down orally from generation to generation by Slow Turtle's forebears, giving it credibility. Here, in a few brief newspaper columns, are expressed many of the most common American stereotypes about Indians—close to nature, primal spirituality, contributors to the tap root of American democracy, symbol of long ago. What the writer did not explain to the newspaper's readers was that this was a skillfully staged media event, one of many organized in this period to support the lobbying effort to persuade Congress to swallow and support the political myth about the Iroquois, and that Slow Turtle and Medicine Story, instead of retelling traditional stories their grandfathers had told them, were reading or quoting from the same press release issued elsewhere.[19]

Being conscious of such cultural knowledge and using it does not include critical awareness of its truth, authenticity, or validity. And there are other features of such knowledge that operate automatically, normally outside consciousness. The most important is the system of principles for assigning racial or ethnic identity. In this respect, for many years, there were important differences between Canadian and American practice. A distinction between *status* and *nonstatus Indians* in Canada was consistently applied, yielding two broad categories, individuals and groups with legally recognized Indian political identity and those without. Status Indians are legally recognized by the government and have all the rights and privileges associated with that social position.

Changed recently by legislation, in Canada access to the status of Indian was obtained either by birth or by marriage, but it differed for males and females. An Indian-status woman who married a nonstatus male, for instance, lost her official position as an Indian and all rights to membership in a recognized band. Moreover, her children could not obtain such recognition. In reverse, Indian-status males who married outside this social category retained their legal identities as Indian, and so did their children. Conversely, women with no Indian ancestry wedded to Indian-status males acquired the official identity of Indian at marriage, but not males of similar antecedents. Thus, a recent Ukrainian immigrant woman who married a Blackfoot man was assigned the identity of a legal Blackfoot, whereas a woman of impeccable Cree heritage and antecedents who married an Irish-Canadian lost her legal identity automatically. This is a patridominant system pure and simple, one that follows a simple rule: women and their children take the legally defined racial or ethnic status of the husband/father.[20]

In the United States, no patridominant rule has ever been consistently or widely applied. But, large numbers of American males and fewer females have acquired the status of Indian, a social position recognized more informally by government authorities if not always by Indian communities, through residence with a recognized Indian group, commonly coinciding with marriage to a person from that community. These individuals include the Squaw Men, made historically infamous by their reputation of having exploited Indian resources through marriage.[21] The phrase is ordinarily applied solely to American men who married women of the Indian societies in Indian Territory (eastern Oklahoma and Kansas), but the practice was nationwide.

In contrast to the Canadian patridominant system, official American practice has limited legal recognition and restricted delivery of federal services to people of more than "one-fourth Indian blood"; but all must be acceptable to existing Indian groups following the rules of their corporate constitutions. The American equivalent of Canadian status Indians, therefore, includes people who claim that at least one-fourth of their ancestors were Indian but only if a recognized group will accept them. In the United States, distinct from Canadian law, such ancestry is traced in both male and female descent lines. However, in recent years—due to pressure from the memberships within federally sanctioned Indian communities and elsewhere—there is a move on to diminish this requirement and to accept as legally recognized Indians persons who can document any Indian blood whatsoever. This development is the consequence of several social processes. One of these is the continuing intermarriage and interbreeding between legally recognized Indians and others. The experience of Maud Clairmont with her children and grandchildren illustrates that process (see Chapter 11). A second process, operating in both Canada and the United States, involves an increasing emphasis on popular notions of biological determinism for fixing social identity, a transition to a full-scale racial definition of Indianness. This means that any individual claiming any degree of Indian blood may assert an Indian identity, and others tend to accept them as such. And, a third process is the increasing popularity of being defined and accepted as Indian in contemporary North America.

The idea of Indian blood is a culturally standardized figure of speech, a folk metaphor for biological ancestry, the old European root of thinking that something called *race* inherently determines the identities and characteristics of individuals and groups. In the United States, through the early twentieth century, at least officially, there was less stress on such racial definitions than on cultural factors, the capacity to learn and master the cultural knowledge and behavioral patterns of Americans of European extraction. Thus, native

Americans were encouraged and pressed to alter their attitudes, values, and behavior, and to take on the characteristics of Euro-Americans. When they did so, they were supposed to have lost their identities as Indians. In practice, this sometimes involved little more than a legal transition from the official status of Indian to that of a citizen, with the loss of the former's and the acquisition of the latter's rights and obligations. Nonetheless, the old Euro-American folk thinking about racial determination of Indian status persisted, as did the assumption that individuals with any degree of Indian blood, whether English-speaking citizens or not, remained inherently Indian. Indeed, this racial style of thinking was often supported by federal court decisions, which held that irrespective of degree of ancestry, place of residence, and style of living, "Indians-by-blood" retained their identities and rights under law.[22]

This culturally determined thinking about racial determinants of individual and group identity and about inborn aptitudes and behavior potentials is European in origin and took root in North America among peoples of European and (eventually) native American ancestry, particularly among persons of composite European, native American, and Afro-American origins. Originally, no native North American society subscribed to the idea of biological determination of identity or behavior. Indeed, the most common identity question asked of strangers was not, "What nation do you belong to?" or "Of what race are you?" Instead, when confronting unknown people, they typically asked, "What language do you speak?" They were disinterested in skin color, the standard Euro-American sign of racial identity. On the contrary, they stressed as criteria of group membership learned aspects of human nature: language, culturally appropriate behavior, social affiliation, and loyalty. This was reflected in their willingness to accept, adopt, and assimilate individuals and small groups of French, English, and others of European origin (see Chapters 2 and 12).[23] However, modern Indians—who are all of composite native and Euro-American biological ancestry, and who have long since absorbed much Euro-American cultural knowledge—think differently. Today, most use the standard American or Canadian principles of assigning group identity, which are determined by blood.

This manner of fixing individual identity by putative biological ancestry has been durable and pervasive. It operates implicitly, automatically, and out of conscious awareness, accepted as if it were primordial and natural. It is, however, a historically derived cultural pattern, reflecting only one of the world's traditional means of defining the boundaries between groups. Its underlying basic principles can be stated briefly. A few basic races are recognized: White, Black, Red (or Indian), and Yellow (Asian). Although in recent years the color/race categories of White and Black remain in daily use, Red and Yellow have fallen into disfavor. In place of the former, the synonym Indian, sometimes the recently coined Native American, is preferred. Normally at birth, individuals are assigned to one or another of these arbitrary social categories, and the associated racial identity. During their lives, individuals repeatedly have these categorical identities attributed to them, are often called on to classify themselves as such (in employment applications and in a census), and will often see themselves belonging to one category. The principles of such classification are simple. Individuals with any known "degree of Black blood" (i.e., any sub-Saharan African ancestry) are automatically classed as Blacks. Similarly, those with any known "degree of Indian blood" are categorized as Indian. On the other hand, only persons with neither Indian nor Black ancestry are regularly categorized as White. People with some combination of Black and Indian, perhaps also with more-or-less White ancestry, on the other hand, form something of an anomaly. Historically, depending on regional social circumstances, individuals and groups with mixed biological antecedents may be classed as Black, Indian, or White, or one after the other in historical or biographical sequence (see Chapters 5 and 8).[24] Underlying this culturally patterned system of assigning individual and group identity by race is a simple, implicit principle: any degree of Black blood or Indian blood overrides an individual's or a group's other antecedents and fixes racial identity.

How this cultural knowledge and the system for ascribing racial identity affects the attitudes, expectations, and behavior of Americans and Canadians is illustrated with several examples. Some years ago, I was asked to serve as a consultant for a program of language instruction on a Canadian Indian reserve. The students and instructor involved in this learning activity were experiencing many difficulties, and the education director wanted advice on how to alleviate them. Mainly adult women, the students were all status Indians under Canadian law, and like the whole population of the reserve, their ancestry—biological, cultural, and linguistic—was mixed. Their several generations distant native Canadian ancestors included many speakers of Ojibwa/Odawa (Chippewa/Ottawa) dialects, some who had spoken related but mutually unintelligible languages such as Delaware, Shawnee, and Potawatomi, and a few who had spoken unrelated Iroquoian languages like Mohawk. But their ancestors also included as many speakers of totally different languages such as English, Gaelic, and French. There were even a few immigrant Slavic grandparents thrown in to further complicate the picture.

The language of instruction was Ojibwa, but few students had ever heard this or any other native language used during their childhood, and students who had heard it could not understand it at the time. Their natal language, therefore, was English, which they had learned in their homes early and used exclusively all their lives. The presenting difficulty was that students complained they were not learning to speak "Indian" fast enough, and they were dropping out of the program. Some of the instructional weaknesses were immediately apparent. The teacher was not trained or experienced in foreign language instruction and was neither a native nor a fluent speaker of Ojibwa: he had only recently learned the rudiments of the language in a classroom. Moreover, these adult, English-speaking students received only four hours of class instruction weekly, and no practice in its use elsewhere. Under such handicaps, few monolingual speakers of any language are likely to become competent bilinguals quickly, if ever.

But there was a deeper problem, the source of much frustration, confusion, and emotional distress. These students were convinced that Ojibwa was not a foreign language to them. They firmly believed that, as Indians, it should come easily and naturally to them, and that they had an inborn capacity for speaking the language. Many students knew that Ojibwa was a "simple" language, reflecting a common European stereotype about the crudity of "primitive" languages. When they failed to master the language readily, they became disenchanted. They did not, however, blame their instructor or the limitations of the program; they blamed themselves. Failure to master their "native" language quickly led to confusion about their identities—one woman confessed, "Maybe it's because I'm only a quarter-blood Indian I can't learn." My explaining that for them to learn Ojibwa under such handicaps was no different from trying to master Japanese or Turkish did not help much.

In part, these students had been penalized by highly inflated expectations, imposed by others and themselves. The expectation that because an individual is an Indian by the conventional categories of social race they should possess special knowledge of Indian culture and language, and special inherent aptitude for mastering Indian ways, is widespread and deep-seated. It is pervasive in our universities, where we expect to find the highest level of critical thinking. I have an acquaintance whose experience will make this and other salient points. To safeguard her anonymity, and to make certain she is accepted as a person and not confused with a tribe, let us call her Victoria.

Victoria was born and raised in a large midwestern city, of a mother who was a member of an Eastern Dakota reservation community, from whom she inherited her legal status as a Dakota. But from her mother and other kin, she learned practically nothing of Dakota culture or language. During her adolescent years and on a few later occasions as a young adult, she visited her mother's home community but developed a lasting personal distaste for the social atmosphere there. Later, thinking of herself as an Indian and seeking more congenial associations, she searched for a suitable Indian population that might accept her. She found a place to lodge her identity in a small, highly conservative, isolated, rural Great Lakes Algonquian community. In this respect, her experience—this quest for a lodgment for her self—is much like that of Joe True (see Chapter 12), except that she is an Indian by blood and that she married a man in her new community and bore several children. The former, given standard American cultural criteria, legitimizes her identity as Indian. However, like Joe True, no matter how she conducted herself she has never been accepted fully by all in her adopted community. The older women there, for example, disparage her as a "foreign Indian," a considerable insult.

A rotund, ebullient, gaily assertive woman, in dress, mannerisms, and complexion, Victoria is readily seen, accepted, and treated as an Indian. (For my part, I have always thought that if she decided to settle in Manhattan and set herself up as a Gypsy fortune-teller, few would be the wiser.) She has no complaint about being so categorized; indeed, she presents herself forcefully as Indian—and much else. However, she regularly experiences a special form of discrimination about which she harbors a strong grievance. As a child, Victoria became a reader, and in school she excelled in literature, later earning an honors degree in American Literature, for which she has a deep and abiding love. Later, several of the professors from her university developed an interest in Indian literature, and they started calling on their star Indian student, Victoria, to visit their classes and lecture on and perform Indian myths, legends, and folk tales.

These same professors repeatedly pressed Victoria to go to graduate school specializing in Native American Literature, which they—all conde-scending smiles—indicate would be a suitable specialty for her, meaning the study of some combination of traditional oral literature and modern authors of Indian ancestry. Victoria finds these experiences highly insulting. She has no special knowledge of the oral traditions of either the Dakota or the Algonquians nor much interest in them; and she appreciates—from the perspective of the traditional people she knows best—that it would be improper, if not dangerously taboo, for her to make such presentations. No one who pressed her to behave as an Indian ever invited her to their classes to speak on her true interests: Poe, Whitman, and Hemingway. When she offers to do so, she is told there is no need for that: the professors have all the expertise required to cover such subjects.

Victoria finds these experiences demeaning and confusing. She remains bewildered because she expects people with Ph.D.s after their names to accept her for who she is, not to force on her their stereotyped expectations for a racial category. Victoria is a woman who is doubly marginal—both socially and culturally. Neither fully socially accepted in the Indian commu-nity where she makes her home, she is not received as an equal, as an individual in her own right, nor in the intellectual community, where she might display her hard-won knowledge and her considerable talents.[25] Unlike Dan Raincloud (see Chapter 10), she is not competent when called on to perform as an authentic Algonquian or Dakota; she knows it; and she is unwilling to pretend. Unlike Mourning Dove (see Chapter 7), when pres-sured to assume a role as cultural mediator to the outside world, which would require much special study, she is too committed to her own interests to conform. And unlike Sylvester Long (see Chapter 8), she is too committed to and content with her own sense of self to adopt a spurious identity that might be profitably enacted before American audiences.

These examples illustrate some of the experiences of people who are legally recognized as status Indians, who have at least some lasting associa-tion with an organized Indian community, and who exhibit some of the physical characteristics commonly associated with being Indian. There are many others in Canada and the United States who lack one or all of these attributes, yet assert an Indian identity. This may be little more than the casual claim of those who, out of the blue in an informal social gathering, will inform others that they are "a little bit Indian." Such an assertion of Indian identity may go no further than such a passing claim to ethnic distinctiveness. But in tens of thousands of instances, it does. The claimants are people who through their lives are ordinarily identified by others as White or Black. These do not, however, include the 11.8 million Mexican-Americans who are largely Indian in ancestry but are content with their existing ethnic identity. And, in Canada, the people known as Métis do not make such claims, although they assert special status as an "original" people. The Métis stem from the early fur-trade years, when many French males settled among and married women from various tribes (see Chapters 3, 4, and 11). Long organized as an occupational subculture that serviced the economic interests of Europeans and Indians, the Métis in Canada eventually emerged as culturally distinctive, organized communities. On the other hand, many Canadian Métis who migrated into the United States assimilated into American Indian communities, since no comparable Franco-Indian Métis communities existed to sustain their identities.[26]

Such tentative or partial assertions of Indian identity are made in many different ways for various purposes. Like other academics who have written about Indians, over the years I have received countless unsolicited letters from individuals making such claims and asking for my help or comments. A selection of these letters illustrates other social and psychological processes involved in being and becoming Indian. An elderly, retired, midwestern, urban woman, for example, writes that in compiling her family's genealogy, she discovered that she had Potawatomi ancestors, only one of whom had a Potawatomi name—the rest, she reported, had been given French names. (In truth, they had French names because they were French.) This woman added that as far as she knows, she is only "one-fourth Potawatomi" (which is highly unlikely), but she is "just as proud as a full blooded [Indian]." This woman is deeply engaged in the pastime much enjoyed by millions of many elderly Americans, tracing her roots. This popular hobby reflects the deep longing many persons—who come from a highly mobile population after generations of migrations—feel about the loss of connection to place and kin-group. The discovery of an illustrious ancestor or two populating the family tree is a major find, enhancing one's pride in self. This is known as *prestige genealogy*. This writer did not indicate if she intended to discover more and seek out her Indian kin in an effort to affiliate herself with them.

Not so for the younger man with an Ed.D. after his name who wrote from overseas, where he was employed on a U.S. government project. His elderly aunt, in searching out the family's heritage, had similarly discovered an Indian ancestress, this time a "Potawatomi princess," some eight generations back (possibly 200 years). Needless to say, the Potawatomi had no royalty, and if there were such a great-great-great-great-great-great-great-great aunt, she was the wife or consort of a French or English trader. However, this writer immediately researched the Potawatomi, came across my name, and wrote asking for addresses and instructions so that he could obtain legal membership in the Potawatomi tribe for himself and his offspring because he wanted to "pass his Indian heritage on to his children." This well-educated man's behavior amply illustrates the generalization offered earlier: for Americans, the presence of any Indian blood, however remote and unconnected the ancestry, often overrides all else. This individual immediately was convinced he *was* an Indian, and he began action aimed at affiliating himself and his offspring with the Potawatomi. Undoubtedly, on government affirmative action forms he classifies himself Indian, as do thousands of others like him.

Another middle-aged man reported how he carried this process further. Not until he was in his forties did his father reveal to him that he was of Métis descent; his ancestors included French officials and traders at Detroit during the French colonial regime and, supposedly, at least one Potawatomi woman. Although he later identified his French ancestors by name, he was unable to do so for his supposed Potawatomi kin. Nonetheless, he believes he is "1/16th Indian" (a generous estimate). But this did not stop him and other relatives: they solicited and obtained legal membership in the Kansas Potawatomi organization, where they are now planning to further their careers. The writer expressed much sympathy to "Native American problems," while also indicating some mild discomfort with the step taken to alter his identity by saying that "we are not much more than 'courtesy Indians.' "

He does not suggest, however, that he and others like him are a serious problem to the genuine Potawatomi. The ancestors he names, for example, were Franco- and Anglo-American bourgeois who, through the last half of the nineteenth century, acting as figureheads for the government and railroad interests, systematically fleeced the Kansas Potawatomi of their land, treaty funds, and goods, leaving them impoverished. The fact that such "courtesy Indians" can four generations later readily obtain recognized membership and rights in an Indian community like this represents another painful defeat for the small band of traditional Potawatomi who, through the mid–1960s, fought to build a protective wall around themselves, desperately wanting to exclude such people. It also represents another step toward imposing an American racial definition of Indianness on such hard-pressed groups.[27]

These few examples are only the tip of a rapidly rising iceberg. Behind them lie hundreds of thousands of others with obscure antecedents who, in the past twenty years, have swapped their ethnic or racial identities for Indian. In 1970, for instance, the U.S. Census enumerated 827,108 Indians (including Inuit and Aleuts), but ten years later, some 1,421,367 reported themselves as Indian, an apparently astounding population increase of some 75 percent. But this does not represent natural biological increase from the 1970 base population. Instead, because of a more generous new definition of Indianness used by the U.S. Bureau of the Census, which allowed people to self-declare race and ethnicity, it consists largely of new additions to the Indian population of 1970 from elsewhere, and subtractions from the totals for other groups.[28] Unquestionably, the 1990 census will report a comparably huge increase, since the popularity of becoming Indian for some purposes has increased in the 1980s.

These transformations of personal identity—the mobility of individuals between ethnic and racial categories—is not new in the history of North America. Indeed, throughout the history of the United States, most formal policies adopted by Congress and implemented by the executive branch have fostered ethnic inconstancy, the movement of individuals and groups from the category of generic White into the category of Indian. This has been true whether the particular policy was designed to foster the deculturation and assimilation of traditional Indians, as most policies did through the 1920s, or whether the policy was intended to guarantee special privileges and rights to legally recognized Indians, which has been the course of private and public intervention since 1934. A generalization summarizes this process: every time the value of being Indian increases, the number of persons of marginal or ambiguous ancestry who claim to be Indians increases. This generalization is stated in terms of the consciousness of persons affected who detect unplanned opportunities and unintended incentives in such policies, not from the perspective of the power holders who formulate such programs and distribute resources and rewards.

The *Indian Trade and Intercourse Act* of 1834, for instance, included a clause that gave preferential federal employment rights in the Indian Service to persons "of Indian blood."[29] Most persons who enjoyed such privileges had mixed antecedents. Similarly, when the federal government and missionary societies inaugurated schools intended to "promote Civilization among the Savages," it was French and Anglo-American fathers who saw the chance of free education for their children by Indian women, whereas Ojibwa and Potawatomi fathers, for example, long resisted this interference in their efforts to educate their children in traditional fashion.[30] The experience of Susette and Susan La Flesche's privileged advancement and of Sylvester Long's indulgent appointment to West Point illustrate this process (see Chapters 6 and 8).

From soon after the War of 1812 until the end of the American treaty-making era in 1871, the United States regularly provided additional incentives and rewards to individuals and groups marginal to Indian societies. They included substantial payments in cash and titles for large land tracts to persons denominated half-breeds or Indians by blood. These payments were deducted from the resources of the Indian community involved, which ordinarily did not consider the recipients as full or legitimate members of their groups.[31] Even during the years of the removal policy (c. 1825–1855), when Indian communities from the East were often obligated to abandon their lands and resettle west of the Mississippi, a policy commonly characterized as the "Trail of Tears," many individuals and families and whole communities saw large incentives in the policy, which for some Indian communities was a highly stressful experience. Two Canadian Indian communities, for example, which were outside the jurisdiction of the United States, discovered in "removal" the opportunity to gain title to tracts of valuable land and voluntarily joined the emigration.[32]

In the last decade of the nineteenth century and the first years of the next century, when the General Allotment Act was implemented, hundreds of people claiming Indian status—none associated with an Indian community—were awarded 160 acres each from the public lands of the United States. The allotment policy, designed to break up collectively owned reservations and Indian governments and move Indians into the mainstream of American life, is generally regarded as extremely damaging to Indian interests. One reason for this judgment is that it caused the loss of more than 60 percent of Indian-owned land. Yet, while communities like the Sauk and the Dakota lost much of their territory, many people of supposed Indian descent gained land. In addition, the implementation of the Dawes Act attracted back to reservations thousands who had earlier abandoned their ties to such communities, and thousands whose connections were often ambiguous.[33] More recently, the Indian Claims Commission Act of 1946, and the deluge of categorical aid programs for Indians passed during the 1960s and since then under the War on Poverty and later social programs, all aimed at benefiting impoverished Indians, have been a bonanza of opportunities for persons who can locate an Indian ancestor somewhere in their family trees.

The Indian Claims policy was intended to settle all Indian claims against the United States for certain abuses once-and-for-all, mainly for inadequate payment for land purchased during the treaty era. Instead, it vastly increased the value of being Indian, and it caused the rise of an entire industry of claims attorneys, researchers, and other experts who enhanced their welfare through servicing Indian clients. For example, attorneys for the small Turtle Mountain and Chippewa-Cree bands of North Dakota and Montana won such a suit before the claims commission. By the time the dust had settled, more than 24,000 individuals (mainly of Canadian Métis ancestry) appeared and clamored for their shares; and the Bureau of Indian Affairs eventually approved some 22,000 persons eligible for cash awards, which were thereby reduced to $43.81 per capita.[34] The small local communities that began the litigation remained impoverished.

The generalization about incentives works in opposite directions for both individuals and groups. During the middle of the nineteenth century, several legally recognized Indian communities gave up their status, became citizens, collected their individual shares of collectively owned property, and passed into the general population. One such group was the Mission Band of Potawatomi, which—after expending its assets within a few years—successfully petitioned for readmission as Indians.[35] In 1839, the Brotherton Indians of Wisconsin voluntarily petitioned Congress for disbandment and became citizens; but 150 years later, their descendants, recognizing the many late twentieth century rewards of being Indian, were busy organizing to renew their status as a federally recognized Nation. In the United States, for many years, it was possible for members of official tribes and bands to cash in their head rights, disavowing their identities as legal Indians, and thousands did so, but in recent years, this election of identity has been made reversible. The career of Eleazer Williams (Chapter 5) illustrates the effects of variable incentives on choices of identity. Exposed to the opportunities of New England Protestant life as a boy, he wanted to cast his lot with his hosts, but he was rebuffed and pressed back to an Indian identity, while in his later years, he eagerly gave it up in favor of the delusion of being the rightful heir to the throne of France.

The example of Billy Caldwell (1780–1841) further illustrates the experiences of persons who attempt a passage from the status of Indian to English, Canadian, or American citizen. The child of a casual liaison between an Anglo-Irish British officer and a Mohawk woman at Niagara in the midst of the Revolutionary War, Caldwell, as an infant, was abandoned by his father, and abandoned as an adolescent by his mother's people. As an adult, his utmost ambition was to make his way and be accepted as a true Briton. Failing that, he migrated to Chicago, where he tried to gain acceptance as an American businessman, but he was labeled an Indian Chief by American authorities, and squeezed into that—for him—most uncomfortable identity and role. For Caldwell, in his time and place, being an Indian was a stigma that he unsuccessfully sought to escape. When chastised by his Anglo-Canadian siblings for assuming such a role, he protested that he was only playing the "political Indian" to serve his Potawatomi associates.[36] In contrast, Sylvester Long (Chapter 8) sought opportunities in the opposite direction, through evading the burden of being a Southern "colored boy" by assuming an Indian identity, which he acted out before Canadian and American—not Indian—audiences.[37] The perception of opportunity through an alternative identity, therefore, is relative to historical era, place, and social context, as well as personal needs.

In this perspective, our era is one where many thousands of persons nominally categorized as White (and, today, much less often, Black) see possible incentives for themselves in becoming identified and accepted as Indian. Such assertions of new public identities may be halting and tentative, temporary or permanent, successfully achieved or failed, partial or exclusive, and acted out in small or large social arenas. Most readers are familiar with individuals who have experimented with identifying themselves as Indians. Moreover, many readers know of people who have been persuaded to assume such new identities by others, by events, or by institutional pressures. The impetus for altering identity is by no means entirely internal and subjective—representing only private, personal wants. Frequently, such identity transformations are caused by external agents and agencies forced on sometimes unwilling people.

Individuals acting as leaders and organizers of efforts to secure federal recognition and support for these small populations of putative Indians spend much time in actively locating and enlisting new members. They search genealogical records, trace distant collaterals and their descendants, and show up at sometimes unsuspecting people's doors proclaiming the rewards of signing on. In addition, at this moment, there are several recruiters traveling the Great Lakes states engaged in a different activity, mustering new members for already organized and recognized Indian communities (whether the communities like it or not). The middle-aged White commercial fisher of Puget Sound, impoverished by federal court rulings that have awarded the Indian communities of the region more than half the allowable catch of migratory fish, represents a different external pressure. Stimulated by a decline in prosperity, he remembers a Skagit great-grandfather and seeks to recoup his fortunes. Whole organized groups claiming to be long-unrecognized Northwest Coast Indian communities have followed suit.

Often such choices are made with great reluctance and are the source of grave, poignant personal conflict. The experience of a young college professor, a specialist in Indian Studies, illustrates this point. Denied tenure at his college, where he was classified under federal and state affirmative action guidelines as White, he recognized that his chances of obtaining another academic position in his specialty were near zero. Proud of his achievements and strongly valuing the principle of merit, he faced a problematic future where opportunities for professional security and development were few and far between. He had always known he had distant Indian ancestors, but had never been associated with the community from which they came, and had never identified or presented himself as an Indian. Yet, he was fully aware that many institutions had reserved positions in his specialty for Indians with professional credentials. At first, he refused to take the needed step, but his disinclination was erased when his young wife pointed at herself and their small children and commanded: "Think of the future of your family!" At that moment, pressed by institutional racism which he loathed, he capitulated and became an academic Indian.

Although both doctrinaire Marxists and devout adherents of the free enterprise system—often joined by Indian communities themselves—equally agree that economic factors are the root motivation for moves from one identity to another, there are many other factors involved.[38] Aside from economic security, the young professor deeply wanted to pursue his chosen academic profession. Unmistakably, Joe True's affiliation with the Kiowa (Chapter 12) was devoid of any pecuniary interest. The elderly woman who discovered an Indian in her family tree expressed little more than pride in ancestry. As a boy, Simon Girty (Chapter 2) had no choice in the matter: being a captive, his identity transformation was involuntary. When the Minnesota fur trade collapsed, Joseph Renville (Chapter 3) might have cast his lot with western Indians and improved his business prospects, but he did not. Joseph La Flesche, on the other hand, saw a political and economic future for himself and his family by becoming Indian (Chapter 6). The variety of satisfactions obtained from assuming an Indian identity, or avoiding the same, are many and are hardly confined to the economic dimension. The 75 percent increase in self-declared Indians between 1970 and 1980 represents the result of many choices and incentives. Among them, the simple prestige of having an Indian ancestor, ego-enhancing for many people, is a motivator, as is the search for a meaningful new identity in a rapidly changing world. Asserting an Indian identity often expresses a substantially cultural drive: embracing a powerful symbol.

Indeed, the increased value of being Indian in the United States and Canada during recent decades has accompanied a decline in capitalism, contrary to the assumption of economic determinists. The social value of being Indian has increased, on the contrary, by extensions of liberal welfare programs. The affirmative action program that trapped the young professor is one example, but there are many other public and private categorical aid programs aimed at benefiting "the Indian." One net effect of these programs is a great increase in the number of people asserting Indian status. The problem is that popular definitions of Indianness are vague, slippery, and rapidly changing. Hence, during the past quarter-century, a considerable dilution of the definition of Indian status has developed.

So eager are many to deliver favors to "the Indian" that they do not always wait for an applicant to appear, instead bestowing this identity on the unsuspecting. Members of a university committee once phoned asking if I thought it appropriate to select the late Dr. Philleo Nash as their institution's commencement speaker. Instantly, the man's credentials flashed through my mind: Philleo Nash—distinguished anthropological scholar; esteemed and effective White House adviser to presidents on race relations; high-quality, practical political leader and former lieutenant governor of his state; acknowledged as one of the best of the Commissioners of Indian Affairs; founder of innovative schools; folk singer extraordinare ready at a moment's notice to break into his native song in a fine baritone with 'Men of Harlech'; in retirement, a happy cranberry farmer on his Welsh great grandfather's homestead. A few seconds later, I offered my judgment, "Philleo Nash would be a perfectly marvelous choice." Before I could list my reasons, the committee's chair replied, "That's fine—we want to do something nice for a Native American." Hence, Philleo Nash became an instant Indian—which is identity by association, while the committee's members congratulated themselves on their generosity.

These illustrations, and the associated considerations and discussion, should show that the uncritical use of culturally derived labels such as White, Indian, and Black for individuals and groups is a misleading and intellectually inhibiting practice. To assume automatically that such nomenclature denotes separate, immutable groups of humans in North America effectively blocks understanding. Yet, their use is common and unquestioned, even by anthropologists and historians who should be wary of historically derived, culturally patterned forms of thought. Rarely do we find a hint that something is amiss. No less an authority than Francis Paul Prucha, for example, raised a question about the use of "Indian" in Indian history, but dismissed the issue in favor of sticking with what has been "sanctioned by long usage" rather than "laborious circumlocutions and hyphenated nouns" such as "Native Americans or Euro-Americans."[39] Prucha is entirely right as far as his commentary goes: the addition of synonyms does not contribute to better analysis and improved knowledge, but it leaves the underlying issues unexamined.

Prucha, like most historians and some anthropologists, favors the use of everyday language in writing about Indians and Whites. Therein lies the root of a serious conceptual problem. Everyday language is inextricably tied to common sense explanations and both are products of a specific cultural heritage. Reliance on both is like wearing cultural blinders, an automatic assumption that the differences between Indian and White are determined by the Laws of Nature. Such an assumption is, in the first place, ahistorical. First coined by Christopher Columbus, the word *Indian*—meaning all the diverse cultures of the Americas jointly—required centuries before it was commonly accepted and standardized, even by peoples of European ancestry. To think otherwise, as Alden T. Vaughn emphasizes, is to distort "the nature of early ethnic relations" and to obscure the development of attitudes toward native peoples.[40] In fact, for nearly three centuries European intellectuals classed these indigenous Americans as essentially White, which in the racial thinking of the time confused inherent biological characteristics such as skin color with cultural and mental attributes. In the earlier era, White included Indian but sharply excluded Black. Not until the American Revolution did the trichromatic racial classification of White, Red, and Black come into standard usage. Of more significance, the cultural assumption that Indians were inherently and/or potentially White lay behind centuries of efforts to "civilize" them, to educate and convert them into English, French, or American citizens.

Centuries passed before many of the politically, culturally, and linguistically separate peoples native to North America willingly accepted and used the word *Indian* as a meaningful appellation for themselves, whether individually, as groups, or collectively. Even today, there are many Hopi, Tlingit, Menomini and others who resent being labeled in this manner. In short, the "Indian" was an invention of people of European origins. This interpretation applies to the name for a presumed "race" as well as the assumptions that people so called shared common characteristics, a special position in the social structure of the emerging nations of Canada and the United States, and a unique destiny.

Furthermore, much of what is written about interactions between the "Indian" and the "White man," especially so in general histories and sociological and anthropological textbooks, deals exclusively with relations between these two "races," as if peoples of European and indigenous extraction had no extensive associations with other emigrants of different language, culture, and "race." The extensive interactions between Indians and Afro-Americans, for example, are rarely mentioned in such sources, ignoring the role of thousands of escaped slaves, Blacks captured and assimilated by Indians, and the many Afro-American trappers, cowboys, and cavalry troopers, for example.[41] Similarly ignored are the important, if less frequent, relationships between native Americans and peoples from Asia and the Pacific Islands of recent decades.

In summary, the uncritical use of Indian, White, and Black, and the associated ethnocentric assumptions about ancient differences in behavior and potentialities, history, and culture effectively block analytic thinking. These historically derived, culturally patterned, institutionally reinforced convictions include such persistent ideas as being and becoming Indian is a matter largely of biological ancestry, that Indianness is fixed by blood. A related assumption is that the labels White and Indian mark sharply defined biological, social, and cultural boundaries instead of conventional social categories—culturally defined ways of sorting diverse peoples into a few classes. A further assumption is that these differences are primordial, inevitable, original, durable, and natural. However, together they represent nothing more than the foundations of North American thinking about social race, the culturally patterned epistemological roots of what is known about Indians. While this footing may not need to be dug up, it must be laid bare and examined critically.

Such an examination must start with a clear view of what has happened to immigrants from Europe, Africa, and elsewhere, and the original inhabitants of North America during the past five centuries. Before 1492, they were entirely ignorant of and had no relationships with each other. But the day Christopher Columbus granted shore leave to his sea-weary crews, the interpersonal isolation ended. At that time, a pattern of biological relations began—interbreeding—which continues today, together with the development of social relationships. On the purely biological level, of the peoples named Indian today, few can trace their ancestry exclusively to pre-Columbian native populations. Genetically speaking, the Indian population of North America is an amalgam of composite indigenous American, European, African, and other ancestries. In truth, many contemporary status Indians, as we have seen, have no native American biological ancestry at all. Conversely, there are millions of Americans who have much native biological ancestry, such as Mexican-Americans, but they are not classed or treated as Indians.

Hence, whether individuals or groups today are accepted as legal Indians is determined essentially by political decisions, decisions sometimes made by the governments of the United States and Canada, by their states and provinces, or by the governing boards of recognized Indian organizations. Such decisions are political because they invariably involve access to resources. The resources acquired by being accepted as Indian range from the legitimation of an asserted identity and other social rewards such as prestige, to tangible assets, a share in the resources owned by or owing to an Indian community, or privileged access to categorical aid programs such as college scholarships and employment. But people can be or become Indian in less formal ways, entirely outside the purview of a formal political process. Over the course of North America's history, the value of being Indian has varied greatly; and definitions of being and ways of becoming Indian have been equally changeable. Today few Indian organizations could withstand the assaults of persons excluded should they insist on admitting only full-bloods, for example, but not too many decades ago, this was common.

Over the years, the points or places of contact between emigrants from Europe and Africa and descendants of the native peoples of North America have changed dramatically, as have the political and social nature of these contacts. These are the frontiers cited in the title of this book. Over several centuries, these contexts of contact were classic frontiers, meaning the farthest extent of the migrations of one society, the places where they came up against the territory of another.[42] Such frontiers were sometimes officially marked by political boundaries, such as the one established by British authorities in 1763, beyond which British subjects were not supposed to go, although they did. This idea of a political frontier, a boundary marking "Indian Country," is still alive, but the territory consists of small, scattered tracts. Frontiers in this narrow sense can also be objectively drawn by historians and social scientists for special purposes, the density of American settlements in contrast to the preponderance of Indian occupation, for instance.

However, anthropologists and sociologists give frontier a different, broader meaning more relevant to the biographical essays and the questions raised in this book. In this sense, a frontier is a social setting, a culturally defined place where peoples with different culturally expressed identities meet and deal with each other. While the migration of one group into a territory inhabited by another group creates one form of frontier relationships, the processes of social and political development in complex societies create others.[43] The movement of Simon Girty's family across the British-proclaimed boundary of 1763 into Shawnee and Delaware territory (Chapter 2) represents the former type of frontier contact and relationship. In contrast, the latter variety of associations and relationships on cultural borders is represented by Augustin Hamlin, Jr.'s, experiences as a novice in Rome (Chapter 4), Christine Quintasket's laboring as a migrant worker on American farms and her efforts to explain Salish culture to Americans as an author (Chapter 7), Dan Raincloud's appearance before an audience of American physicians (Chapter 10), and Joe True's visit as a spectator at an Oklahoma Powwow.

This distinction is expressed as a difference between external and internal social boundaries or frontiers. So long as the native societies of North America were populous, powerful, and independent, they could maintain firm exterior political boundaries recognized by colonial authorities and the young nation states developing on the continent. Once the United States and Canada emerged as continental nations, however, these formerly independent Indian communities were incorporated politically and socially into their social systems. Their basic relationships with other Americans and Canadians, since then, have been on interior lines, a system of ethnic groupings. Such relationships are dynamic. During the past twenty years, for instance, a counter trend has emerged, with Indians and their supporters proclaiming a doctrine of local sovereignty. Through skillful manipulation of the political process in Canada and the United States, many Indians today are striving to convert ethnicity into nationality. The aim is to carve part of the territories of the United States and Canada into several hundred petty states, so many miniature Indian Monacos and Liechtensteins.[44] The relationship between Dan Raincloud and the American Indian Movement leaders (Chapter 10), the activities of the young Shoshone militants who ousted Maud Clairmont and others of the old guard from power (Chapter 11), and the leadership role taken by Ooleepeeka in pan-Inuit (Chapter 13) organizations are three of many expressions of this recent movement toward greater political autonomy.

The recent political movements are an outgrowth of features of ethnicity that are obscured by popular understanding of this technical term. Ordinarily, ethnicity is understood as an odd-lots collection of surviving cultural traits or customs that distinguish a particular group from others. That ethnic groups have a historical and cultural heritage is accepted implicitly. That much of this history and heritage has been recently invented is less appreciated.[45] However, anthropologists and sociologists understand ethnicity in different, analytic, and more useful ways. In this way of thinking, over the course of the history of North America, as continent-wide nation-states developed, formerly independent Indian societies were embraced in the emerging social and political systems. This process of incorporation consisted of fitting Indians, as individuals and groups, into a system of social stratification. The core of this new system of ethnic (and other forms of) stratification was the imposition of ideas about and means of imposing special forms of inequality on the descendants of the peoples indigenous to the continent. In historical process, the native societies lost their political autonomy, control of their resources, and often their identities, with some groups being absorbed into others.

It is easy to overemphasize the negative side of this development. This is because it is seen as having violated deep-seated modern values about freedom—personal and group autonomy in decision making, as well as the ideal of equality—the equivalence of individuals in enjoying unrestricted access to the good things in life. The consequence of both violations has been a lasting sense of irrational guilt, whether individual or collective. Modern Indian leaders, often joined by church groups and other allies, have developed fine skills in manipulating such guilt feelings for their political purposes, mainly aimed at securing a larger share of the resources available in Canada and the United States. The name of the game being played is interest-group politics, and in the late twentieth century, the Indian has emerged as a significant player on the local and national scenes. However, such emphasis on the negative ignores the positive aspects and consequences of the encounters on external cultural and societal borders and internal ethnic boundaries. Such settings are generally locations for high rates of creative innovation in social and cultural forms.

One of these innovations has been the idea of the Indian, and the notion of commonality of interest, situation, and purpose between individuals and groups that earlier had scarcely known of one another's existence. It is in this larger sense that the Indian is an invention of Euro-Americans, and it is on this basis that Indians today operate as an interest group. To be more accurate, the historical process of reducing various groups of Indians to a common status as one ethnic group among others with greater power and wealth has promoted a reaction—the development of a shared identity. This is further stimulated by the continuing tendency of thinking about Indians in racial terms, a form of thought regularly used by modern Indians.

North Americans regularly mix and confuse ideas about race and ethnicity when thinking about Indians in ways social scientists do not. Both represent forms of social stratification, social means of allocating inequality in prestige, privilege, and power, but they are analytically distinct and different in their effects on people.[46] In contrast to the layer-cake horizontal tiers of social class stratification, both racial and ethnic divisions are vertical; they cut across lines of social class, dividing people into distinct categories and groups. The difference between racial and ethnic groups, however, is dissimilar. The classification and the treatment of people by race presumes that they share inherent, intrinsic, inescapable characteristics. They are of a race automatically at birth, in the American idiom *by blood*, and this is a status and identity they cannot escape by their achievements, accomplishments, or any form of mobility. Indeed, the presumption is that they will always show evidence of their inherent racial nature in physiognomy and in their behavior. Ethnicity, in contrast, is understood in different ways, being defined by mutable, extrinsic characteristics. Ethnicity is marked by a group's style of dress, by speech, by their learned, culturally patterned behaviors. The presumption is that people joined in an ethnic group share a common historical and cultural heritage, but this is not immutable. What is learned can be unlearned or abandoned and new mannerisms and fashions can be mastered. There is, in addition, always the possibility of mobility from one ethnic status to another for both individuals and groups.

The difficulty is that Indians are seen and treated in terms of both race and ethnicity. Often, they are applied at different times, in different contexts, for different purposes, but they are sometimes confounded. The editor of a university press who questioned the inclusion of essays about Sylvester Long and Joe True in this book because neither was "truly Indian," for example, seemed to apply a standard American racial criterion. Neither possessed "Indian blood," she complained, while Sylvester "looked Black" and Joe surely did not have the "features of an Indian." This is a distinction that would have made no sense to traditional Delaware and Kiowa, however, else the former would not have bothered to go out and capture White children, nor would the Kiowa elders have bothered to instruct Joe True in the tenets of their rituals. The doctrines of social race were alien to the thinking of both. However, another consequence of contacts between traditional Indians and Euro-Americans is that most of the former eventually absorbed American and Canadian ideas about race to define their memberships. There are, nonetheless, still persistent exceptions. The conservative Eastern Iroquois, for example, continue to apply matrilineal criteria. Children born of Iroquois mothers are Seneca or Mohawk, but not children born of mothers from other communities. They may be Indians as far as Canadians, Americans, and others are concerned, but they are not legitimately Iroquois.

Part of the confusion of race and ethnicity is that features of both are ordinarily acquired by accident from birth and early learning. The social learning of later years, which can lead to partial or comprehensive identity transformation, is easily forgotten. Birth from parents of the same "race" generally means that children receive biological and cultural characteristics from their parents, although in entirely different ways. Hence, culturally determined patterns are often confused with the few obvious physical characteristics that are inherited genetically. However, sensitivity to such physical characteristics as skin color or hair, and what is made of them, is a historically derived cultural pattern. This pattern emerged among Europeans but was at first absent among traditional Indians. That modern Indians often define their memberships in terms of "degree of blood," placing greater value on a "full blood" than a "quarter blood," is a practice acquired from Euro-Americans. That hundreds of thousands of people not associated with Indian communities nonetheless believe they are "Indians by blood" with rights as such represents another example of this racial thinking, and it is the outgrowth of centuries of both biological interbreeding and the invention of new ways of thinking. That they are often accepted as legitimately Indian by Americans and Canadians represents a victory of the principles of racial stratification over ethnicity.

Historically, there was much interbreeding between Europeans and Indians in North America for more than two centuries before there was a commonly accepted label, and a social category, for the children of such unions. When terms such as *half-breed*, *mixed blood*, and *"brulé"* (burned) emerged, they were coined by the English and French, and reflected exclusively European preoccupations with racial classification. However, the identities attributed to such children, and its influence on their careers, were highly variable—reflecting local social conditions and attitudes that were not uniform or stable.

Billy Caldwell, for example, born of a Mohawk mother and an Anglo-Irish father, by the conventional standards of his mother's people was a Mohawk, but he was socialized in a school for orphans. Caldwell later spent most of his adult life identified and associated with Anglo-Canadians. In all the records and correspondence surrounding him in this period, there is no hint that he was socially identified as Indian or half-breed by others. He made his career without the support of either his father's or his mother's people, and he identified himself as a Briton of Irish ancestry. Only in his later life, after he had migrated into the United States, was he so classified, identified, and treated. The experience of Mary Muskgrove, an early seventeenth century Carolina woman, presents a different picture. Like Caldwell, she had a British father and a mother from a matrilineal society, the Creeks; but unlike Caldwell, she enjoyed the full support of both her father's and her mother's people. In effect, she had two sociological fathers, her biological father from a strongly patridominant community who acted as her sponsor in Anglo-Carolina settlements, and her mother's brother from the matrilineal Creek, who supported and aided her there. Educated, accepted, and active in both communities, her career as an accomplished frontier entrepreneur-diplomat is striking.[47]

Children born of unions between Euro-Americans and Indians, therefore, had different experiences that affected their later identities and careers. They might become identified as a member of one, two, or no ethnic groups, depending on the nature of the cultural frontier where they were born and lived. As we have seen, even children born of British fathers and women from matrilineal societies had different childhood experiences with important consequences for their adult personalities and careers. On the other hand, children born of French or English fathers and mothers from strongly patrilineal Indian communities had a different set of experiences. Such children, because of their fathers' ethnic status, did not easily obtain recognized status as Ottawa, Ojibwa, or Potawatomi. As the career of Chief William Berens shows (Chapter 9), among such patrilineal peoples, it made a difference whether an individual's father or mother was of European extraction. Berens was unusual in fur-trade society because his mother was of English ancestry. He could not have inherited his position as tradition chief had his father been English. Indeed, it was in the Great Lakes area during the fur-trade era, on the edges of such patrilineal Algonquian societies, that a distinctive new type of community emerged—the Franco-Indian Métis—after generations of such interbreeding. Rejected as not fully Indian by local native communities and not accepted as appropriately White by Euro-Americans, they emerged as an ethnic group in their own right.[48]

During the middle nineteenth century, a full-blown, well-known, widely accepted body of ideas emerged about such people, who were products of biological unions between Indians and Euro-Americans. This amounted to a persistent popular stereotype, drawn up and disseminated by literary figures obsessed with thinking about the incompatibility of different types of blood and the "clash of cultures." The accepted image of the half-breed was, however, no more than a literary caricature.[49] One widely accepted feature of the supposed half-breed character was that such people were incapable of adjusting to either Indian or American societies. The most common metaphor used to describe this condition was that they were "suspended between two cultures." Curiously, this American literary stereotype was later adopted by sociologists interested in migration and assimilation, and became part of the early formulations about social marginality, expressed in the marginal man characterization, complete with the use of the suspension metaphor.[50] In this manner, science copied art. The vitality of this stereotype and the "suspended between cultures" metaphor is remarkable. It is still found in use characterizing, for instance, the experience of Indian children in Indian Service boarding schools.

Since all fourteen individuals whose lives are closely examined in this book are marginal men and women, people whose lives were spent on the borders between ethnic groups, readers may ask if they acted as if they were inertly "suspended between cultures" or immobilized by the clash of cultures or races within their own identities. On the contrary, in their experiences, there were creative efforts to cope with and to surmount the conflicts and frustrations of such settings.

Anthropologists, particularly those concerned with the effects of cultural change on personality, have drastically revised this way of thinking about the identities of people whose lives are spent on cultural frontiers. And sociologists and psychologists studying contemporary religious and political conversion have added to this knowledge. The older popular stereotype was that culturally marginal people became psychologically diminished, losing key elements of the ability to live effectively in the community where they were originally socialized without gaining enough of another culture to become comfortably adjusted there.

That the experience of crossing cultural boundaries—of operating first within one ethnic group and then within another or on the edges between both is inherently disabling—is contradicted by the evidence. On the contrary, such people become more complicated psychologically. Biculturism is one name given to this development, meaning that in such settings, people master knowledge of both cultures, which is used to organize their behavior as called for and appropriate in different social contexts. Such people become, not diminished, but culturally enlarged, as Malcolm McFee points out with his apt phrase, "The 150% Man."[51]

Although the mental transformations of people who become involved with and in several cultures includes motivational and emotional aspects, cognitive processes seem especially important. Anthony F. C. Wallace once conceptualized the cognitive world of an individual living in a single cultural world under the rubric *mazeway*. He coined this word deliberately to mean the individual's unique cognitive maps, the mental images of positive and negative goals, the pathways toward these goals, and a complex set of images about persons, places, and things, including a view of the individual's own identity. When people begin interacting with others of different cultures, their mazeways become more complicated. Images of the self change; new goals, values, and skills are added; and different knowledge of the social and physical environments join earlier ones. Arden R. King carries this idea forward to include the experiences of people like our fourteen subjects. Their cognitive worlds, rather than being like simple mazes, become more like stratified labyrinths, he suggests. In their minds are complex sets of cognitive maps, layers of them, each with elements fitting various different cultural settings. Of special importance is the understanding that on cultural and ethnic frontiers, people learn to assume, accommodate, and coordinate different roles.[52]

These thoughts sharpen our insights into the examples discussed in this essay and the fourteen individuals whose life histories are examined in detail in the following essays. Of the three letter writers, for instance, although none had any experience living in an Indian community, each had ideas about being and becoming Indian, namely that the status of being Indian is inherited biologically. Moreover, on discovering an Indian ancestor, this addition to their knowledge became a path toward something desirable, little more than an enhanced sense of self for the elderly woman, but the possibility of a new career track for the "1/16th courtesy Potawatomi." On the other hand, although the young professor had long known of a few Indian ancestors, his personal values said not to manipulate this fragment of his biography to advance his professional prospects—until severe disadvantage dictated otherwise. In the first three examples, we see an emotional gain, a new and refreshing sense of self. But in the last example, there was some loss of self-esteem, for this young man was averse to assuming an Indian role for any purpose.

All these examples and others in this book indicate that there is something wrong with conventional thinking about the idea of the social process known as assimilation. In popular thinking, assimilation as a social policy has recently had a nasty reputation. It is usually described as something the White forces the Indian to do, to become more and more White. It is thought of ordinarily as a policy adopted by powerful groups and imposed on weaker ones with an aim of cultural homogenization. Assimilation is also understood as one-way, permanent, and irreversible. The few examples just given contradict such characterizations. In the first place, the individuals involved were never culturally Indians. Three of them, during their adult years, defined themselves as Indian merely on the basis of the Euro-American racial blood idea, and they and recent ancestors were raised and identified as generic White Americans. To think of these people and others like them as "assimilated" Indians is to remain confused by conventional racial thinking. Instead, these were individuals who assumed the identity of Indian, as did Sylvester Long and Joe True in larger ways (Chapters 8 and 12). Moreover, as discussed earlier and seen in the careers of Simon Girty (Chapter 2) and Joe True (Chapter 12), the practice of assimilation has not been limited to powerful nation states or dominant ethnic groups, nor is it permanent and irreversible.[53]

Defined in the language of social science and seen from the perspective of individuals, being an Indian means to occupy a particular social position (or status). Always, such social positions exist in some relationship with other statuses.[54] Being Indian, therefore, is an aspect of the self, one that affects a person's rights and obligations, always in association with others occupying complementary social positions. Victoria's experience illustrates this idea. Seen as an Indian by her professors who wanted her to serve their interests, and who felt obliged to offer her an opportunity to describe her Indian culture to their classes, she was called on for a public presentation. However, Victoria knew too little to act out this role and was placed in an uncomfortable position. Even a man as deeply involved and expert in his "Indian way" as Dan Raincloud, when called on to describe Ojibwa medical knowledge or to offer tr..ditional prayers in strange contexts, was placed in strained circumstances. On the other hand is the example of Sylvester Long, by self-definition, become Chief Buffalo Child Long Lance, who gladly traveled the continent speaking and writing about the Indian experience, although his knowledge was piecemeal and entirely secondhand, if not simply invented.

These examples, and others throughout this book, mark a feature of cultural frontiers that must be emphasized. When peoples of different languages, cultures, and identities meet and deal with each other, they develop special channels of communication and role networks played by individuals assigned to organize their relationships, which anthropologists call *boundary*, *broker* or *intermediary roles*. The responsibilities of individuals who occupy such intermediary positions are varied. They may translate from one language to another, for instance, or explain the expectations and customs of one group to another, or represent the political-economic interests of one community in the councils of another, or simply model the behavior of their people for the edification or amusement of aliens.[55] Assuming such special responsibilities means enlarging the cognitive worlds of the individuals involved. From Simon Girty to Ooleepeeka, all our subjects assumed and acted out such roles in the cultural middle ground where they lived.

Simon Girty, once he had been captured and resocialized as a Seneca, was equipped linguistically and culturally to act as a cultural broker. Alternating between Indian, British, and American communities, he worked as an interpreter, intelligence agent, low-level diplomat, and guerrilla leader—a late eighteenth century one-man special forces unit. Joseph Renville, in contrast, with his double Dakota and French socialization and identity, built a distinctive bicultural community in which he lived out his life, largely managing economic relationships between the Dakota and Americans. Augustin Hamlin, Jr.'s, life presents a different contrast. Although he was not their first choice, nor was he fully accepted as an Ottawa, the leaders of that society deliberately selected him for advanced education intending that he would serve their political interests as their agent, which he did more-or-less sincerely throughout his life.

In Eleazer Williams's life, we can see elements of the bizarre, perhaps bordering on the pathological. Raised in a missionized Indian community that was culturally marginal, he was embraced and educated by New England Protestants and displayed a willingness to make his career in their communities; but he was turned back to a role they assigned him as a go-between, a missionary to Indians, which brought him no lasting satisfaction. Susette and Susan La Flesche's identities and experiences as Omaha Indians, deliberately arranged and limited in their effects by a father who had larger aspirations for them, were distinctive. Becoming the proteges of an Eastern elite, and thoroughly committed to their styles and mannerisms, both made careers on the middle ground between Indians and Americans, the one serving as a journalist, the other as a medical missionary. Starting near the bottom of the social class ladder, Christine Quintasket's role as Mourning Dove was self-initiated and later enhanced by American patrons. Hers was a life of ceaseless menial toil, in which she regularly cycled between being an impoverished author producing for American audiences and refreshing herself as a Salish woman in Salish ways.

For Sylvester Long, becoming an Indian provided an escape from the stigma and restrictions of being Black in the early twentieth century American South. His was an adopted ethnic identity pure and simple, one which he enacted as a solitary performer before exclusively Canadian and American— never Indian—audiences, an identity that allowed him to realize much of his talent and potential but at a terrible, ultimately fatal cost. Chief William Berens, in contrast, stood firmly within a community created by his Saulteaux ancestors, where he inherited an honored role played out amidst both Indian and Canadian counterparts. To this political role, as leader and representative of his community, he added several other parts including the responsibility of acting as cultural guide for anthropologist A. Irving Hallowell, which had large and lasting effects. Also rooted in his home community, but in a different position as a principal religious leader, Dan Raincloud's career was marked by the constant need to make demanding choices, and the strains of balancing traditional constraints with novel calls on his expertise, requests that he serve and perform in contexts not known to his predecessors, the ethnic frontiers of the twentieth century.

Still enjoying a life that looks as if it will extend over the entire twentieth century and beyond, Maud Clairmont has experienced and coped with more changes than most humans will ever know. Coming from a large western frontier family with antecedents in many different ethnic groups, her career in the Shoshone reservation community expressed continuity with a distinctive family ethos, one dedicated to meshing Shoshone with American ways. If Malcolm McFee can speak of 150% Blackfoot men, certainly Maud Clairmont is at least that, maybe a 200% Shoshone woman. Joe True, on the other hand, became a Kiowa ritualist only temporarily. Once adopted and educated by his Kiowa sponsors, he was responsible for acting as their missionary among Americans and other Indians. This special role temporarily suited his drive toward discovering personal spiritual truths, a consuming need that later moved him to a distinctive, self-generated role as pastor for his own flock. Finally, the careful, formal comparison of the lives and personalities of Ooleepeeka and Mina makes a significant point. Not all people raised in the same culturally distinctive community become equally well-equipped to cope with the problems of living in an increasingly complex world. Ooleepeeka's stable, supportive, and successful family gave her a base for adult competence that Mina's contrasting childhood experiences did not.

NOTES

1. Eleanor B. Leacock and Nancy O. Lurie, eds., *North American Indians in Historical Perspective* (Prospect Heights, IL: Waveland Press, reissued 1988 [1971)], pp. 418–80.
2. The best single overview of such changing images is Robert F. Berkhofer, Jr., *The White Man's Indian: Images of the American Indian from Columbus to the Present* (New York: Alfred A. Knopf, 1978).
3. See John A. Price, *Native Studies, American and Canadian Indians* (Toronto: McGraw-Hill Ryerson, 1978), pp. 200–216.
4. Rodney Needham, *Exemplars* (Berkeley: University of California Press, 1985), p. 190.
5. *U.S. Senate Concurrent Resolution 76*, September 16, 1987. For an authoritative study of this invented tradition, see Elisabeth Tooker, "The United States Constitution and the Iroquois League," *Ethnohistory* 35 (1988, in press).
6. See Rudolph Kaiser, " 'A Fifth Gospel, Almost', Chief Seattle's Speech(es), American Origins and European Reception," in Christian F. Feest, ed., *Indians and Europe: An Interdisciplinary Collection of Essays* (Aachen: Rader Verlag, 1987), pp. 505–26.
7. Victor W. Turner and Edward M. Bruner, eds., *The Anthropology of Experience* (Urbana: University of Illinois Press, 1986), pp. 139–53.
8. For the purposes of his own narrative account, Bruner exaggerated the uniformity of anthropological views and activities in this period. Those most concerned with the development of acculturation theory fully recognized that there were several potential alternative outcomes of culture contact other than just assimilation of small, powerless groups. These alternatives included rebellious separatism and progressive mutual adjustments leading either to stable cultural pluralism or the fusion of two or more existing cultures into a distinctive new system. For a systematic discussion of these lesser known ideas, see, Homer G. Barnett, et al., "Acculturation: An Exploratory Formulation," *American Anthropologist* 56 (1954), pp. 9732–1002, especially Barnett's dissenting appendix to that report; and, Edward H. Spicer, ed., *Perspectives in American Indian Culture Change* (University of Chicago Press, 1961), pp. 517–44. Bruner's abbreviated perspective on anthropological thinking in this period is part of the later dominant story line that replaced it.
9. In the field of history, there are a few critics of these developments. See Wilcomb E. Washburn, "Distinguishing History from Moral Philosophy and Public Advocacy," in Calvin Martin, ed., *The American Indian and the Problem of History* (New York: Oxford University Press, 1987), pp. 91–97; and, Thomas Hagan, "Full Blood, Mixed Blood, Generic, and Ersatz: the Persisting Problem of Indian Identity," *Arizona and the West* (1986), pp. 309–26; also, James A. Clifton, "The Political Rhetoric of Indian History," *Annals of Iowa* 49 (1988), pp.101–11.
10. The absence of systematic analysis and the concealment of anything that might be a blemish distinguishes much of the writing in this genre. For examples, see, R. David Edmunds, ed., *Studies in Diversity: American Indian Leaders* (Lincoln:

University of Nebraska Press, 1980); Margot Liberty, ed., *American Indian Intellectuals* (St. Paul, Minn.: West Publishing Company, 1978); and, L. G. Moses and R. Wilson, eds., *Indian Lives; Essays on Nineteenth- and Twentieth-Century Native American Leaders* (Albuquerque, N.M.: University of New Mexico Press, 1985). For an alternate perspective in studies of nonheroes, see James A. Clifton, "Personal and Ethnic Identity on the Great Lakes Frontier: the Case of Billy Caldwell, Anglo-Canadian," *Ethnohistory* 78 (1978), pp. 69–94; and, "Simon Pokagon's Sandbar," *Michigan History* 71 (1987), pp. 12–17.

11. The best dispassionate overview of such developments in the United States is in Francis Paul Prucha, *The Great Father, The United States Government and the American Indians*, 2 vols. (Lincoln, University of Nebraska Press, 1984), 2, pp.1017–1207. For a good discussion of similar happenings in Canada and more on the United States, consult Price, *Native Studies*. For an excellent study of the Lumbee, the largest of the recently "reconstituted Indian" communities, see Karen I. Blu, *The Lumbee Problem: The Making of an American Indian People* (New York: Cambridge University Press, 1980). For a study of the triracial Nanticoke, also recently resuscitated as official Indians, see Frank W. Porter III, *The Nanticoke* (New York: Chelsea House, 1987); and the same author's *Strategies for Survival, American Indians in the Eastern United States* (Westport, Conn.: Greenwood Press, 1986). Also compare J. Anthony Parades, "The Emergence of Contemporary Eastern Creek Indian Identity," in Thomas K. Fitzgerald, ed., *Social and Cultural Identity: Problems of Persistence and Change* (Athens: University of Georgia Press, 1974), pp. 63–79. Parades, who does not subscribe to the dominant plot, shows how and why a group like the Eastern Creek set out to obtain federal recognition as Indians. James A. Clifton's *The Pokagons* (Washington, D.C.: University Press of America, 1984), was written on behalf of a community of Catholic Potawatomi seeking such recognition.

12. A recent description of this inhibiting process is in Loretta Fowler, *Shared Symbols, Contested Meanings: Gros Ventre Culture and History, 1778–1984* (Lincoln, Neb.: University of Nebraska Press, 1987), pp. xi–xii.

13. It is difficult to imagine an American anthropologist reporting as frankly the insults experienced while working among the Navajo and Hopi as Armin W. Geertz did in his "Prophets and Fools: The Rhetoric of Hopi Indian Eschatology," *European Review of Native American Studies* 1 (1987), pp. 33–46. Also, see similar, more detached essays in Feest, ed., *Indians and Europe*.

14. See David Henige, "On the Contact Population of Hispaniola: History as Higher Mathematics," *Hispanic American Historical Review* 58 (1978), pp. 217–37; "If Pigs Could Fly: Timucuan Population and Native American Historical Demography," *Journal of Interdisciplinary History* 16 (1986), 701–20; and "Primary Source by Primary Source? On the Role of Epidemics in New World Depopulation," *Ethnohistory* 33 (1986), pp. 293–312.

15. See, Henry Steele Commager and Elmo Giordanetti, eds., *Was America a Mistake? An Eighteenth-Century Controversy* (New York: Harper and Row, 1967); and, Percy G. Adams, "Benjamin Franklin and the Travel Writing Tradition," in J. A. G. Lemay, ed., *The Oldest Revolutionary: Essays on Benjamin Franklin* (Philadelphia: University of Pennsylvania Press, 1976), pp. 45–48.

16. For other examples of such representations, inert and two-dimensional or three-dimensional and mobile, see Plates 7–1, 8–1C, 11–1, and 12–1 in this book. Also see Christine Turnauer, "Contemporary Plains Indians Portraits," *European Review*

of Native American Studies 1 (1987), pp. 25–32; and Hugh Honour, *The New Golden Land, European Images of America From the Discovery to the Present Time* (New York: Pantheon Books, 1975), especially pp. 242–47.

17. For a full account of the historic Squanto and this event, see Lynn Ceci, "Fish Fertilizer: A Native North American Practice?" *Science* 188 (1975), pp. 26–30.

18. For a history of this legend, see James Axtell and William C. Sturtevant, "The Unkindest Cut, or Who Invented Scalping?" *William & Mary Quarterly*, 3 ser. 37 (1980), pp. 451–72.

19. Elisabeth Tooker, "The United States Constitution and the Iroquois League," *Ethnohistory* 35 (1988, in press). The Wampanoag nation is one of the tiny remnant triracial eastern groups recently resurrected (in April 1987) and given official tribal status by the Bureau of Indian Affairs.

20. For a discussion of the implications and consequences of this, see R. Bruce Morrison and C. Roderick Wilson, eds., *Native Peoples: the Canadian Experience* (Toronto: McClelland and Stewart, 1986), especially pp. 523–28.

21. See, Prucha, *The Great Father*, 2, pp. 649–50; and Arrel M. Gibson, *The American Indian: Prehistory to the Present* (Norman: University of Oklahoma Press, 1969) pp. 453–54.

22. See Marvin Harris, "Race," in D. L. Shills, ed., *International Encyclopedia of the Social Sciences*, 13 (1968), pp. 263–67.

23. For further discussion, see James A. Clifton, *The Prairie People: Continuity and Change in Potawatomi Indian Culture, 1665–1965* (Lawrence, Kan.: Regents Press of Kansas, 1977), pp. 250–59.

24. For a marvelous exposition of this process, see Virginia R. Dominguez, *White by Definition, Social Classification in Creole Louisiana* (New Brunswick, N.J.: Rutgers University Press, 1986); and her article "The Marketing of Heritage," *American Ethnologist*, 13 (1986), pp. 546–55; also, Blu, *The Lumbee Problem*.

25. Anne Wortham, in *The Other Side of Racism: A Philosophical Study of Black Race Consciousness* (Columbus, Ohio: The Ohio University Press, 1981), especially pp. 75–79, addresses these issues regarding American Blacks. For a full analysis of a comparable situation involving a Mexican community, see Judith Friedlander, *Being Indian in Hueapan: A Study of Forced Identity in Contemporary Mexico* (New York: St. Martin's Press, 1975).

26. See Jacqueline Peterson and Jennifer Brown, eds., *The New Peoples: Being and Becoming Métis in North America* (Lincoln, Neb.: University of Nebraska Press, 1984); and Thomas K. Flanagan, "Louis Riel and the Dispersion of the American Métis," *Minnesota History* 49 (1985), pp. 179–90.

27. See Clifton, *The Prairie People*, especially pp. 361–403; also see H. Craig Miner and W. E. Unrah, *The End of Indian Kansas: A Study of Cultural Revolution, 1854–1871* (Lawrence, Kan.: Regents Press of Kansas, 1978).

28. See Hagan, "Full Blood, Mixed Blood, Generic, and Ersatz" pp. 317–19; and Stephen E. Feraca, "Why Don't They Give Them Guns": The Great American Indian Myth (In press), chapter 1.

29. Francis Paul Prucha, *American Indian Policy in the Formative Years: The Indian Trade and Intercourse Acts, 1790–1834* (Cambridge, Mass.: Harvard University Press, 1962).

30. Clifton, *The Prairie People*, pp. 250–52; and "Chippewa Death March: Explaining the Extremes in Old Northwest Indian Removal," *Transactions of the Wisconsin Academy of Arts, Letters, and Sciences* (1987, in press).

31. Most treaties in this period contain lists of such payments. See Charles J. Kappler, ed., *Indian Treaties: 1778–1883* (New York: Interland, 1972), especially pp.145–781.
32. See Clifton, "Chippewa Death March."
33. See Frederick E. Hoxie, *A Final Promise: the Campaign to Assimilate the Indians, 1880–1920* (University of Nebraska Press, 1984), for an overview of the Dawes Act and some of its social and economic consequences. Like many scholars, Hoxie does not deal with Indian status or identity critically.
34. Feraca, *"Why Don't They Give Them Guns"*, chapter 2.
35. Clifton, *The Prairie People*, pp. 379–403, 433–34.
36. Clifton, "Personal and Ethnic Identity"; also,"Merchant, Soldier, Broker, Chief: A Corrected Obituary of Captain Billy Caldwell," *Journal of the Illinois State Historical Society* 71 (1978), pp. 185–210.
37. Before the Civil Rights Movement era, Sylvester Long was by no means the only "Black" who assumed an Indian identity and a helping role with respect to Indian communities. See Susan K. Postal, "Hoax Natavism at Caughnawaga: A Control Case for the Theory of Revitalization," *Ethnology* 4 (1965), pp. 266–81; and Clifton, *The Prairie People*, pp. 430–31.
38. Jay O'Brien, "Toward a Reconstitution of Ethnicity: Capitalist Expansion and Cultural Dynamics in Sudan," *American Anthropologist* 88 (1986), pp. 898–907. The Catholic Potawatomi of Michigan, often besieged by claimants when they assemble to discuss their economic future, have coined an English word, *meandom*, to express their distaste for what they see as a mercenary attitude toward being Indian. Clifton calls this process the *Indian windfall syndrome*. See his "Chippewa Death March."
39. *Indian Policy in the United States: Historical Essays* (Lincoln, Neb.: University of Nebraska Press, 1981), pp. 2–3. In her "Pagans, Converts, and Backsliders, All: A Secular View of the Metaphysics of Indian-White Relations," in Martin, *The American Indian and the Problem of History*, pp.75–83, Mary Young raises a similar issue about the racial antecedents of some "Indians" but does not follow through systematically.
40. "From White Men to Redskin: Changing Anglo-American Perceptions of the American Indian." *The American Historical Review* 87 (1982), pp. 918–19.
41. For glimpses of such relationships, see Charles Hudson, *The Southeastern Indians* (Knoxville, The University of Tennessee Press, 1976); Brewton Berry, "Marginal Groups," in Bruce G. Trigger, ed., *Handbook of North American Indians: Northeast* 15, (Washington, D.C.: Smithsonian Institution, 1978), pp. 290–95; and William C. Sturtevant, "Creek into Seminole," in Leacock and Lurie, *North American Indians*, pp. 92–128.
42. Walker D. Wyman and Clifton B. Kroeber, eds., *The Frontier in Perspective* (Madison, Wis.: The University of Wisconsin Press, 1965), pp. xiii–xx.
43. See Charlotte Seymour-Smith, *Dictionary of Anthropology* (Boston: G. K. Hall, 1986), p. 125; and A. Irving Hallowell, "The Backwash of the Frontier: The Impact of the Indian on American Culture," in Wyman and Kroeber, *Frontier in Perspective*, pp. 229–58.
44. For a full presentation of the legal and political myths used by advocates of this developing Indian nationalism, see Charles F. Wilkinson, *American Indians, Time, and the Law* (New Haven, Conn.: Yale University Press, 1987).
45. See, Eric Hobsbawm and Terence Ranger, eds., *The Invention of Tradition* (Cambridge University Press, 1983).

46. Gerald Berreman, ed., *Social Inequality: Comparative and Developmental Approaches* (New York: Academic Press, 1981), pp. 1–30.
47. Clifton, "Personal and Ethnic Identity"; and Michael Green, "The Enigmatic Mary Muskgrove," paper presented at the 1987 Meetings of the Western History Association.
48. Peterson and Brown, *The New Peoples*.
49. William J. Scheick, *The Half-Breed: A Cultural Symbol in 19th-Century American Fiction* (Louisville, Ky.: The University Press of Kentucky, 1979).
50. Robert E. Park, "Human Migration and the Marginal Man," in Ralph E. Turner, ed., *Robert E. Park on Social Control and Collective Behavior: Selected Papers* (Chicago: The University of Chicago Press, 1967), pp. 194–206.
51. Steven Polgar, "Biculturation of Mesquakie Teenage Boys," *American Anthropologist* 62 (1960), pp. 217–35; and Malcolm McFee, "The 150% Man: a Product of Blackfoot Acculturation," *American Anthropologist* 70 (1968), pp. 1096–1107. Also, see David G. Bromley and James T. Richardson, eds., *The Brainwashing/Deprogramming Controversy: Sociological, Psychological, Legal and Historical Perspectives* (New York: Edwin Mellen Press, 1983).
52. Anthony F. C. Wallace, *Culture and Personality*, 2d ed. (New York: Random House, 1970), especially pp. 15–20; and Arden D. King, "A Stratification of Labyrinths: the Acquisition and Retention of Cultural Identity in Modern Culture," in Fitzgerald, *Social and Cultural Identity*, pp. 106–17.
53. See A. Irving Hallowell, "American Indians, White and Black: the Phenomenon of Transculturation," *Current Anthropology* 4 (1963), pp. 519–31.
54. Ward Goodenough, "Rethinking Status and Role: Toward a General Model of the Cultural Organization of Social Relationships," in M. Banton, ed., *The Relevance of Models for Social Anthropology* (New York: Praeger, 1965), pp. 3–8.
55. Barnett, "Acculturation: An Exploratory Formulation."

CHAPTER 2

Simon Girty: Interpreter and Intermediary

Colin G. Calloway

PRESENTING SIMON GIRTY (1741–1818)

Simon Girty's life spanned the last decades of American colonial dependency, the emergence of a young United States, and seven decades of nearly constant frontier conflict in the Great Lakes-Ohio Valley region. At the heart of these clashes were the vital political and economic interests of British loyalists, Americans, and Indian societies in the area. Girty's adult career was fixed by a feature of these rivalries little known today: the Indian communities in the vicinity regularly replenished their populations by forcibly abducting children and young people from their neighbors, commonly from American frontier communities. Such captives, violently separated from family and community, were transported spatially and culturally into the villages of their captors, where they were often successfully assimilated, their social identities transformed, becoming accepted and behaving as Shawnee or Delaware or Wyandot men and women. Taken captive at age fourteen with the surviving members of his family in 1755, the experiences of Simon and his brothers illustrate the variable reactions of such prisoners to Indian efforts to resocialize and convert them. Elder brother Thomas escaped and made his way back to an American community. Younger brother George, although with Simon in 1758, given the opportunity of returning to his home, voluntarily maintained his affiliation and a Delaware identity until the end of his life. Simon Girty, however, accepted his liberation but spent the rest of his life in a series of occupational roles on the margins between Indian and English-speaking communities. There, he constructed a distinctive career, built on his dual identity, his multilingual skills, and his knowledge of both Indian and American cultures. There, also, he acquired a contemporary and an historical reputation as a vicious, untrustworthy, disloyal frontier Tory and renegade, a "White savage." As the author points out, however, Simon Girty was never fully Indianized, nor was he ever entirely content with a peaceful life spent wholly within any American or Canadian community. His life was spent on extraordinarily conflicted ethnic and national borderlands, exposed to and involved in all the violent controversies such mercurial conditions dictated. (J. A. Clifton)

As a student of British-Indian relations in the generation after the American Revolution, I became intrigued by members of the British Indian department who functioned as intermediaries between the Redcoats and the tribes with whom they dealt. Further delving into colonial and frontier history heightened my interest in the experiences of Euro-American captives who remained in or on the edges of Indian society. Having just relinquished a secure academic position in England for an uncertain future in the United States with my American wife, I was particularly struck by Everett Stonequist's description of "the marginal man" as: "The individual who through migration, education or marriage, or some other influence leaves one social group or culture without making a satisfactory adjustment to another finds himself on the margin of each but a member of neither." My interest in marginals grew even as my feelings of marginality diminished, and I focused on the individuals whom social elites and folklore had dubbed outcasts.[1]

Of all the categories of marginal people that emerged on the frontier, renegades—those who joined the Indians and fought against their own kind—aroused the greatest hatred and detestation. Paranoia, fear, and rumor colored contemporaneous stereotyped reactions to renegades and established them in popular imagination as degenerate turncoats who surpassed their Indian friends in cruelty and treachery. No renegade—perhaps no individual in American frontier history—enjoyed such notoriety as Simon Girty. But Girty's reputation rests on the vociferousness of hostile commentary rather than the fullness of the records, and his historical image has been blackened and dimmed by the hatred of some contemporaries and the judgments of later writers. In American eyes, loyalists who served in the British Indian Department were double traitors who had forsaken both their country and their race. Having cast his lot with the losing side, Girty became an easy target for writers and historians who readily accepted the judgments of hostile witnesses like Moravian missionary John Heckewelder, who pronounced him "as brutal, depraved, and wicked a wretch as ever lived."[2]

Most accounts of Girty have been written by Americans and fall into two broad categories. Traditional narratives portrayed him as a sadistic traitor who abandoned "civilization" for the company of Indian "savages" and their British paymasters. More moderate discussions have attempted to show that Girty was not as much of a devil as he has been painted, but nonetheless dwell on the sensational aspects of his life and rarely manage to depict him as anything better than a scoundrel. The purpose of this essay is neither to review and refute the extensive apocrypha surrounding Simon Girty nor to whitewash his character. Even from nonjudgmental records, Girty emerges as a volatile individual who could be violent, vengeful, and drunken, and who frequently displayed moodiness, insecurity, and hypersensitivity, attributes which were common among others on American frontiers. This essay offers a short biographic portrait of the man, sympathetic to the extent that it is written from the perspective of his British and Indian friends, not that of his American enemies, and focuses on his occupational roles as interpreter and intermediary at a crucial period of Anglo-American Indian relations.

Simon Girty's Old Northwest

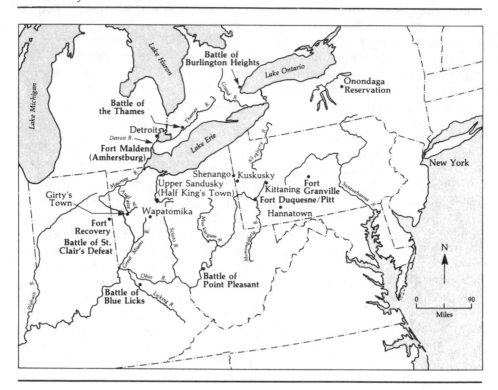

The key to understanding Simon Girty and the forces that moved him is to consider him not as a renegade beyond the pale of American society but as a marginal individual who moved freely and functioned as an intercultural broker between Indian and British. Americans regarded Girty as scum; the British valued his services and utilized his talents but did not attach the importance to him that American accounts would suggest. However, Girty's role and standing among the Indians offers perhaps the best clues to his abilities, character, and identity.

Accustomed to chiefs who fulfilled transactional roles in times of contact and crisis, the Indians found it easy to accept a man like Girty and to place confidence in him. A former captive, married to an Indian, knowledgeable in Indian languages and customs, yet experienced in the ways of frontier Americans, Girty was well-qualified to serve as a pivotal person at a time when tribal relations with the British assumed critical importance. That Girty achieved respect and prestige among the Indians testifies to his talents as an interpreter and his usefulness as an intermediary. Such acceptance also indicates that Girty displayed characteristics that Indians valued: courage in war, integrity in personal relationships, generosity to the less fortunate, and honesty, which was important to Girty's role as a trader and dispenser of goods from the King's stores. Simon Girty was a complex and multifaceted individual; we have a long way to go to get behind his historical image and understand him as the Indians evidently did.

Simon Girty was the second son of an Irish immigrant who came to America around 1730 and settled in Pennsylvania. Simon Girty, Sr., took up business as a trader at Chambers Mill and in 1737 married an English girl, Mary Newton, who bore him four sons: Thomas, Simon, James, and George. Simon was born in 1741. When the boy was eight years old, his father moved the family across the Susquehanna River to Sherman's Creek, where a dozen families had erected cabins on Indian lands. The authorities of newly formed Cumberland County soon took steps to remove the squatters, and in 1750, Simon Girty, Sr., and the others were charged with trespass and bound to appear at the next county court. Some of the squatters' cabins were put to the torch: they were "of no considerable Value, being such as the Country People erect in a Day or two."[3]

The Girty family returned to Chambers Mill. There, in 1751, occurred the first of a series of tragic incidents that marred the early years of the Girty brothers and created the impression that Simon was bred to violence. According to tradition and the accounts of Girty's biographers, Simon Girty, Sr., was killed in a drunken brawl with an Indian called The Fish. But, in fact, Girty, Sr., was killed in a duel with a man named Samuel Saunders, who was accused of murder and tried at the Pennsylvania Supreme Court in 1751, with the jury returning a verdict of manslaughter.[4]

Girty's widow soon remarried a neighbor, John Turner, who moved the family back to the Sherman's Creek area in the summer of 1755. But Braddock's rout on the Monongahela and Neyon de Vellier's Franco-Indian expedition from Fort Duquesne sent the settlers scurrying to Fort Granville for protection. When the Fort was surrendered and burnt, the Girty family was captured and taken to the town of Kittaning on the Allegheny, headquarters of the Delaware war chiefs Shingas and Captain Jacobs. The Indians tortured and killed John Turner in the presence of the other captives, but fourteen-year-old Simon, his brothers, and mother were earmarked for adoption. When Colonel John Armstrong attacked and destroyed Kittaning, a handful of captives escaped and made it back to Fort Pitt. Thomas Girty was one of the persons rescued. But the Indians fled into the woods with the other prisoners, who were divided as the Indian force dispersed. Mary Girty, her newborn infant, and George were taken by the Delawares, who withdrew to less-exposed villages at Shenango and Kuskushy (near Sharon and New Castle, Pennsylvania, respectively). James was given to the Shawnees, and the western Senecas took young Simon for adoption.

The Girty brothers were captured at an age when they were particularly susceptible to pressures for reeducation and resocialization exerted by their Indian captors. Thomas, the eldest, escaped and resumed life in the Pittsburgh frontier community, where he achieved respectability. George, the youngest, by many accounts was almost totally "Indianized" and later took to living almost exclusively among Indians. Some reports referred to him as Indian Girty. Simon presumably underwent customary Seneca adoption rituals and for three years he lived as a Seneca, learning the language and following their customs.

General John Forbes captured Fort Duquesne in 1758; the next year, the Ohio Indians made a treaty with the British in which they agreed to hand over their prisoners. To judge by the emotional strain commonly generated on such occasions, Girty's liberation constituted another upheaval in the youth's already turbulent life. Returning to Fort Duquesne, he was united with his mother and brothers. The family probably sought shelter at Fort Pitt during Pontiac's War, and around 1765, Mrs. Turner and her five sons settled in the Squirrel Hill district of Pittsburgh. The sons apparently blazed trees, claiming a large tract of land by "tomahawk right," and built a log cabin for the family. In 1769, Thomas, Simon, and George each made application for large tracts of land, part of which included their mother's claim. Subsequent years saw the Girty brothers again separated. The younger Girty brothers forfeited all their land on Squirrel Hill when they sided with the British during the Revolution, but Thomas Girty lived there until sometime before 1792, when he moved his family to Girty's Run on the Allegheny River. Girty's half brother, John Turner, grew up and lived at Squirrel Hill as a land dealer and agent until his death in 1840, at age eighty-five.

Simon, George, and James earned a living as traders and interpreters. An account book of Baynton, Wharton, and Morgan at Fort Pitt shows that the company had thirteen traders employed in 1767, including the Girty brothers.[5] With numerous Virginia and Pennsylvania merchants operating out of Fort Pitt, Simon's services were in demand as an interpreter, mainly to the Delawares. He evidently earned the Indians' esteem because about this time a Delaware named Katepakomin took the name "Simon Girty" for himself. This was a common Delaware practice; adopting another's name displayed both respect and an interest in acquiring some of the special power enjoyed by the original holder. Katepakomin was delivered as a hostage to Bouquet under the name Simon Girty in 1764, and in 1765 this Indian Girty was listed as a noted warrior of the Delawares, along with Wingenum, Captain Pipe, White Eyes, and Captain Johnny.[6] The original Simon Girty's employment as an interpreter indicated that he was held in no mean respect by the British as well: the British Indian Department looked for men "of the best Character, and knowledge of the Indian language" to serve as interpreters; and in the fall of 1769, Girty was the translator at a private conference held at Fort Pitt between the officers and the chiefs of the Six Nations.[7] Already, it seems, Girty was a man with a command of various languages, well-accepted in several cultures.

As a young man, Girty lived in turbulent times and the conflicts were not only between Indians and frontier Americans. In 1771, he voted in the first election ever held in Bedford County, Pennsylvania. For inhabitants of the

Pennsylvania frontier in the early 1770s, the major issue was not yet Patriot versus Tory, but the dispute between Virginia and Pennsylvania for jurisdiction over the forks of the Ohio River. Both claimed the region and both sold land there to home seekers and speculators. When the Pennsylvania and Virginia factions divided into armed camps, Girty sided with the Virginians and was soon involved in several scrapes. At the October 1773 session of the Westmoreland County court, "a true bill for misdeameanour" was found against him by the grand jury and a "process" was issued for his arrest, although he evidently escaped prosecution. In May 1774, an altercation occurred at the house of a Pennsylvania man named Aeneas McKay, in which a blow was struck at McKay's wife, "but Simon Girty, who stood by, parried off the Stroke with his hand." The following year, McKay accused "the perfideous Savage Simon Girty" of making a mob drunk and inciting them to violence. Similarly, on Christmas Eve 1774, Girty was a leader of an armed gang that marched on the Westmoreland County jail in Hannastown and ordered the jailer to release one of their comrades.[8] Girty's alignment with Governor Dunmore of Virginia and his agent, Dr. John Connolly, brought him into the camp of those who would soon prove loyal to the Crown, at a time when events were in motion that would lead to revolution and independence.

When tensions between westward-driving frontiersmen, speculators, and angry Shawnee warriors erupted into Dunmore's War, the British Indian Department played a key role in preventing the formation of a multitribal confederacy and keeping the Shawnees isolated. Simon Girty functioned as a capable and trusted interpreter in the process. In the fall of 1773, various Indian delegations had assembled at Pittsburgh to complain of liquor dealers and encroachments by settlers. Following the council, Girty accompanied the Seneca statesman Kayashuta on his journey to carry his report and recommendations to the Six Nations Iroquois of New York, and to Superintendent Sir William Johnson, Colonel Guy Johnson, Kayashuta and several other Indians. Girty was rewarded: for his services he was paid five shillings a day, earning £45 10s between September 1773 and March 1774.[9]

As depredations against the Indians escalated in the spring of 1774, Girty was increasingly active. When he learned of Michael Cresap's unprovoked attack on a group of Shawnee chiefs, Alexander McKee, deputy Indian agent for Sir William Johnson, dispatched Girty to bring in the chiefs living nearest to Pittsburgh. McKee met with Kayashuta, White Mingo, and the Six Nations delegates, assuring them that the recent murders were unauthorized and that the Governor of Virginia would make ample restitution. Girty returned with White Eyes, Captain Pipe, and other Delaware chiefs, whom after spending the evening in consultation with McKee and Kayashuta, agreed to help in trying to restore harmony. White Eyes volunteered to carry word to the Ohio tribes, but frontier settlers were in a less pacific mood and Simon Girty had to escort White Eyes's family to Croghan Hall, protecting them against vigilantes.[10] Continued Virginian aggression negated these peace efforts but the Indian Department successfully dissuaded the westernmost tribes from supporting the Shawnees and the Ohio Valley Iroquois (then called Mingoes).

Girty served as a scout and interpreter with Lord Dunmore, and was one emissary the governor sent to the Shawnees with an offer to negotiate after the Battle of Point Pleasant. The Shawnee chiefs, Cornstalk and White Fish, were induced to come in and make peace, accepting the Ohio River as their southern border. Girty is also reputed to have brought the Mingo chief Logan's famous speech back to Camp Charlotte at this time and to have recited it from memory. Dunmore apparently had Girty and his half brother, John Turner, do an Indian dance one evening in camp, "which they did, with accompanying with songs, kicking fire brands about etc."[11]

Girty accompanied Dunmore back across the Ohio where, while world-shaking events gathered momentum, the mundane questions of life also demanded attention. In January 1775, Girty paid £1 10s for a pair of breeches in Pittsburgh; the following June, the man who became the terror of the American frontier had his breeches washed at a cost of 2s and 6d.[12] On February 22, 1775, the Virginia Court for Augusta County convened at Fort Dunmore. Simon Girty took the usual oath of allegiance to King George III, subscribed to the abjuration oath and test, and was ordered certified as a lieutenant of militia in the Pittsburgh region.[13] Two months later, the American Revolution erupted.

The outbreak of the conflict guaranteed that Girty's services as an interpreter would again be in demand—not only by the Americans and the British. In July 1775, a spokesman of the Six Nations told the Virginian representatives in a council at Fort Dunmore:

"Brethren: As we cannot well do without a person who understands the Language of the six Nations, We therefore desire that Simon Girty should be appointed to interpret any matters we may have to say to you hereafter upon Public Business; and if it is agreeable to you we desire that your string [of wampum] may accompany ours to the six Nations upon this Subject to let them know of such agreement."[14]

The opening months of the American Revolution, therefore, found Girty assisting the Virginia commissioners, and he made several journeys into the Ohio country on their behalf.

In July and August 1775, he accompanied Captain James Wood as an interpreter in a tour that embraced the Ohio villages of the Delawares, Senecas, Wyandots, and Shawnees. Girty's services were well-rewarded the following January.[15] In the spring of 1776, Congress took direct control of Indian affairs and appointed George Morgan Indian agent at Fort Pitt, with orders to try to keep the Indian tribes neutral. On May 1, Simon Girty was appointed interpreter to the Six Nations for the rebellious colonies at the rate of five-eighths of a dollar per day, and in the middle of the month, Morgan dispatched him with a belt of peace and friendship to the Six Nations Council at Onondaga, where delegates from all except the Mohawks had assembled.[16] Girty was earning a living as a specialist on a cultural—as well as a revolutionary—frontier, brokering relations between all comers, Indians and non-Indians. Despite his oath of allegiance to the Crown, Girty displayed little hesitation in serving the rebels' cause. But Morgan and he came from vastly different backgrounds and evidently did not get along. Within three months, Girty was discharged.

Hanging around Pittsburgh, with no pay and no commission, his talents unused, Girty became increasingly alienated. He enlisted men in the Pittsburgh region for service in the Patriot army and apparently expected a captain's commission as his just reward. Instead, he was made a second lieutenant in Captain John Stephenson's company, a position he resigned in August 1777. According to one informant, the refusal to give Girty a captain's commission was natural, "he being a drunken and unfit person," but frontiersman Simon Kenton held Girty in consistently high regard and thought he was greatly wronged.[17]

As the Year of the Three Sevens neared a close, Girty continued working for the Patriot cause among the tribes, carrying word of the victory over Burgoyne to the Seneca towns at the head of the Allegheny River and gathering information on the activities of Indian war parties. The Senecas apparently "told him they looked on him as a Spy" and threatened to hand him over to the British at Niagara. Clearly, Girty's standing with the people who had adopted him in his youth could change with circumstances. But when faced with the Senecas' threat, he seized an opportunity to make good his escape and reported back to Fort Pitt by the beginning of December.[18]

That same month, however, rumors of a Tory conspiracy led to Girty's being thrown into the guardhouse at Fort Pitt. Alarmed by reports that plans were afoot to murder all the Patriots and hand over the fort to the British, General Edward Hand had Girty arrested, along with other suspects George Morgan, Colonel John Campbell, and Alexander McKee. According to one story, Girty escaped from the guardhouse one evening, slept in an apple tree in the orchard next to the fort, and gave himself up the next morning "to show that they could not keep him." Subsequent examination of the prisoners revealed little or no evidence implicating a conspiracy. Girty was examined before a civil magistrate and acquitted.[19] Temporarily reinstated in the Patriots' confidence, he participated in General Hand's "squaw campaign" in February 1778.

However, Girty's Tory sympathies strengthened as his sense of ill treatment by the Patriots grew. Finally, on the night of March 28, 1778, together with Alexander McKee (who had lost his position as a Patriot Indian agent), Matthew Elliott, McKee's cousin Robert Surphit, a man named Higgins, and two of McKee's Black servants, he fled from Pittsburgh to Detroit and offered his services to the British commander, Henry Hamilton. The defection of Girty, Elliott, and McKee, three of the frontiersmen most influential among potentially hostile Indians, spread alarm through the frontier settlements. They were denounced as blackhearted rogues who had betrayed their countrymen to British scalp collectors; and each was proclaimed guilty of high treason against the Commonwealth of Pennsylvania.[20] In addition, Girty forfeited his property, the improvements made thereupon, and left "a pretty good farm" to his half brother John Turner. The records of the Loyalist Claims Commission show that Girty claimed he lost a total of 873 acres, of which 300 were in Kentucky. He claimed payment of £521 from the British and was awarded £235.[21]

In the conditions of the time, however, Girty's decision to side with the Crown was logical and understandable. He was a subject of the King and had taken a binding oath of loyalty to George III. When Simon Kenton was captured later that year, Girty reminded him of the oath they had both taken and asked him how he managed to get out of it.[22] Moreover, the Patriot cause looked weak and Congress's efforts to secure the neutrality of the Indian tribes were failing. In the face of American suspicion and rebuffs, it made complete sense for a man with Girty's connections and expertise to go the way the wind was blowing and offer his services where they would be best appreciated, used, and rewarded. Having made his decision to adhere to the Crown, Girty was consistent in his actions and his loyalties. James and George Girty soon followed suit and joined their brother behind British lines, although Thomas Girty and half brother John Turner elected to remain in Pennsylvania.

The British Indian Department was keen to secure the services of men with influence and experience among the tribes, and Girty and McKee quickly obtained positions, although Hamilton did not fully trust Elliott, and that Irishman was not employed until later in the year. The Indian Department was a multicultural institution. Prominent members were of Scots and Irish ancestry; agents wore a mixture of Indian and European clothing and frequently developed extensive kinship ties by marrying Indian women; and business was conducted at frontier posts where Redcoats, French Canadian traders, Indian, and Métis families, together with delegates from tribes far and near, rubbed elbows in fluid and heterogeneous communities. Girty's experience and talent made him a natural participant in this multiethnic world, where cultural intermediaries were valued not despised. Although Girty lived at Detroit, he moved freely back and forth to the Indian towns, and though he claimed kin with the Mingoes and was most fluent in Seneca, he knew Shawnee, Delaware, and other languages. According to the recollections of one who knew him, Girty "would live sometimes in one town, and sometimes in another—kept changing."[23]

Girty's polyglot facility made him a valuable addition to the British at a pivotal place and a crucial time. He was one of eight interpreters present at a council held in Detroit in June 1778 between Lieutenant Governor Hamilton and delegates from the Ottawas, Chippewas, Hurons, Wyandots, Potawatomis, Shawnees, Delawares, Miamis, Mingoes, Mohawks, and Senecas. On the second day of the council, Girty "was then brought forward and declared

Interpreter, as having escaped from the Virginians and put himself under the protection of His Majesty, after giving satisfactory assurances of his fidelity." Girty was promptly entered on the department's books at Detroit as an interpreter for the Six Nations.[24] From June 1778 to June 1783, the British held about thirty major councils in the Detroit-Sandusky region. At a time when the going rate for an interpreter seems to have been eight shillings a day, Girty as "interpreter to McKee" was paid ten, the equivalent of a captain's pay.[25]

Throughout 1778 and 1779, Girty was active in the British service as an interpreter, scout, messenger, and ranger. The Girty brothers accompanied the Shawnees on a raid against the Kentucky border in 1778. On their return to the Indian town of Wapatomica, Simon saved the life of the recently captured Simon Kenton by having him transferred to the British in Detroit. In January 1779, Girty ambushed an American resupply party on its return to Fort Laurens, capturing several important letters and boasting of his exploits in the Delaware towns. That winter and spring he was busy carrying news of American movements and keeping the British abreast of developments in the Indian country. Even when no other Indians would turn out to join the British in May 1779, "a little band of Senecas called Mingalis, [Mingo] consisting of twenty or thirty led absolutely by Girty" rallied to the cause.[26] Later that year, Simon, his brother George, and Matthew Elliott accompanied a large war party of Shawnees, Wyandots, and Mingoes, who defeated Captain David Rodger's command at the mouth of the Licking River near Cincinnati.

The Rebels offered $800 bounty for Girty's scalp. Those Delawares who were still neutral or in the American interest also suffered at the hands of McKee's Shawnees and Girty's Senecas, and the Delawares were offered "60 Bucks" for McKee and "20 Bucks for any of the Girtys." Enemies and allies alike recognized Girty's importance. Lieutenant Henry Bird assured his superiors that Girty "is one of the most useful disinterested friends in his Departmt Government has."[27]

The Girtys, Elliott, and McKee spent the winter of 1780 in the Shawnee villages. They returned to Detroit in March with news that the Americans had built two forts in Kentucky. Simon Girty, McKee, and Elliott led the contingent of Indians that accompanied Captain Henry Bird's expedition from Detroit to destroy the fort established by George Rogers Clark at the falls of the Ohio. The Indians compelled Bird to alter his plans, turned to attack Ruddel's and Martin's Stations, and spent the summer harassing the Kentucky settlements.

Girty was equally active in the King's service the following year, leading Indian scouting and raiding parties, bringing in prisoners to Detroit, and trying to keep the Indians amply supplied and supported. Early in the year, he took up residence at Upper Sandusky in the Wyandot country. Major Arent Shuyler De Peyster, the new commanding officer at Detroit, felt that Girty would be more effective and valuable among that tribe than among the Mingoes, desiring him to interpret for the Wyandots and go to war with them when necessary. It was the beginning of a long and close connection with this tribe, although he seems never to have become as fluent in their language as in Seneca. By early March, Girty had completed the first successful raid from his new base of operations, with a party of Wyandots and Shawnees bringing in three prisoners.

In May, Girty reported to De Peyster that the Wyandots were discouraged by news of American successes and by lack of provisions. Reporting on one trader who had run off when he heard the rebels were in the Indian country, Girty commented: "He minds Trading more than king's Business." Girty, by contrast, seems to have put the King's business first. He ended his report to De Peyster with a request for "a little Provision for myself, as I was obliged to give mine to the Indians."[28]

That spring, Girty used his influence among the Wyandots at Upper Sandusky to intercede on behalf of a prisoner, Henry Baker, who was sent to Detroit and released by the British. Captive Samuel Murphy, who was under the care of British surgeons at Detroit in 1781, asked to see Girty, whom he remembered from Pittsburgh. Girty did not recognize Murphy but, shortly after, he sent the prisoner a pound of tea tied up in a new handkerchief and five or six pounds of sugar. "Girty was good and kind to me," Murphy assured historian Lyman Draper many years later, "this is as true as you are sitting there." Murphy also recalled that Girty would dress like an Indian when he was out on service with them, but would don American-style clothing when he returned to Detroit.[29]

In August 1781, the British and Indians ambushed Colonel Archibald Lochry's command, marching from Fort Pitt to Sandusky. Shortly after the victory, Girty was involved in an altercation with the Mohawk war chief, Joseph Brant, which left him with an ugly saber wound on the right side of his head. Since Girty was able to interpret at a council in Detroit less than two months later, the severity of the wound may have been exaggerated, but it affected his sight in later years. His daughter-in-law believed the wound had damaged the optic nerve and caused his eventual blindness; his daughter remembered that it forever after affected his mind "more or less."[30]

In 1779, Girty had apparently been involved in a plot to capture Moravian missionary David Ziesberger, an attempt foiled by the timely intervention of two Delawares. In the fall of 1781, he was instrumental in removing the Moravian missionaries and their converts to Upper Sandusky, where the British at Detroit could keep an eye on them. British policy demanded the move as a security measure, although the Rev. John Heckewelder accused Girty of fabricating evidence that the Moravians were communicating information to the enemy and of instigating the Wyandots against the missionaries.[31]

Early in 1782, Girty left Sandusky for Captain Pipe's Delaware town on the Tymochtee, and in March he crossed into Pennsylvania with Scotosh (the son of a Wyandot chief, Half King) and eighty warriors. By April, he was back at Sandusky, from where he reported to De Peyster on the massacre by

Virginia militia of ninety-six Moravian Delawares at Gnadenhutten.[32] He was in Half King's town on the Sandusky River when word came that another American expedition was invading the Indian country. Half King and Girty dispatched a runner to De Peyster and raised the alarm among the Wyandots, Delawares, Shawnees, and Mingoes. Led by Captain Pipe's Delawares, the Indians scattered the American force in June 1782, taking prisoner its unfortunate commander, Colonel William Crawford.

The grisly story of Crawford's torture at the hands of Delaware warriors is well-known, and Girty is supposed to have looked on with cool indifference if not sadistic pleasure, refusing Crawford's plea to shoot him. Girty's role at the Battle of Sandusky and its aftermath remains open to debate, however. Eye witnesses recollected that he tried to parlay and, riding toward the American lines on a gray horse, called on Crawford to surrender. Girty said that he did everything in his power to save Crawford, and traditions handed down by Indians and others support his story. According to these accounts, he offered the Indians money, his horse, and his rifle to spare Crawford. But Girty's influence lay with the Wyandots, not with the Delawares, who were determined to exact revenge for the slaughter of their relatives at Gnadenhutten. The Delawares not only refused Girty's offers but threatened to put him in the doomed man's place. If Girty tried to save Crawford, no mention of it was in British reports of the incident, which is significant since Girty's superiors abhorred the torture and lamented the effects it would produce among the Indians.[33]

The story of Girty's presence at Crawford's execution was fundamental to his evil reputation, but other accounts show Girty in a much more favorable light and indicate the effectiveness of his intermediary role. He twice intervened to save Simon Kenton's life, and other captives also looked to him for salvation. Margaret Handley Erskine was captured by the Shawnees and plagued by the fear of being forced into marriage with one of her captors, even though they assured her this was unlikely. Mrs. Erskine recalled, "I was further relieved by Simon Girty who soon after I was captured came to see me and inform us that we need have no fear on that score as they were not the people to compel any one to such a course." She saw Alexander McKee and the Girty brothers often during her five-year captivity and noted that the Indians thought highly of McKee and Girty.[34]

Young John Burkhart, captured in the spring of 1783 when Girty led a raid from Sandusky to within five miles of Pittsburgh, was similarly well-treated by Girty, who handed the boy over to De Peyster for release.[35] One female captive, on watching Girty's arrival in the Indian village, grabbed his stirrup and begged for help as he rode by. Girty made light of the incident, but nevertheless paid her ransom and she was released.[36] Girty was also present at the council that decided Thomas Ridout should be taken to Detroit and ransomed, and was instrumental in effecting the release of James Moore's sister. Liberated captive William May recounted simply that he "was condemned to die, but saved by Simon Girty."[37] Girty exerted significant influence except when constraints existed, such as the barriers that doomed any attempt to relieve William Crawford of his torments.

Soon after Crawford's death, Girty figured in another disaster for the Americans, who by now persistently overestimated his role. In mid-August, a large force of Indians "under the command of the noted Simon Girty, and many other white men" laid siege to Bryant's Station in Kentucky. When Colonel John Todd and a relief column of Kentucky militia arrived, Captain William Caldwell, Girty, and the Indians lured them into ambush and totally defeated them at the Battle of Blue Licks.[38] By the fall of 1782, the American cause in the West looked bleak. With Caldwell, Elliott, McKee, and Girty active in the Indian country, the British were rallying the tribes for a new offensive. After Blue Licks, Americans regarded Simon Girty as the driving force in the British-Indian war effort in the West, and "flushed with so many victories, to his natural boldness, he will be confident."[39] Moreover, Girty's role in the American's military discomfort was inferior to that of his superiors Caldwell, Elliott, and McKee; his official responsibilities were as an interpreter, not a troop leader.

At the peace negotiated in Paris, Britain agreed to independence for the Americans and—without the consent or even consultation with Indian combatants, handed over the vast territory stretching to the Mississippi and the Great Lakes. In the tense months that followed, Girty played an important role in negotiations between the British and their disgruntled Indian allies. Peacetime retrenchment brought discharges and paycuts in the Indian department. George Girty, interpreter to the Delawares, had his pay cut in half; but Simon's salary as Six Nations interpreter remained unchanged at sixteen shillings a day.[40] He was in attendance at crucial councils following the Revolution, most notably the multitribal summer gatherings at Sandusky when Joseph Brant and the Indian Department began to organize the western tribes into a defensive alliance to resist American expansion. Girty was indispensable as interpreter to McKee and Elliott as they implemented postwar British Indian policy among the Ohio tribes.

American claims to the contrary, Simon Girty never became fully "Indianized." From August 1778 to August 1783, he spent much of his time with the Mingoes and the Wyandots but he never lived with either tribe exclusively. He was constantly on the move carrying news, messages, and speeches between Detroit and the Indian country, and once peace was made, he chose to live among British subjects—not with the tribes he had long known and served. Even before 1796, when Britain abandoned Detroit and other posts on American soil, he had made his home in Malden Township near the juncture of the Detroit River and Lake Erie, where British troops, Indians, and loyalist settlers began mingling in the postwar years.

While in British eyes, Girty and his fellow "Indian officers" were deserving refugee loyalists, titles to land did not come automatically or easily. These veterans of the western campaigns determined to secure real estate in Canada to replace what was lost when they sided with the Crown. After negotiations during the winter of 1783–84, the Hurons and Ottawas around Detroit agreed to cede a seven-mile-square tract of land at the mouth of the Detroit River to a group of Indian officers and interpreters who had served with them during the war, even though the cession contravened Governor Haldimand's instructions and long-standing Crown policy prohibiting the cession of Indian lands to individuals. The wartime comrades-in-arms turned peacetime land sharpers included Matthew Elliott, Alexander McKee, William Caldwell, and Simon Girty. This negotiation provided the veterans a claim but not clear title to the estates they desired.

Thus, in June 1786, Elliott, McKee, and Girty set off for Quebec to petition for their rights to Canadian lands—as payment for the services they had rendered during the war. Simon, George, and James Girty each received lots on the north side of Lake Erie, where disbanded troops and refugee Loyalists were settled, "from a Creek, 4 miles from the mouth of the River Detroit, to a small creek about a mile and half beyond Cedar River." In October 1789, a memorandum listing the lots to be measured off for "the Gentlemen designed by the Commissioner in chief to settle on the land near the mouth of the River given by the Indians, to the king for that purpose," included a parcel "for Mrs. S. Girty." Simon, James, and George later petitioned the Land Board for the District of Hesse as United Empire Loyalists for additional tracts. On Christmas Eve 1793, the Surveyor General's Office at Detroit listed as approved awards for "Simon Girty—One thousand Acres on the North Side of River La Tranche (present Thames River)," while in March 1798, the Crown granted him another tract in the township of Malden (presently Amherstburg).[41]

Girty had a wife in the Indian country, but in 1784, he married Catherine Malott "& put away the other." Catherine had been captured by Indians during the war and Girty became acquainted with her, perhaps, according to one account, even arranging for her release. They were married at the mouth of the Detroit River by a German preacher and settled at Girty's home just south of Malden. The early years of marriage were marred by tragedy, with their first born child dying in infancy. A daughter, Ann, was born in 1786, followed by Sarah, Thomas, and Prideaux, the last child named after Prideaux Selby of the British Indian Department.[42] Meanwhile, Girty's turbulent temper earned him notoriety on the British side of the border, as it had in Pennsylvania. In August 1791, tanner George Setchelstiel swore a complaint against Girty who, he claimed, had attacked him without provocation as he rode along the King's highway, trying to seize his bridle and hurling stones at him.[43]

During the postwar years, McKee, Elliott, and Girty continued their political associations with the tribes, persistently advocating that the north-western Indians insist on the Ohio River as the boundary to American settlement. Their work among the Indians in this period further fueled the hostility of Americans, who attributed every manifestation of Indian resistance to the intrigues of British agents and the "implacable malice" of Girty and his colleagues. As the struggle for the Old Northwest came to a head, Girty played an increasingly central role. He led the Wyandot contingent in the utter destruction of Governor Arthur St. Clair's army in November 1791, for example, where he displayed such courage that the Indians presented him with three captured cannon.[44]

As was true of earlier periods in his career, much of our information about Girty at this time comes from the accounts of American captives. Oliver Spencer, for instance, met him in Blue Jacket's Shawnee village on Ohio's Au Glaize River and thought him "the very picture of a villain." Despite Spencer's prejudices, and Girty's undoubted attempts to unnerve the captive as he interrogated him, Spencer's account of the meeting offers a picture of a man who still felt ill-used by the Americans, resentful of his treatment, and anxious to justify his conduct. Girty was dressed like an Indian but without any ornamentation, and instead of a hat, he wore a silk handkerchief that hid the unsightly wound on his forehead. Girty said he had received the wound at the rout of St. Clair. He questioned Spencer closely about American troop strengths and intentions, as well as about his family and the circumstances of his capture. "He spoke of the wrongs he had received at the hands of his countrymen, and with fiendish exultation of the revenge he had taken," and ended by telling Spencer that he would never see home but he might make a chief if he proved to be a good warrior or hunter. Spencer, understandably, was glad to get away from him.[45]

Captive William May reported how, in September 1792, Girty and 247 Wyandots and Mingoes with two guides had set out to strike the American supply column between Fort St. Clair and Fort Hamilton, intending to create as much mischief as possible before a peace council could be convened between the Indians and Americans. Messengers reported that Girty was present when the Indians attacked Fort Jefferson and, according to May, Girty said "that he would raise hell to prevent peace."[46]

The old frontier brawler could do just that. In December 1792, Secretary of War Henry Knox reported to President Washington that, at the recent council held by the Indians at the Au Glaize, "no other white persons was admitted but Simon Girty, whom they considered as one of themselves."[47] The American commissioners treating with the Indians in the summer of 1793 saw Girty's handiwork behind the Indian answers and demands. On August 1, a Wyandot chief, speaking through Girty as interpreter, said the Indian delegates would convey the commissioners' words to the warriors gathered on the Maumee River, but added that the commissioners might as well go home. As the council began to break up, Matthew Elliott took the Shawnee Chief, Kakaipalathy, to one side and told him the speech was wrong. Girty insisted that he had interpreted accurately what the Wyandot had said, although Reverend Heckewelder suspected that the interpreter had taken the liberty of adding the last sentence. After a hurried consultation, Girty asked the commissioners to wait until the Indians had time to consult with their head warriors.[48]

Two weeks later, two young Wyandots arrived with a message for the American negotiators. According to Heckewelder, "The language in the speech was such that no person having knowledge of the Indians and their modes of expression, would believe it an Indian speech." Having delivered their message, the Wyandots departed, "agreeably to Simon Girty's orders." The commissioners sent after them, requesting that they take an answer back to the council, reporting: "We saw quite plainly that the Indians were not allowed to act freely and independently but under the influence of evil advisers."[49] According to one tradition, reported by Heckewelder, Girty demonstrated his contempt for the American commissioners and proclaimed his Indian sympathies during these negotiations by wearing a quill driven crossways through his nose, but his daughter Sarah had no recollection of this.[50]

With the breakdown in negotiations, the Indians looked to the British Indian Department to assume a more active role in defense of their homelands. In the fall of 1793, McKee dispatched Girty to report on the progress of the American army. As General Anthony Wayne's well-trained legions advanced, Girty's position became increasingly precarious. While the Americans offered $1,000 for his scalp, Indian leaders issued a proclamation requiring all loyalists in the area to don Indian dress and join them in resisting their common foe.[51]

When the Indians attacked Fort Recovery in 1794, some British soldiers and Detroit militia blackened their faces and fought along side them. Wayne's Choctaw and Chickasaw scouts, sent out a few days before the attack, fell in with a large body of Indians at Girty's town and reported large numbers of Britons and Canadians (Métis) with the Indians. Others reported that a considerable number of men urged the Indians on from the rear during the attack. Except for three red-coated officers, all had their faces blackened, and it is likely that Girty was among them.[52]

At the Battle of Fallen Timbers, however, while William Caldwell's Detroit militia fought a rearguard action to cover the Indians' retreat, Girty, Elliott, and McKee watched the battle from a safe distance near the river.[53] When the British closed the gates of Fort Miami (at modern Toledo) against the fleeing Indians, Wayne's victory was complete. But Girty's services were again in demand as the British endeavored to heal the resulting breach in Indian relations. In the months between Fallen Timbers and the Treaty of Greenville, Girty acted as scout, messenger, and spy for the Indian Department.

There is a tale told that when the Americans took possession of Detroit in 1796, Girty spurred his horse off the wharf and swam to the Canadian shore, waving his hat and cheering for King George. The story is probably apocryphal, but it symbolizes the end of an era in Girty's life. It does not seem that he ever set foot again in the United States. Like Elliott and McKee, his life might have been forfeited had he been caught on American soil.

In later years, he became increasingly concerned with domestic life and his failing health: scattered references also mark a general decline in his fortunes. A broken right ankle, sustained about 1800 as he slipped climbing some snow-covered steps (more dramatic accounts attribute it to a riding accident), left him with a limp for the rest of his life. His eyesight continued to fail; he continued to drink heavily; and always a thick-set man, he put on much weight. His daughter-in-law, Catherine, remembered Girty as "a fine looking man, even to old age," but his daughter Sarah described him as having black eyes, a pug nose and a thick neck, and his black hair turned steadily white.[54]

Sarah claimed her father could not write, that having been raised among the Indians he had no chance to learn. The Girtys' biographer agreed. Nevertheless, Sarah showed Lyman Draper two old letters from Girty, and these are preserved in the Draper manuscript collection. One letter, written in 1804 to his half brother John Turner, refers to Girty's separation from his wife some six years previously owing to his drinking and unkindness to her. Catherine left Girty to live with her brother Pater Malott and then, in her old age, with her daughter Sarah Munger. Girty and his children lived together and, he wrote Turner, were doing as well as could be expected under the circumstances. The letter also shows the exiled Girty's desire to visit again the country around Pittsburgh, and he asked Turner to send him news of the area. Girty had made a will and deposited it with his half brother. Now, after talking with his children and his friends, he decided to make a new will and he asked Turner to send him the old one. Turner and Girty remained close: Girty willed a portion of his property to his half brother, which Turner willed back to Girty's descendants.[55]

In 1808, with Britain and the United States again on the brink on war, the Indian Department geared itself for renewed conflict by strengthening its ties to the tribes. William Claus, the Deputy Superintendent of Indian Affairs, thought many of the old guard were incompetent, however. James Girty was strongly recommended and appointed interpreter at Amherstburg but, Claus told Prideaux Selby, "S. Girty is incapable of doing anything."[56]

When war came in 1812, it brought the aging Girty further misfortune. His son Thomas, an ensign in the First Regiment of Essex militia, died from a fever, apparently the result of overexertion and drinking from a puddle of polluted water as he carried a wounded officer from the battlefield. Girty buried his son in his orchard.

He was too old for active service. Now frail and portly, his head "as white as a sheet," he had become partially blind and his sight deteriorated steadily until he was completely blind for two years before his death.[57] After Commodore Perry's 1813 victory on Lake Erie, Girty retreated from Fort Malden with General Procter, Tecumseh, and the remaining British-Indian forces. Before the retreat, Elliott had ordered the Indians and their families to provision themselves from Girty's cornfields (a service for which Girty subsequently claimed payment from the government). Although he could barely see enough to follow the road, Girty accompanied the retreating army up the Thames. Contrary to reports that he was cut to pieces at the Battle of the Thames, Girty withdrew to Burlington Heights, where he sat out the remainder of the War of 1812.

The peace of 1815 marked the end of an era for a whole generation of agents and officers in the British Indian Department. Alexander McKee died in 1799, Matthew Elliott in 1814. In May 1815, William Claus included Simon Girty in "a return of officers & others whose services I think may be dispensed with, and a return of Interpreters whose age and Infirmities render them totally unfit for further service." In July, both Simon and James Girty were admitted on the pension list of the Indian Department of Upper Canada, listed as "Superannuated Interpreters." Girty continued to receive this pension until he died. In 1816, he returned to his home near Fort Malden, where he lived out his last few years, a shadow of the man who had terrorized the American frontier.[58]

By now, Girty was blind and plagued by rheumatism, "an object of great pity," according to U.S. Indian agent John Johnston. His heavy drinking continued. Even totally blind, he was reported as drinking himself into insensibility whenever he visited Malden. Although credited with a naturally friendly disposition, he evidently could not control his temper when intoxicated—"liquor would easily craze him."[59]

Some months before his death, however, according to his daughter-in-law, Girty made a pledge to stop drinking and he lived up to it. He continued to attend Indian councils up to the end. His daughter Sarah recalled that, about a month before he died, he told his wife that he would not live until spring. His final illness lasted only a few days and he lay unattended, for his physician was away. The old man refused to eat, asked his wife's forgiveness for his unkindness to her, evinced much penitence, and declined rapidly. On February 18, 1818, at nearly eighty years of age, Girty died on his farm at the mouth of the Detroit River. A detachment of troops from the garrison at Malden attended the funeral and Girty was buried with full military honors near his son in the orchard to the west of the house, although no memorial stone marked the grave.[60]

Girty left behind a large family of descendants. A daughter of his dead son, Thomas, lived in Michigan. His daughter Ann had several children, while Sarah had ten or eleven. His youngest son, Prideaux, had seven children and a dozen grandchildren. A nephew, George Girty, was a secondary chief or councilor of the Delawares and migrated west with them in 1822–23. Girty's roving and adventure-filled career had not shattered his family ties, either among his natal kin or his own descendants. When John Turner died, he remembered the children of his "renegade" half brother, leaving $1,000 to Prideaux Girty and to Sarah, and only $500 to the son of Thomas Girty who had remained in Pennsylvania.[61]

Simon Girty's varied activities raised questions of personal and ethnic identity as well as of national loyalty among his contemporaries and for later generations of commentators. To Americans, he was a traitor and a "renegade"; to the British, he was a loyalist; and to the Indians, he was a former captive adopted and resocialized as one of their own, a man who continued to operate in their interests. The social world Girty inhabited was both an embattled political and a conflicted ethnic borderland, where American frontiersmen, British Redcoats, Canadian traders, loyalists, and Indians of various tribes and dispositions mingled in communities molded and shaken by revolutionary forces.

Girty's talents and his long association with the Indians assured him a special place in that turbulent world, enabling him to function as a bridge between cultures. Familiar with the languages and the ways of different communities, he facilitated communication between friends, and between friends and foes. As an interpreter and an intermediary, he played a pivotal public role in British-Indian relations and he exerted significant behind-the-scenes influence in council-fire diplomacy. But Girty's importance was of that world and declined as times changed. He devoted the best years of his life to the British-Indian cause in the Old Northwest, only to see his efforts and sacrifices wasted, his Indian friends betrayed and abandoned, and American control over the region confirmed. British need for his services decreased even as Girty's faculties declined, and he outlived the final British-Indian defeat in the Old Northwest by only a few years. American history—or legends—portrayed Girty as an outcast and accorded him undeserved celebrity status as a villain of larger-than-life proportions. In reality, Simon Girty's identity and his career were fashioned out of the imperatives of the Great Lakes-Ohio Valley frontier, where he made his home and played his part in the middle ground of British-Indian relations. The importance he enjoyed stemmed only from the effectiveness as interpreter and intercultural broker between English-speaking and Indian peoples. For this he may be remembered as noteworthy, not notorious.

NOTES

1. Everett V. Stonequist, *The Marginal Man: A Study in Personality and Culture Conflict* (New York: Russell & Russell, Inc., 1961), pp. 2–3. Colin G. Calloway, "Neither White Nor Red: White Renegades on the American Indian Frontier," *Western Historical Quarterly* 17, no. 1 (1986), pp. 43–66; "Rhode Island Renegade: the Enigma of Joshua Tefft," *Rhode Island History* 43 (1984), pp. 136–45; "Arapaho Renegade: Robert North and the Plains Indian Wars of the 1860s," *Essays and Monographs in Colorado History* (1984), pp. 1–20.
2. Rev. John Heckewelder, *History, Manners, and Customs of the Indian Nations Who Once Inhabited Pennsylvania and the Neighboring States* (New York: Arno Press and the *New York Times* reprint edition, 1971), pp. 152ff.
3. *Pennsylvania Archives*, 8th series, 4 (1931), p. 3, 325; A.T. Volwiler, *George Croghan and the Westward Movement, 1741–1782* (Cleveland, Ohio: The Arthur H. Clark Company, 1926), p. 71.
4. C. W. Butterfield, *History of the Girtys* (Cincinnati, Ohio: Robert Clarke Co., 1890), pp. 4–5. Lyman Draper Mss., Wisconsin Historical Society, microfilm edition, 10E:

144 (Hereafter DRMss); *William and Mary Quarterly* 5 (1897), p. 270; *Pennsylvania Archives*, 8th series, 4 (1931), p. 3, 427.

5. *Western Pennsylvania Historical Magazine* 29 (1946), p. 144.
6. James Sullivan, et al., eds., *The Papers of Sir William Johnson*, 14 vols. (Albany, N.Y.: The University of the State of New York Press, 1921–1965) 11, pp. 436–37, 723–24. C. A. Hanna, *The Wilderness Trail* (New York: Putnam, 1911), p. 380.
7. *Johnson Papers* 12, p. 85; 7, p. 186.
8. *Pennsylvania Archives*, old series 4 (1853), pp. 565–66; *Pennsylvania Magazine of History and Biography* 29, no. 3 (1905), pp. 369–70. *Pennsylvania Colonial Records* 10 (1852), p. 227.
9. *Johnson Papers* 12, p. 1,044.
10. *Johnson Papers* 12, p. 1,100.
11. DRMss 3S, p. 11.
12. *Western Pennsylvania Historical Magazine* 4 (1921), pp. 188, 274.
13. *Pennsylvania Magazine of History and Biography* 7, no. 2 (1833), p. 151. Butterfield, *History of the Girtys*, pp. 341–42.
14. *Virginia Magazine of History and Biography* 14 (1906–07), p. 67.
15. R. G. Thwaites and L. P. Kellogg, eds., *The Revolution on the Upper Ohio, 1775–1777* (Madison, Wis.: Wisconsin Historical Society, 1908) 28, pp. 34–66. *Virginia Magazine of History and Biography* 26 (1918), p. 399.
16. Barbara Graymont, *The Iroquois in the American Revolution* (Syracuse, N.Y.: Syracuse University Press, 1972), pp. 101–02, 329.
17. DRMss 3S, pp. 18–20; 2S, pp. 103–04; 20S, p. 209; 5S, p. 105.
18. R. G. Thwaites and L. P. Kellogg, eds., *Frontier Defense on the Upper Ohio, 1777–1778* (Madison, Wis.: State Historical Society of Wisconsin, 1912), pp. 178–81
19. *Pennsylvania Magazine of History and Biography* 40, no. 3 (1916), p. 468; DRMss 3S, pp. 19–20.
20. *Pennsylvania Archives*, 4th series 3 (1900), pp. 684, 940.
21. *Pennsylvania Archives*, 6th series 13 (1907), p. 29; DRMss 3S, p. 21; Gregory Palmer, *Biographical Sketches of Loyalists of the American Revolution* (Westport, Conn.: Meckler Publishing, 1984), p. 317.
22. DRMss 8S, pp. 45–46.
23. DRMss 11C, pp. 6,230, 6,233.
24. Haldimand Papers, *Michigan Pioneer Historical Collections* 9 (1886), pp. 442–44, 470 (Hereafter *MPHC*).
25. Haldimand Papers, British Museum, Additional Manuscripts, 21756, p. 383; and 21769, pp. 26–27.
26. *MPHC* 19 (1892), p. 413.
27. DRMss 1H, pp. 18–21; L. P. Kellogg, ed., "Frontier Retreat on the Upper Ohio, 1779–81," *Collections of the State Historical Society of Wisconsin* 24 (1917), p. 299. *MPHC* 19 (1982), p. 413.
28. *MPHC* 10 (1886), pp. 478–79.
29. DRMss 3S, p. 22.
30. I. T. Kelsay, *Joseph Brant, 1743–1807: Man of Two Worlds* (Syracuse, N.Y.: Syracuse University Press, 1984), pp. 311–14. DRMss 17S, p. 198; 20S, pp. 196–99.
31. John Heckewelder, *Narrative of a Mission among the Delaware and Mohegan Indians*, (Philadelphia, Penn.: McCarty & Davis, 1820), pp. 204–05, 304–09.
32. Haldimand Papers, British Museum, 21762, pp. 13–14.
33. DRMss 2S, 37; 4S, pp. 137–38; 20S, pp. 200–01; 11C, 6,233–6,234; 10E, pp. 146–47, 152; U11, 10, 30. Butterfield, *History of the Girtys*, pp. 174, 179–80, 187–89, 355–60.

Haldimand Papers, British Museum, 21762, p. 80. C. W. Butterfield, ed., *Washington-Irvine Correspondence* (Madison, Wis.: David Atwood, 1882) pp. 372–74.

34. *West Virginia History* 23 (1961–62), pp. 290–91.
35. Butterfield, *Washington-Irvine Correspondence*, p. 418.
36. R. G. Thwaites, ed., *Chronicles of Border Warfare . . . By Alexander Scott Withers* (Cincinnati, Ohio: The Robert Clarke Company, 1903), p. 372.
37. *Western Pennsylvania Historical Magazine* 12 (January 1929), p. 28. *Virginia Historical Register* 4 (1851), p. 154. *American State Papers: Indian Affairs*, 2 vols. (Washington, D.C.: Gales and Seaton, 1832–34), p. 243 (Hereafter *ASPIA*).
38. *Calendar of Virginia State Papers* 3 (1883), pp. 280–83, 300–301.
39. *Calendar of Virginia State Papers* 3 (1883), p. 338.
40. Haldimand Papers, British Museum 21783, p. 294; 21882, p. 50.
41. 3rd Report of the Ontario Bureau of Archives 20 (1905), pp. 29–30, 88–91, 151, 148, 281.
42. DRMss 2S, pp. 103–04; 17S, pp. 193–95; 20S, p. 206.
43. M. M. Quaife, ed., *The John Askin Papers*, 2 vols (Detroit, Mich.: Detroit Library Commission, 1928–1931) 1, p. 385.
44. *ASPIA*, 1, pp. 243–44.
45. M. M. Quaife, ed., *The Indian Captivity of O. M. Spenser* (New York: Citadel Press, 1968), pp. 92–93.
46. *ASPIA*, 1, p. 244.
47. *ASPIA*, 1, p. 322.
48. "Journal of a Treaty held in 1793, with the Indian Tribes North-west of the Ohio, by Commissioners of the United States." *Collection of the Massachusetts Historical Society*, 3d series 5 (1836), p. 150; *ASPIA* 1, pp. 352–54; E. A. Cruikshank, ed., *The Correspondence of John Graves Simcoe*, 5 vols. (Toronto: Ontario Historical Society, 1923–1931) 1, pp. 405–09; 2, pp. 29–30; Heckewelder, *Narrative of a Mission*, p. 403.
49. Cruikshank, ed., *Simcoe Correspondence* 2, p. 24.
50. DRMss 20S, pp. 209–10.
51. Cruikshank, ed., *Simcoe Correspondence* 2, pp. 128, 258; William Claus Papers, Public Archives of Canada, Ottawa, MG 19 F1, p. 164.
52. R. C. Knopf, ed., *Anthony Wayne, A Name in Arms: The Wayne-Knox-Pickering-McHenry Correspondence* (Pittsburgh, Penn.: University of Pittsburgh Press, 1960), pp. 345–49; DRMss 1YY, p. 17.
53. *ASPIA* 1, p. 494. Cruikshank, ed., *Simcoe Correspondence* 3, p. 13.
54. DRMss 20S, pp. 207–08; 17S, p. 198.
55. Butterfield, *History of the Girtys* 99, pp. 399–400. DRMss 20S, pp. 213, 222; and U12, p. 16.
56. Claus Papers, MG 19 F1, 9, pp. 171–75.
57. DRMss 17S, pp. 174, 191, 215–16.
58. *MPHC*, 16 (1890), pp. 115–16; and 23 (1895), p. 109. DRMss 17S, p. 191.
59. DRMss 1YY, p. 113; and 17S, pp. 216, 244; U11, p. 30.
60. DRMss 20S, pp. 207–08; and 17S, pp. 191, 198–99.
61. DRMss 20S, p. 215; and 1YY, p. 40. *Western Pennsylvania Historical Magazine* (1924), pp. 196–97.

CHAPTER 3

Joseph Renville and the Ethos
of Biculturalism

Gary Clayton Anderson

PRESENTING JOSEPH RENVILLE (1779–1846)

Joseph Renville's life was spent in an early Minnesota community that developed amidst, depended on, and endured only as long as there was a viable fur trade. This pattern of economic exchanges connected Indians—the primary sources of peltry—to distant consumers through a chain of manufacturers and suppliers. A critical link in this complex cultural-economic network was the local trader, who coped with the often-conflicting demands of both sides of the system in face-to-face relationships with Indian producers. Renville's father was one local trader, a French-Canadian voyageur, who, in the "custom of the country," took a Dakota wife, young Joseph's mother. The boy experienced a dual socialization, first informally among his Dakota kin, followed by years of formal French Catholic education in Quebec at his father's behest. Returning to Minnesota, the young man soon established himself in his father's place, eventually building a multicultural community with himself as patron and master, home to Dakota kin groups, Franco-American employees and their families, and eventually American missionaries. Like a self-made frontier Baron, Joseph Renville successfully presided over this bicultural estate, for many years delivering satisfaction to all involved, until inescapable economic changes threatened its demise. At his Lac qui Parle establishment was the critical link between two radically different economic systems, the Dakota one, based on generous reciprocal exchange of valued goods and services, and the European-American profit-and-loss system of capital investment and gain. So long as there was an ample supply of furs for trapping and enough consumers wanting them, the system was well-balanced. When both the supply of and demand for Indian-produced raw materials dropped, the system fell into disrepair and Renville's little community collapsed with it. As the author shows, Joseph Renville worked to cope with such changes, foreseeing a future where his novel community would have to be transformed. In this he failed, undone by his enduring commitment to the Dakota ethos, the configuration of social values and expectations he had absorbed as a child from his mother's people. Then, unwilling to uproot self and community and move west into potentially richer hunting grounds, equally unwilling to take a more exploitative stance toward his Dakota clients and kin, he could not deliver the generosity his life-long associates expected of him, and his last years were spent in poverty. Joseph Renville's public identity was as inextricably tied to time, place, and economic circumstances as few others, but his larger choices were personal, as the Dakota side of his bicultural identity won out in the end over the entrepreneurial French. (J. A. Clifton)

Nineteenth century immigrants from Europe generally found a place for themselves in some corner of American society. While the first generation often had problems depending on their social, economic, religious, and linguistic backgrounds, their children and grandchildren most often readily passed into the main corridors of American life. Within a few generations, most had become, in their own identities, Americanized, perhaps clinging to some minor traditions of national origin, identifying themselves as ethnic hyphenates: Irish-Americans or Swedish-Americans, for example.

The same was less often true of peoples stigmatized by identification with a racial category, the people "of color." Among them was a special class of frontier folk, the descendants of generations of interbreeding and social intermingling between native and immigrant Americans. Such people, called *half-breeds*, *mixed bloods*, or *breeds* in the language of the time, had fashioned small communities on the borders between cultures, where they played significant roles mediating relationships between Indians and Americans during the colonial and early national eras.

These were the sons and daughters—unto the great-great-great-grandchildren—of Indians on the one hand and Euro-Americans, occasionally Afro-Americans on the other hand. The majority were connected with Indians through bonds of marriage and, as the generations passed, descent. Their ties to Indian communities were personalized, intimate, and binding. They were involved in a web of mutual obligations and rights which, after a few generations, evolved into a distinctively bicultural pattern of values and sentiments neither traditional Indian nor European in character. Instead, they lived out an emergent ethos, in essence, the creative product of the cultural frontiers they inhabited.

So long as the frontiers endured, they occupied a significant, influential place, particularly so in economic and political affairs. On the Great Lakes fur-trade borderland, most were Franco-Indians, called *Métis*, although more than a few Anglo-Indians or Scots-Indians, joined by occasional Afro-Indians, were also involved. Persons of partial French descent, especially, became the heart and soul of the western fur trade, helping to open the West to commerce and settlement. They developed their own local dialect, a *lingua franca*, and their own communities such as Prairie Du Chien, Green Bay, and Fort Wayne. As important as their contributions were to the frontier economy, their accomplishments certainly should have brought them an important place in the developing American West.[1]

Joseph Renville's Frontier

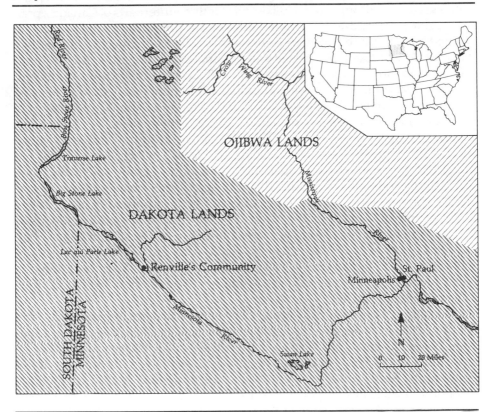

But this was not always the case. Despite such important services, the descendants of these culturally marginal people were mostly unable to capitalize on the fruits of their ancestors' labors in seeking upward mobility in the American class system. All indications suggest that many such people, most of whom could trace their European antecedents to the first colonists on the Atlantic seaboard, commonly moved down the social ladder during the early nineteenth century. Unlike Irish, German, and later Slavic or Italian immigrants, who moved into a broad spectrum of social classes within a few generations, these bicultural people—the mixed bloods—seem to have failed to adapt to the changing social system of the young United States.

This dramatic decline in their economic security, standing, and influence —their downward social mobility—was associated with the collapse of the fur trade, on which their communities and identities had been founded. By tracking the fate of such communities, and the key figures who populated them, we can see that the positive experiences and public behavior that gave them meaning and a place on the borders between Indian and American societies gradually disappeared. Unlike their Métis counterparts of Canada's prairie provinces, Franco-Indian communities in the United States did not remain isolated for long. As the fur-trade communities collapsed, the communities they had created were soon penetrated and dominated by numerous Americans of different ancestry. These new arrivals quickly became competitors of the old-line marginals of mixed French and Indian antecedents, and shortly replaced them in the commercial, administrative, and other occupational roles that were the economic foundation for the latter's earlier prominence.

Newly arriving Americans carried negative attitudes and convictions about "race" mixture or the "mingling of blood," which exposed the old marginals to prejudice and open discrimination. These Americans were increasingly conscious of and unwilling to accept these bicultural peoples as equals. No separate, distinct social category or group identity, such as the Métis people of Canada or the Mestizos of Mexico, emerged in the United States. Americans, increasingly, were intolerant of these ambiguous, "in-between" people who were thereby faced with an either/or proposition. Either they were Indian or they were racially White, and Americans, ranking racial blood in a scale of value, considered them Indians by blood, thus inferior and stigmatized.

Bicultural Franco-Indians were also closely tied to Indian tribes, and continued to draw benefits from this relationship. By 1830, the eastern tribes were being systematically displaced from their old habitats and resettled in new lands in the West, in a territory reserved exclusively for Indians, if but temporarily. So with the reduction of the fur trade and intense competition from other Americans, opportunities for the mixed bloods in the Great Lakes area declined. Hence, as the tribes moved west, many of the cultural marginals accompanied them. Those who did so were apparently unwilling or unable to begin again in new occupations in developing communities in the settled portions of the United States.

Simultaneously, a widely accepted, stereotyped popular image of such mixed bloods emerged. Mixed bloods, Americans commonly believed, were passive in nature, lacking the stamina needed to compete in a capitalistic marketplace. They were, in the self-serving rationalizations of this ethnic stereotype, a lazy and incompetent people, carefree souls who were capable of handling a boat but little else.[2]

Such popular images expressed collective American fantasies about earlier frontier peoples, which were products of the racial thinking that pervaded American popular culture in the period. Except that the bicultural folk were exposed to and had to contend with such demeaning images, they tell us little of how these in-between people viewed and coped with the dramatic changes going on around them.

Not all responded alike to the alterations in their social and economic positions. The issue facing all, however, was one of choice. Confronting

Mary Riggs' Sketch of Renville's Community

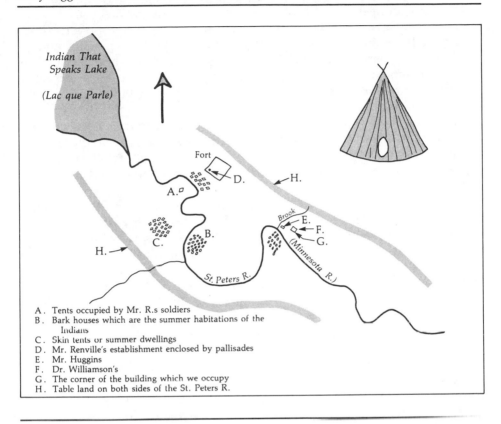

A. Tents occupied by Mr. R.s soldiers
B. Bark houses which are the summer habitations of the Indians
C. Skin tents or summer dwellings
D. Mr. Renville's establishment enclosed by pallisades
E. Mr. Huggins
F. Dr. Williamson's
G. The corner of the building which we occupy
H. Table land on both sides of the St. Peters R.

pressures from the dominant culture, some elected to move away from their heavy reliance on Indians. They sought to adapt by assimilating into American society, to work with historical currents rather than against them. Others went the opposite route, moving in with their Indian relatives. But a third group remained committed to an ethos of biculturism. Convinced of the benefits of understanding and working with both Indian and American societies, they struggled to confront and to surmount the changes they were experiencing. While those who tried to adapt, seeking new roles and relationships, were likely not a majority, they had one characteristic in common: they were more extensively and effectively bicultural than others. One such man was Joseph Renville, a French-Dakota trader who, in the 1830s, determined that change in roles and values was essential if he and his family were to survive and prosper.

Contrary to stereotypes of the frontier half-breed, Renville was a man vigorously seeking control of his destiny, a person who sought to manage the future. He was rightfully proud of his past accomplishments, for he had built a successful commercial establishment, attaining enough wealth to win the respect of Indians, other marginal peoples, and Americans. Nevertheless, during the 1830s and 1840s, Renville saw that the frontier was passing, and he decided that his large family and his many Indian relatives should assimilate into the dominant society. But, at the same time, Renville also worked to sustain the bicultural community he had created on the upper Minnesota River at Lac qui Parle. Thus, an examination of his career affords a vantage point, a way of developing insights into the dilemmas and trials faced by such composite Indian-American communities. In his attempts to adapt, we can see Joseph Renville and his kin applying an older bicultural ethos to new economic imperatives, changing social contexts, and altered cultural values and goals.

Renville was born in 1779, the son of a Dakota (Eastern Sioux) woman and a French Canadian voyageur, usually identified as Joseph Rainville (or Rinville).[3] A nineteenth-century traveler who met the younger Joseph later in his life attested to his "Indianness," once describing him as a "dark looking Indian with strong features, and black hair, and short in person, [he] has some French features and a very wily physignony [sic]."[4] Judged solely on physical appearance, Americans were prone to identify Joseph Renville as Indian.

Renville's mother, Miniyuhe, came from Little Crow's Kaposia band of Dakota Indians. This village, one of seven belonging to the Mdewakanton Sioux tribe, was situated on the Mississippi River below present St. Paul. Miniyuhe's mother seems to have come from Wabasha's village, also on the Mississippi, downstream of Lake Pepin. Given Dakota rules of exogamy, which prevented a man's taking a wife from his own village, Miniyuhe's mother had to come from a village other than Kaposia. Renville later married an important woman from the Kaposia band, the daughter of a particularly influential chief, Little Crow.[5]

The social position of Renville's Dakota mother and wife provided him extensive kinship ties within several Dakota communities, and his numerous Dakota relatives played major roles in his early education. Since his father was absent for long periods during his youth, the boy spent the first ten years of his life in a traditional Dakota setting, mastering the language, learning Dakota institutions, and living by their values. Missionaries later claimed Renville spoke Dakota better than any other mixed blood in their country.[6]

One of the most significant lessons absorbed during his Dakota socialization was the great importance of cooperation within the primary community, a critical survival value in their dangerous environment. Another core lesson was the central value placed on reciprocal sharing, of generous giving. The Dakota shared because they realized how difficult it was for individuals and isolated families to survive in their environment, and because all at one time or another experienced want or plenty. The leading men in the community where Joseph Renville grew up always shared whatever they had with their kin, demonstrating a willingness to sacrifice for the benefit of the whole.

About 1789, this Dakota training came to an abrupt end. According to oral accounts, that year Renville's father took the ten-year-old boy to eastern Canada. There, young Joseph was subjected to formal schooling, studying with a priest, learning Catholicism and the rudiments of the French language.[7] This part of his education continued for six or seven years until, as a young man, Renville returned west to work in the Dakota trade.

Over the next twenty years, Renville was increasingly active and successful in the Indian trade, and his name appears in the journals and letters of most early traders and explorers ascending the Mississippi River. Much of this time was spent in the employ of the noted Scots trader, Robert Dickson. Renville's services were fundamental to Dickson's enterprises, for he was able to use his kinship ties with the eastern Sioux or Dakota tribes—Mdewakanton, Wahpekute, Wahpeton, and Sisseton—to help Dickson control the commerce of the upper Mississippi. When the War of 1812 came, and Dickson joined the British Indian Service, Renville, too, received a commission and served loyally for the British. By the end of the war, Renville was identified by his contemporaries as the leading mixed-blood trader on the upper Mississippi River.[8]

Nevertheless, the British surrender of sovereignty over the upper Mississippi valley in 1783, at the close of the American Revolution, foreordained eventual American rule, although actual control of the region did not pass into the hands of Americans until the end of the War of 1812. Then came rapid American occupation and many substantial changes. Two major events promoting such developments were the opening of Fort Snelling in 1819, and the first run by a steamboat up the Mississippi River to the fort four years later. The American entrepreneurs who followed the army, and the improved communication and transportation facilities provided by steamboats on the Mississippi's waterways, slowly eroded the social-political structure of the region. Franco-Indian marginals suffered as a result, finding employment as traders, interpreters, clerks, blacksmiths, teamsters, and boatmen increasingly difficult.

But the pressures undermining the position of the older masters of the trade built slowly, since there were still fur-bearing animals on Dakota lands and a need for experienced, well-established intercultural brokers like Renville to help in obtaining them. Indeed, the arrival of the first American authorities failed to produce any immediate transformation, because established British and Scots traders simply acquired American citizenship and moved their operations to the new trade-administrative-military entrepôt growing near Fort Snelling, at the juncture of the Mississippi and Minnesota Rivers.[9]

At first, perhaps fearing a trading system dominated by American citizens, Renville resisted these changes. Unlike others, he did not immediately apply for citizenship. Instead, he convinced most of his relatives at Little Crow's village to follow him west to Lake Traverse, where, in 1819, he joined Duncan Graham, whose supplier was the Hudson's Bay Company. At Lake Traverse, Renville and Graham built an extensive commercial post, where they employed about twenty mixed bloods and gave extensive credits and presents to Indian relatives. This venture did not prosper because of the high costs of presents and growing competition from the Northwest Company.

By 1822, Renville lost his connection to the Hudson's Bay Company, and he turned to an association with the Columbia Fur Company, newly organized by Kenneth MacKenzie and William Laidlaw.[10] Within five years, this minnow was swallowed by the fur trade's whale, John Jacob Astor's American Fur Company, which held a virtual monopoly of the trade after 1827. During these years of commercial maneuvering, Renville settled at Lac qui Parle, a pretty spot located about thirty miles below Lake Traverse on the Minnesota River. There, he finally made his peace with American authorities at Fort Snelling, and in 1826, he was joined by many of his Dakota relatives from Kaposia. The new community that he founded at Lac qui Parle—part commercial outpost, part Dakota village—remained intact until Renville's death in 1846.

At Lac qui Parle, Renville built a unique, bicultural community, one that attracted a substantial body of Indians and several French-Indian voyageurs and their families. In outward form, Renville's community remained European both in profit-orientation and in its well-built living quarters, storage buildings, and shops. But in social organization and ethos, especially regarding cooperation, reciprocal sharing, and prescribed etiquette, the community was traditional Dakota. No doubt Renville believed his community was blending the best of both worlds and serving two sets of cultural ends.

His was a specialized community that exploited the fur trade through manipulation of Dakota communal institutions, especially kinship networks, while working within the imperatives of a profit-and-loss-driven market economy. For over a century, frontier communities that were similarly organized and oriented had been successfully managed by people of French and Indian ancestry. They were several different kinds of social places: the homes of the proprietors, their kin, and their clients and employees; a neutral ground where traders and natives could come together and commune socially; and a marketplace.

While estimates vary, during the 1830s, Lac qui Parle was home to about seventy Dakota families, or some 500 to 700 people. The half-dozen Franco-Dakota households added another thirty or forty people to the total population.[11] The community resembled a small fiefdom, with common fields of corn tended by Dakota women, adjoined by open pastures containing herds of horses, cattle, and sheep belonging to Renville and used to occasionally feed his Indian relatives. In the center, Renville built a substantial stockade, in which he, the patron, lived with his wife and eight children.[12]

Although Renville was not an autocratic man, he possessed an unusual amount of power, a capacity to influence the behavior of others generated by the ties he maintained with his surrounding Dakota relatives and by the wealth he controlled. The key social element in this system was the *Tocadan*, the "Kit Fox Society." It consisted of about fifteen warriors who lived in the small village of twelve lodges next to Renville's stockade. Although Joseph Nicollett, the French traveler who visited Lac qui Parle in the late 1830s, suggested that this Dakota warrior's association was founded in 1830, it probably functioned earlier, since its membership was dominated by the Mdewakanton relatives Renville brought west with him in 1826, and because it played such a vital role in Renville's commercial enterprise.[13]

The Tocadan was headed by Renville's Mdewakanton brother-in-law, Left Hand, who led the Mdewakanton migration to Lac qui Parle in 1826 from Little Crow's village, Laposia. The principal soldiers in the lodge were directly related to Renville, including Cloud Man and Wamdiokeya, both cross-cousins. The Kit Fox Society stemmed from a traditional Dakota institution called the soldiers' lodge, which had been used, probably for centuries, to control the behavior of men engaged in collective hunting. Such control was necessary to prevent one hunter from spooking game herds and causing the entire village to go hungry. Renville, however, had adapted the functions of this long-established institution to fit and serve the needs of the fur trade. The Tocadan soldiers policed the region around Lac qui Parle, collecting furs for Renville when necessary, ensuring that hunters who received credit in the fall turned over the pelts taken during winter only to their trader-patron, Renville, in the spring. The Tocadan operated as Renville's enforcers. The Dakota now saw his establishment as a mainstay of their collective well-being.[14]

Nearly all early travelers visiting Lac qui Parle in the 1830s left comments about the Tocadan. John C. Fremont noted that because of it, Renville's "good will" acted as a "passport" through the entire country.[15] Nicollett was no less praising, calling the dozen or more members of the society "faithful and brave." Nicollett relied heavily on members of the society to protect his expedition, which went out onto the forbidding Dakota plains.[16] However, perhaps the best evidence of the effectiveness of the Kit Fox Society is found in the correspondence of missionaries who came to live at Lac qui Parle in 1835. Thomas S. Williamson, after watching the men of the society work for over a year, concluded that while they could not prevent an occasional cow or sheep from being killed, they were so effective as guards that Renville could confidently allow his extensive cattle, horse, and sheep herds to graze freely on the prairies near Lac qui Parle.[17]

The influence of the Tocadan was further enhanced by marriages between its members and the women of other Dakota bands and tribes. Cloud Man, for example, took a Sisseton woman as his wife, while Left Hand married two Wahpeton Dakota women. Finally, Renville's sons took Dakota women from the surrounding bands as their wives, bringing together a kinship network that gave Renville influence among all the upper Minnesota River Sioux bands.[18] Such a network was important because the Dakota people believed strongly in relationships transcending local band communities, relationships fostered by intermarriage that required affinal kin to do what was necessary to help their distant in-laws.

Renville recognized that such a network had to be reinforced through generous giving. Only then could he expect reciprocal aid and support. Dakota Indian attitudes about material possessions differed markedly from Euro-Americans. Indeed, sharing was the rule. There were good reasons for such generosity. Irrespective of the vegetable food produced in their women's gardens, the Dakota tribes on the upper Minnesota River were dependent on hunting and gathering. They knew how precarious food supplies were, necessitating cooperative work in groups called *Tyospayes*, to most effectively exploit food resources. Tyospayes literally means lodge group or band of relatives. Traditionally, everyone needed to sustain relationships with such relatives by reciprocal giving, since there would always be a time when one had food and other members of the Tyospayes did not. Thus, as missionary Stephen Riggs noted, it was common for the husband to tell the wife of his lodge, "Be very liberal of food, as many men as come to visit you give them something to eat . . . If you are stingy, I shall be ashamed."[19]

Aliens living among the Dakota quickly appreciated the importance placed on gift-giving. "Bona fide presents were given by friends and relatives to each other much more than among us," missionary Samuel Pond wrote of the Dakota people. "There was much also given to the poor, such as widows and orphans, especially food, for none were ever suffered to starve if there were provisions in the camp."[20] Persons who gave important presents were "highly esteemed," and the recipients were certain to traverse the village announcing in public their good fortune and the generosity of their benefactor. "This is sometimes repeated for several days," Pond indicated, and after the announcements were over, the receiver was just as likely to give the gift away himself.[21]

Renville did his best to live by the rules of reciprocity, knowing that his relatives expected him to share. One of the wives of the Lac qui Parle missionaries noted Renville's great generosity at Christmas time, when the Indians "are accustomed to received many presents from traders."[22] Even other Indians, writing of Renville twenty years after his death, mentioned his generosity; Lorenzo Lawrence recounted that Renville "was always very merciful to the Indians."[23]

Renville's role in helping the Dakota of the upper Mississippi expanded further after the buffalo herds of the region diminished in the 1820s. One witness to the event, during the particularly difficult winter of 1834, described how Renville had slaughtered thirty to forty head of cattle to keep the Indians at Lac qui Parle alive. Moreover, even after he began suffering large losses in the fur trade, Renville continued delivering presents and food to his many relatives. As the missionary Williamson wrote: "in the time of his [Renville's]

MICHAEL RENVILLE (1822–1899). Michael was one of Joseph Renville's eight children. He spent several years studying the Dakota and English language at the Lac qui Parle Mission School. This sketch, by Frank B. Mayer, was done in 1851, probably while Mayer was observing the treaty negotiations with the Sissetons and Wahpetons at Traverse des Sioux. Little is known of Michael's career, although he was possibly involved in the fur trade along the James River with his brothers, young Joseph and Antoine, and his uncle, Gabriel Renville. (Courtesy of the Edward E. Ayer Collection, the Newberry Library; and the Minnesota Historical Society.)

greatest prosperity, such was his kindness to the poor, that he accumulated very little; and in his latter years, when the profits of his business were so reduced that he could purchase but a little more than a sufficiency of food for his own family, he gave a part of that to the Indians; so that for several months of every year, he and his family suffered."[24] Renville never forgot his Dakota upbringing.

The goods Renville distributed took the form of presents, such as the food and gifts that he handed out at Christmas, or credits—supplies and equipment delivered to hunters in the fall so that they might seek fur-bearing animals in the more isolated river valleys north and south of Lac qui Parle. Recipients of Christmas gifts or food were not bound to any specific, timely return exchange. Credits, on the other hand, were different. Hunters receiving them were obligated to balance the transaction in the spring by delivering the pelts they had taken. Often, however, the take in furs did not cover the credits, causing losses for traders like Renville.

Such failures of this Dakota-style exchange system conflicted with Renville's obligations to his distant suppliers, who operated under different economic principles. So as the number of fur-bearing animals along the upper Minnesota River declined through the 1830s, his financial losses increased. Dakota hunting grounds no longer held adequate numbers of the valuable beaver, martin, mink, or deer. Plenty of muskrats still could be taken on the sloughs southwest of Lac qui Parle, but a muskrat skin was worth only a dime, while a beaver pelt generally brought three dollars. As revenues fell, the Indians at Lac qui Parle relied more heavily on Renville's generosity, while he fell increasingly in debt to the American Fur Company.[25] By the early 1830s, Renville realized that he could not sustain this composite exchange system—part traditional reciprocity, part capitalized market—for many more years. While Joseph Renville might feel adequately compensated by the social credits delivered by his Dakota kin, especially their esteem and loyalty, his own creditors, the stockholders of the American Fur Company, demanded a different type of compensation.

In the same years, Renville's Dakota hunters also recognized that they were not producing the required quotas of peltry. Most preferred to blame the neighboring Ojibwa bands for their economic woes. The Ojibwa, long-time rivals and often enemies of the Dakota, lived northeast of Lac qui Parle in the woodlands around the headwaters of the Mississippi River. There was some truth to Dakota suspicions, for Ojibwa hunters were hunting farther south each year, edging into the Sauk and Crow River valleys just north of Lac qui Parle. This invasion brought bloody clashes throughout the 1820s, causing government officials near Fort Snelling much consternation, followed by unsuccessful efforts to end the cycle of raids and ambushes.

In a great intertribal treaty conference negotiated at Prairie du Chien in the summer of 1825, under Superintendent of Indian Affairs William Clark from the St. Louis superintendency and Governor Lewis of Michigan Territory, the Dakota, Ojibwa, and other tribes supposedly made a "firm and perpetual peace," accepting boundary lines separating their territories. The Dakotas' Indian Agent, Lawrence Taliaferro from Fort Snelling, was especially active in securing their consent to the agreement. The Dakota-Ojibwa boundary extended roughly across the mid-section of the future state of Minnesota. But years passed before it was surveyed, while neither Dakota nor Ojibwa hunters were prone to respect an abstract line of demarcation.

Concerned with Ojibwa incursions, during the summer of 1832, Renville finally took matters into his own hands. He encouraged the Kit Fox warriors to attack these competitors, sending his own brother, Victor, on the raid. Left Hand led the attacking Dakota marauders deep into Ojibwa country. After failing to find their enemies, however, the party pillaged the American Fur trading post on the Crow Wing River, probably expecting to find several Ojibwa inside. On their return trip, an Ojibwa war party ambushed the

Dakota, killing Victor Renville and two other men. If the loss of his brother was not a severe enough blow to Joseph Renville, his sponsorship of the raid brought sharp protests from the traders at Crow Wing and the Ojibwa to American authorities.[26]

Lieutenant Jefferson Vail, commanding officer at Fort Snelling, learned of the attack in February 1833. He promptly wrote Washington, concluding that "if Mr. Renville does not excite the Indians to war, he has sufficient influence to prevent them from pillaging a trading establishment of the same [American Fur] Company." Vail also heard that other war parties were forming at Lac qui Parle and that Renville and his son were urging them on. In the Dakota social system, brothers had exceedingly close ties; hence, it was essential for a man in Renville's position to seek revenge for the loss of Victor. Wishing to prevent such intertribal raiding, after some high-level military debate, the army decided to use gifts and persuasion to stop the warfare that was escalating across central Minnesota.[27]

While high American authorities seemed unwilling to exert the military effort required to end the fighting, Taliaferro felt that, at the least, Renville should have been arrested and brought to trial. Renville, however, denied any wrongdoing and refused to appear at Fort Snelling to answer charges. Instead, he was reported as preparing his Indian followers for a military invasion, allegedly proclaiming the contents of a fictitious letter from the British King, which indicated that the Sioux would be welcome in Canada. Officers at Fort Snelling even reported at one point that Renville was distributing British medals to the Indians, but this was a rumor. Fortunately, the fighting subsided in 1835 and with it the concern of government officials about the role and loyalty of Joseph Renville and his Kit Fox warriors.[28]

Renville's support of intertribal war may have reflected his growing economic difficulties, but this is uncertain. Nevertheless, the decline in trade caused havoc everywhere along the upper Mississippi watershed, and Renville's actions fit a widespread pattern. Traders farther east, who worked the Blue Earth and Mississippi River valleys, resorted to reclaiming goods given on credit when Indian hunters failed to turn over the required skins in the spring. The new head of the American Fur Company, Henry Hastings Sibley, in 1834 encouraged more entrenchment, telling his traders to credit only Indians who were young and strong, and thereby likely to meet the required spring quotas in pelts.[29] Renville, with his strong personal ties to Dakota kin and clients, was unable to make such "rational" reforms. His response was in line with what was considered proper and acceptable among the Dakota.

Partially expressing Dakota understanding of the causes of their problems, Renville hoped to use warfare to push the Ojibwa back from prime hunting grounds, thereby enhancing the take in skins. He was far more committed to reinforcing kinship ties and helping and encouraging his relatives in terms they preferred than the traders operating farther east, many of whom also had Dakota relatives. Nevertheless, his actions also illustrate the growing conflict that came with his distinctive bicultural status. Support-ing intertribal warfare may have suited the wishes of angry Dakota warriors, but it ran counter to government Indian policy, and it even injured the fur trade, since fighting made it impossible for hunters to safely go about their occupation.

The events of the early 1830s made Renville reevaluate his role both at Lac qui Parle and as a fur trader. Too many people relied on him for aid and support, including close relatives living at Lac qui Parle and the hundreds in his extended kin networks who lived among the Mdewakanton, Wahpeton, and Sisseton Sioux tribes. He also employed several Franco-Indian clerks and had eight children dependent on him. Renville's two eldest children, Joseph (1805–1856) and Antoine (1810–1884), had started their own families, but they still worked with him in the trade and knew no other profession. More significantly, Renville's other six children were growing up in a community their father had created, but it did not offer the minimal educational advantages he had received as a child. There is no doubt that Renville wondered and worried what would become of them.

Such concerns likely convinced Renville in 1835 to welcome missionaries and to encourage their establishment at Lac qui Parle. Thomas S. Williamson and Alexander Huggins of the American Board of Commissioners for Foreign Missions, a Presbyterian-Congregational group, were at Fort Snelling that summer looking for a new field for their endeavors. When introduced to Renville by agent Taliaferro, who wanted someone to keep an eye on this overly independent Lac qui Parle trader, the missionaries quickly agreed to come to Renville's settlement and open a station. Renville, for his part, offered them shelter and help in transportation. He expected the missionaries would open a school and a church, and introduce the benefits of "civilization" to his community. Two years later, Stephen Return Riggs and his wife Mary joined the Lac qui Parle establishment, and in the years to come, several other Protestant mission workers, including Samuel and Gideon Pond, came and went. Under Renville's strong patronage, the Lac qui Parle mission pros-pered.

While it is not clear that the missionaries ever fully understood Joseph Renville or his motives, from the start they often found themselves contributing to the welfare of his bicultural community. Williamson, for example, reported in May 1836 that Renville had over fifty head of sheep but his people lacked expertise in spinning yarn. The missionaries promptly introduced weaving. Another development lay in increased food produc-tion. "Mr. Renville who first induced them [his relatives] to plant corn here [Lac qui Parle]," Williamson continued, made it clear that he "wishes them to raise a sufficiency for their subsistence the whole year." Recognizing Renville's desire to foster animal-powered farming—agriculture proper rather than the woman-powered gardening of prior years—the missionaries brought in plows and introduced new crops, such as spring wheat.[30] While this new and more balanced economic diversity caught on slowly with the Indians, it became an important part of the missionary program, and both

GABRIEL RENVILLE (1825–1892). Gabriel was the son of Joseph's brother, Victor, who was killed in the 1833 raid against the Ojibwa. In contrast to Joseph, Gabriel Renville was unsympathetic to the missionaries' cause when he took over his uncle's position in the fur trade during the 1840s and 1850s. Gabriel later served as Chief of the U.S. Army Indian Scouts during the Dakota War of 1862, and then emerged as an extremely astute, hard bargainer on behalf of the Dakota. He literally put together the Sisseton treaty of 1867, when that people's present South Dakota reservation was established, and during the 1870s and 1880s he remained the principal spokesperson for the Sisseton. Gabriel's facial features, and the deceptive conventional image created by the photographer, Steinhauer (complete with frock coat, cravat, silver-headed walking stick, and top hat), do not reveal Gabriel's self-image or cultural inclinations. He never spoke English and throughout his life he remained adamant in his support and use of Dakota customs. (Courtesy of the Minnesota Historical Society.)

Riggs and Williamson often wondered whether their move to Lac qui Parle was encouraged because of their agricultural expertise rather than their spiritual guidance and virtues.

Perhaps the most obvious interest behind Renville's support of missionaries was the educational opportunities they offered his children. Renville placed all eight of his children in school and encouraged his clerks and the members of the Kit Fox Society to do the same. He constantly supported the missionary school with presents, and his children, especially the girls, made much progress. After the missionaries created a thirty-two syllable writing system, the children learned how to read and write in the Dakota language. Unfortunately, they never seemed to make much headway with English. As one of their teachers noted, "the daughters do not make that progress in learning English . . . [since] they are surrounded with a few exceptions, only by those who talk Sioux." The two oldest Renville boys were more interested in the fur trade than education, although the younger ones attended classes.[31]

The missionaries were convinced the major obstacle to their success in educating Renville's children, and those of other biculturals at Lac qui Parle, was their composite social environment. Mary Riggs noted in 1839 that Renville's children had been raised by a Dakota mother—their earliest training was "like that of Indian children." Yet, from early childhood, the Renville offspring seemed to sense that they were different, for they soon began dressing "nearly like" Whites. Their clothing often was changed, however, when it came to play, for the Renville children were not "ashamed," as Mary Riggs put it, to use leggings and rawhide skirts when the opportunity came to frolic with their Dakota cousins. Also characteristic of being in-between, the children frequently joined in Dakota feasts and amusements but refused to chop and carry fire wood, as was expected of their Dakota female kin and companions. The Renville boys similarly demonstrated bicultural patterns of behavior. While they remained heavily involved in the fur trade, they made, according to Mary Riggs, "their mothers, wives & sisters their servants, almost as much as do Indian men."[32]

Missionaries naturally viewed such anomalous behavior as the epitome of irresponsibility. It seemed to express a lack of cultural commitment that even Indian children did not exhibit. What the missionaries were witnessing and describing were children who grew up in an uncommon environment, picking and choosing the mode of life which met their fancy at any given time, demonstrating as well that they recognized they were the daughters and sons of the elite in this small community, the children of the village's patron founder.

Promoting the acceptance of Christianity in such an environment proved equally frustrating for the Lac qui Parle missionaries, although Joseph Renville supported the infant mission church in many ways. When the Missionaries first arrived, he ordered the lodge used by the Kit Fox warriors to be employed as a church, and its members even agreed to change the name of their association to "the friends of the Holy Book."[33] Evidence suggests that the members of the soldiers' lodge had little if any understanding of this change. Only Renville seemed aware of the significance of Christianity. While he had been baptized as a Catholic and his marriage had been consecrated by the church, in 1836, he was the first resident of Lac qui Parle to join the new Protestant mission. His wife and three of his children followed shortly there after. The first services were preached in English, translated to French, and retranslated into Dakota by Renville. The Lac qui Parle trader also opened and closed meetings with a prayer, in the Dakota language, behaving much like a Dakota *Wicasta wakan*, or shaman.[34]

The missionaries' progress was from the top down. Renville's role in the religious conversion process increased during the late 1830s, despite his Catholic background. Most of his immediate family soon joined the church, as did many of his Dakota kin, especially women. By 1840, the Lac qui Parle church numbered some forty members. It became obvious, however, that the church was as dependent on Renville for its existence as many of the Indians were for their economic well-being. This point was driven home forcefully in 1837 when the missionaries subjected the Renville girls to stringent tests of their qualifications for church membership.

According to standard Presbyterian and Congregational canons, the neophytes had to manifest evidence of deep personal piety and of being reborn in Christ. Obtaining clear evidence of such a conversion experience, however, was no simple task. Samuel Pond, who watched the interview process, noted that the Reverend Williamson asked questions in English, which were translated into French by Renville's clerk, which were further translated to the girls in Dakota by their father. The girls answered yes and no, without elaborating. Later, the clerk quietly told Pond that one daughter was "very wicked," and on being so informed, Williamson, the head of the mission, refused her admission to the church.

Not long after this rebuff, Renville, his family, and the Indians at Lac qui Parle stopped attending Sunday service. Williamson, seeing that his mission hinged on Renville's goodwill, soon reversed his decision. Pond, who later wrote about the American Board's mission establishments, noted that Renville was the driving force behind the Lac qui Parle church and that he had never been particularly concerned with disguising his role. At one point, Renville told Pond that *he* had made the decision to boycott the church "with the Indians *whom I have converted.*" Pond, who had a mission elsewhere, indicated he could have had many such converts if he had willingly adopted such minimal standards.[35]

Obviously, the Renvilles, especially the children, viewed Protestantism far differently than the missionaries. They lacked the philosophical indoctrination that came with growing up in a Christian church and, thus, they never developed a deep-seated adoration and understanding of its rituals and symbols. Without an historical appreciation of the holy land, an understanding of the notion of original sin, or for that matter, an acceptance of the idea of the trinity, the Franco-Indian children at Lac qui Parle would never be successful Christians. The lifestyle of the fur trade also stood in the way of missionary progress. This was a highly mobile business, frequently necessitating long trips that often stretched over weekends. But the Missionaries adamantly refused to allow travel on Sunday, arguing forcefully that to travel on the seventh day was a sin.

Renville tried to comply with these wishes, despite his disagreement with the concept. His children, in contrast, never disguised their views on the subject. After one of Renville's sons was caught hunting on Sunday,

Williamson did his best to find an excuse for this behavior, asking the young man if not hunger or want had driven him to sin. But all inquiries produced a simple "no." In the end, young Renville confessed that he knew it was wrong to hunt on Sunday, but he expected to "repent of it when he got home."[36] His notion of Christian repentance differed markedly from that of the missionaries. Here, religious practices appropriate to an agricultural or an industrial work week conflicted with the demands of hunting and trapping economy, and the Renville children never understood the symbolic importance of replenishing one's spiritual commitment to God on a seven-day cycle.

Perhaps the most remarkable contrast regarding the acceptance of Christianity, however, came when the Renville family experienced death. Then a striking conflict between two fundamentally different systems of values and beliefs appeared. The first occasion for the missionaries to view such a scene came in February 1839, when a young son of Joseph's oldest son was buried. During and after the funeral, the family proceeded to give away many of their worldly possessions, including clothing and provisions. This act was common among the Sioux tribes, for it demonstrated grief and concern for the spirit of the departed. But, it was alien to the expectations of the Protestant missionaries.

Preparing for the rites, the boy's grandfather, Joseph Sr., killed a beef and fed all comers. In the room where the casket lay, shades had been drawn and small candles had been placed on either side of the coffin. "The females had their hair half unbraided & flowing gracefully upon their shoulders, the mother & grandmother wore common Indian blankets . . . & had all the appearance of desolation [desolation]," according to a missionary. The coffin had been closed, the missionaries assumed, to hide the usual utensils that Dakota mourners sent along with their dead. More shocking, however, was the fact that "the child bed & cradle or Indian board were deposited in the grave." After leaving the grave site, the missionaries noted that "moaning and wailing" commenced. It lasted all night and into the next day. Mary Riggs could only lament that the example given by the supposedly Christian Renville family "should be thrown upon the side of heathenish superstition."[37] The next year, when Renville's wife passed on, the missionaries made a point of not disturbing her while she was on her death bed. As Williamson said in a private letter to Gideon Pond, "I had doubts about whether the family wished me to converse with her." Even so, after his wife died, Renville put the best face on his loss, telling Williamson that his wife's last words were that "her Savior was with her."[38] He was more sensitive to the feelings of the missionaries than the reverse.

The missionaries hoped that the Renville family would come to see death as a release from the drudgery of everyday life and that it would lead to eternal life with their Christian God. They believed that all Christians, at conversion, had a saving experience that made death insignificant when compared to eternal life in the hereafter. The missionaries constantly looked for this saving experience among the native and culturally marginal members of the bicultural community at Lac qui Parle; they were regularly disappointed. What seemed to them as casual identifications with doctrine and ritual, and a flexible, partial adherence to Christian obligations by their "converts" in Renville's community, prevented them from ever accepting the neophytes on an equal footing. Their lingering prejudices about the physical appearances and heathenish customs of their congregation did not encourage them toward tolerance.

Joseph Renville saw Christianity in a different light. Socialized into the basic ethos of the Dakota as a child, subsequently catechized in Catholic forms, his view of religion was more tolerant and eclectic than the doctrinaire Protestants. He was, moreover, working almost single-handedly to transform his community in ways that would better fit them into the new social world developing on the Minnesota frontier. The terms of this cultural transformation, as he saw them, necessarily included minimal, formal Christianization of his people. Accordingly, Renville supported schools and churches and translated the Bible into the Dakota language, and he served the mission church as a loyal member.

In later years, Williamson saw the immense importance of Renville's early role: "I have of late often suspected that during the early years of this mission we were much more indebted to him [Renville] for protection—ourselves and our property—and inducing the Indians to attend our school and meeting for worship than any of us at the time supposed."[39] Nevertheless, Renville's support came at the price of compromise: the missionaries reluctantly took into their church the people that Renville wanted as members, and the Lac qui Parle missionaries realized it was futile to attempt altering such long-standing, sacred practices as property distribution after a funeral or gift-giving, both of Dakota origin. So many compromises occurred—in effect, syncretic recombinations of Dakota and Protestant forms, that these Protestant missionaries' plans of remaking the members of the Renville community over to fit their ideal models was doomed from the start.

Any opportunity for Renville to orchestrate a major cultural transformation ended quickly in the early 1840s. Then, his world began to fall apart completely, prompted by continued economic decline and the final collapse of the fur trade. When Renville could no longer support his Dakota clients and kin with generous giving and ample winter credits, they were forced to move away from Lac qui Parle. Even his own children turned elsewhere for a livelihood. The two oldest boys, Joseph and Antoine, moved into eastern Dakota territory, trading most frequently on the James River.[40] Renville's two oldest daughters married mixed bloods, to the dismay of the missionaries who had hoped for better matches. One such marriage, that of Magdeline to Louis Martin, lasted only a short time.[41] Joseph Renville, Sr., however, kept his post open until his death in 1846, but in the early years of the decade, he fell so heavily in debt to eastern merchants that they would no longer deliver goods on credit. Eventually, this proud, resourceful man was forced to ask the missionaries for aid, an act that must have been extremely demeaning for him. The American Board responded by sending him $200. After his death, his extended family scattered to various localities.[42]

What stands out in the career of Joseph Renville, this Franco-Dakota proprietor of a fur-trade emporium and ethnically composite community on the Minnesota frontier? By the 1830s, he had sensed the winds of great changes coming, and he determined that his personal community—his own children, his Dakota kin, and his employees—would have to change to meet and to surmount the challenges of the future. Also, he sought more than mere survival for his people: he desired them to prosper. The issues he faced were how to change and what was needed. An intelligent, educated, and broadly experienced man, he saw that formal education and knowledge of American ways was vital. However, he was also convinced of the advantages of remaining bicultural. The future he saw for his children and for the Dakota would incorporate elements of the old with features of the new. It was a transformation of the existing bicultural ethos he tried to encourage, not slavish, wholesale imitation of the models advanced by the Protestant missionaries.

Renville saw the adoption by his community of elements drawn from American culture and Protestantism as instrumentalities, hence, he was often content with surface forms and nominal observances. The missionaries defined this as inadequate, if not anathema, for they involved matters that were sacred and compelling to them. Renville sought adjustment to the future while preserving the fundamental core of his community's bicultural ethos. The missionaries sought its uprooting and replacement. Renville was convinced that the flexibility inherent in his biculturism was essential to meeting future changes. The missionaries saw such composite mixtures as anomalies. However, he and the missionaries agreed on one thing: when his children playfully picked up and then casually dropped an element of American practice in their daily lives, returning to older forms and habits, they were not seriously mastering the skills and attitudes they would need in years to come. Instead, they were clinging to the comforts of the older variety of biculturism tied to the fur trade, which was rapidly disappearing.

Renville wanted for his family and people a future tied to the habitat they had known. Williamson discussed this with him in 1838. "Mr. Renville knows something of the state of society on the frontier," he wrote, and "dreads" taking his children back east to live in such a world.[43] Such an uprooting would have meant his abandoning, not only the physical environment where he had matured and for so long prospered, but the people and social relationships that had provided him security and esteem. Unfortunately, during his later years, Renville's experiences were driving home an unavoidable lesson: the kind of life that existed at Lac qui Parle would soon disappear forever.

It was this dual fear, of the loss of a way of life and of the threat of relocation into a completely alien environment, which prompted Renville to look closely at the possibilities of change in place, at adapting the biculturism of himself and his community to meet coming challenges where they were. An adaptive person, a properly bicultural man who appreciated and blended elements of Dakota, French-Canadian, and American ways into a creative synthesis, Renville had lived well by the terms of a composite ethos.

Thus, he mourned his dead Dakota fashion, while advocating conversion to Protestantism and the acceptance of formal education. He was willing to adopt the surface trappings of one version of Christianity, without binding himself to its moral directives stressing personal accumulation of wealth and individualism. Indeed, it was his unique blend of Indian and American ways that was his undoing. Had he been less committed to the Dakota ethos of sharing and more the French bourgeois, he might have built his own capital and provided a substantial inheritance for his children. Some other Franco-Indian contemporaries did so. They survived the demise of the fur trade and the transformation of the frontier economy by ruthless exploitation of their relationships with Indians, extracting every dollar they could from their associations even after the fur trade expired. They became successful entrepreneurs—merchants, lumberjacks, and even industrialists in locations near where they had prospered as fur traders; not Joseph Renville. Following the dictates of his personal ethos, he spent his financial capital in Dakota ways, accumulating many social credits, which had no market value in a capitalized economy.

NOTES

1. For general information on mixed bloods in the United States, see Robert E. Bieder, "Scientific Attitudes Toward Indian Mixed-Bloods in Early Nineteenth Century America," *Journal of Ethnic Studies* 8 (Summer 1980,) pp. 17–30. A new study of the Métis is by Jacqueline Peterson and Jennifer Brown, *The New Peoples: Being and Becoming Métis in North America* (Lincoln, Neb.: University of Nebraska Press, 1984).
2. See Bieder, "Scientific Attitudes Toward Indian Mixed-Bloods," pp. 17–30.
3. Two early articles on Renville are Rev. E. D. Neill, "A Sketch of Joseph Renville, A 'Bois Brule,' and Early Trader of Minnesota," *Collections of the Minnesota Historical Society* (St. Paul, Minn.: Minnesota Historical Society, reprint 1902) 1, pp. 157–65; Gertrude W. Ackerman, "Joseph Renville of Lac qui Parle," *Minnesota History* 12 (September 1931), pp. 231–46.
4. George W. Featherstonaugh Diary, 1837, microfilm, Division of Archives and Manuscripts (DAM), Minnesota Historical Society (MHS).
5. See Gary Clayton Anderson, *Little Crow, Spokesman for the Sioux* (St. Paul, Minn.: Minnesota Historical Society, 1986), pp. 185–86.
6. Thomas S. Williamson to David Greene, August 5, 1835, American Board of Commissioners for Foreign Missions (ABCFM), Papers, typescripts, DAM, MHS.
7. Neill, "A Sketch of Joseph Renville," 158–59; Thomas Hughes, *Indian Chiefs of Southern Minnesota* (Minneapolis, Minn.: Ross & Haines, Inc., reprint, 1969), p.112.

8. Neill, "A Sketch of Joseph Renville," pp. 158–60; Hughes, *Indian Chiefs*, pp. 112–113.
9. See Gary Clayton Anderson, *Kinsmen of Another Kind: Dakota-White Relations in the Upper Mississippi Valley, 1650–1862* (Lincoln, Neb.: University of Nebraska Press, 1984), chapter 5.
10. For a detailed discussion of these years, see Robert Tiling, "Joseph Renville, a Biography," unpublished manuscript, Alan R. Woolworth Files, Minnesota Historical Society, pp. 11–19.
11. See, for example, Williamson to Greene, August 5, 1835, ABCFM Papers; Amos Bruce to Robert Lucas, September 30, 1840, National Archives Record Group (NARG) 75, Letters Received (LR), St. Peter's Agency.
12. Stephen Return Riggs, *Tah-koo Wah-kan; or, The Gospel among the Dakotas* (Boston: Congregational Sabbath-School and Publishing Society, 1869), pp. 154–162; Williamson to Greene, August 5, 1835, ABCFM Papers.
13. Bray, Edmund C., and Martha Coleman Bray, trans. and eds., *Joseph N. Nicollet on the Plains and Prairies: The Expeditions of 1838–39 with Journals, Letters and Notes on the Dakota Indians* (St. Paul, Minn.: Minnesota Historical Society, 1976), pp. 108, 235–36, 242, 277, 279; Riggs, "Dakota Portraits," *Minnesota History Bulletin* 2 (November 1918), pp. 528, 536–37, 553.
14. Bray and Bray, trans. and eds., *Nicollet*, pp. 277–78; Riggs, "Dakota Portraits," *Minnesota History Bulletin* 2 (November 1918), pp. 532–37, 553.
15. John C. Fremont, "Excerpt From the Memoirs," in *The Expedition of John C. Fremont* 1, ed. Donald Jackson and Mary Lee Spence (Urbana, Illinois: University of Illinois Press, 1970), p. 17.
16. Bray and Bray, trans. and eds., *Nicollet*, pp. 235–236.
17. Williamson to Greene, August 5, 1835, ABCFM Papers.
18. Anderson, *Little Crow*, pp. 188, 192–93; Riggs, "Dakota Portraits," *Minnesota History Bulletin* 2 (November 1918, pp. 532–37, 547–52, 561–68; Indian Reserve Papers, NARG 75, Bureau of Indian Affairs.
19. Riggs to Greene, September 10, 1839, ABCFM Papers.
20. Samuel Pond, *The Dakota or Sioux in Minnesota as They Were in 1834* (St. Paul, Minnesota: Minnesota Historical Society, reprint 1986), p. 170.
21. Samuel Pond letter (unaddressed), January 22, 1841, John Howard Payne Papers, Edward E. Ayer Collections, Newberry Library, Chicago.
22. Mary Ann Longley Riggs to Alfred Riggs, December 30, 1837, Longley Papers, DAM, MHS.
23. Lorenzo Lawrence, "The Story of Lorenzo Lawrence," unpublished manuscript, DAM, MHS.
24. Renville obituary, *The Missionary Herald*, May 15, 1846.
25. For a general discussion of the fur trade in this period, see Anderson, *Kinsmen of Another Kind*, chapters 4 and 5.
26. William Atkin to C. R. Williams, February 5, 1833, and W. Baker to Bureau of Indian Affairs, February 8, 1833, NARG 75, LR, St. Peter's Agency.
27. Quotation in Vail to Clark, March 4, 1833, NARG 75, LR, St. Peter's Agency. See also Elbert Herring to Clark, April 6, 1833; Taliaferro to Clark, June 7, 1833; and Colonel Zachary Taylor to Lieutenant A. S. Johnston (Assistant Adjutant General), June 23, 1833, NARG 393, LR, Jefferson Barracks, 1831–53.

28. Major John Bliss to General Henry Atkinson, April 28, May 3, May 23, and May 26, 1834, NARG 94, LR, Adjutant General's Office; Taliaferro to Clark, June 7, 1833, NARG 393, LR, Jefferson Barracks, 1831–53; Clark to D. Kurts, NARG 75, LR, St. Peter's Agency; Taliaferro Journal, June 6, 1835, DAM, MHS.
29. Sibley to Ramsay Crooks, April 29, 1835, American Fur Company Papers, LR, photostats, DAM, MHS.
30. Williamson to Greene, May 16, 1836; ABCFM Papers; Riggs, "Dakota Portraits," *Minnesota History Bulletin* 2 (November 1918), p. 536.
31. Quotation in Mary Riggs to her mother, November 8, 1838, ABCFM Papers. See also Williamson to Henry Hill, June 14, 1836, and School Reports, 1839, 1844, and 1846, ABCFM Papers.
32. Mary Riggs to her sister, December 28, 1839, ABCFM Papers.
33. Williamson to Greene, May 4, 1836, ABCFM Papers.
34. Williamson to Greene, October 1, 1836; Williamson to Samuel Pond, February 8, 1837; and "Sermon," entitled "Planting of the Gospel in Minnesota and Among the Dakotas," by T. S. Williamson, ABCFM Papers; Renville obituary, *The Missionary Herald*, May 15, 1846.
35. Pond, "Reminiscences," no pages.
36. Pond, "Reminiscences," no pages. See also Stephen and Mary Riggs to "mother," October 8, 1837, Riggs Papers.
37. Mary Riggs to her parents, February 9, 1839, Riggs Papers.
38. Williamson to Gideon Pond, February 24, 1840, Pond Papers.
39. Williamson to Greene, December 19, 1840, ABCFM Papers.
40. Williamson to Sibley, August 16, 1839; Renville to Sibley, October 20, 1842; and Martin McLeod to Sibley, February 21, 1845, Sibley Papers; Williamson to Greene, May 28, 1840, May 5 and December 19, 1843, ABCFM Papers.
41. Mary Riggs to her mother, August 23, 1838, Riggs Papers; Williamson to Greene, June 12, 1846, ABCFM Papers; Indian Reserve Papers, NARG 75.
42. Williamson to Greene, December 19, 1843; Riggs to Greene, February 14, 1844; Williamson to Henry Hill, July 18, 1844; and Williamson to Green, November 30, 1846, ABCFM Papers.
43. Williamson to Greene, May 10, 1838, ABCFM Papers.

CHAPTER 4

Augustin Hamlin, Jr.: Ottawa Identity and the Politics of Persistence

James M. McClurken

PRESENTING AUGUSTIN HAMLIN, JR. (1813–1862)

Augustin Hamlin, Jr.'s, place was among the Ottawa, Franco-Indian, and American entrepreneurs of the nineteenth century's outstanding center of the Great Lakes fur trade, Mackinac Island. Most of his adult life was spent with his ambitions pressing against the restrictions placed on him mainly by his Ottawa sponsors and by American rivals such as Henry R. Schoolcraft. Born in a Michigan village of a Métis father and an Ottawa mother, as a child that tribe's leaders selected him as one of several talented youths to be sent away for formal education, first in local mission schools, later in Ohio, and lastly in Rome. If the old leaders had their way, young Hamlin might have become a priest beholden to themselves, their loyal, chosen instrument serving exclusively Ottawa interests. Their aims included preservation of their identity and as much of their autonomy as could be sustained in the rapidly changing western Great Lakes region; they faced their future determined to manage the course and content of social change on their terms. Hamlin's larger, multiethnic regional community stressed achievement and open social mobility—for men and women—whether vertically, across ethnic boundaries, or horizontally, from positions of less wealth and prestige to more. As Americans increased their presence and power, however, these social values changed toward a restricted social class system with rigid boundaries between groups defined in racial and ethnic terms. Through much of his abbreviated life, Hamlin was prompted by his Ottawa patrons to manage relationships with the U.S. government, helping them avoid dislocation and resettlement and helping negotiate treaties. In practice, the quality of service he delivered was diluted by his aspirations. Likely modeling himself after the forceful prelates he had known in Rome's hierarchical institutions, he wanted to become a paramount chief appointed by federal officials, wielding centralized power and absolute decision-making authority. The Ottawa, however, had no place for an upstart satrap; they thwarted his ambitions, without alienating Hamlin or dispensing with his services. His later efforts to obtain Superintendent Schoolcraft's office was similarly frustrated, and Hamlin had to remain content with lesser positions, which occupied and supported him until the end of his life. His career, therefore, was marked by much compromise between the wants, opportunities, and limits set by the Ottawa, the lures

offered and restrictions established by American officials, and his profound ambitions for self-advancement and power. In the end, the Ottawa endured—with
much aid from Augustin Hamlin, Jr., their well-managed servant. (J. A. Clifton)

I am an Indian by birth—by education, whatever it is, a white man. I have tread
in the path of civilized life, and that my countrymen may also be civilized is my
utmost wish and endeavor—and whenever I see things or the actions of men,
however plausible they may appear, tending towards the subversion of this end,
I am filled with resentment and am ready to have recourse to the sources of
power in the government whence alone effectual redress may be expected. I now
write in the name of my tribes—the Ottawas and part of the Chippewas in
Michigan as head-chief.

Letter to President Martin Van Buren, June 29, 1837[1]

At age twenty-four, Augustin Hamlin, Jr., thus emphasized the dual nature of
his public identity. He was, as he informed the president in this official
communication, an "Indian by birth," but he was also a "civilized" man by
later education. Then hardly two years from Rome, where he had studied for
the priesthood, Hamlin was embarked on a new, different career. Although
he exaggerated his position by claiming to be the "head-chief" of Michigan's
Ottawa and Chippewa, he was acting for the traditional leaders of these
communities, who had only recently selected and instructed him to represent
their interests before the high authorities of the United States.

Hamlin was born south of the Straits of Mackinac on July 12, 1813, among
his mother's family in the region the Ottawa called *Waganagisi* (Crooked Tree).
Just north of Little Traverse Bay, in today's Emmet County, this area was
known to the French and later to the Americans as L'Arbre Croche; and it had
long been a main center of Ottawa occupation and power. He was the eldest
child of Augustin Hamlin, Sr., a voyageur-trader of French, Ottawa, and
Chippewa descent based on Mackinac Island, and the Ottawa woman
Angelica Kiminchigan.[2] At the moment of Augustin's birth, the entire social
system of the region lay on the edge of dramatic change. At that time, the
Ottawa, allied to the British in the War of 1812, still held their territory firmly;
but in 1815, the British withdrew their garrisons from Fort Mackinac, leaving
local residents to make their own accommodations with the new regime.
From then on, American officials engaged in political contests for control of
the region and its economy, battles fought most intensively between 1820 and
1855. After reaching adulthood, Augustin, also known by his Ottawa name
Kanapima, played a central role in these engagements. At stake was not only
the security of the Ottawa, but the future of the entire regional economy, built
on the fur trade and a multiethnic local population.

Augustin Hamlin, Jr.'s, Landscape

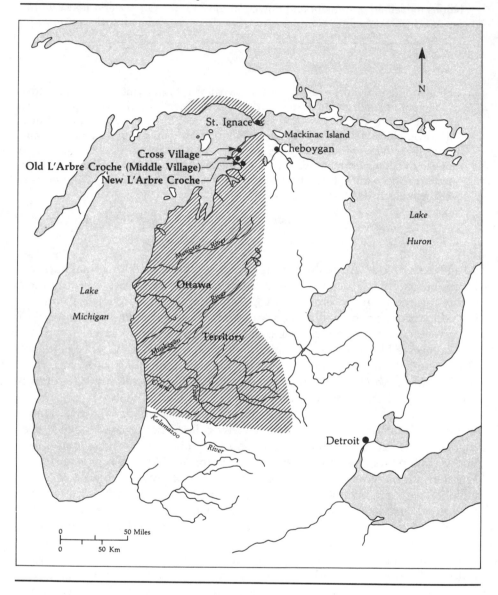

The roots of young Hamlin's social identity, and his distinctive career, lay in the L'Arbre Croche economy and its ties to the multiethnic regional community. French and British colonial authorities had governed the western Great Lakes as they did many other far-flung outposts of imperial power, exerting only enough political presence and physical force to maintain a mutually beneficial economic relationship with the peoples who lived there. Both tolerated, indeed, they encouraged local cultural accommodations with indigenous peoples who provided useful services to colony and empire.[3]

Ottawa contributions to this frontier social system were substantial and varied. Occupying a territory with fertile soils and a growing season unusually long for these latitudes, from 1672 until the American occupation, they raised large surpluses of corn and vegetables, produced fish and, later maple sugar, and manufactured canoes, snowshoes, and clothing essential to the Great Lakes fur trade. As a result of Ottawa production and the needs of the French (later the British, as well), the two peoples formed a symbiotic and mutually beneficial relationship in the region centered on Mackinac Island. These relationships were constantly reconfirmed by partnerships between French traders and Ottawa suppliers, especially when French males married into Ottawa kin groups. Through such marital alliances, the interests and fortunes of two societies became tightly linked in mutually understood and honored bonds, difficult to sever, perpetuated in the highly visible, emotion- • ally bonding contract of children. Soon after the British arrived in 1761, they incorporated these local political-economic-kinship structures into their imperial design, but only after the Ottawa and their allies had driven home an unforgetable lesson in the rebellion known as Pontiac's War.

In 1813, when Augustin Hamlin, Jr., was born, some 1,300 Ottawa lived in or near the two large villages of *Ahnumawautikuhmig* (Pray Tree Place, or Cross Village) and *Waganagisi* Village. Both major settlements contained as many as 500 residents apiece, who lived in bark houses built on tablelands overlooking Lake Michigan. Some smaller villages scattered along the Lake Michigan shoreline later merged and, joined by families of Catholic converts from the large villages, formed *Weekwitonsing* (Small Bay Place or Little Traverse, later Harbor Springs).[4] Storable crops and abundant fish allowed many residents to remain in or near their villages throughout the long, cold winters—a pattern that historically distinguished Ottawa cultural adaptation to their environment.

Jesuit priests, in 1671, established a mission for several tribes on the north shore at St. Ignace. But when the Ottawa exhausted their fields at the straits, the priests followed the Indians to Cross Village, where they continued their missionization work from the 1740s until the 1760s. The Catholic priests legally sanctioned marriages between the French and Ottawa, like that of Augustin's parents, and promoted social harmony essential to the trade. Although the Jesuits left the Ottawa village in the late 1760s, the kin relations they blessed remained. In later years, when Ottawa leaders reflected on the miseries and problems of their lives, they remembered and dreamed of a return to this golden age.

In 1820, the multiethnic settlement—the regional trading center—at the foot of Fort Mackinac's white-stone bastions housed as many as 400 permanent residents. When Americans first landed at Mackinac Island, they found a three-class social system. Its elite was composed of fur-trade entrepreneurs, wealthy and influential French Canadians and British men, aided by a leavening of skilled and semiskilled Métis craftsmen, clerks, and laborers. On the edges of this settlement were the Ottawa and Chippewa. Many of the elite had married daughters and granddaughters of important Ottawa leaders.

The settlement had between seventy and one hundred log and bark houses. In contrast, the wealthiest families lived in large frame dwellings filled with luxuries suitable for entertaining dignitaries from European countries and the most refined American visitors, in a fashion well beyond what was possible in most frontier outposts. The elite families sent their children away for education at Catholic institutions in Europe and the larger Canadian and American cities. Many of the young people, after exposure to the values and styles of the metropolis, once their educations were complete, returned to the Straits of Mackinac and assumed positions in the fur trade.

Although the L'Arbre Croche Ottawa and the Mackinac Euro-Americans formed geographically distinct communities, their mutual economy and strong kinship ties assured that the boundaries between the two remained highly permeable. The Ottawa women who married traders, for instance, freely accompanied their husbands on annual trade expeditions or visited Ottawa villages alone, renewing their kinship ties. Hence, when Angelique Kiminchigan gave birth to Augustin, she did so at her home village. Ottawa women also became wives of bakers, shoemakers, blacksmiths, fishermen, carpenters, and other laborers; as such they provided hospitality and services to their Indian relatives. During the summer, Indians from all over the upper Great Lakes pitched wigwams along the Mackinac Island shore and enjoyed several weeks of unrestrained celebration and trade. The hospitality granted by these women assured a continued flow of goods from the outlying areas to Mackinac traders.

During the French and British eras, individuals like Augustin of mixed European and Indian descent who lived at the Straits of Mackinac, faced few barriers to full participation in the fur trade economy and local society. They lived in a primarily egalitarian, pluralistic, face-to-face, achievement-oriented frontier community where national or racial status were of little significance in limiting social mobility or fixing group boundaries. With the arrival of American officialdom and private parties, however, this system experienced much pressure for change. Once they had finally established the Mackinac community as within the effective jurisdiction of their nation, Americans began imposing on the local population their values and views of a proper social order. Whether elite or laborer—French, Scots, Métis, or Ottawa—all old settlers experienced great tension in being incorporated into the American national social system.

Augustin Hamlin, Jr., came of age during the height of American pressure for social transformation of the network of Mackinac communities.

He witnessed American efforts to impose ranked categories of social race—White, Half-Breed, Indian—on the population, and further efforts to revise the distribution of already limited resources according to such racial categories. The largest share of local power and wealth was destined to fall into the hands of incoming Americans. However, instead of simply accepting the stigma Americans attached to persons of mixed ancestry, Hamlin and his peers used their dual identity to seek and to achieve a more satisfactory division of political and economic resources during the middle years of the nineteenth century.

Augustin spent much of his life coordinating the political actions of both the L'Arbre Croche Ottawa and Mackinac residents. The old settlers jointly opposed American policies that threatened their rights to remain at and make a living from resources at the Straits of Mackinac. The most ominous policy was a later effort to implement the Indian removal policy, which aimed at a wholesale uprooting of the Ottawa and their resettlement west of the Mississippi River. By the 1820s, the Ottawa *Ogamuk* (leaders)—the most influential male family heads—also recognized other threats posed by Americans, the demand for land cessions being first among these. The L'Arbre Croche Ogamuk had already witnessed the effect of the 1821 Treaty of Chicago on the *Owashshinong* (Far Away Place) or Grand River Ottawa, where Protestant missionaries had moved onto southern Ottawa lands, generated factional disputes, imposed a foreign morality, and acted as a vanguard for settlers bent on acquiring Ottawa lands.

In 1823, a few prominent L'Arbre Croche Ogamuk began working to retain a position for themselves in what promised to be a radically altered society. Augustin's uncle *Mackatabenese* (Black Hawk) joined *Apakosigan* (Smoking Mixture), the most influential L'Arbre Croche war leader and another of the boy's close relatives, in a movement to transform their society.[5] Their goals were to preserve Ottawa cultural identity and social autonomy; their tactics were the politics of persistence. These men won the support of other leading Ogamuk, including Augustin's grandfather *Kiminchigan* (Bustard). Together these leaders petitioned the Bishop of Detroit for a missionary to live in their village. In the context of regional politics, this was a radical political act, for by seeking the support of Catholic missions, they stood in defiance of Protestant American authorities. This move soon involved Augustin as a central actor, shaping the major events of his lifetime and the direction of his career.

Until the 1820s, the few Americans who lived on Mackinac Island cooperated with the old settlers, working within the norms of the established community, relying on locals to conduct trade and provide food. For the most part, they ignored cultural practices that offended them. In 1823, however, the Reverend William Ferry began a government-sanctioned Presbyterian mission school for the northern Indians, which he staffed with teachers from New England. The newcomers' diligent search for converts soon spread beyond the school proper, as they sought to impose their religious beliefs and morals on the "free-livers, free drinkers and infidels" at Mackinac.[6] Soon, these Protestant pacesetters polarized the entire straits population. While many recently arrived American immigrants favored the Protestants, the older Mackinac residents were committed to Catholicism. Old regime Catholics were set thus against newly settled Protestants. By inviting Catholic clergy to live in his village, Apakosigan clearly threw his weight behind the former.

Augustin Hamlin and a few other local Indian children briefly attended Ferry's school and learned much, acquiring rudimentary English and the basics of other studies.[7] As the Catholic and Protestant factional disputes intensified in 1824, however, their parents withdrew them from this institution. Countering this step, between 1823 and 1827—when a priest at last arrived to reside among the Ottawa—the Presbyterians many times asked Ottawa leaders for permission to establish a mission school in their villages: each time they were refused.

The forward-looking Ottawa leaders faced other hazards besides rivalries with Protestant clergy. Their efforts to obtain a Catholic missionary also involved them in the internal politics of the major L'Arbre Croche villages, since many of their traditionalist constituents opposed importing any alien religious practitioner, whether Catholic or Protestant. Those persons who hewed strongly to customary Ottawa religious institutions knew Catholic missionaries would demand cultural change, especially suppression of feasts and rituals essential to promote the well-being of their people through supplication of the spirit forces around them. The pro-Catholic Ogamuk, therefore, had to avoid alienating a large, influential part of their communities. While trying to usher the entire Ottawa community into the American era, they needed a strategy that would avoid potentially disruptive factional disputes, which unchecked might destroy their society.

Those Ogamuk who favored inviting the priests presented their case as a revitalization of traditional Ottawa subsistence and other economic activities. Catholic clergy had lived in their St. Ignace, Michilimackinac, and Cross Village homes during the height of Ottawa influence, and there they had made substantial contributions to upgrading the local economy. The Ogamuk reasoned that the Catholics would again bring financial aid to help the Ottawa develop their horticulture and fishing, the proceeds of which they would sell to Americans, assuring their continued survival in their homelands. Moreover, native catechists were employed to spread church teachings, and they cast Catholic doctrines in the forms of traditional Ottawa beliefs. These doctrines were redefined as complementary sources of spiritual power, which could be invoked by performing new kinds of rituals, songs, and prayers directed at the Christian pantheon, in much the same manner as the Ottawa addressed other spirits who inhabited their universe. These syncretic practices, the Ogamuk believed, would enhance—not destroy—Ottawa culture. In this respect, affiliation with Catholicism offered opportunities that contrasted sharply to the imperious demands from the rigidly individualistic and moralistic Presbyterians. The choices became clear—to redefine the nature of their culture under locally popular Catholic auspices, or to invite the American-backed Protestants to destroy it.

Both as symbols of their commitment to winning Catholic support and as instruments for implementing their designs, the Ottawa leaders selected three of their most promising children for advanced education under church auspices. In 1826, they sent Augustin Hamlin, Jr., and William (*Petawanequot*) and Margaret Blackbird (Mackatabenese's children) to a Catholic seminary in Cincinnati, Ohio.[8] These youngsters were ideal candidates for the new roles envisioned by the Ogamuk. All were related to the most influential Catholic leaders, while both Augustin and William had learned some English at the Presbyterian school. Moreover, the Ogamuk believed that powerful spirit beings had chosen William to lead the Ottawa when he was still a small child. Margaret, in her turn, would give her attention to L'Arbre Croche females. The three, once educated, could serve both church and Ottawa leaders.

The Catholic Ogamuk wished these children would learn skills essential to survival in American society and use them, on their behalf, to preserve Ottawa cultural integrity and political autonomy. The Catholic clergy, on the other hand, desired to train young Ottawa religious leaders fluent in their native language to become translators and catechists who would convert their kin to the ways of the church.

Once at Cincinnati, Augustin, William, and Margaret worked diligently at their studies. Thomas McKenney, then head of the United States Indian Office, later lamented that Augustin had an "Indian's" lack of ambition and could not overcome his inherent native traits, which made him—so McKenney believed, a mediocre student.[9] However, after three years in Cincinnati, the youngsters' instructors chose Augustin and William to attend the School of the Propaganda in Rome, an assessment of their merits that did not bespeak lack of ambition. Since all three students were probably bilingual in Ottawa and French but spoke little English and no Latin, they had to overcome handicaps that McKenney himself probably could not have surmounted. That they did so and were prepared for advanced education in only three years indicates stronger incentive and dedication than McKenney could recognize.

Augustin and William sailed for Rome in 1829, leaving Margaret to finish her education in Cincinnati. William's brother, Andrew Blackbird, later reported that even though Augustin's complexion was darker than William's, he was presented in Rome as half French.[10] Blackbird's observation indicates that, in the eyes of the Ottawa, Augustin was marked with few if any genetic traits that might distinguish him from his Indian relatives.

In Rome, the boys' studies demanded constant labor, from sunup until sundown. On holy days, they saw the sights of Rome and the Vatican and heard mass spoken by the Pope. William's powerful, eloquent oratory marked him as "promising" to the Italians who knew him, while Augustin's friendship with William clearly shaped his later role in L'Arbre Croche political affairs. Even in Rome, the lads were not isolated from affairs affecting their people. President Andrew Jackson took office the year the boys arrived, and soon rumors and speculations about his plans for new land cession treaties and for dislodging all Eastern Indians reached the students. William adamantly opposed any land sale, writing his kinsmen and advising them not to treat with the United States, even if threatened with physical violence. He promised that when he returned home, he would help them negotiate a favorable settlement.

Then tragedy struck, ending the career of the Ottawas' chosen young leader, and starting the career of his cousin, Augustin. On the evening of June 25, 1833, the evening before William's ordination, Augustin came to his room to discuss affairs at home. According to Andrew Blackbird, William vowed that when he returned to L'Arbre Croche, the Ottawa would not be removed to the west. Blackbird does not record Augustin's response to these plans, but within hours of the conversation it developed that he, not William, would spend the next twenty years fighting the threat of the Indian removal policy.

The following morning, William did not appear for breakfast. A messenger was dispatched and discovered the Ottawas' great hope in his chamber lying dead in a pool of blood. Augustin rushed to the room where, although authorities had immediately removed William's body, he saw evidence of murder. The Italians suspected an American student, someone jealous of an Indian mastering the sciences, an Indian who was more than his equal, but never apprehended the murderer. At L'Arbre Croche, the people believed someone had assassinated their brightest young leader because he advised them not to sell land. Augustin returned to the United States in 1834 without receiving ordination to the priesthood.

When, in 1835, Michigan's population grew faster than any other state or territory in the nation, its territorial representatives worked hard for statehood. Henry Rowe Schoolcraft, head agent of the Michigan Superintendency and Augustin's primary antagonist, along with many other Michigan residents wanted the entire state cleared of Indian title and opened for settlement. Before Hamlin arrived at L'Arbre Croche, Schoolcraft had won assurances from important Ottawa Ogamuk, including Apakosigan, that sale of a large tract in Michigan could be arranged for a proper financial consideration.

Upon his return to Michigan, Hamlin began teaching school at the Catholic Ottawa village on Little Traverse Bay.[11] From the first days of his residence at L'Arbre Croche, the Ogamuk considered him an important member of their society, one with credibility strong enough even to change the minds of leaders who had supported Schoolcraft. On May 3, 1835, leading Ogamuk from all L'Arbre Croche settlements signed a document certifying their acceptance of the young man and appointing him as their representative. They confirmed that, because they "placed special trust and confidence in the integrity ability and learning" of young Hamlin, they were assigning him the legal right to "execute and perform all the duties pertaining to that appointment."[12]

The specifics of Hamlin's "appointment" were defined vaguely, but the document's text implies that Augustin would become an Ogema of the same status as his grandfather, Kiminchigan. That is, he was accepted as a respected man allowed to express his positions and those of his family in council. The document, however, coupled this traditional authority with the

American concept of power of attorney to summarily execute the signatories' business. Edward Biddle and Samuel Abbott, two Mackinac traders married to Ottawa women and desiring the Indians' continued patronage, supported the Ogamuk and witnessed the signing. They registered the document with the Mackinac county clerk to make Hamlin's authority official under American law. The Ogamuk, however, never intended to delegate full decision-making authority to a twenty-two year old man whose wisdom was incomplete and whose political standing in the L'Arbre Croche community not fully established. Instead, they acknowledged Hamlin as "a minor or young chief" of the L'Arbre Croche Ottawa, signifying their respect for his knowledge and language skills, both of which they would use in forthcoming councils with Americans.[13]

The Ogamuk attending the council at L'Arbre Croche in May 1835 discussed with Augustin a plan of action to alleviate their immediate economic need and continue the development begun in the 1820s. These ends they sought without having to sell their claims to all their Michigan lands. Instead, they proposed disposing of only the Manitou Islands in Lake Michigan, and Upper Peninsula lands shared with the Chippewa. With the cash proceeds, they proposed paying $40,000 in debts to traders, liabilities accrued since the start of the American regime. To assure their wishes reached President Jackson directly, Augustin proposed that the most important Ogamuk accompany him to Washington and personally present their offers. This would bypass agent Schoolcraft, whom Hamlin thought untrustworthy and likely to oppose this limited cession.[14] Hamlin's speech, his visible political connections to local traders and the bishop at Detroit, and his knowledge of the outside world persuaded the Ogamuk to take his advice.

When Commissioner of Indian Affairs T. Hartley Crawford received the Ottawa petition drafted in May, he interpreted the imperfectly worded document as delegating total authority to Hamlin as "head chief." Crawford believed it could do little harm to so recognize Augustin, for many Ogamuk had signed the petition and two reputable merchants verified it. To the commissioner, it appeared that Hamlin already held the Indians' confidence, and United States recognition of his position, while adding formal approval to a potentially favorable political situation for the young man, could work to the advantage of the United States. Crawford's hopes for Hamlin were expressed in his comment that, "Such a man might by a prudent and conciliatory course be easily constrained from error."[15]

Henry R. Schoolcraft, however, opposed Augustin's promotion and his activities. Eventually, as a result of their political clashes, Schoolcraft would challenge the validity of Hamlin's Indian identity in American circles of power. Their first conflict occurred when, citing departmental policy, the Michigan superintendent denied the Ottawa leaders permission to visit Washington. Schoolcraft planned to visit the capital in the fall of 1835, hoping to convince Secretary of War Lewis Cass that the nation's best interests demanded a major Michigan Indian land cession. Nonetheless, Apakosigan, Hamlin, and several other L'Arbre Croche Ogamuk left for Washington at the end of October without government sanction, intending to block Schoolcraft's efforts.[16]

When the L'Arbre Croche delegation arrived at the capital in early December, they found government officials inclined to hear their requests but slow to act. Michigan Territory's representative, John Norvell, met them but took no action, hoping the Indians would leave quickly. While they also met with President Jackson, their conversations with Lewis Cass, until recently the governor of Michigan Territory, promised more positive results, since Cass proposed that the delegates present written requests for his department's consideration. On December 5, 1835, Hamlin submitted the Ottawa agenda. He asked that the government arrange to give the Ottawa "the quiet possession of our lands, and to transmit the same safely to our posterity."[17] The Ogamuk clearly and emphatically refused to move west of the Mississippi River. In return, they offered for sale the lands identified during the May council.

Augustin used the well-rehearsed phrases, key symbols, and oratorical style of a traditional Ottawa speaker to represent the position of his constituents, saying:

> It is a heart-rending thought to our simple feelings to think of leaving our native country forever; the land where the bones of our forefathers lay thick in the earth; the land which has drank, and which has been bought with the price of, their native blood, and which has been thus safely transmitted to us. It is, we say, a heart-rending thought to us to think so; there are many local endearments which make the soul shrink with horror at the ideal of rejecting our country forever—the mortal remains of our deceased parents, relations, and friends, cry out to us as it were, for our compassion, our sympathy and our love.

> But, we are aware of this plain fact, that we Indians cannot long remain peaceably and happy in the place where the tribe is at present if we persist in pursuing that way and manner of life, which we have hitherto loved although now in a less degree. We now deem the life of a savage incompatible with that of a civilized man; and therefore we would wish to exchange the former with the latter.[18]

Allow the Ottawa to remain in their heartlands, and they will promise to become "civilized" in a fashion acceptable to Americans. This was the clearly defined position expressed by Hamlin. It remained his primary goal in all future dealings with the government.

Cass responded favorably to the proposal, but rightly noted that Hamlin and his companions did not represent all Ottawa and Chippewa claiming the regions that these few delegates proposed to sell. The government would require a full council of representatives from all interested bands before any negotiations could begin, he countered. When Schoolcraft arrived in late December, Cass immediately authorized him to negotiate a treaty, not for the limited territory Hamlin proposed, but for all unceded Michigan lands. Cass instructed him to assemble a full delegation of Ogamuk with full authority to negotiate on these terms. To win the support of the Ogamuk already in Washington, the secretary of war then promised Hamlin employment at

L'Arbre Croche, and sent him home to recruit a more representative delegation.[19] Defeated in attempts to negotiate a fast settlement on their terms, the delegates returned to Michigan to begin preparations for full-scale treaty deliberations.

News of the upcoming negotiations reached Michigan well before Hamlin arrived, creating turmoil among the entire Ottawa population. The Grand River Ottawa opposed sale on any terms and threatened to kill any Ogema who cooperated with Americans. After nearly two months of counseling with their traders and missionaries, these southern Ottawa dispatched a delegation of young men supervised by three Ogamuk. But the Grand River bands forbade their delegates to make a treaty and instructed them to obstruct any move the L'Arbre Croche Ottawa might make toward such an agreement.[20] At L'Arbre Croche, most Catholic Ottawa opposed the comprehensive land cession, and their leaders feared signing a document supporting any sale whatever. Local traders and other members of the Mackinac Catholic community contributed to the already painful Ottawa disunity. They opposed a negotiation in a distant place, where they could not voice their opinions and use their influence with the Indians to demand a cash settlement for their debt claims.

Hamlin's plans for Ottawa development, however, required a large infusion of money. With hopes for a small land sale dashed, he pressed the Catholic Ottawa to accept a larger cession—on the condition that large reservations be made and removal be omitted from the treaty's terms. A leading Grand River trader reported that Hamlin visited the southern villages, presumably arguing this case. But however hard he pressed them, the resolve of the southern delegates to prevent land sales remained firm.[21] There is no indication that Hamlin was successful in persuading even the L'Arbre Croche or Mackinac communities to support such a large sale, although he returned to Washington as a delegate and participated in the negotiations, presumably after winning at least partial approval from some.

On March 15, 1836, the Indians and government negotiators assembled in Washington D.C.'s Masonic Hall and held their first recorded treaty discussions. Augustin Hamlin, Jr., the "half-breed, and delegate from L'Arbre Croche," spoke only once, according to the official record, although he interpreted throughout the proceedings. In his one recorded speech, Hamlin made clear his self-identification as a member of the Ottawa "nation," suggesting that if the "white men" who accompanied the Ottawa delegates would cease trying to influence and confuse the Indians, they would all approve the government's proposition for a larger cession.[22] The consensus Hamlin had failed to obtain among the Ottawa while in Michigan, he sought to win around the conference table in the Masonic Hall.

In councils closed to the Ottawas' "friends," Apakosigan offered to sell all lower peninsula lands south of an East-West line beginning north of the Manistee River, and he invited the Grand River Ottawa to join his people in the north. When the government offered the Ottawa two large, permanent reservations north of the Manistee River, all Ottawa present agreed to approve the treaty. However, they wanted their trusted "friends" to scrutinize the draft of the document and verify its contents. Many local traders were kin; they controlled the Indian's credit; hence, their wishes had to be considered in any settlement. The L'Arbre Croche Ottawa, however, selected Hamlin as their treaty inspector. In the end, all parties approved the terms of the agreement, which sold all but 141,000 acres of the Ottawa's Michigan lands. The treaty met the Ogamuk and Hamlin's goals by providing land to develop for agriculture, cash to invest in the project, continued access to fishing grounds, and no removal clause.

The treaty had to be approved in Michigan by all Ottawa Ogamuk, in open council where they were exposed to the gaze of their constituents and the actors on the margins of their communities. It was important, therefore, for all interested parties to receive some benefits from the treaty, including the Mackinac Métis. Article Six set aside $150,000 for the "Half-Breed" kin who did not live in L'Arbre Croche villages but claimed rights to share land and natural resources by descent from an Ottawa ancestor. The treaty provided three levels of such payments, depending on how closely such marginal folk identified with the Indians, their ability to provide for themselves, and their history of and potential for providing services to Ottawa communities. This provision thus codified American imposed racial categories in the Mackinac community. Descent and degree of social distance from the Indians were criteria for group membership now made explicit, and they would have unexpected political consequences for Hamlin and other Mackinac residents.

As Blackbird later noted, Hamlin was phenotypically indistinguishable from the Ottawa. His close kin relations with the most influential Ogamuk, their selection of him for education and a leadership role, and the use they made of his acquired skills all show Hamlin's strong bonds to the Ottawa community. But under the 1836 treaty, Augustin received payment as a specially favored "half-breed" for whom the Ottawa had "a strong consideration for aid rendered," receiving $1,600 of a special $48,148 fund.[23] Such payments to the Ottawa marginals were in lieu of personal reservations, the blocks of land that in earlier treaties had been used as payments or rewards for individuals closely associated with but not fully acceptable as Indians.

Because Augustin accepted this payment, government agents did not place his name on the tribe's annuity rolls, and he was not officially recognized as a proper Ottawa. On the other hand, he had become an important member of the Ottawa community even though he did not make a living by farming, fishing, or hunting. He clearly demonstrated his political skills by helping negotiate a settlement that community members could support—however reluctantly—at a time when government officials pressed for even greater concessions. To Americans, however, payment to Hamlin and other Mackinac Métis in a category distinct from Indians gave this classification a firm reality, one strengthened by legal contract.

The treaty, which Augustin and the Ottawa hoped would settle their affairs beneficially, in the end left them in worse condition than before the negotiations began. Senator Hugh White, chairing the Senate Committee on

YOUNG AUGUSTIN HAMLIN, JR., IN WASHINGTON. This lithograph was painted during the winter of 1835–1836, while Hamlin was negotiating the Treaty of 1836. He was also known as Kanapima *(One Who Is Talked Of). The original painting was by Bass Otis, and it first appeared in McKenney and Hall's* Indian Tribes of North America. *The fashionable image he displays was acquired during his years of education in Cincinnati and Rome, and it demonstrates his willingness to adopt aspects of American culture. His accomplishments and arguments helped convince American officials of the Ottawas' capacity for making desirable accommodations to their policies, which is precisely what Ottawa leaders desired him to do. Hamlin continued to dress in American middle-class fashions throughout his lifetime. (Courtesy of the Grand Rapids Public Library, Michigan Room Collections. From James D. Horan, ed.,* The McKenney-Hall Portrait Gallery of American Indians. *New York: Crown Publishers, 1972.)*

Indian Affairs and wanting to embarrass President Jackson, amended the treaty, deleting the guarantee of permanent reservations in Michigan, limiting tenure of these lands to five years, and inserting provisions for removal of the Ottawa into the western Indian Territory. With this amendment, Senator White restricted the number of presidentially controlled, vote-winning patronage positions available, positions for blacksmiths, farmers, carpenters, and agents to supervise reservation development. The amendment also obligated the government to finance an exploring expedition southwest of the Missouri River and to create a new reservation there, "as soon as the Indians desire it."[24] As a result, the Ottawa received the capital needed for enhancing production from their now severely restricted land base, but their guaranteed tenure of these reservations was limited to five years, subject thereafter to unilateral extensions of occupation rights by the United States. For this grave legal uncertainty, the Ottawa had ceded title to half the state of Michigan.

In Michigan, Ottawa leaders were understandably reluctant to ratify the Senate's amendments. Only when Henry R. Schoolcraft assured them that they could not be removed without their consent, and with his guarantee that the United States would honor the treaty's 13th Article stipulating "for the right of hunting on the lands ceded, with the other usual privileges of occupancy until the land is required for settlement," would they give their reluctant approval.[25] The 1836 treaty was then finally ratified by the U.S. Senate. However, for the next nineteen years, the Michigan Ottawa Ogamuk worked constantly to clarify their ambiguous status, to win permanent title to their reservation lands, and—once and for all—to end the threat of removal.

Augustin Hamlin, Jr., played a less active role in Ottawa politics after the treaty's ratification. Unlike mainstream Ottawa leaders, he married late, not until a few years before his death. Through most of his adulthood, Augustin dedicated much of his time and energy to managing the affairs of his Ottawa kin. He resided at Little Traverse, presumably still employed as a teacher at the Catholic Indian school there. By 1840, however, he lived near his natal family at St. Ignace, assisting with his father's Indian trade affairs.[26] There, he acquired a reputation as a good business leader. Throughout this time, Augustin used his understanding of local politics and closeness to officials and events to keep his Ottawa friends and family informed and advised. In July 1837, for instance, he wrote some of the most influential Ogema at Cross Village, Little Traverse, and Cheboygan, alerting leaders about an effort to promote their removal to the west. Hamlin assured them that the treaty they signed explicitly provided they could not be required to migrate against their will, and advised the Ogamuk to say nothing to agents dispatched to advocate removal. They had many influential local allies, he observed, informing them that the Mackinac trader community wanted the Indians to remain in their homes forever.

Hamlin's position in the trader community at Mackinac, together with his behind-the-scenes political maneuvers, eventually threatened his credibility in the Ottawa community, straining the foundation of his Indian identity. During the crisis period surrounding the treaty negotiations, the Ogamuk had allowed the young leader much scope, particularly the assumption of important responsibilities in negotiating and verifying the 1836 treaty, a role for which his education qualified him. In Washington, however, Hamlin pressed his campaign for a comprehensive power of attorney and government recognition as head chief. This action his Ottawa kin could not accept. They did not share his vision of a formal, power-laden office, from which he could dictate developments. Indeed, the Grand River Ottawa openly distrusted him, while at L'Arbre Croche, not even his closest kin would validate the interpretation he placed on the 1835 petition. If Hamlin wished to become a respected leader, the Ottawa insisted, he would have to recognize the limitations of his age, the proper boundaries of authority, and work with—not above—other community members for resolution of issues that influenced all of them.

Hamlin avoided open censure from the Ogamuk by working discretely within the community; however, at the same time, he campaigned vigorously for formal recognition as head chief through private communications with officials in Washington. The ambitious young man again lobbied Congressman John Norvell, who in turn approached Commissioner of Indian Affairs, Carey Harris. The commissioner demurred: he would not appoint Hamlin "principal chief" until Schoolcraft could be consulted.[27] After receiving this news, he asked President Van Buren on June 28, 1837, to validate his status as head chief, and requested a presidential medal as a symbol of office, justifying his request with the claim, "I am an Indian with very little of the white man's blood in me."[28] Further, he claimed responsibility for conducting the Indians to Washington for the 1836 treaty, and referred the new president to the May 1835 petition of the L'Arbre Croche Ogema.

No friend of Hamlin's, Schoolcraft instead saw the young man as a competitor, someone attempting to carve out a new role standing between his and the Ottawa leaders. Indeed, he resented Hamlin's disruption of his 1835 treaty plans and Augustin's continued opposition to Michigan Indian Agency appointments and policies. On June 16, 1838, Schoolcraft replied negatively to the commissioner's inquiry, citing Hamlin's mixed descent as an obstacle to such an appointment. He added that on the last occasion, when the Ottawa asked to have Hamlin made a "chief," he told them Augustin was "a mere youth, the son of a French half-breed trader at Point St. Ignace, and not a native even of their district . . . That the President required me to transact the public business with the Indians and not with other persons who made themselves busy in Indian affairs."[29] He advised the commissioner that Hamlin had been educated with some care and that his knowledge of the Ottawa and English languages could benefit the Ottawa and others if he would not overstep his position. His assessment of Hamlin's potential—for aiding the interests of the United States, was summed up with the remark: "I do not think it is his *Forte* to rule in their political affairs. At least thus far he has not evinced that foresight in pointing out the present and probable condition, and *true* policy of the Indians or firmness and consistence in counselling them which are deemed essential . . . and unhappily he has been found opposed to policy of the department in every instance known to me." Hamlin's claim to the position of high chief should be rejected outright, Schoolcraft recommended.

By 1838, however, Schoolcraft had few Ottawa supporters at L'Arbre Croche. His failure to accept the Indians' potential for increased participation in American society was at the heart of their discontent with this administrator. From the perspective of Ottawa leaders, they were actively and successfully pursuing the assimilation policies that the American government had promoted since the republic's founding. But while Schoolcraft acknowledged they had already made much progress toward becoming yeomen farmers, that many could pass as citizens, and that most local Americans had a "friendly feeling towards them," he was convinced these efforts would be no more successful in Michigan than those made by other Indian communities. "There are," he said, "a thousand causes of latent dislike and disunion between the two great stocks of human race, who are also different in their leading traits, physical and intellectual, as the American Indian and the Teutonic or Celtic."[30] Faced with such overt racism, Hamlin drafted petitions for the Ottawa and joined forces with dissatisfied Mackinac traders, many of them—like himself, also of plural ancestry and heritage. Joining forces, these allies sought to force Schoolcraft's dismissal from office.

Firm in his beliefs, Schoolcraft pressed for Ottawa removal. In 1838, he authorized his brother, James, to raise an Ottawa exploring delegation to travel southwest of the Missouri River. The Grand River Ottawa sent only two Ogamuk, while the L'Arbre Croche people flatly refused to participate until Schoolcraft intimidated them, issuing scarcely veiled threats to cut their annuity provisions and services. Since fear of removal had been the single most important issue inducing the Ottawa to negotiate the 1836 treaty, and because Schoolcraft had previously promised that the Ottawa would probably not ever be removed—certainly never against their will—the superintendent severely damaged his credibility. Although the delegation explored Kansas lands, no Ottawa agreed to relocate to the west.

In May 1839, rumors swept through the population at the Straits of Mackinac: the government, many believed, planned to load the Ottawa on steamboats and send them to western lands without their consent. In response, more than 250 persons from L'Arbre Croche and Cheboygan loaded their canoes and moved their families into British territory on Manitoulin Island. Others threatened to leave. Schoolcraft responded by deleting those who left from the annuity roles.

With Schoolcraft's actions causing serious agitation in the Ottawa community, the Ogamuk again called on Hamlin to play a prominent public role in their political affairs. Again, this reinforced his standing in the Ottawa community and his Indian identity, despite Schoolcraft's efforts to diminish the former and to deny the latter. In July 1839, several leading Ogamuk petitioned Michigan's Governor Stevens Mason asking for the right to buy reserve lands on Little Traverse Bay, and for citizenship. They cited their progress toward becoming American-style Christian agriculturists as reason to grant them permanent right to remain in Michigan. Augustin drafted and signed this petition.[31]

In 1840, the Hamlin-Schoolcraft rivalry climaxed. The most recent removal threat had strengthened the L'Arbre Croche Ottawas' resolve to purchase land, but for this they badly needed cash, just at the moment when a major national depression made money even more scarce than normal on this frontier. To obtain additional capital, Hamlin worked with the Ogamuk to gain access to the nearly $150,000 "debt fund"—the unallocated part of the

$300,000 appropriated under the 1836 treaty to pay debts to traders made before the document's ratification—plus accrued interest.[32] In February, Augustin went quietly to L'Arbre Croche, where he discussed the Ogamuks' wishes, finally requesting expenses to visit Washington, where he would lobby on their behalf, seeking release of the debt fund.

Schoolcraft, in turn, seriously miscalculated his personal standing in the eyes of both the Ottawa and the Mackinac trader community. Both groups harbored a degree of vexation about his dealings well beyond what he could recognize or accept. Thus, he wrote Acting Commissioner Potts to report that the locals held, "Some petty misrepresentations against this office, which are not deemed entitled to notice."[33] At the February council, Hamlin teamed up with Schoolcraft's brother-in-law, William Johnston, to accuse the superintendent of intentionally and illegally withholding the debt fund. The Ogamuk added their own charges—that Schoolcraft withheld treaty stipulated goods and services, employed incompetent female interpreters, and failed to carry out key provisions of the 1836 treaty to survey their reservations.

The Ogamuk sent Hamlin and Johnston to Washington with their complaints and the promise of a thousand dollars to pay for their travel, on the understanding that the money would be drawn from their annuity, and that any additional expenses would be met from the debt fund.[34] The pair arrived about April 1, met Crawford, and made formal complaints against Schoolcraft. Because of their protests and letters received from other Mackinac residents, the commissioner appointed two prominent Michigan traders to examine the charges. A formal investigation began May 19, 1840.

Hamlin and Johnston won support from Mackinac traders, the priests, and from other citizens in their efforts to remove Schoolcraft from office. Each of these groups had their reasons for wishing him gone. Traders reasoned that, should the Ottawa receive the debt fund, they would receive a share for the credit they had advanced since the 1837 payments. Moreover, some local merchants and community leaders had strong connections with the Whig party and opposed Schoolcraft's staunch Democratic affiliation. Others in these cash-poor times were desperate for government jobs as carpenters, farmers, and interpreters—salaried positions that Schoolcraft handed out liberally as patronage favors to his trusted relatives. Catholic missionaries, who maintained schools in Ottawa villages, had received little of the treaty-stipulated funds for missions from the Presbyterian churchman Schoolcraft. Together, the Ottawa and their political allies—traders, Catholic missionaries, job hungry laborers and craftsmen, Whig party aspirants—all hoped for more under a new superintendent.

Schoolcraft's closest adherents argued that the Indians had little to do with the complaints filed against him. One claimed that Hamlin and Johnston had secretly collected a few Ogamuk in a Mackinac store where they persuaded the Indians of Schoolcraft's bad faith and promised to recover much money by going to Washington. Because the Ogamuk's petition was, in fact, drawn up in L'Arbre Croche, where many well-known leaders signed the charges, it appears that this friend of the superintendent both over-estimated Hamlin's influence in the Ottawa community and misunderstood Indian opposition to the man who pushed for their removal. This critic also attempted to defuse Hamlin and Johnston's lobbying effort in Washington, claiming that the pair had won an agreement from the Ogamuk for a payment of half of whatever funds their trip produced. Indeed, Johnston later submitted a claim for payment of $4,000 for this journey—$1,000 to repay the Ogamuk for a travel advance, and the rest for the pair's additional travel expenses, in addition to his claim for a private fee for services rendered. Johnston was, indeed, notorious as a scoundrel, a tool of whoever would pay him; but even the man who criticized the pair's trip noted that Hamlin more closely represented the Indian's wishes than his partner. Unlike Johnston, for whom this trip was a money-making enterprise, Hamlin had good reason for not claiming personal payment. Still seeking recognition as the Ottawas' head chief, had he done so, he would have lost credibility.

Hamlin's personal goals in lobbying for Schoolcraft's dismissal are clear. Success would remove a major obstacle to his central ambition, official government recognition as paramount chief of the Ottawa. During the Schoolcraft investigation, Hamlin again requested that Commissioner of Indian Affairs Crawford grant him the title. When informed of the commissioner's inclination to do so, Schoolcraft bowed slightly to administrative authority and agreed to put Hamlin's name on the Ottawa payroll and to recognize him as an Indian, but only if the department insisted. Nonetheless, he believed it was an unsound policy, even though it might "quiet fears and disturbance of those people [the L'Arbre Croche Ottawa] on designs and policy of the government." He continued, depreciating Hamlin, adding that the Indian Department would not "find another John Ross, in Mr. Hamlin, who is, I am free to say, a young man of correct habits, a plain education and conscientious [sic] feelings, but inheriting the bias of opinion peculiar to the aboriginal races."[35]

The core of Schoolcraft's case against Hamlin was that, despite the young man's sincerity, he would be easily influenced by the sinister "*clique* of Indian traders" who opposed him as superintendent, the department, and official American policies. Schoolcraft's allusion to the Cherokee leader John Ross marks a key ingredient in this dispute, one which went beyond the personal antagonism between him and Hamlin. What was involved was an administrative step away from direct management of an Indian community's affairs—through an American official—toward indirect rule through a government-appointed high chief.

Thus, despite Schoolcraft's objections, Crawford recommended that Hamlin be recognized as head chief of the Ottawa. Three days later, on August 21, the Commissioner of Indian Affairs addressed himself directly and officially to Hamlin, outlining the findings of the commission to investigate Schoolcraft, a *de facto*, if partial, recognition of his newly enlarged leadership role in Ottawa society. Crawford reported that no legal grounds for Schoolcraft's dismissal had been discovered, hence he would remain in office.

Therefore, Schoolcraft remained at Mackinac, his position diminished, unwilling to bend to the wishes of Hamlin and his political backers, an act he believed would cause the utter collapse of his authority.

Schoolcraft continued using Hamlin's "half-breed" heritage to impede the new "chief's" ambitions. He soon again raised that issue to avoid paying a $300 claim, which Hamlin and Johnston requested from the autumn annuities for travel expenses above the cash advanced by the Ogamuk for the spring trip to Washington. Although this amount was small, Schoolcraft argued that both Hamlin and Johnston had received payments under the half-breed provision of the 1836 treaty, were not included on later payrolls, and, hence, were not Indians. The treaty barred non-Indians from receiving annuity funds, he argued.[36] With such legalisms, the superintendent squeezed his rival, but he also sought to thwart the directives of his superior in the Indian Office, a risky game, indeed.

He continued his anti-Hamlin campaign by seeking the approval of the L'Arbre Croche Ogamuk, whom he called into council on September 19, 1840. At this meeting, Schoolcraft carefully questioned Apakosigan about the intention of the L'Arbre Croche leaders in their 1835 petition. According to Schoolcraft, Apakosigan and other Ogamuk who witnessed the signing of the petition were "surprised and disavowed" having sought Hamlin's appointment as head chief.[37] They had, Schoolcraft reported, merely wanted him recognized as a young leader. The likelihood that these Ogamuk were genuinely uninformed of Hamlin's bid for government recognition is slight. News traveled too quickly between the Straits communities for Hamlin to have kept so large a political secret for five long years. Moreover, Apakosigan spoke French and visited Mackinac Island regularly, both increasing his opportunities to learn of Hamlin's ambitions and activities.

More likely, the Ogamuk were using this meeting for their own purposes, as an opportunity to force onto Hamlin a greater measure of conformity to Ottawa leadership standards. When Schoolcraft introduced the matter of Hamlin's parentage and the original omission of his name from the payrolls, Hamlin's Ottawa relatives for the first time publicly classified the young man as a "half-breed." Apakosigan offered an economic explanation for doing so, saying that the treaty had drawn a line between the Indians who lived by "hunting"—a contemporary American stereotype for most Eastern Woodland peoples, which only partially fit the Ottawa—and those affinal kin who did not. Hamlin, who worked as a trader and did not reside at L'Arbre Croche, fit in the second category.

The young man was, moreover, educated in an European style of life, which the Ottawa appreciated as sometimes useful to themselves. However, Apakosigan added, if all their affinal kin and their descendants—the "mixed bloods," shared in the treaty provisions, there would be little left to support the L'Arbre Croche villagers. Both politically and economically, even though all the Ottawa Ogamuk were "most favorable to Hamlin's pretensions among them" and were "kindly disposed" to him, they did not regard him as head chief or entitled to pay for his services. While hobbling Hamlin's overweening ambitions, the L'Arbre Croche Ottawa were trying to draw an ethnic boundary around themselves, guarding their limited resources against distribution to the affiliated marginal folk.

To influence the commissioner's decision, Schoolcraft then described the role expectations held by the Ottawa for their Ogamuk. Such leaders, he explained, had little formal authority and only local influence and jurisdiction; they were chosen by popular voice—verbal or tacit consent—not appointed by written documents granting full authority to make decisions for the entire society. Schoolcraft argued that if the United States issued a written commission, the Indians would be suspicious, "especially when [the appointee was] not of pure Indian blood and acknowledged [as a] member of the tribe."[38] He reasoned that when Ottawa leaders arose with temporarily broader authority and responsibilities to meet the demands of unusual situations, little harm and no permanent results would occur. However, if the department formally recognized such an office, and if it gave written authorization to the appointee, then it would be difficult to withdraw. The commissioner of Indian Affairs accepted Schoolcraft's cultural analysis and political logic and did not award Hamlin further official recognition.

Hamlin and Johnston returned to Washington in the winter of 1840–1841 as "agents of the Ottawa and Chippewa tribes."[39] Once again, they protested Schoolcraft's handling of Ottawa affairs and his continuation in office. Apparently this trip brought no successful results, for the following April they again requested permission from Secretary of War John Bell to conduct a delegation of some four to six Ogamuk to Washington to protest Schoolcraft's behavior, this time directly to the president.

There was, indeed, critical business needing attention, for the five-year tenure of the Ottawa reservations granted in 1836 would soon expire. Meanwhile, back in Michigan, Schoolcraft still refused to take any action except preparation for removal. Except for persons who had purchased land, most Ottawa were in an exceedingly tenuous position, living on and developing reservations whose permanency were subject to the unilateral decisions of the president. Hamlin and Johnston's overtures were well-timed, for the twelve-year reign of the Jacksonian Democrats had been broken. Their first success came soon after President William Henry Harrison was inaugurated, whereupon Henry R. Schoolcraft was at last separated from his authority over Michigan Indian affairs.

The closing events of Schoolcraft's administration show that the L'Arbre Croche Ogamuk continued to accept Hamlin as a respected community member. Nonetheless, that powerful outsider, Schoolcraft, continued emphasizing a personally politicized ethnic boundary, one arbitrarily separating Augustin Hamlin, Jr., from other Mackinac residents whom Schoolcraft recognized as Indian. His personal conceptualization of Hamlin's social identity went far to block the latter's political aspirations. When all other attempts to curtail the influence of this popular marginal leader failed,

Schoolcraft drew on the American concept of racial status, ascribed by descent, to block Hamlin's progress.

Although the Ogamuk seemed to support Schoolcraft's contention that Hamlin's descent from only one wholly Ottawa parent prohibited his sharing full rights in Ottawa property, their interpretations were not based on the American myth of blood. Unlike Schoolcraft, they recognized Hamlin as a man well-qualified to deal with American authorities on every level, aided by advanced formal education, experience, and skills. They did not share Schoolcraft's ire or his racial convictions—that Hamlin was inherently inferior because of his "mixed blood." However, while they recognized and welcomed him as a member of their community, it was their community and its values they worked to preserve, and their political system held no place for an autocrat.

Following Schoolcraft's dismissal, Augustin became more intimately involved in L'Arbre Croche community affairs, promoting local economic development and working to end the threat of removal. In June 1841, the Presbyterian minister of Grand Traverse Bay, Peter Dougherty, observed Augustin accompanying a Catholic priest to the villages there as an interpreter, holding services and baptizing the resident Ottawa and Chippewa. Such ritual activities likely marked an important symbolic feature of Hamlin's growth as a traditional leader. For among the Ottawa, secular influence often rested on a specially demonstrated relationship with the spiritual beings who inhabited their cosmos. By working with the priest, Hamlin made his spiritual power known; and once again he strongly identified himself with politically potent Church institutions. Hamlin also requested appointment as government interpreter at Little Traverse, a position that would have added income and bolstered his secular influence in the village, but he did not receive the job.

While the new Whig administration would not guarantee an end to the possibility of removal, Robert Stuart, the new head of the Michigan Indian Superintendency, supported the Ottawa's efforts to remain in the state. At this point, Hamlin severed his political connections with William Johnston, who also had not received the government job he sought. Johnston had turned against Superintendent Stuart, whose early activities promised some limited benefits to the Ottawa. Among the new superintendent's first moves was an attempt, at last, to obtain release of the 1836 treaty debt funds. While he may well have had in mind the obligations of his former employer, the American Fur Company, this was a step sought by the Ottawa in their own right. However, like Schoolcraft, Stuart favored the appointment of Presbyterians to other government posts, and he refused to pay Hamlin and Johnston any portion of their $4,000 claim beyond the sum advanced them. Unlike Johnston, Hamlin kept a low profile, working quietly within the community to promote the Ogamuk's long-term goals.

Apakosigan and the senior Ogamuk of L'Arbre Croche continued their movement toward partial assimilation into American society and regularly petitioned against removal. Hamlin's name did not appear on another petition until December of 1843, and then it appeared as a witness—not as "chief." However, the substance of that document—sent to the Michigan Legislature and requesting citizenship, clearly bears Augustin's mark. The text opens with a variation on a biblical theme, saying "we are not strangers in a strange land, but are strangers in our own land." It argued that the Ottawa were becoming "civilized" and their old customs were "ameliorated by the influences of Christianity." They had made comfortable homes "in imitation of the white men and are maintaining their families by cultivating the soil."[40] Hence, they should not be sent to live among uncivilized Indians but granted citizenship. The petition reached the legislature March 11, 1844.

By the mid-1840s, many Ottawa lived in log houses. They had much increased the size of their fields, and agricultural surpluses were sold to support an ever more sedentary life. Fish and maple sugar became more important than ever as salable commodities in a wider American market, and the Ottawa augmented these with wheat, rye, and root crops—especially potatoes. However, the growing American population began spreading southward along the north shore of Michigan's lower peninsula and increasingly competed for resources that the Ottawa relied on. The L'Arbre Croche people complained of squatters cutting their maple groves and intruding on their lands.[41] By the 1850s, Little Traverse Bay's most accessible fishing grounds became so depleted that many Ottawa farmed for their complete subsistence, until lumber companies began stripping northern timber in the 1870s, bringing new economic opportunities.

These Indians had purchased thousands of acres with annuity funds; still, the title to even these lands remained in doubt. The status of reservation lands, occupied and exploited only during the "president's pleasure," was even more unsettled and insecure. On the other hand, legally the Ottawa remained wards of the federal government; hence, the property they owned could not be seized for debts or other reasons, nor could it be taxed, which marked them a significantly different category of Michigan resident. American merchants at Mackinac held large claims against the Ottawa during the 1840s and 1850s and anxiously awaited the day their clients would become citizens, holding land in fee simple, which could be attached for debts. While some government officials and citizens strongly favored granting all Ottawa full citizenship, others sought to preserve a protected status for the uneducated Indians. The Ottawas, their defenders believed, could not defend themselves in an increasingly complex, Americanized society.

Hamlin's drive to win citizenship for the L'Arbre Croche Ottawa placed him at the forefront of this new political and economic debate. His goals were several. Obtaining Ottawa citizenship and full rights to participate in the American system was one. Ending the ever-present possibility of removal, and guaranteeing Indians the right to defend themselves in the courts were others. He criticized even the Catholic clergy, whom he believed hampered Ottawa chances to achieve this new status. So long as the citizenship and land tenure questions remained unresolved, Mackinac merchants placed a high priority on receiving payments from the "debt fund." Robert Stuart and his successor attempted to persuade the Indians to release this money throughout their tenure in office, but so long as merchants—and not Indians—would be the beneficiaries, Hamlin opposed distribution of the fund.

Hamlin became Indian interpreter at Mackinac, December 3, 1849, finally receiving a formal, government-sanctioned role in Ottawa affairs. Then, in 1850, the Michigan legislature added a clause to the new state constitution, which granted citizenship to any Indians renouncing their "tribal" affiliation. Hamlin had worked long years to preserve the Ottawa hold over their homeland and this constitutional opening, by itself, almost settled the matter.

In the eyes of Michigan's legislature, the provision was designed to provide for and to protect the enfranchisement of Mackinac County residents of mixed ancestry, especially those who had contributed greatly to the Democratic party. By the 1850s, however, many Americans failed to distinguish "half-breeds" from their Indian relatives, and classified the two as a single ethnic group. Because the legislation failed to distinguish between Métis and Ottawa residents of the region, its provisions applied to nearly all L'Arbre Croche residents. Neither did the legislature define explicit criteria for determining when an individual's tribal affiliation "ended." However, this ambiguity allowed any Ottawa desiring the right to purchase and hold land, to defend their claims in Michigan courts, and hence the right to remain in their homelands as citizens of the state.

Nonetheless, an uncertain relationship with the federal government still clouded citizenship and land tenure rights of the L'Arbre Croche Ottawa. Hamlin, meanwhile, in contrast to his conflicted relationships with earlier Indian agents, had gained high standing and a sterling reputation in the mind of the new agent, Henry Gilbert. This positive relationship influenced Gilbert's thinking about Ottawa citizenship, for he subsequently recommended to the Commissioner of Indian Affairs, George W. Manypenny, that these questions be settled. The commissioner, who was in process of ending the old removal policy, and who much favored Indian development in place, responded by dispatching a special commissioner to investigate relationships between Michigan's Indians and the Americans settled nearby. These investigators reported that the Ottawa had made great strides toward "civilization" as market farmers and commercial fishermen, and that the citizens who lived near them opposed their removal.

On receiving this report, Commissioner Manypenny authorized Henry Gilbert to make plans for new treaty negotiations, to be held during 1855. Hamlin interpreted for the L'Arbre Croche delegation at these meetings in Detroit. Although Hamlin did not speak in his own right for the official record, the delegates certainly knew his views. The old Ogema, Apakosigan, with whom Augustin worked for so many years, died shortly before this council. By this time, Hamlin had become a leader of some prominence, who made his opinion known in private Ottawa councils, as well as translating for the public record the words of the Ottawas' chosen speaker, Assagon. When completed, the 1855 Treaty of Detroit granted the Ottawa legal right to remain in their homelands, gave them firm titles to their reservations, and the right to seek resolution of unsettled claims in federal courts. Augustin Hamlin signed the document as interpreter and witness on March 28, 1855.

Once the treaty was ratified and proclaimed the following year, the Ottawa had at last won the secure right to remain in their home territory. This right did not, however, guarantee them open access to all opportunities available to other Michigan residents. They and their Métis relatives, for instance, were systematically excluded by American racial stereotypes from salaried public jobs. The Ogamuk addressed this issue in 1856, when an attempt was made to remove Augustin Hamlin from his position as interpreter. Michael Kewa, the first elected county clerk in the newly formed, Ottawa-administered Emmet County, wrote a petition in Hamlin's favor. Twenty-eight leading L'Arbre Croche Ogamuk, including Hamlin's uncles, J. Kiminchigan and Mackatabenese, joined in signing this document. The petitioners protested his dismissal, arguing he had done nothing wrong and should not be replaced. If he must lose his job, they requested that Hamlin be given a position as school teacher.[42]

While marking and defending Hamlin as one of their own, Ottawa leaders argued a broader case, for employment discrimination against him was only the tip of the racial iceberg. In their tightly reasoned petition, the Ogamuk demanded that Indians be employed in all jobs connected with their reservation. They protested that a non-Indian had already received the blacksmith's post when a qualified Ottawa man was available. Using phrasings we, today, would call a "self-fulfilling prophecy," they cogently argued that while Americans spent much money educating Indian children for participation in American life, they then blocked growth by asserting "an Indian will [always] be an Indian," meaning there was no hope for success in the American system.[43] In this manner, the Ogamuk pointed out, by denying access to entry-level, semiskilled and skilled occupations, Americans removed incentives and prevented an Indian from obtaining anything but the most menial employment. The Ottawa objected to being locked into the lower reaches of the increasingly rigid American class system. Once again, they used Augustin Hamlin, Jr., as their best example in seeking larger benefits.

Agent Henry Gilbert agreed with Kewa and the Ogamuk. Writing to Commissioner Manypenny about their petition, he emphasized, "there is certainly much good sense in it and it shows very clearly what is really the fact, that the Indians there are doing all they can towards becoming a civilized people." Gilbert went on to inform Manypenny of the Ottawas' "remarkable" advancement. Despite living almost entirely isolated from other citizens of Michigan, he stressed, they "have an organized county and with some help manage to get along with their business."[44]

Through his political ties with the Office of Indian Affairs, Hamlin helped direct Ottawa business. Recognizing this, his ally, Gilbert, refused to remove him from his post as interpreter. Indeed, Gilbert had plans for a promotion and a new role for his associate, reporting:

> I had the removal of Hamlin suggested before. He is a very excellent man and shall be continued in his place as long as I have anything to say about it. I have made arrangements with him to remove to Little Traverse in the spring and with his wife take charge of the school there.[45]

Hamlin's reputation held firm when Andrew M. Fitch replaced Gilbert as Indian Agent in 1857. That year, his old partner, William Johnston, made a fresh bid for Hamlin's job as interpreter, with the much exaggerated charge that the latter made $1,000 a month salary for interpreting at Mackinac and teaching at Little Traverse, even though he did not adequately serve the Democratic party, which had appointed him. Agent Fitch, however, would have none of this, responding with:

> Hamlin has acted as interpreter for many years, is an Indian, a member of the tribe and for which he acts. He was educated in Rome, Italy, speaks several languages, is a very good business man, is studious and industrious, I have every reason to believe [Hamlin] a man of strict integrity. He is a good Democrat, has acted with the party, and to my certain knowledge interested himself and labored in last canvass to secure success of Democratic cause.[46]

Such incidents mark further developments in Hamlin's career, identity, and roles. While accepted by the Ottawa as a valued member of their community, he had established himself across the cultural border as a trusted supporter of the American political process, at least as a good Democrat. In his middle years, Hamlin had become a leader respected for his knowledge and skills, and at the same time, had built a strong network of supporters in local and federal governments, through which he served the needs of the Indian community. With the support of the Ottawa leaders at L'Arbre Croche and the help of agents Fitch and Leach, Hamlin retained his employment.

In his forty-nine years, Hamlin played a large part in preserving Ottawa political autonomy and access to their essential natural resources, in locales of their choice. Well before he reached maturity, the L'Arbre Croche Ogamuk had set their sights on economic development in their old homeland. They fashioned their responses to policies formulated by the American regime, and Hamlin was selected as one of their chosen instruments. Once properly educated under the auspices of the Catholic church, he worked both at helping them understand American ways and wants, and at mediating the political-economic transition they faced.

The Ottawa had to move quickly. Only recently had they been politically autonomous, prosperous horticulturists and fishermen producing for a regional fur-trade economy. Suddenly they were faced with the threat of political submission and drowning in a market economy. They knew perfectly well, from the experiences of Indians from Ohio, Indiana, and Illinois who had been moved west, that their main option was resettlement in an unfamiliar and unsuitable habitat. The old Ogamuk used Hamlin's education and talents many times in negotiations crucial to the successful attainment of their goals. In the end, the Ottawa prevailed, and Augustin Hamlin, Jr., prospered. Living as a culturally distinctive people within the bounds of their old territory, the Ottawa avoided both removal and wholesale assimilation. Indeed, they not only survived, but it came to pass, as their neighbors recognized, that they excelled in the "arts of civilization."

None of these developments came easily. Nor was the education of Augustin Hamlin, Jr., complete for many years. He began his life as an atypical child, distinct from others in the L'Arbre Croche community. Advanced for special Catholic training, he returned from the ancient seat of Mediterranean civilization filled with high ambitions for himself and a proclivity for back-stage political maneuvers, which were not valued much by the Ottawa. They had no place for a stripling satrap, and he had much more to learn before he and the Ogamuk could strike a positive balance.

Moreover, his advanced education, his occupation as trader, and his residence at Mackinac clearly separated him from the ordinary run of Ottawa life and society. Still, he maintained kinship ties with his mother's people and, under proper supervision, exercised all his skills to promote the program chosen by Ottawa Ogamuk. Augustin Hamlin, Jr. was no lone hero, single-handedly winning the goals sought by Ottawa. Indeed, he functioned most effectively when he pursued the wishes of his Ottawa constituents. As his repeated efforts to obtain American recognition as a paramount chief show, he was capable of overstepping the bounds of Ottawa propriety. However, when corrected, he conformed to a culturally defined status more proper for his rank. The Ottawa fashioned him in styles appropriate to their ethos. He, in turn, contributed his share to the politics of Ottawa persistence.

Americans of the new community at Mackinac thought of Hamlin variously as an "Indian," a "Half-Breed," or a "White." The sequence and contexts of such ethnic categorizations suggest that, once the peak political tensions of the area ended, racial boundaries at the Straits again became permeable. In his later years, Hamlin lived modestly, on the social fringes of the largely immigrant population, supporting himself on his salary as a government interpreter. Like many other old-line Mackinac residents, his siblings who remained in the vicinity lived by typical Indian occupations—fishermen, servants, and day laborers. Thus, he achieved for himself a modest position in one—the American—community, and won for himself a position of some prominence in another, among the Ottawa. When Hamlin died "from a lingering illness" on July 12, 1862, he left few debts, an American wife named Catherine, and no children.[47] His legacy rests in his personal contributions to the political success of the Michigan Ottawa, who today persist as a people with a distinct identity in twentieth century Michigan.

NOTES

1. Augustin Hamlin, Jr., to Martin Van Buren, June 29, 1837, National Archives Microcopy M234, Correspondence of the Office of Indian Affairs (Central Office) and Related Records—Letters Received, Record Group 75 (Washington D.C.: National Archives Microfilms), reel 402, frame 338 (hereafter NAM M234).

   More complete documentation of topics discussed in this essay are provided in the author's previous texts on the Michigan Ottawa, see "Strangers in Their Own Land," *Grand River Valley Review* 6 (1985) pp. 2–25; "Ottawa Adaptive Strategies to Indian Removal," *Michigan Historical Review* 12 (1986) pp. 29–55; *We Wish to be Civilized: Ottawa-American Political Contests on the Michigan Frontier* (Ann Arbor, Mich.: University Microfilms, 1987).

   For additional background on Ottawa history and culture see W. Vernon Kinietz, *The Indians of the Western Great Lakes, 1615–1760* (Ann Arbor, Mich.: University of Michigan Press, 1965), pp. 226–307; Elizabeth A. Neumeyer, "Indian Removal in Michigan, 1833–1855" (M.A. thesis, Central Michigan University, 1967); Johanna E. Feest and Christian F. Feest, "Ottawa," in *Handbook of North American Indians—Northeast*, ed., Brice Trigger, vol. 15 (Washington, D.C.: Smithsonian, 1978), pp. 772–773.

2. Louis Hamlin and Others Claim 20 per Treaty of July 29, 1837, Box: Petitions, Indian Claims, Lucius Lyons Collection, 1822–1852, William L. Clement Library, University of Michigan, Ann Arbor, Michigan; National Archives Microcopy M234, Office of Indian Affairs—Letters Received, Record Group 75 (Washington, D.C.: National Archives Microfilms), reel 407, frame 155–159.

   The most important government document collection used for this essay was National Archives Microcopy M1, Records of the Michigan Superintendency, 1814–1851, Record Group 75 (Washington, D.C.: National Archives Microfilms) [hereafter NAM M1].

3. Jacqueline Peterson, "Many Roads to Red River: Métis Genesis in the Great Lakes Region, 1680–1815," in *The New Peoples: Being and Becoming Métis in North America* (Lincoln, Neb.: University of Nebraska Press, 1985); Lyle M. Stone, *Fort Michilimackinac, 1715–1781* (East Lansing, Mich.: The Museum, Michigan State University, 1974).

4. Odawa place names and translations were provided by Wesley Andrews, a Little Traverse Bay Bands Ottawa, in an interview conducted in March 1986.

5. The best information on the Ottawa-Catholic relationship at L'Arbre Croche is found in John G. Shea, *Catholic Missions among the Indian Tribes of the United States* (New York: Arno Press and the *New York Times*, 1969); *Annales De L'Association De La Propagation De La Foi Lyon* (Lyon: Chez M. P. Rusand), vols. 2–8.

6. Henry R. Schoolcraft, *Personal Memoirs of a Residence of Thirty Years with the Indian Tribes on the American Frontiers: With Brief Notices of Passing Events, Facts, and Opinions, A.D. 1812 to A.D. 1842* (Philadelphia: Lippincott, Grambo).

7. *Annales De L'Association*, 4, pp. 302–03; Andrew Blackbird, *History of the Ottawa and Chippewa Indians*, p. 35; H. Schoolcraft to T. Hartley Crawford, September 29, 1840, NAM M1 R.38, p. 360.

8. Blackbird, *History of the Ottawa and Chippewa Indians of Michigan*, pp. 35–37; *Annales De L'Association*, 6, pp.179–181; Richard Smith to Charles E. Mix, June 9, 1862, NAM M234 R.407, pp. 155–159.

9. James D. Horan, ed. *The McKenney-Hall Portrait Gallery of American Indians* (New York: Crown Publishers, 1972), p. 342.

10. The most detailed account of Hamlin's Italian education is found in Blackbird, *History of the Ottawa and Chippewa Indians of Michigan*, pp. 35–37.

11. Rev. J. Bruyn to H. Schoolcraft, October 30, 1835, NAM M1 R.72, p. 291.

12. Nisawakwat et al., to To Whom it May Concern, May 3, 1835, NAM M234 R.424, p. 88.

13. H. Schoolcraft to T. H. Crawford, September 29, 1840, NAM M1 R.38, p. 360.

14. H. Schoolcraft to Elbert Herring, October 30, 1835, NAM M1 R.69, p. 137; Bishop Frederic Rese to John Norvell, November 18, 1835, NAM M234 R.421, p. 768; John Clitz to H. Schoolcraft, November 26, 1835, NAM M1 R.69, p. 149; Augustin Hamlin, Jr., to Lewis Cass, December 5, 1835, NAM M234 R.421, p. 723.

15. T. H. Crawford to Joel Poinsett, August 18, 1840, NAM M1 R.49, p. 83.

16. H. Schoolcraft to E. Herring, October 30, 1835, NAM M1 R.69, p. 137; School-craft *Personal Memoirs*, pp. 532–36; Rix Robinson to Charles Trobridge, February 1, 1836, NAM M1 R.72, p. 410.

17. F. Rese to J. Norvell, November 18, 1835, NAM M234 R.421, p. 768; A. Hamlin, Jr., to L. Cass, December 5, 1835, NAM M234 R.421, p. 723; Journal of the Ot-tawa–Chippewa Treaty of Washington 1836, Henry R. Schoolcraft Papers, 1806–1875 (hereafter HRSP), (Washington, D.C.: Library of Congress Microfilms), R.25, p. 13,930.

18. A. Hamlin, Jr., to L. Cass, December 5, 1835, NAM M234 R.421, p. 723.

19. A. Hamlin, Jr., to L. Cass, July 21, 1836, NAM M1 R.41, p. 95; Ramsay Crooks to Gabriel Franchere, January 2,1836, American Fur Company Records, Aa-61, Box 1, folder 3, Baylis Public Library, Sault Ste. Marie, Michigan; Noah-qua-ge-shik et al., to Andrew Jackson, January 27, 1836, NAM M234 R.422, p. 146; R. Robinson to C. Trobridge, February 1, 1836, NAM M1 R.72, p. 410.

20. Charles J. Kappler, ed., *Indian Affairs: Laws and Treaties*, 2 (New York: Interland Publishing Company, 1972), pp. 454–55; Isaac McCoy, *History of Baptist Indian Missions*, (New York: Johnson Reprint Corporation, 1970), pp. 494–96; Mary Holiday to R. Crooks, March 5, 1836, American Fur Company Letters (New York: New York Historical Society Microfilms, 1952), reel 23, frame 1350.

21. Noah-qua-ge-shik et al., to A. Jackson, January 27, 1836, NAM M234 R.422, p. 146; R. Robinson to C. Trobridge, February 1, 1836, NAM M1 R.27, p. 410.

22. Journal of the Ottawa-Chippewa Treaty of Washington 1836, HRSP R.25, p. 13,930.

23. Kappler, *Indian Affairs: Laws and Treaties*, pp.453–454.

24. McCoy, *History of Baptist Indian Missions*, p. 497; Schoolcraft, *Personal Memoirs*, p. 538; Kappler, *Indian Affairs: Laws and Treaties*, p. 453.

25. H. Schoolcraft to L. Cass, July 18, 1836, NAM M1 R.37, p. 168; H. Schoolcraft to C. Harris, February 27, 1837, NAM M1 R.37, p. 168; Kappler, *Indian Affairs: Laws and Treaties*, p. 454.

26. H. Schoolcraft to Carey Harris, June 16, 1838, NAM M1 R.37, p. 507; H. Schoolcraft to Potts, February 24, 1840, NAM M1 R.38, p. 224.

27. A. Hamlin, Jr., to M. Van Buren, June 28, 1837, NAM M234 R.402, p. 335; A. Hamlin, Jr., to M. Van Buren, July 29, 1837, NAM M234 R.402, p. 338.

28. Commissioner of Indian Affairs to J. Norvell, May 29, 1837, National Archives Microcopy M21, Correspondence of the Office of Indian Affairs (Central Office) and Related Records—Letters Sent, Record Group 75 (Washington, D.C.: National Archives Microfilms), reel 25.

29. H. Schoolcraft to C. Harris, June 16, 1838, NAM M1 R.37, p. 507.
30. H. Schoolcraft to H. Crawford, September 24, 1840, *Annual Reports of the Commissioner of Indian Affairs* (New York: AMS Press), pp. 340–350.
31. Apakosigan, et al., to the President of the United States, May 23, 1840, NAM M234 R.424, p. 50.
32. Petition to His Excellency, Stephen T. Mason, July 2, 1839, Records of the Executive Office, RG 44, B 157, F 6, State Archives of Michigan, Lansing, Mich.
33. H. Schoolcraft to Potts, February 24, 1840, NAM M1 R.38, p. 224.
34. H. Schoolcraft to H. Crawford, February 24, 1840, NAM M1 R.38, p. 225; H. Crawford to H. Schoolcraft, September 2, 1840, NAM M1 R.49, p. 149; Ruben D. Turner to M. Van Buren, June 8, 1840, HRSP R.32, p. 17, 960.
35. H. Schoolcraft to T. H. Crawford, July 29, 1840, NAM M1 R.38, p. 312.
36. H. Schoolcraft to T. H. Crawford, September 28, 1840, NAM M1 R.38, p. 358.
37. H. Schoolcraft to T. H. Crawford, September 29, 1840, NAM M1 R.38, p. 360.
38. Ibid., p. 360.
39. William Johnston and A. Hamlin, Jr., to John Bell, April 30, 1841, NAM M234 R.424, p. 705.
40. Ottawa to Legislature of the State of Michigan, March 11, 1844, American Indian Correspondence: Collection of Missionaries' Letters, 1833–1893 (Washington, D.C.: Library of Congress Microfilms), Box 7, vol. 3, p. 103.
41. W. Norman Macleod to R. Stuart, September 16, 1844, NAM M1 R.57, p. 270.
42. Daniel Mokiwina et al., to George Manypenny, September 18, 1856, NAM M234 R.405, p. 341; Henry Gilbert to G. Manypenny, December 26, 1856, NAM M234 R.405, p. 226.
43. D. Mokiwina et al., to G. Manypenny, September 18, 1856, NAM M234 R.405, p. 341.
44. H. Gilbert to G. Manypenny, December 26, 1856, NAM M234 R.405, p. 226.
45. Ibid., p. 226.
46. Alpheus Fitch to James Denver, January 28, 1859, NAM M234 R.405, p. 309.
47. Richard Smith to C. Mix, June 9, 1862, NAM M234 R.407, pp. 155–59.

CHAPTER 5

Eleazer Williams: Elitism and Multiple Identity on Two Frontiers

Geoffrey E. Buerger

PRESENTING ELEAZER WILLIAMS (1788–1858)

A man who regularly carved and recarved his own epitaph, Eleazer Williams was a man of serial public identities, most of them carefully fashioned by himself. He spent his adult life in nearly constant motion—geographically, socially, and psychologically. Born of a composite Anglo-Mohawk ancestry to a family from the Quebec community of Caughnawaga, his mixed ancestry proved both an advantage and a handicap, a source of perennial ambivalence. Being a descendant of the famed "unredeemed captive," Eunice Williams, provided him an entrée to the northeastern American elite, an opportunity for formal education, and a dream of upward mobility in New England communities. But his status as a half-breed was a stigma that blocked his youthful ambition of acquiring a pulpit on his own merits. Pushed by his hosts toward the role of Protestant missionary to the Iroquois, he eventually found a larger place in a lesser arena among the Oneida of upstate New York, in whose language he had been fluent since childhood. Serving his Protestant sponsors as an agent of civilization, he also obliged the demanding leaders of the Oneida community, who manipulated him for their own ends. His were relationships of reciprocal exploitation with several interested parties, Indian and American, variously serving their ends and his own driving aspiration for fame and advancement. Not content with his successes as missionary, business manager, real estate agent, and negotiator for the Oneida, along the way he commissioned himself a colonel in the U.S. Army, also concocting a heroic role during the War of 1812 for this officer who never was. Not content with such invented prominence, in his last years, he went further and laid claim to the glory of being the long missing rightful heir to the French throne, for which he may be forgiven but never forgotten. His contemporaries, and unwary historians, prejudged him as a maniac, impostor, and con artist. Looking back at his life career of serial assumed identities from the perspective of our era, we can see in him a person who vaulted from one persona to another, sequentially affiliating himself first with one ancestral line then another as he sought advantage in the plural alternative lifestyles available to him during the first half of the nineteenth century. Was there, however, a stable, core identity behind the many masks he wore? This is a question difficult enough to answer for the numerous mutable personalities of our time. An incomplete historical record of Eleazer Williams' several lives—accounts often deliberately and selectively erased, skillfully edited to fit his most current public image, and retranscribed by himself—makes the query more difficult to settle satisfactorily for this illusive, self-proclaimed luminary. (J. A. Clifton)

Eleazer Williams first crossed my path while I was researching an undergraduate seminar paper on the Deerfield Massacre of 1704. One of my sources mentioned that the tradition of the St. Regis Bell, which offers a romantic but fabricated explanation of the motive for the attack, could be traced to Eleazer Williams, an "Indian" descendant of a Deerfield captive. Williams, according to this account, also claimed to have his great-great-grandfather's Bible and other relics of the Massacre. Because I needed to determine the veracity of the St. Regis Bell story (and since, like all novice historians, I was thrilled by the prospect of working with little-used documentary materials), I arranged to study microfilm copies of the Eleazer Williams Papers from the State Historical Society of Wisconsin.

At the same time, I began a search for biographical materials that might suggest how reliable the Williams Papers' testimony would be. The Memorial Libraries in Deerfield yielded William Ward Wight's sulphurous 1896 exposé, *Eleazer Williams—His Forerunners, Himself*, and from its pages emerged a fascinating portrait of a rogue and a con man.[1] Wight denounced Williams as *falsus in uno, falsus in omnibus*, and condemned as unreliable Williams' biography of his father, Thomas. Curiously, however, Wight used this book in fashioning his characterization of Eleazer Williams. Obviously, Wight was selective about the "evidence" he used, accepting what embellished the portrait and omitting what did not.

Wight used few documents in writing *His Forerunners, Himself*. Instead, the bulk of his text was drawn straight from popular magazine articles and from the recollections of men who knew Williams. This testimony had all been written years after Eleazer's disgrace (an important and revealing point needing special attention later). Moreover, in introducing these pieces, Wight stressed the admirable personal attributes of their authors, as though public reputation were the essential yardstick of reliable testimony. Wight's book was more likely caricature than biography. Yet, it showed that Eleazer Williams was strikingly controversial, even in death. What had he done in life to deserve such hostile attention? What were the other sides to Eleazer Williams' story?

When the microfilmed copies of the Williams Papers arrived, I soon discovered that these suggested an entirely different, and equally unlikely, interpretation. From the papers, Eleazer emerged as a long-suffering, misunderstood clergyman whose life-long labors on behalf of the New York

Eleazer Williams' Communities

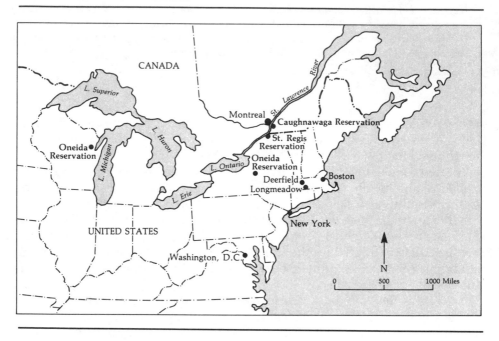

Indians had brought him only censure. Internal contradictions and evidence of multiple revisions, however, indicated that these documents could not be accepted uncritically. Moreover, from records of interviews he gave, it was evident that the public image he projected often sharply conflicted with his private accounts. Apparently, this was a man with a keen eye for the good opinion of posterity, someone interested in managing his own historical reputation. Aside from the controversies about his character and worth, Eleazer Williams was neither a simple personality nor an uncomplicated historical figure. Not only did Wight's questionable and selective evidence require careful scrutiny, therefore; so, too, did Eleazer's representations (or misrepresentations) of his life. Understanding him would be no easy task.

Nonetheless, behind the controversies lay a strong thematic core. Eleazer Williams gradually emerged from the documents as a man seen by others as an Indian—but as one with a different view of his identity, a man seeking to cross the social boundary separating his natal community from the main-stream of early nineteenth century Anglo-American society. In the process, he became caught in a vortex of change on two frontiers, changes in which he participated and to which he contributed, but which were not wholly of his own making. He was a man driven by unusually strong needs for recognition and power, but his status as a "half-breed" denied him the opportunity to achieve in any conventional way the success he desired. Thus, he was forced to adopt unconventional means, particularly the role of an intercultural broker. His performance in this role, coupled with his powerful drive for social rank and recognition, ultimately proved his undoing, and also set in motion the controversies that surrounded him in life and afterward.

Eleazer Williams' shifting accounts of his antecedents provide a revealing view into the core of the man. He several times pruned, grafted, and even replanted his family tree, demonstrating a profound need, bordering on a compulsion, to shake off his ascribed "Indian" identity and win acceptance as a "White Man." And, he was not content with being accepted as just any ordinary American. On the contrary, he yearned both for high position and for a suitably prestigious, even royal, pedigree. That he struggled so creatively to achieve these ends should have brought him more credit than it has; that he struggled in vain tells us far more about the social and historical contexts of his life than has been appreciated.

In the fuller records of Eleazer Williams' life are a compelling combination for closer study: a culturally marginal figure with a complicated personality and several ethnic identities, misrepresented alike by friend and foe, together with limited, sometimes contradictory, often unreliable evidence, all wedded to a morass of earlier portraits of the man. Together, these are too much to resist. Scholars are obligated to bring order out of chaos. How, then, to find valid insights amidst the apparent jumble of Eleazer Williams?

Only a biographer possessing either a sense of irony or extraordinary charity could introduce a life of Eleazer Williams by claiming he was *not* a charlatan of the first water. During his career, Williams embraced three religions and as many sets of ancestors, assumed several fictitious titles, authored a variety of historical fabrications, and left behind him both a trail of debts and an astonishing reputation for mendacity. Late in his life, Eleazer invented his most notable persona—the "Lost Dauphin" and rightful Louis XVII—which has dominated assessments of his career. Indeed, it is nearly impossible to find a standard reference account of his life that does not mention his fantastic claim to the throne of France. This has had a doubly damaging effect on his place in the historical record: on the one hand, his claim to Bourbon parentage has focused the attention of his few admirers on the least plausible aspect of his career, while on the other hand, it has given his critics a club to beat him with.

Eleazer comes off badly in the books and articles written by his detractors, who took advantage of his Dauphin pose to dismiss him altogether as a crackpot. Even descriptions of Williams by men who knew and worked with (or against) him were written almost exclusively after he had become the object of national notoriety—that is, after he had been "revealed" as the Dauphin. These are colored by the 20–20 hindsight of individuals who "knew all along that he was a fraud." Later assessments of his career were fundamentally skewed by the implicit position of these writers that, since he falsely claimed to be the King of France, Williams was probably guilty of all sorts of other intrigue and villainy.

The label beside the portrait of Eleazer Williams in the Neville Museum in Green Bay, Wisconsin, gives a standard summary of this famous missionary's modern reputation: "In the early 1800s, Eleazer Williams, an Episcopal lay minister and missionary in New York, dreamed of relocating the state's six Iroquois nations west of Lake Michigan. There he would create and lead an Indian empire."[2] The distinguished Wisconsin historian Reuben Gold Thwaites went further, claiming that Williams, "an erratic quarter-breed" and "a born intriguer," aimed to be "dictator" of an Indian government in the Green Bay area.[3] A later writer, in the context of his time, brought this line of thought to its logical conclusion by likening Eleazer to Adolf Hitler.[4]

Such characterizations are neither enlightening to those interested in Williams as a person nor useful to those delving into New York Indian history or the development of early nineteeth century America. Indeed, the standard dismissal of Williams as an ambitious "mixed blood" with delusions of grandeur obscures the true circumstances of his role in the migration of many New York Indians to Wisconsin. Moreover, when viewed dispassionately, Eleazer's career sheds light on many aspects of the Indian removal policy. To relegate him to the lunatic fringe is to squander an opportunity to view the dynamics of two frontiers from an intimate perspective.

To understand the development of Eleazer's character, we must begin long before his birth. In 1704, a force of French-Canadians and mission Indians raided Deerfield, Massachusetts, and destroyed about half the town. This Deerfield Massacre was part of a campaign to keep the English, who vastly outnumbered the combined populations of the French and their Indian allies, too busy protecting their own frontiers to launch a major attack on Quebec. One inhabitant of Deerfield taken prisoner by the raiders was Eunice Williams, the daughter of the town's minister. Eunice became famous as the "Unredeemed Captive" for her refusal to come back to New England when her father and neighbors were released. She eventually married an Indian and settled at Caughnawaga (today Kahnawake), on the St. Lawrence River opposite Montreal.[5] Throughout her life, the Williams family in New England sought to persuade Eunice to return home, but never succeeded. She was fond of her family, generally kept in touch with her brother, and visited Deerfield several times, but could never be brought to see The Light.[6] Perhaps because of her steadfast refusal to return to the fold, she became and remained a powerful symbol for the Williams clan. Eleazer, one of thirteen children of Thomas Williams (Eunice's only grandchild) and Mary Ann Rice, was Eunice's great-grandson.

Eleazer was probably born in May of 1788, at his family's seasonal camp in upstate New York, though his name does not appear in the baptismal records of the Catholic mission in his parent's community at Caughnawaga. There is no evidence to suggest his childhood was substantially different from that of any other Caughnawaga boy. Indeed, depositions collected from that community's elders in the 1850s to refute his claims to royal French ancestors affirm that Eleazer enjoyed an ordinary childhood in this Catholic Iroquois community.

One decisive event of his early life occurred on January 23, 1800, when Thomas Williams brought Eleazer and another son to Longmeadow, Massachusetts. There the boys were placed in the care of Deacon Nathaniel Ely, a Williams relative. We can only speculate on the precise nature of the arrangement, but it was surely not a spur-of-the-moment decision, for the boys' support was paid jointly by the American Board of Commissioners for Foreign Missions and the state of Massachusetts.

While in Deacon Ely's care, the boys became the objects of much attention. Their presence in New England, enjoying the advantages of a proper Protestant upbringing far from the savagery of Caughnawaga and the perfidious influence of the French papists, was in an important sense the fulfillment of a mission: having failed to reclaim Eunice, the righteous succeeded at least in redeeming her posterity.

The adolescent lad was much affected by this migration from French Canada to English Massachusetts—Eleazer apparently enjoyed the notoriety attached to his person as the grandson of Eunice Williams. Indeed, he took pains to identify himself with his romantic New England forebear, while doing all in his power to deny his former ethnic identity and to expunge his Mohawk heritage. He had a good reason to do so, since his great-grandmother's name appeared to be a veritable passport to success in the Anglo-American world of the early 1800s, while his Mohawk relations were a distinct liability to such advancement.

With his vicarious celebrity came an opportunity which, properly exploited, might help him escape the dismal lot usually reserved for missionized Indians in the eastern United States. Eleazer was not slow to take advantage of this change in his fortunes. In fact, the young man cannily capitalized on opportunities to remind his hosts of their implicit obligation to him. Thus, in his personal journal (a record regularly subject to the paternal scrutiny of Deacon Ely), he reported:

> January 23, 1805
>
> Toward night, I entered into the valley of Deerfield, with a heavy heart, endeavored to dissipate those melancholy scenes which the first settlers of the town experienced at various times especially, when its inhabitants were taken captives in 1704.[7]

In these few lines, Eleazer proclaimed his identification with the good people of Deerfield, displaying a youthful talent as master of the pregnant hint. Much later, this skill, sharpened by a lifetime of experience, was used to reap numerous if dubious rewards.

During his years in Longmeadow, Eleazer attended school, labored on the Ely farm, and received a strict grounding in the prayers, psalms, hymns, and sermons of his Congregational sponsors. By 1804, Ely could declare his charge an "apt scholar."[8] Perhaps this was merely a euphemism expressing the Deacon's low expectations for an Indian boy, but he allowed Eleazer an increasing amount of sophistication in his studies. From Eleazer's complaint to a contemporary about the necessity of studying Greek, it is clear that his curriculum included subjects appropriate to formal theological study.

During the latter part of his stay in the Ely household, Williams traveled among relatives and their Yale connections throughout southern New England. At least ten ministers took an interest in the youth, providing him a thorough exposure both to the business end of preaching and to the high social position of the Protestant elite. He became aware of both the great spiritual influence of his hosts and their temporal prominence in their communities. Although the days of Puritan dominance were past, clergy in the early nineteenth century remained the first citizens of their towns. Small wonder that Eleazer was dazzled, having made the leap from poverty at Caughnawaga to sitting at table or at prayer with the elite in New England. Seeking to identify himself with them, he declared his ambition to become a clergyman.

Eleazer may well have seen himself as an apprentice minister of the gospel, but his patrons saw him in a far different light. To win him from the errors of his Romish persuasion, to wean him from the ways of the Savage, to redeem the unredeemed captive through her posterity—such were the goals of the successors to the Puritans who sponsored his move to New England. Eleazer was the object of a mission that, once fulfilled, absolved his patrons of further obligation to him. At a time when access to the status of Congregational clergy was so restricted as to make this occupation caste-like, none of the incumbents would have seriously entertained the possibility of allowing an Indian to ascend to a New England pulpit as a colleague. Attitudes and opportunities for social mobility had not changed much, as far as Indians were concerned, since the days when the brilliant Samson Occum had been refused admission to colonial society a half century earlier. Eleazer, however, was refusing to identify himself as an Indian, and apparently did not recognize that others considered him as such. His letters from this period were as full of religious exhortation and scriptural quotations as those of any aspiring minister.[9]

The blow to Williams' designs came in 1807, when in obscure circumstances, he was dispatched to Moor's Charity School, then newly located in Hanover, New Hampshire. Arriving there in early November, he stayed only one week. Of his few days at this institution for Indian youth, we know only of his arrival, where he slept and took his meals, and of his departure.[10] Late in life, he made a game attempt to gloss over this episode by claiming he had made this northern sojourn voluntarily, "for his health," even gilding the lily by describing fanciful conversations with the president and members of the teaching staff at Dartmouth College. The fact was, however, that his Massachusetts patrons had sent him north to continue his education in an institution they considered suitable to his antecedents and social standing.

Brief though it was, this interlude at Moor's Charity School must be considered in any analysis of his career. It was, of course, a significant cut below what Eleazer had come to regard as his proper social station. His sudden departure is evidence of the mortification he must have felt at finding himself enrolled at an Indian school. More to the point, his relegation to such an institution must finally have shown him how he really stood with his patrons, that realization coming as a blow both to his pride and to his powerful, if naive, ambitions. Perhaps, it was intended to be so. Nonetheless, Eleazer did not passively accept this demotion and apparent repudiation. On the contrary, he drew money for a greatcoat to warm him on the road back to Springfield, where he declared as he left Moor's, he was going to fit himself for the ministry.[11]

Deacon Ely, probably less than pleased with Eleazer's precipitate return, died soon thereafter. From 1809 until August 1812, Williams was nominally the pupil of the Rev. Enoch Hale of Westhampton. Contemporary sources for this period in his life are sketchy at best, but in his journals Eleazer claimed to have spent much of 1810 and 1811 traveling. In April of 1810, he went "southward," presumably to New York City, where he met the future Bishop John Henry Hobart, and laid the cornerstone for his adult career. Then about twenty-two years old, Eleazer Williams was seeking his own patrons and opportunities.

Williams also claimed that in January of 1811 he was dispatched to the St. Regis reserve (another Catholic Iroquois community farther up the St. Lawrence, near the Thousand Islands), which had active ties to Caughnawaga, to "see about converting the Indians." If true, this latter journey suggests that Eleazer's sponsors among the clergy of New England had finally found some means of bringing his career among them to a close, the Moor's Charity School scheme having proven a bust.

Two possible explanations of this episode fit the few established facts. Eleazer may simply have been ordered to go home, for his father and siblings then lived at St. Regis. If so, then his later Journal entry was fabricated to make it appear that he had been dispatched on an important mission, and such self-serving falsifications of his personal record were common. On the other hand, his Congregational sponsors may have seized on such a role for him because of its double satisfactions: they could realize some return on their investment by producing a missionary, while gracefully ending their responsibility to him. If the latter were true, however, it is doubtful whether even these rigid theocrats of the Connecticut Valley anticipated that Eleazer might truly wean his Iroquois kith and kin away from Rome. Their principal goal was to terminate their relationship with Eleazer, and characterizing the journey as "a mission" would have been the sugarcoating that made his departure acceptable to him. Once again, however, Williams did not accept his exile passively. Shortly thereafter he converted to Episcopalianism, abandoning one set of patrons and adopting another.

Williams was not long in St. Regis before the War of 1812 erupted, putting the advancement of his spiritual career on hold. The St. Regis population divided over the war, and Eleazer followed his father's example in supporting the American side. What he really did during the hostilities remains something of a mystery, for there are few records to support his wildly embellished accounts of his military exploits. Among his papers, however, were a pair of probably genuine ledger entries. From these we can see that in January 1814, he was in the Albany, New York, area, where he took lodging with one Moss Philips on April 21 (without paying his rent). His diet at the time included bread, cheese, beef, and gin as staples, but beyond such documented crumbs, there is little direct evidence to support Eleazer's recollections of his adventures and contributions to the war effort.

These fill roughly one-fourth of the pages of what was billed as Eleazer's biography of his father, *Life of Te-ho-ra-gwa-ne-gen, alias Thomas Williams*.[12] According to his own testimony—wholly unsubstantiated by hard evidence—Eleazer began as a lieutenant colonel in General Dearborn's army, and was then rapidly promoted (within a few pages) to full colonel, negotiator with the British, secret intelligence agent, and superintendent general of Indian Affairs for the northern frontier. He also credited himself with commanding the artillery battery that proved so important in the Battle of Plattsburg, and with devising the cunning stratagem that ultimately won the crucial contest. However suspect this account of his wartime deeds, his portrayal of himself provides some insight into the personality that invented the later Lost Dauphin persona.

Particularly revealing is the account of his imagined meeting with Sir John Johnson to arrange the neutrality of the border Indian tribes, which includes a fanciful transcript of their negotiations:

> It was remarked by Sir John, that young Williams argued like a young lion upon the subject; that he not only pleaded upon principles of humanity and civilization, but of religion, which would not add savage barbarity to the other evils of war. "Your king," said he [Williams], "styles himself *Defender of the Christian Faith*, and will he league himself with the ruthless savages of the wilderness, whose tender mercies are to be manifested by the tomahawk and the scalping-knife—and that not only upon the wounded and captive of the American soldiery, but upon defenseless women and children? Sir, I have too exalted an opinion of British humanity . . . to admit this unholy alliance."[13]

This fabrication illustrates how much Eleazer wished to dissociate himself from the Indians. His language is as intemperate regarding his family and home community as that of the most racist of his Anglo-American contemporaries.

This preposterous account of a negotiation with Sir John Johnson is noteworthy for more than Eleazer's attempt to place himself on the side of Civilization and against Savagery. He also wrote himself onto center stage, there engaged in diplomatic transactions with powerful officials, sharing the limelight with no others. He does not present himself merely as General Henry Dearborn's interpreter nor even as his aide-de-camp, but as the sole,

American negotiator. The most telling feature of this scenario is that Eleazer imagined himself dealing with a British baronet on terms of easy equality. No tableau could have been more pleasing to a man such as Williams.

While it is tempting to dismiss these inventions as the work of an old man's lonely imagination, written as they were during his exile in upstate New York toward the end of his life, it would be inaccurate simply to regard them as products of mental deterioration. To the contrary: these passages are splendid examples of the distinctive style that characterized Eleazer's bids for fame throughout his career. In the fabrication of plausible scenarios, Williams had few peers; he always associated himself with events in which his role might be acknowledged as central, but for which documentary evidence was sufficiently scant to hamper disproof of such inventive fictions.

Eleazer also carefully explained away the absence of previous public acclaim for his contributions. Why, for instance, had he never received credit for the bold stroke that caused the British to retreat at Plattsburgh? Because, "it is stated," his true role in "this important affair had been *kept down* by generals Macomb and Mooers, lest their own fame in the victory of Plattsburgh should be lessened in the public view."[14] Moreover, in describing such incidents, he skillfully reinforced their rhetorical effects by wrapping himself in the third person, implying that his account carried the authority of a detached commentator, rather than openly claiming honors in the first person. If such accounts were truly delusional, Eleazer Williams was shrewd enough to know how they should be packaged for public consumption.

When the War of 1812 ended, Williams wasted little time reestablishing his connection with Bishop Hobart. The bishop, who had a special interest in resuming the missionary activities among the Indians that the Anglican church had carried on before the American Revolution, must have found Eleazer a godsend. In short order, Williams was dispatched to Oneida Castle to serve as lay reader, catechist, and religious instructor to the New York Iroquois, traveling there in March 1816.

On arriving among the Oneida, Williams found the population much divided. Since 1805, religious differences had separated the "Christian Party," dominated by adherents of their late missionary, Samuel Kirkland, from their "Pagan Party" rivals. Moreover, the tribe was split on other pressing issues of the day. Some elements among the Oneida were actively considering selling their remaining lands and emigrating to the West; others were adamantly opposed both to the move and to further alienation of tribal land; and yet others may have been selling off the right to occupy and use bits of their remaining territory to the land companies—particularly the Ogden firm—which owned the right to extinguish Indian title to that real estate.

There were several reasons, both external and internal, for this cultural and political divisiveness. The Oneida were under heavy and mounting pressure from their increasingly numerous American neighbors to cede their remaining lands. These pressures came not only from local settlers and large-scale speculators, but also from agents of the federal, state, and local governments. Even those who considered themselves friends of the Indian—including many of the churches—saw the sale of the Oneidas' estate and their resettlement beyond the New York frontier as a constructive step that would ultimately work to the benefit of the Indians. Assailed on all fronts, it is small wonder that the Oneida weighed the alternatives of moving or staying put, and that each perspective had its supporters.

Into this unsettled situation moved the ambitious, arresting Eleazer Williams, who quickly filled a void in the religious leadership among the divided Oneida. Williams was a complete contrast to Samuel Kirkland, the missionary who spent many years among these Indians in the waning years of the previous century. Where Kirkland was an unpleasant, dour, monolingual English-speaking Presbyterian, Williams was an outgoing, gregarious, bilingual English- and Oneida-Mohawk-speaking Episcopalian. Bishop Hobart described key features of Williams' success to the Episcopal Convention: " [our previous] exertions . . . for the conversion of the Indian tribes, have not been successful . . . principally because religious instruction was conveyed through interpreters, by those unacquainted with their dispositions and habits, and in whom they were not disposed to place the same confidence, as in those who are connected with them by the powerful ties of language, or manners, and of kindred. The religious instructor of the Oneidas [Williams] . . . enjoys all these advantages."[15]

Eleazer soon justified Hobart's confidence, and satisfied his own deep need for a leadership position, by converting several hundred of the Pagan Party to Episcopalianism. His forceful personality, together with his special linguistic skills and sensitivity to Iroquois ways, overcame the antipathy that many in this numerous, traditionalist faction probably felt toward Kirkland as an advocate of Christianity. Williams preached with vigor and prepared religious texts in their language. Perhaps most important, he showed by example that Christian and Indian were not mutually exclusive terms. Even his enemies conceded that "he had good qualities for evangelizing work among the aborigines."[16]

Williams was more than simply an Iroquois-speaking preacher: he was also the protege of the bishop of New York. Eleazer thus represented the power of an elite church establishment, and his prominence soon made his personal endorsement essential to any enterprise involving the Oneida. He quickly carved out for himself the role of broker between the Oneida and the outside world, a pivotal position he relished. In this capacity, he represented the Oneida in their dealings with local citizens, the Ogden Land Company, officials of the state of New York, and the United States government. No one could deal effectively with the Oneida except through Eleazer Williams.

From the time Eleazer Williams was sent to Longmeadow onward, he was a person seeking a place where he could play an important part in public affairs. A need for power and fame spurred him, and when denied full access to a New England congregation, he was forced to look elsewhere. Only after the War of 1812 did he find, in Bishop Hobart, a willing patron, and in the position of missionary to the Oneida, a place where he could realize his ambitions. At Oneida Castle, working on the border between an Indian community and American society, he suddenly became a great success, achieving the importance he desired. But there he was also tempted into the great blunder that eventually ruined him. He became embroiled in the major political and economic issues dividing the Oneida, adopted a partisan and often self-serving stance, and mixed his role as missionary with that of political and economic broker. In the end, he neutralized his many advantages as missionary to the whole Oneida people, forfeited his unusual position, and fell victim to the political turmoil within the tribe.

The most common historical criticism of Eleazer Williams' career concerns his supposedly single-handed role in causing the displacement of the Oneida and other New York Indians, and effecting their resettlement in Wisconsin. Broadly speaking, he has been painted as the principal—if not sole—actor responsible for contriving these events, as the prime mover who conceived the scheme and foisted it on the Oneida. Such simplistic blaming does grave disservice to the Oneida and other New York Indians actively involved in this development, to the various other private citizens and public officials involved, to Williams himself, and to the historical record. A central image in this interpretation, which made the Oneida naive and passive victims, was a common stereotype in the nineteenth century, when many believed Indians could be treated like helpless children. In such a context, Eleazer Williams was naturally painted as a grasping villain. However, well before he arrived at Oneida Castle, many Oneida and other New York Iroquois, together with allied Algonquians such as the Stockbridge and Brotherton, were already contemplating the advantages of such a migration. To condemn Williams as the scheme's inventor and prompter, we would have to assume that the Oneida were sufficiently childlike to be easily manipulated by a glib Episcopalian newcomer. To do so confuses Eleazer Williams' true role in the affair.

When Williams arrived on the upstate New York scene, the resident Iroquois were facing increasing pressure on their lands, experiencing increased competition for nearby resources, and steadily losing their power and autonomy. They were, consequently, exploring a variety of options. Among them was the possibility of emigration to new lands in the West. As early as 1817, Secretary of War John C. Calhoun had before him a proposal that would have transplanted these Indians to lands in the Arkansas Territory, a plan carrying the endorsement of Congressman David A. Ogden—who had personal vested interests in this scheme—and an anonymous Oneida Chief. For unknown reasons, this first removal plan came to nothing; but it is significant that Eleazer Williams was not involved with it. On the contrary, at the time, he was fully occupied with missionary tasks, such as revising Iroquois translations of the *Book of Prayers* and other religious texts, and working toward the completion of St. Peter's, the tribe's own Episcopal church. Moreover, Williams had established a good relationship with the Oneida, was well regarded by the clergy of upstate New York who periodically visited the Indians to distribute the sacraments, enjoyed the full confidence of his bishop, and had won admission to candidacy for Holy Orders.[17]

Yet in June 1821, Eleazer left Oneida Castle with a delegation of Oneidas, Onondagas, Tuscaroras, and Stockbridges, bound for "the country west of Lake Michigan, to treat with the Western tribes for a cessation of lands, [and] for a new home for themselves."[18] There are several possible explanations for his change of direction. The most favorable alternative is, Bishop Hobart having consecrated the completed St. Peter's in 1819, Eleazer was looking for new challenges. An equally benign possibility is that he became convinced that the Oneida no longer had a viable home in New York, and that he shopped around for the best alternative for his charges, settling on Wisconsin. On the other hand, Williams may have been looking for a way out of New York and for new opportunities for himself, in which case association with the delegation would have concealed his personal interests. Albert Ellis, his assistant for some years and later one of his chief detractors, reported that before this trip, settlers and businessmen near Oneida Castle "were coming to him almost daily with claims, large and small, for labor and for supplies, which claims he was always contesting," and that he was widely suspected of having skimmed off a substantial proportion of the mission funds raised to build St. Peter's.[19] In short, New York may have been getting just a little too hot for Eleazer.

Another suggested explanation for Williams' new enthusiasm for emigration to the West asserts that he was on the payroll of the Ogden Land Company, which owned preemption rights to much of the Iroquois' New York lands, including those of the Oneida. So long as the Oneida occupied and used their estate, the Ogden Company was blocked from putting the lands on the market and realizing large profits. While there is no evidence placing Williams directly in the employ of the company, it is difficult to avoid this interpretation since the firm paid part of the expenses of the delegation. As a congressman, David A. Ogden played a major role in promoting the Arkansas resettlement scheme, and he was later a central figure in obtaining new lands in the West for the use of Eastern tribes when and if they could be persuaded or forced to relocate. Congressman Ogden also championed Thomas Williams' claims for compensation for lands lost during the War of 1812, when he and his son had sided with the Americans.[20] If, in truth, Eleazer Williams entered into a *quid pro quo*, or even salaried, relationship with any party that had a vested interest in dislodging the New York Indians, it was undoubtedly Ogden with whom he did so.

It is unlikely, however, that the Oneida leaders in this delegation would have responded as they did had they seen Ogden's hand behind the Wisconsin proposal, unless they, too, were quietly involved in the transaction. The Oneida knew perfectly well why Ogden was promoting their move out of New York; and they probably would not have cooperated in this exploration of the Green Bay area without some understanding of the benefits that might flow to themselves.

It is more likely that Eleazer was enlisted in the cause of emigration by more prestigious and less personally interested parties. The famous churchman-geographer Jedidiah Morse explored the Green Bay area, and later visited the Oneida in October of 1820, as part of his tour "for the purpose of ascertaining, for the use of the government, the actual state of the Indian tribes in our country."[21] Part of Morse's commission was to locate a new homeland in the Lake Michigan area for Indians of the Northeast. Albert Ellis, himself much involved in arrangements for relocating the New York Indians, later reported how Morse had found Eleazer Williams "already ripe for the adventure."[22] Since Ellis joined Williams at Oneida Castle only a month after Morse's departure, and because Morse left no records substantiating this recollection, Ellis's testimony may be suspect. However, Eleazer must have found this renowned scholar an imposing figure, for he came with credentials from both the secretary of war and church mission groups, charged with the responsibility to locate suitable new lands for the New York and other Indians. An association with Secretary Calhoun's personal representative, a man whose work was also blessed by influential mission societies, would have brought him a fresh source of prestige and patronage—a nearly irresistible temptation for Eleazer. The prospect that he might have refused personal solicitations from Morse is unlikely.

In the background was Eleazer's growing reputation, for earlier Bishop Hobart had used Williams as an example when he wrote to Secretary Calhoun boasting about the Episcopal Church's success among the Indians. Eleazer Williams, therefore, was a name well-known to federal authorities even before Morse's trip. As an influential missionary and the ranking non-Oneida in the community, he was an obvious contact for Morse during his research and promotion tour. From the perspective of the federal government, Eleazer Williams represented a valuable source of influence in the tribe. Moreover, he also had the unqualified support of the Episcopal church. Since federal removal policy at the time stressed both the consent of the Indians before their resettlement and cooperation with church groups and other private interests, securing Eleazer Williams' services was imperative, because his influence rested on his position between these parties. His opposition could have impeded the planning; his support would ease any effort to persuade the New York Indians to move. The United States needed an already established broker, and Eleazer was the man on the spot.

This was, indeed, heady stuff for Eleazer, who saw himself solicited by Washington to play a leadership role in a great plan to improve the Indians. Just as he had been dazzled by the dream of standing above a New England congregation in his pulpit, and the later fantasy of rising above his Indian heritage and being a high army officer and statesman, now he saw himself as serving the higher interests of the United States, the church, and the Indian. More than simple missionary concern marked the great vigor Eleazer displayed as he undertook the task of moving his flock from the New York frontier to the wilds of Wisconsin. His were the movements of an ambitious

ELEAZER WILLIAMS AS EPISCOPAL MINISTER. George Catlin was determined to capture on canvas the Indians of what he and others at the time believed to be the "fast disappearing" North American frontier. His subjects included "other principal personages" as well as chiefs, and on several occasions he painted Indians who had become Christian missionaries. Eleazer Williams sat for Catlin in 1836 when the artist visited Green Bay, and the result is striking. There is no question that Catlin considered Williams an appropriate subject for his work. Possibly Williams was unaware that Catlin was painting only Indians, but it seems more likely that his desire to be immortalized overcame his reluctance to be considered an Indian. (Courtesy of the State Historical Society of Wisconsin. Eleazer Williams, painting by George Catlin.)

man seizing a promising new opportunity. He must have known that the move west with the Oneida would end his chances for the Episcopal priesthood and a prestigious pulpit in the settled East. Only some significant new opening could have led him to shrug off the significant personal cost of his jump onto the removal bandwagon. The chance to be agent plenipotentiary for both the secretary of war and the Episcopal church on the raw western frontier would undoubtedly have been such a consideration.

The appearance by Morse and the later support given Oneida removal by both the federal government and the Episcopal church certainly strengthened the position of the tribal factions favoring such a move. Since Eleazer Williams had been chosen by these two powerful institutions as their representative to the Oneida, the leading advocates of emigration among the tribe undoubtedly decided that their preacher should also be their spokesman to the Anglo-American world. It was a circular process that thus placed Eleazer at the heart of the Oneida move to Wisconsin. The external agencies promoting the move saw that he had the support of the tribe, and the removal-minded of the tribe saw that he had the support of those external agencies. In such a way, Williams came to be the broker between disparate groups with different motives and goals. So long as he retained the support of both, he was secure and rewarded. But his was a precarious position, for he could remain effective only so long as others found him useful. Once negotiations with Wisconsin Indians for lands were complete and had obtained informal approval in Washington, and once the Oneida migration was well underway, the goals of the key parties were realized. Then, Eleazer Williams found himself embroiled in intense competition with other contenders for the Oneidas' and federal favors, and his position became untenable. His success in facilitating the removal and resettlement of the Indians, ironically, proved his undoing.

To sustain his role as an intercultural broker, by 1821, Williams required the support of reliable leaders among the Oneida, and of government authorities and private interests with whom the Oneida were dealing. He was, therefore, under enormous pressure—implicitly or explicitly—from all sides interested in promoting the move west. If he did not himself create the wave of migration, he rode its crest. To have opposed it would have been professional suicide—the end of Eleazer's career with the government, among the Oneida, possibly even with his church. His activities, therefore, were determined by his sponsors, patrons, and clients both within and outside the tribe. He was a man caught in circumstances over which he could exert little control, where his prominent role promised as much risk as reward.

Unfortunately, Williams being Williams, he later claimed that the move to Wisconsin was all his idea, just as he claimed he had personally saved the day during the Battle of Plattsburgh. This self-serving confession has allowed some scholars to pass over both the complicated internal divisions within the Oneida community and the external conditions that strengthened the hand of the party favoring emigration. Such treatment is typical of how Eleazer has fared at the hands of writers for whom the Dauphin fantasy has been the central feature in his life, and who have gone to great lengths to show how unreliable Williams' testimony was, yet have quoted him as final authority when it suited their purpose. In short, Williams has been made into a historical scapegoat, while for a century and a half we have had to do without a useful history of the Oneida migration to Wisconsin.

Secretary Calhoun did all in his power to expedite the Williams mission, and the delegation that left New York for Green Bay in 1821 did so supported by the agents, policies, and resources of the Department of War.[23] The group reached their destination without mishap, and directly entered into negotiations there with the Menominee and Winnebago tribes. By August 11, they had obtained what they called a "treaty," an agreement supposedly selling a substantial tract of land intersecting the Fox River to them for $1,500. Thereafter, the negotiators returned to New York.

Their reception at Oneida Castle was not encouraging. Criticism and resistance came from many sides. The Oneida were then divided politically and religiously into the First Christian Party (Pagans recently converted by Williams), who remained politically estranged from their brethren, the Second Christian Party (who had been converted earlier), and the remaining Pagan (or Orchard) Party. Of them, only Eleazer's First Christian Party converts were strong supporters of emigration, so it is not surprising that the Second Christian and Orchard Parties sought repudiation of the Wisconsin "treaty." That the First Christian Party also raked their delegates over the coals, however, indicates the purchase was not seen as much of a deal for all Oneida. While no written record exists of actual tribal debate on the subject, the pro-emigration faction may have been ridiculed by their political opponents for advocating an abandonment of the tribe's remaining lands in New York for an unknown and less valuable tract far to the West. Embarrassed, the advocates of removal, perhaps, turned on the representatives who had produced what was proclaimed as a bad deal, and so Eleazer Williams and his supporters caught it from all sides.

The foes of emigration were not content with ridiculing the 1821 purchase of Wisconsin land. Viewing Williams as a threat to their intention to remain in New York, they set about securing his dismissal. Williams was a far greater threat personally than the pro-emigration faction he championed. He was dangerous to the traditional elements in the tribe for precisely the same reasons that he was useful to the First Christian Party: he enjoyed the support of the Episcopal church, and, through the church, of the U.S. government. His influence could not be eroded by merely humiliating him in council, as a tribal leader's influence might be, so it was essential to discredit him in the eyes of his patrons in the church.

Eleazer's political enemies began their campaign to get rid of him by addressing a request for his recall to the source of his authority, Bishop Hobart. Eleazer mobilized his supporters, however, and sent off a counterpetition assuring his Bishop that the letter of complaint was merely the work of a few malcontents.[24] For the better part of the next two decades, this same pattern continued. Accusations about Williams would be sent to his superiors, and Eleazer would respond by denouncing his critics as scoundrels who represented no one's opinion but their own.

The counterpetitions defending Williams are crucial documents in an attempt to identify which Oneida supported emigration. While Eleazer probably wrote or dictated the letters (who better, after all, to judge what words would have the best effect in New York or Washington?), the consistency of the signatures appended to them shows that there was a pro-Williams "party" among the Oneida. While he had the support of the principal figures from that faction, he could (and did) claim that the prominent men in the tribe as a whole upheld his ministry. Eleazer presumed that, since he was serving the interests of his close supporters, he could count on their fidelity in return. However, when even these men abandoned him (as they finally did in 1832), his position became untenable and he fell from grace.

Williams led a second delegation to Green Bay in 1822 to seek more lands, and met with far better success. The Winnebagos declined further participation in the negotiations, but some Menomini leaders eventually agreed to allow the New York tribes joint occupancy of part of their lands. Although the Menomini repudiated the agreement almost immediately, the government declined to acknowledge their change of heart. Any progress toward dislodging the New York Indians from their old homes the president and the secretary of war intended to preserve.

So, Eleazer's machinations received the approval of the executive branch of the U.S. government. That endorsement proved critical, for the War Department had two outraged parties on its hands. The Menomini complained that they had granted only temporary rights to use part of their lands for all New York Indians, both the Iroquois Six Nations and the composite, Christianized Algonquian communities associated with them; they had not approved an outright sale to the fragments that Williams and others led to Wisconsin. They further complained that the Menomini chiefs who signed these two "treaties" had no authority to do so. On the other hand, the majority of the Oneida and other Iroquois argued that they did not need to leave their New York lands to find suitable homes, and that the Wisconsin lands just acquired were a poor exchange for their ancestral territory.

In the end, only some Oneida, emigrating in small groups over the next several years, joined the emigrant Brotherton and Stockbridge Indians in Wisconsin. The territory assigned the New York Indians jointly was further defined and successively reduced in three full-scale treaties—at Prairie du Chien (1825), at Butte des Morts (1827), and in Washington (1831)—negotiated by the United States with the tribes native to Wisconsin, which held aboriginal rights to the lands claimed by the New York Indians. In the end, the emigrant Oneida wound up settled on a tract on Duck Creek, as a result of a final treaty of their own negotiated in Washington in February 1838. This tract, comprising one hundred acres for each Oneida actually residing in Wisconsin, totalled 65,540 acres. It was hardly an "Indian Empire."

Indeed, disillusionment with the reality of life and opportunity in Wisconsin almost certainly contributed to the sharp drop in Eleazer's stock among the Oneida. It was a decade before the bottom dropped out from underneath him altogether, but it is clear that his career among the Oneida had passed its zenith even before the first emigrants reached the Fox River valley.

This was not readily apparent during Eleazer's early years in Wisconsin, however. In addition to arranging and leading the actual relocation of parties of Oneida, he was busy establishing the spiritual community at Duck Creek, constructing a log church similar to St. Peter's, and preparing for the deaconate. He also sought to extend his ministry to the Menomini, Winnebago,

ELEAZER WILLIAMS AS LOST DAUPHIN. The most famous likeness of Eleazer Williams, this portrait was executed in 1853, at the height of his celebrity as The Lost Dauphin. The painting is attributed to the prominent artist, Guiseppe Fagnini, which is ample testimony to Williams' prestige during that period. Clearly accentuating facial features that the artist considered "Bourbon," since its first appearance, this image has been a mainstay of articles on the Lost Dauphin (and is frequently cited as evidence of Williams' royal blood). However, Fagnini saw a face that might have been Louis XVII, and drew a portrait that is nothing less than a triumph of art over reality. (Attributed to Guiseppe Fagnini. Courtesy of the National Portrait Gallery, Smithsonian Institution, Washington, D.C.)

bago, and Métis—with less than total success. Finally, he reached out to the tiny American community in nearby Green Bay, joining the Masonic Lodge and entering an arranged marriage with the daughter of a local French merchant, Joseph Jourdain. It is a measure of the Midaslike influence of Williams' later Dauphin pose that by the middle of the century Jourdain was popularly transmuted into a relative of one of Napoleon's marshals.[25]

In these years, Eleazer probably enjoyed his greatest success in crossing the social barriers separating Indian from White. The social flexibility of the frontier, coupled with the prestige guaranteed him by his position, enabled him to hobnob with the cream of Green Bay society, such as it was, and to establish himself as a prominent citizen in that community. Moreover, he traveled widely to New York and Washington D.C., representing the interests of the Oneida and other Indians. For a time, he maintained both the fiction of his leadership and his broker role, and while it lasted he made the most of it. Wisconsin may then have lacked some of the amenities of New York, but Williams surely had reason to be pleased with his gains.

Those gains were jeopardized on the arrival of other Episcopal clergy-men, who came to Green Bay to take up the burdens of schoolmaster and missionary. Eleazer's preparation for the deaconate consumed an unusually long time—he was finally ordained a deacon in 1826, eight years after his admission to candidacy. This, together with his frequent absences from Duck Creek, had obliged the church to appoint others to positions of spiritual authority among the Oneida. Eleazer, having lost two important elements of his complex role, was thereby placed in a difficult position. These newcom-ers, particularly the Rev. Richard Fish Cadle and the Rev. Solomon Davis, were unquestionably threats to Eleazer's position. Not only did they, as priests, displace him as the senior agents of the Episcopal church, and therefore as the brokers through whom outsiders would seek to influence the Oneida, but they defined Williams as a rival and supported efforts to have him removed. They complained of him, accusing him of neglecting his own ministry and of interfering with theirs. Indeed, during the period between 1824 and 1842, Eleazer was accused of everything that could be construed as a betrayal of his sacred trust short of rape and pillage.

Eleazer responded to the attacks on him in typical fashion, claiming that a small, unrepresentative clique was in conspiracy against him. Few were safe from his accusations of complicity: at one point he even denounced the local grocers as having an interest in his ruin. When Bishop Jackson Kemper admonished him in 1842 and forbade him to officiate at Episcopal meetings within Wisconsin, Williams replied with a torrent of abuse, attacking the bishop's information, informants, action, and place in the Apostolic Succession.[26] All this was to no effect; neither the Oneida nor the Episcopal church in Wisconsin wanted him any longer. His career in the West was over.

During his forced retirement, Eleazer found he was without much credit as a man. He had no official position; his personal behavior was increasingly erratic; his influence was negligible; and his resources were few. Aware that he was being stigmatized as "a fat, lazy, good-for-nothing Indian,"[27] Williams apparently concluded that his Caughnawaga heritage was to blame for his fallen state. He began—consciously or not—to prune the Native American branches of his family tree, grafting on more European stock. The first cut and implantation came when Stephen W. Williams approached him while com-piling his genealogy of the Williams family in America. Eleazer told him that an English physician, the son of the Bishop of Chester, had married Eunice Williams' daughter while he was in Canada as a captive during the last of the French and Indian wars.[28] This revision provided Williams with another illustrious ancestor, a prestigious forebear who was at once an Englishman, a doctor, and the son of a prominent cleric. This was not the only alteration Eleazer made in his ancestry. By the time he was "revealed" as Louis Charles, rightful King of France, his pedigree had undergone other advantageous refinements.

Precisely when Eleazer hit on the idea of proclaiming his Bourbon birthright is not clear; but his emergence as the Lost Dauphin is a fascinating study. Although he supposedly was claiming royal blood as early as 1838, no evidence remains that he did so until some time shortly before or early in 1849, when Williams was featured as the Dauphin by two national magazines. The appearance of these articles at that time is worth noting: Eleazer had tried to reestablish himself as a missionary on the St. Regis reservation after his expulsion from Wisconsin, but by 1848 even that venture had failed. Moreover, Thomas Williams died in 1848, eliminating the most serious obstacle to any effort by his son to obscure his origins. With his own career in tatters, Eleazer was pressed by desperation; with his father dead, he was free to concoct his hoax.

Like other aspects of his career, however, even the authorship of the Dauphin pose has been disputed. A Wisconsin lawyer, Colonel H. E. Eastman, claimed that he had written a romance about the Dauphin with "facts drawn entirely from imagination," and, on a whim, cast Williams as the hero of his tale. This account was supported by Colonel Eastman's former law partners. He lent Eleazer his manuscript, Eastman reported afterward, whereupon Williams had it copied during the summer and winter of 1847. As Eastman expressed it to the Wisconsin Historical Society, "you were none of you so much astonished as I was when I . . . bought a number of *Putnam's Magazine*, containing the startling discovery of the mislaid Dauphin, in my own language."[29]

The *Putnam's* article that caught Eastman's eye was John H. Hanson's February 1853 piece, "Have We A Bourbon Among Us?" Eleazer first met Hanson in 1851 in a chance meeting on a train, while Williams was beginning a trip back to New England to visit old friends and haunts. Hanson, who just had read a magazine article proclaiming Eleazer the Lost Dauphin, was enchanted by the story, and completely taken in. His *Putnam's* article, describing the interview and supporting Williams, was the first shot of what proved to be a prolonged, contentious, occasionally acrimonious debate between adherents of the Lost Dauphin theory and the debunkers who were outraged that such a transparent confidence man should be allowed to put one over on the public.

Williams could not have invented a better advocate for his Dauphin pose than Hanson. As a clergyman, he possessed public credibility, while as an individual he exhibited remarkable credulity. Hanson believed everything that Williams told him, drew all the proper inferences from Eleazer's coy hints, accepted all the documents put before him at face value, and generally leapt on the story of Louis XVII like an abbot on a newly discovered relic. He made Eleazer's cause his own, and set out to champion it with his book, *The Lost Prince*.[30]

The story Hanson told was simple enough: the Dauphin had not died in the Tower, but (as indeed many claimed) had escaped both his prison and the French Revolution. He had been whisked away to America by royalists, where he was brought to the least likely (and therefore safest) refuge imaginable—an Indian reservation near Montreal. Periodically, money was brought to support the boy, always by a man with a French accent, one of whom saw scars on Eleazer's legs and kept crying, "Pauvre garçon! Pauvre garçon!." The poor boy, Eleazer (or Louis Charles), remembered nothing of his early years because of the maltreatment suffered in prison, which reduced him to near idiocy. Diving into the waters of a lake, however, he struck his head sharply, and so recovered mental competence.

Supposed proof of Eleazer's royal birth came in 1841, when (as related by Hanson) the Prince de Joinville, son of Louis Phillipe, approached him while touring America and requested him to sign a paper abdicating his rights to the throne of France. De Joinville acknowledged the meeting, but denied that it occurred other than by chance, categorically rejecting the allegation that he had asked Williams to abdicate. But Eleazer, again capitalizing on an absence of contrary evidence, crafted a plausible account, and succeeded in leaving the impression that they had discussed dynastic matters and that the prince was only covering up in Louis Phillipe's interest.

Exactly how much of this Williams explicitly told Hanson will never be known, for Eleazer was a master of suggestion as well as a gifted dissembler. A contemporary captured the aura of unquestionable sincerity that this Pretender could project:

> However the story of his titled ancestry, suffering, and sequestration, may have originated, it is believed no person intimately acquainted with Mr. Williams will deny, that he possessed an ingenious faculty for collating the plausible coincidences which make up the warp and woof of the narrative, and that few who heard from his own lips the various incidents which tended to confirm the theory, could withstand the conviction that the whole chain of evidence *was extremely like truth.*[31]

While certainly gullible, Hanson did not fashion the substance of *The Lost Prince* out of mere stories, and he conscientiously sought to substantiate the details of Eleazer's fantasy. Williams became openly culpable in the fraud by soliciting signatures to affidavits and letters from others that he had drafted— he even deceived or intimidated his mother into saying he was not her child. Between them, Hanson and Williams assembled a tall stack of "evidence," which purportedly proved everything from Eleazer's resemblance to a young boy seen in Albany, to the common knowledge that Thomas Williams had accepted French money for the support and education of his son.

The Lost Prince, predictably, attracted heavy fire from skeptics, while its principals hurried to defend the account. Williams fanned the flames warming his newfound celebrity identity by writing letters to the editor under an assumed name, attesting to the veracity of his own story. Hanson, in contrast, dealt with contradictory opinions and conflicting testimony with a bludgeon, accusing Eleazer's detractors of being either liars or dupes. So vigorous were his assaults on Father Marcoux, the Roman Catholic priest at Caughnawaga at the time of the controversy, that one critic was moved to muse, "we are almost tempted to inquire where the Rev. Mr. Hanson studied theology to acquire such remarkable notions of moral accountability."[32]

This brief but intense burst of notoriety ultimately availed Eleazer little. He became enough of a celebrity to warrant portraits by such prominent artists as Guiseppe Fagnani and Matthew Brady, and the public's interest in him continued sporadically until his death. This was not enough, however, to rehabilitate his reputation or salvage his career. Eleazer spent his last years writing the biography of his father, preparing his papers, and declining into obscurity. The failed missionary and latter-day Dauphin died in poverty at the St. Regis reserve in Hogansburg, New York, on August 28, 1858.

After Eleazer's death the Dauphin debate revived, raging in the 1890s and on into this century. To this day, his claim to Bourbon blood has its adherents, and he has become something of a folk hero. He was lampooned by Mark Twain in *Huckleberry Finn* as "Looey the Seventeen . . . the wanderin', exiled, trampled-on, and sufferin' rightful King of France," and he was also featured, in later years, as the subject of a widely popular novel, a successful play, a short Metro-Goldwyn-Mayer film, and even an opera.[33] "Lost Dauphin" landmarks remain tourist attractions in both Wisconsin and New York, and both states have embraced him as a colorful part of their past—to such an extent that the possession of his remains was a heated issue as late as 1947.

In standard assessments of Eleazer Williams' career, far too much attention has been given to the Lost Dauphin fantasies of his retirement years. If in old age he became a fraud, as a young adult he was a brilliantly successful missionary and an architect of voluntary removal for many New York Indians—neither achievement easy or common in the United States of his lifetime. He was sufficiently important in his own day to have had an important hand in the development of the Old Northwest, and this aspect of his career has been unfairly neglected by biographers who have sought either to canonize or to crucify him.

Lost altogether has been the significance of his "half-breed" status, which shaped his career more profoundly than any other single influence. Eleazer was a youth on the fringe of American society early in the nineteenth century, and as an ambitious man with a socially imposed handicap, he seized at every available opportunity to vault the color line. Given a taste of the good life in New England by the Congregational establishment there, when rejected, Eleazer found opportunity among the Oneida on the upstate New York frontier. This eventually took him down the cul-de-sac of his role in moving the Oneida to Wisconsin. There, on another rapidly developing frontier, the emergent establishment—both Oneida and American—frustrated his desire to maintain the influential place he had achieved for himself. Small wonder that he ultimately took refuge in fantastic creations that purged his pedigree of his Indian handicap. Williams sought prestige and prominence; and when he failed to win these through conventional careers, he tried to achieve them through clever manipulation of public credulity—succeeding after a fashion. Eleazer Williams was no Indian dictator, merely a man caught between his own ambition and the social realities of his day. His sins brought their own reward in his lifetime; if he does not now merit kind remembrance, at the least he deserves empathetic understanding from the posterity that so long villified him.

NOTES

1. Milwaukee: Parkman Club Publications 7 (June 9, 1896).
2. Caption next to Charles V. Bond portrait (1844) of Eleazer Williams in the Neville Museum, Green Bay, Wisconsin.
3. Reuben Gold Thwaites, *Wisconsin: The Americanization of a French Settlement* (Boston: Houghton Mifflin, 1908), pp. 213–15.
4. Milo M. Quaife, *Lake Michigan* (Indianapolis, Ind.: Bobbs-Merrill, 1944), p. 324.
5. Representative of "Unredeemed Captive" literature is Clifton Johnson, *An Unredeemed Captive* (Holyoke, Mass.: Griffith, Axtell, & Cady, 1897).
6. See Alexander Medlicott, Jr., "Return of This Land of Light: A Plea to an Unredeemed Captive," *The New England Quarterly* 38, no. 2 (1965), pp. 202–16.
7. From a diary in the Eleazer Williams Papers collection of the State Historical Society of Wisconsin (herafter, SHSW).
8. "Deacon Ely's Journal," from the Eleazer Williams Paper collection of the Missouri State Historical Society.
9. See especially Eleazer's correspondence with Aaron Burt, in the Eleazer Williams Papers, SHSW.
10. See the Register of Moor's Charity School, unpublished manuscript in the Special Collections of Baker Library, Dartmouth College, Hanover, N.H.
11. Register of Moor's Charity School.
12. Eleazer Williams, *Life of Te-ho-ra-gwa-ne-gen, alias Thomas Williams, a Chief of the Caughnawaga Tribe of Indians in Canada* (Albany, N.Y.: J. Munsell, 1859).
13. *Williams, Life of Te-ho-ra-gwa-ne-gen*, pp. 67–68.
14. Williams, *Life of Te-ho-ra-gwa-ne-gen*, p. 87.
15. *Journal of the Convention of the Diocese of New-York*, 1818, pp. 18-19.
16. Wight, *Eleazer Williams*, p. 160.
17. *Journal of the Convention*, 1818, p. 20.
18. A. G. Ellis, "Fifty-Four Years' Recollections of Men and Events in Wisconsin," *Report and Collections of the State Historical Society of Wisconsin*, 7 (1876), p. 210.
19. A. G. Ellis, "Recollections of Eleazer Williams," *Report and Collection of the State Historical Society of Wisconsin*, 8 (1879), pp. 325–26.
20. David Odgen to Secretary Calhoun, in W. Edwin Hemphill, ed., *The Papers of John C. Calhoun*, 11 (1817-1818) (Charleston, S.C.: University of South Carolina Press, 1963), pp. 183, 185, and 190.
21. Jedidiah Morse, *A Report to the Secretary of War of the United States on Indian Affairs, Comprising a Narrative of a Tour Performed in the Summer of 1820, Under a Commission from the President of the United States, for the Purpose of Ascertaining, for the Use of the Government, the Actual State of the Indian Tribes in Our Country* (New Haven, Conn.: S. Converse, 1822).
22. Ellis, "Recollections of Eleazer Williams," p. 327.
23. *Papers of John C. Calhoun* 4 (1969), pp. 656–58.
24. See, for example, the letter to the Secretary of the Domestic and Foreign Missionary Society of the Protestant Episcopal Church in the United States dated April 5, 1824, in the Archives of the Protestant Episcopal Church.

25. T. Wood Clarke, *Emigres in the Wilderness* (New York: Macmillan, 1941), p. 191.
26. Both Kemper's letter and Williams' reply are in the Eleazer Williams collection, SHSW.
27. John Y. Smith, "Eleazer Williams and the Lost Prince," *Report and Collections of the State Historical Society of Wisconsin*, 6 (1872), p. 330.
28. Stephan W. Williams, *The Genealogy and History of the Family of Williams in America, More Particularly the Descendants of Robert Williams of Roxbury* (Greenfield, Mass.: Merriam & Mirick, 1847).
29. Smith, *Eleazer Williams*, pp. 337–41.
30. John H. Hanson, *The Lost Prince: Facts Tending to Prove the Identity of Louis XVII, of France, and the Rev. Eleazer Williams, Missionary Among the Indians of North America* (New York: G. P. Putnam, 1854).
31. Franklin B. Hough, "Introduction," in Eleazer Williams, *Life of Te-ho-ra-gwa-ne-gen*, p. 11.
32. Smith, *Eleazer Williams*, p. 11.
33. The novel is Mary Hartwell Catherwood's *Lazarre* (Indianapolis, Ind.: Bowen-Merrill, 1901), adapted for the stage by Otis Skinner. The film is a historical short by M-G-M entitled *King Without A Crown* (1937). Two operas have been written about Williams as the Dauphin, but neither has been published.

CHAPTER 6

Susette and Susan La Flesche: Reformer and Missionary

Jerry E. Clark and Martha Ellen Webb

PRESENTING SUSETTE (1854–1903) AND SUSAN (1865–1915) LA FLESCHE

The identities of Susette and Susan La Flesche, like their siblings and half siblings, were ordained by a decision made by their father. Like other Métis merchants of the middle nineteenth century, Joseph La Flesche perceptively examined his future and that of his posterity in the new continental United States, where Indians would be restricted to reservations and subject to programs of directed change aimed at incorporating them individually as American citizens. Of Franco-Ponca ancestry, with no legitimate claim to the status of Omaha, he elected to build his future and that of his children among this strongly patrilineal people. Arranging to be appointed the principal chief of the Omaha reservation community, he fashioned for himself an influential political-economic role, for he was also one of two merchants monopolizing their trade. Thus, Susette and Susan, with Joseph's other children, were born into an emerging reservation elite, of questionable ethnic antecedents. Joseph carefully managed their early education, seeing to it that they were sufficiently exposed to Omaha ways to claim an Indian identity, without becoming so traditionally Omaha that they would be stigmatized, their futures as Indians on a larger American stage curtailed. Both girls experienced some aspects of Omaha life, and the best formal education locally available. Prepared in this way, both became proteges of eastern liberal Americans, the crusading Christian advocates of an Indian reform movement directed at detribalization and Americanization. Educated in eastern schools at the expense and under the benevolent supervision of these inflexible, upper-class proselytizers, both prepared for professional careers suitable to the ideals and goals of their sponsors. Susette became a campaigning journalist, regularly exploiting her identity as the Omaha woman Bright Eyes to advocate such causes as Free Silver and the plight of the Sioux at Wounded Knee; Susan became a medical missionary to the Omaha and the larger community in which this reservation existed. Interestingly, living in this late nineteenth century American rustic hinterland, both modeled social roles and cultural styles absorbed from their eastern mentors, whether as highly educated, vociferous professional women, or as champions of eastern hair and dress styles, indoor plumbing, public health measures, or Indian causes. Coming from—but not fully involved in—the lives of ordinary Omaha, the targets of reform for Susan and Susette included both Indians and neighboring Americans. Many Omaha, in particular, remained ambivalent about their ministrations and the legitimacy of the La Flesche family's status as tribal members. Although in 1986 a new wing of the Omaha clinic was named in honor of Susan, for instance, twenty-four years earlier a faction in the tribe had sought to have the names of Joseph La Flesche's descendants expunged from the roll, on the grounds that they had never rightfully been Omaha according to traditional principles. (J. A. Clifton)

The lives of Susette La Flesche Tibbles (1854–1903) and Susan La Flesche Picotte (1865–1915) span the most dynamic and devastating sixty years of Omaha tribal history. Susette was born in 1854, the same year the Omaha ceded nearly 5 million acres of land in eastern Nebraska, retaining only 330,000 acres in what is today Thurston County for a reservation.[1] Within twenty years, half their lands had been sold for a Winnebago reservation and to make way for railroad construction. The last annual buffalo hunt took place in 1876, ending a way of life that had supported the Omaha for centuries. In 1882, the tribal status of the Omaha was terminated and land was allotted to individuals. Omaha judged competent were awarded title to their land in 1910. By the time Susan died in 1915, nine out of ten Omaha holding individual titles to their land had disposed of it.

U.S. government Indian policy leading to these events was designed, in part, to "civilize" the Omaha and make them productive citizens. After the Civil War, liberal reformers took up the cause of the American Indian with considerable fervor. Just as the reformers had seen slavery as a violation of the natural rights of man, they also viewed Indian segregation onto reservations and their restricted status as wards of the United States as alien to the philosophy they perceived to be the guiding morality of the United States. These reformers, primarily Eastern philanthropists and members of missionary societies, strove to put the Indian on an equal footing with other Americans. They advocated educating Indians and eliminating their dependency on the government by terminating the protection of the tribal reservation and granting full citizenship. Susette and Susan were exceptional products of this move to alter the status of Indians. In fact, they became active reformers themselves, and worked to acculturate the Omaha to what they saw as the advantages and superiority of the dominant American culture.

Susette and Susan were born to Joseph La Flesche and Mary Gale. Joseph (Iron Eye) was one of the last recognized chiefs of the Omaha, even though his father was French and his mother was a Ponca. Joseph had lived with both his uncle, a captive adopted by the Sioux, and his father, who traded out of St. Louis with the tribes of the upper Missouri River. But he chose to make his permanent home with his Ponca mother, who had been taken in by and lived with the Omaha. Joseph had been adopted by Big Elk, the principal Omaha chief, and on Big Elk's death in 1853, Joseph succeeded him as chief.[2]

Omaha Reservation Setting

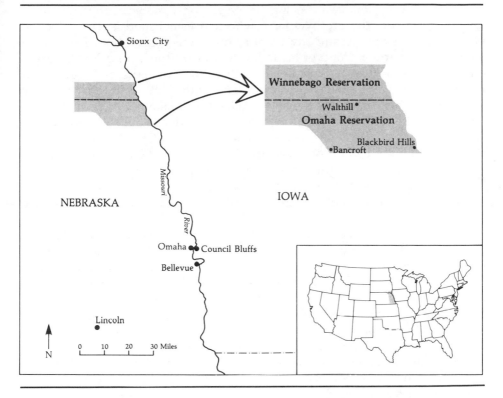

Mary Gale, Joseph's first wife, was the daughter of a U.S. Army physician. However, she was primarily raised by her Omaha mother after her father abandoned them when Mary was an infant. Her mother, Nacomi, then married an American trader, Peter Sarpy. It was probably at Sarpy's trading post in Bellevue, Nebraska, where Joseph met Mary Gale. Mary joined Joseph among the Omaha and bore him a son, Louis, and four daughters. Susette was the oldest daughter and Susan was the youngest, with Rosalie and Marguerite between them. Joseph also took a second, additional wife, Ta-in-ne, by whom he had three children: Francis, called Frank, Lucy, and Carey. Although Joseph quietly separated from his second wife—to conform to the teachings of the Presbyterian missionaries—he supported her and saw to the care of all his children. Joseph was aware that his children were going to live in a more complex, changing world, and so he insisted they acquire needed experience and skills, especially formal education. All the La Flesche children went to the local Presbyterian Mission School or the Agency School, and all but Rosalie went beyond local schooling to schools in the East. The encouragement of their father set the La Flesche children apart.

In 1854, Joseph was a party to the treaty where the Omaha ceded their lands in eastern Nebraska. Seeing the need for a modernizing influence, Joseph asked that the Presbyterians, who had established a school for the Omaha in Bellevue, accompany them to their new reservation. Even more significant, he and a group of his followers called "the Young Men's Party" chose to build a village of frame houses rather than live in the traditional earth lodges. They even divided up their land into plots and farmed it as individuals. This village was derisively called the "Make Believe White Man's Village" by the more traditional members of the tribe. Thus, all his children were raised in a frame house, went to school, adopted Christianity, and were taught to read, write, and speak English. But, as a chief of the Omaha, Joseph was also committed to preserving the Omaha's identity. The traditional customs and values that Joseph believed important were passed on to his children. It was this blend of cultures in which the La Flesche children were raised.

When Susette was able to walk, she went through the traditional Turning of the Child Ceremony, which symbolized her formal admission into the tribe. It was at this ceremony that she received her new name, Inshtatheamba (Bright Eyes). Bright Eyes was five years old when she accompanied her family on her first buffalo hunt. While yet a small girl, she observed a variety of traditional Omaha activities such as hunting, building an earth lodge, the sacred pole ceremony, traditional medical practices, and even a mixture of Christian and traditional funeral practices when her brother Louis died at the age of twelve. At age six, Susette was enrolled in the Mission School. There, while excelling in her studies, she also adopted many of the values of the crusading missionary teachers. This greatly influenced the direction her life would eventually take. She also developed an interest in drawing, which she continued to adulthood. Unfortunately, her only surviving art works are the illustrations for Fannie Reed Griffen's book on Omaha, Nebraska, published for the Trans-Mississippi Exposition in 1898.

After the government cut off funds for the Presbyterian Mission School in 1869, education was offered at a daytime Agency School. But Susette was too old for this school. After three years, a former teacher, Nettie C. Read, then the headmistress of the Elizabeth Institute for Young Ladies in Elizabeth, New Jersey, arranged for the young woman's education at the Institute. Susette left the reservation in 1872 to enroll there.

When Susan was born, June 17, 1865, the traditional Omaha way of life was quickly "disappearing," and the Omaha were uncertain what their future would hold. Just before her birth, they had signed the treaty selling part of their land to the government for a Winnebago reservation, and just after she was born, the Nebraska Territorial legislature voted to ask the federal government to expel all Indians from the state. Life for the La Flesche family became even more uncertain when the agent removed Iron Eye from his position as chief of the Omaha in the Spring of 1866. He and his family left the reservation for about a year. Susan received her earliest education at the

Agency School. During the last year she attended the Agency School, her sister Susette was among its teachers. Until September of 1879, when Susan left for the Elizabeth Institute, both La Flesche daughters were little known outside the Omaha reservation.

Susette graduated with honors from Elizabeth Institute in 1875. On returning home, however, in spite of petitions to the Commissioner of Indian Affairs, she could not secure a teaching position on the reservation. Nearly two years later, she discovered a rule governing reservations giving any qualified Indian employment preference for any position in the Indian Service. Taking advantage of her Indian ancestry and quoting this provision, of which the commissioner should have been aware, she wrote again to the commissioner, adding:

> It is all a farce when you say you are trying to civilize us, then, after we educate ourselves, refuse us positions of responsibility and leave us utterly powerless to help ourselves. Perhaps the only way to make ourselves heard is to appeal to the American public through the press. They might listen.[3]

Her threat apparently worked, for she was appointed teacher at $20 per month and taught in the Agency School from 1877 through 1879.

The trial of the Ponca chief, Standing Bear, in late April 1879, proved to be a turning point in Susette's life. The Ponca, who were closely related to the Omaha and spoke the same language, were moved against their will to Indian Territory in 1877. Several Ponca died en route and epidemic disease caused many more deaths in the first year there. After the death of his son, Standing Bear and thirty others left Indian Territory and returned to northeastern Nebraska, where they were given land by the Omaha. Interior Secretary Carl Schurz ordered their return and dispatched General George Crook to escort them back. The Ponca group was arrested and taken to Fort Omaha, where they were jailed until arrangements could be made to return them to Indian Territory. That is as far as they got. Thomas H. Tibbles, a sometimes preacher, newspaper editor, storyteller, and professional reformer, became interested in their plight. In his role as assistant editor for the *Omaha Herald*, Tibbles publicized the Ponca cause and convinced two lawyers from Omaha to obtain a writ of *habeas corpus* to prevent their removal to Indian Territory. Susette was asked to contribute her knowledge of the case and thus became involved in this famous trial. Federal Judge Elmer S. Dundy handed down a landmark decision declaring Indians to be *persons* under the law and thus protected by a writ of *habeas corpus* against incarceration without just cause.

After the trial, a committee of preachers and laymen from Omaha asked Susette and her father to make a fact-finding visit to the Ponca reservation. On their return, the young woman presented her findings to the committee and a congregation in that city. Thus was born her career as a crusading reformer.

In late October of 1879, Susette began a lecture tour of eastern cities aimed at bringing the plight of the Ponca to the attention of philanthropists who might finance a court case against the government. With Tibbles and Standing Bear, the Elizabeth Institute graduate spent six months speaking to audiences in Chicago, Pittsburgh, Boston, New York, and Washington, D.C.

On July 23, 1881, she married "T. H.," as Tibbles was known by the La Flesche family. By then, Tibbles had become a professional crusader involved in several causes. Besides the Ponca case, he became involved in efforts to increase money and credit to midwestern farmers, most notably bimetallism and populism. He and Susette lived on the reservation between lecture tours and jobs writing for or editing newspapers championing the cause of the Indians, the Bimetallic League, and finally the Populist Party. One tour in late 1887 and early 1888 took them to England and Scotland. Susette assisted T. H. in his work by lecturing, writing, and editing. Both were correspondents of the *Omaha World Herald* in 1890, and they were on the scene of the Wounded Knee Massacre as reporters. From 1894 to 1900, they lived a sedentary life in Lincoln, Nebraska, where T. H. edited *The Independent*, a Populist newspaper. Ill health drove Susette back to the reservation to be with her family, and she died there on May 26, 1903.

Although the efforts of Joseph La Flesche and his family to find a place in the larger society often placed them at odds with more traditional Omaha Indians, Susette had no desire to deny her origins. Susette's Omaha Indian identity was an active part of who she was. Even as she fought to have the Indians granted American citizenship, she identified strongly as an Indian. In the introduction to T. H. Tibbles' *The Ponca Chiefs*, Susette wrote of "my people" and "my race." She also signed the introduction with her Indian name, *Inshtatheamba*.

As an adult, Susette looked back with resentment on some things done by missionaries in the name of "civilization." For those who ran the Mission School on the Omaha reservation, formal education meant replacement of anything Indian. So they gave European names to the pupils, arguing that they were easier to pronounce. The missionaries selected for the children biblical names such as Gideon, Abraham, Job, and Isaac; political names like Edwin Stanton and Ulysses S. Grant; or names of military heroes such as Philip Sheridan and William T. Sherman. She also felt that the practice of cutting Omaha boys' hair was degrading. When her older brother, Louis, was chastised by the missionaries as being a savage for embarking on a vision quest, the young girl was perplexed. The vision quest was an essential part of an Omaha boy's transition to manhood. While Susette saw the need to acquire a formal education, she resented the notion that to do so required abandoning all Omaha culture. Her approach to acculturation was essentially pluralistic. She accepted the new culture and expected others to accept and tolerate her Omaha Indian culture as well.

While Susette identified with the Omaha and worked for what she believed to be the good of all Indians, in many ways she did not fit in with the Omaha or even her own family. Joseph wanted his children to participate in the larger society. Thus, the La Flesche girls did not receive the traditional symbolic marks the Omaha tattooed on a girl's forehead and neck as symbols of honor. As a chief who could "count" many honors, Joseph and his family were entitled to these traditional badges of rank. But, convinced that his daughters would have to function in the larger society, Joseph refused these honors and the permanent markings that would forever identify them as members of an Indian culture.

In 1872, Susette became the first of her tribe to go away to finish her education. This came at a time when the more traditional Omaha were even opposed to sending their children to school on the reservation. Indeed, the education she received at the Elizabeth Institute set her apart from most girls in Nebraska, not only the Omaha Indians.

Furthermore, the three years of almost complete resocialization made her reentry into Omaha society as an Omaha difficult. The niche she eventually filled on the reservation was one that was previously occupied by missionaries. She became a teacher dedicated to preparing other Omaha youth for involvement in the larger society. The new role she assumed, therefore, had roots outside Omaha culture.

Nonetheless, more than anything else, it was Susette's ties with Tibbles that estranged her from the Omaha and her own family. The problem was not that he was non-Indian. Other Omaha had married non-Indians and continued to function within Omaha society, including Susette's sister Rosalie. But like many who had taken up the Indian crusade, T. H.'s dogmatic style and his condescending, paternalistic attitude toward Indians annoyed them greatly.

More than interpersonal style was involved in this conflict. The positions Susette and Tibbles advocated on various Indian issues alienated many Omaha generally and the La Flesche family in particular. For example, they crusaded for the immediate implementation of full citizenship for the Omaha, with all accompanying rights and responsibilities, a change numerous Omaha opposed. Similarly, T. H. attacked the voluntary self-government plan supported by Joseph and Rosalie. His activities generated a legal investigation into the pasture program, which used unallotted lands as a communal pasture and was operated by Rosalie's husband Ed Farley. After Tibbles tricked Joseph and other Omaha into supporting a scheme that would destroy the pasture program, Joseph commented that Tibbles "doesn't care how his gun is loaded; usually it has nothing but powder in it and when it goes off there is a great deal of noise and that is all."[4]

Frank, Susette's half brother, probably despised Tibbles more than any other family member. T. H.'s amorous overtures toward Susette—even before Tibbles' first wife's death—irritated him, so he disliked Tibbles from the beginning and he conveniently managed to be away when the two were married. Frank later worked with Alice Fletcher, an anthropologist studying the Omaha Indians. Their relationship became close—Fletcher often referred to Frank as her son. However, insidious rumors regarding their relationship existed. Frank was convinced the rumors were started "by that nasty, dirty

SUSETTE LA FLESCHE—INDIAN ADVOCATE, REFORMER, SYMBOL. Susette La Flesche Tibbles was the eldest daughter of Joseph La Flesche or Iron Eye, the Franco-Ponca man who became the last recognized chief of the Omaha tribe. A forward-looking man, La Flesche sought the best advantages for his children, so Susette was educated in mission schools and the Elizabeth Institute for Young Ladies in New Jersey. After teaching in the Omaha agency's school, she married a newspaper editor and Populist reformer, Henry Tibbles, and soon became a major advocate for Indian rights, a journalist, a popular public speaker, and a symbol of Indian success for the philanthropic eastern reformers who had aided her career. (Courtesy of the Nebraska State Historical Society. From the Thomas Henry Tibbles Picture Collection.)

man that Susette has given us for a brotherinlaw [sic]."[5] Nevertheless, in spite of T. H.'s activities and Frank's dislike of him, most of the family tried to maintain close ties with Susette.

Tibbles' style, his exaggerations, as well as his inflated sense of importance and place in history, alienated him, and thus Susette, from more than her family. His autobiography, *Buckskin and Blanket Days*, is almost comic melodrama. In it, he placed himself, often in heroic proportions, at the center of virtually every major historic event on the American frontier during his lifetime, which moved Francis Paul Prucha to call Tibbles "one of the strangest characters in the history of Indian reform."[6] When Susette married Tibbles, Assistant Secretary of the Interior Alonzo Bell commented,

> I was greatly rejoiced on my return from the sea-trip to find that the Ponca case was at last ended, that Bright Eyes had capitulated to Tibbles, and that Tibbles

had surrendered to Bright Eyes. I very much fear, however, that this last act of the pale-face is in the line of other wrongs perpetrated upon this most unfortunate band of Indians, and that the confiding Indian maiden will some day feel that the fate of Big Snake [the Ponca chief who had been murdered] was preferable to the unhappy one which she has chosen. . . . I fear poor Bright Eyes has made a mistake, but I am willing to forgive her if the act has effectively disposed of Tibbles. Even so great a sacrifice may be rare economy if it gives the Nation a rest from the vexatious borings of the Tibbles school of philanthropy.[7]

Local officials, too, were disturbed by Tibbles. G. W. Wilkinson, the treasurer of Dakota County, was upset about Tibbles' crusade and implied that Tibbles had to go east to Boston to gain a hearing because he could not command a following locally.

The Ponca case provided a role for Susette, bringing her into contact with liberal Christian reformers fighting for their vision of Indian rights. The missionaries and teachers at Indian schools came out of the same milieu as temperance crusaders and former abolitionists, and Susette was likely influenced by their rhetoric and style as well as Tibbles'. Her report to the Omaha Committee on Ponca conditions certainly reflects this. The truth was horrible enough, but newspaper accounts of her reports about the Ponca reflect embellishments and exaggerations in the true spirit of a crusader, less concerned with truth than with what made good press.

As "Bright Eyes," Susette became a national celebrity. She was accepted by the eastern reformers as representing "her people." As such, many doors were open to her among the well-to-do and famous in eastern society. Liberal politicians, judges, literati, and philanthropists shared the stage with Susette and became her acquaintances in the reform movement.

On her tours, Susette shared the platform with and met such distinguished people in Boston as author Henry W. Longfellow, publisher H. O. Houghton, Justice Oliver Wendell Holmes, abolitionist Wendell Phillips, Mayor Fredrick G. Prince, and Helen Hunt Jackson. In fact, Bright Eyes was a major influence in Jackson's involvement in the Indian cause. Jackson became a regular at public lectures and was motivated in 1891 to write the most important book of reform literature, A Century of Dishonor.

Additionally, the lectures of Bright Eyes and Tibbles in Boston inspired Amelia Quinton and Mary Bonney to establish the Women's National Indian Association (WNIA). The Boston Indian Citizenship Committee, another major Indian reform group, also grew out of the furor of the Ponca affair.

As a lecturer, Susette sought to reform existing laws and policies to get equal rights and protection for American Indians. She had adopted the liberal reformer's belief in the importance of American law and that to be equal under the law was essential if Indians were to be successful. In the introduction to Tibbles' book, The Ponca Chiefs, she stated that the Indians were asking for "their liberty, and law is liberty."[8] Most of the crusaders' attacks were aimed at government policy and officials, a group Tibbles called the "Indian Ring," and naturally many of them fought back. Carl Schurz, the Secretary of the Interior, was the focus of much of the reformer's criticism, particularly in the Ponca case. Helen Hunt Jackson kept up a running diatribe against Schurz in the press, which was designed to embarrass the secretary into supporting the Ponca cause. Schurz, a master at dealing with the public himself, backed up his position with a good command of the facts of the case. At one point, he took Bright Eyes to task on the Ponca case and called her a "phenomenal liar." In fact, Schurz's ability to refute the exaggerated tales of the reformers often decreased their credibility to the public.

Susette and the Ponca lecture party spent most of their time in Boston, though stops were made in Chicago, Pittsburgh, New York, and Washington, D.C., because the Boston elite had money and political clout in these places. The young crusader's lectures helped set in motion a chain of events that led to the passage of the Dawes Bill in 1887. Senator Henry Dawes, representing the Boston philanthropists in Washington, proposed the bill, which broke up the reservations and allotted the land to individual Indians.[9] This was seen by the reformers as a large step toward "civilizing" the Indians and protecting their individual rights under the law.

After the flurry of activity surrounding the Ponca case subsided, Susette continued to be involved with political causes and journalistic writing, primarily as an aide to her husband. Her involvement was not as an Indian *per se*. She was with Tibbles at Wounded Knee in 1890, where he covered the massacre as a correspondent for the *Omaha World Herald* and other papers. She was a reporter for *The Nonconformist*, a newspaper of the Bimetallic League. During the 1890s, when Tibbles served as editor of *The Lincoln Independent*, Susette regularly wrote for the paper. Her articles were often placed on the front page as if they were news items. But, in reality, they were editorials praising Populist and pro-silver senators and congressmen, attacking universities as being run to suit the views of millionaires and corporations, describing how the gold standard had wrecked the economy of England, and so forth. Although these were not Indian issues, she wrote under the byline of Bright Eyes.

In spite of throwing herself into transforming Indians into acceptable citizens of the United States, Susette felt some bitterness toward her mentors. She was bothered by the missionaries' attempts to obliterate traditional Omaha culture. As she grew up, Susette saw and heard of many depredations perpetrated against Indians. For example, in 1863, a party of fifteen Poncas on their way home from a visit to the Omaha were attacked by soldiers from the Seventh Iowa Cavalry. Three women and a girl were killed, and the rest were wounded. The soldiers, however, were never punished. In another case, the Omaha Agent, in 1865, ordered that military passes were necessary for all Omaha wishing to leave the reservation, which made them virtual prisoners. The young girl was also undoubtedly aware of the petition passed by the Nebraska Territorial legislature in 1866, requesting the federal government to remove all Indians from the territory. Her bitterness and sarcasm are obvious in a letter published in 1880 in *St. Nicholas* magazine. In it she inquired, "DEAR ST. NICHOLAS: I do not know whether you allow 'Savages' in your 'Letter Box'. . . ." Later in the letter she commented, "I never knew him [her six-year-old brother] to be afraid of anything except white men, when he saw a good many of them together."[10] Undoubtedly, lessons she learned in the Ponca case also contributed to her ambivalent anger and made her aware that as an Indian she, too, was a victim of prejudices and government policies. The lecture tour gave her numerous occasions to tell of mistreatment of the Indians. But her full anger was focused on the governmental "Indian Ring" and was not aimed at the general population.

Obviously, Susette felt considerable ambivalence over her role as a reformer and her continuing identification as an Indian. There was also the conflict between her loyalty to a strong and opinionated husband and her sense of disloyalty to family and community. This can be seen in the undisguised hostility in her letter to *St. Nicholas* magazine. It was also expressed in the overly romanticized and nostalgic article she wrote in 1883 and published in another children's magazine, *Wide Awake*. While she may have accompanied her family on a tribal buffalo hunt, it certainly was not as idyllic as she remembered:

> When thinking of those old days—so happy and free, when we slept night after night in a tent on the wide trackless prairie, with nothing but the skies above us and the earth beneath; with nothing to make us afraid, not even knowing we were not civilized, or were ordered to be by the government; not even knowing there were such beings as white men; happy in our freedom and our love for each other—I often wonder if there is anything in your civilization which will make good to us what we have lost. I sometimes think not, unless it be the wider, fuller knowledge of God and his word.[11]

In her later years, Susette questioned the fruits of her labor. In spite of allotment and citizenship, the Omaha had not successfully assimilated and had, indeed, lost most of their land. The traditional Omaha were far worse off than before citizenship.

Susette's sister Susan's experiences in the Omaha and larger social worlds were somewhat different, yet similar. In September 1879, the young girl followed Susette's lead and attended the Elizabeth Institute. After three years of studying arithmetic, reading, writing, philosophy, physiology, and literature, she returned home in the summer of 1882; the following year, she worked and taught small children at the Mission School.

In 1884, Susan entered Hampton Normal and Agricultural Institute, an Eastern school admitting Indians. General Samuel C. Armstrong had established Hampton in 1868 for Blacks, but Indians were first admitted in 1879. Although Hampton was a teachers' college, various industrial arts, military drills, and physical work were required of students to build spiritual, moral, and intellectual strength. The bright young Omaha woman graduated with honors on May 20, 1886. As salutatorian, she spoke to her fellow Hampton students on the topic of "My Childhood and Womanhood." In addition to being salutatorian, she received the Demorest Prize, a gold medal, for earning the highest examination scores in her junior year.

Early in 1886, Susan determined to continue her schooling after graduation from Hampton, but she chose an unusual career to pursue—that of a physician formally trained in western "scientific" medicine. Young Indian women did not practice medicine in traditional Omaha society, and even Indian men did not attend formal medical schools. Moreover, it was only in 1848 that American medical schools begrudgingly admitted their first female student. In the 1880s, women were still frequently denied admission on grounds of their sex alone.[12] In addition, there was a problem of money for the recent Hampton graduate to reckon with. Fortunately, in May 1886, the Connecticut branch of the WNIA, known as the Connecticut Indian Association, awarded her educational funds. They enrolled her in The Woman's Medical College in Philadelphia and, assisted by the U.S. Bureau of Indian Affairs, provided financial support for her professional training.

On October 7, 1886, Susan arrived in Philadelphia to begin medical school. At The Woman's Medical College, she pursued the "Three Years' Course," much of which she described in her letters home. In the summer of 1887, the young medical student taught briefly at Hampton, visited the Connecticut Indian Association in Hartford, and resumed her medical studies. After almost two years' absence, she returned home to Bancroft, Nebraska, in 1888. She spent the summer there and then resumed her studies in Philadelphia the following fall. On March 14, 1889, Susan graduated from medical school at the top of her class. Shortly thereafter, she served a four-month internship at the Philadelphia Woman's Hospital.

Late that summer, the first formally trained female Indian physician returned to the reservation. On August 5, she became physician at the Omaha Agency School. That winter, however, she was appointed one of two Agency doctors, a post she held for some four years. When the other physician left, she became sole physician to over 1,200 tribal members. Around 1891, she was also appointed Medical Missionary of the WNIA among the Omaha. As her responsibilities to the tribe increased, Susan's health grew increasingly poor. Then, in 1891 and 1892, she began missing entire days of medical practice.

In spring 1892, the young doctor traveled to Hampton to present its twenty-fourth commencement address, where she spoke on the topic foremost in her mind, "My Work as Physician Among My People." She also addressed the Washington branch of the WNIA about alcoholism among the Omaha before returning to the reservation.

Despite her own illness, this determined young woman continued her medical practice until the autumn of 1893. She then chose to temporarily abandon her profession to devote full-time care to her aging mother. Susan's frailty and their fear she might abandon medicine altogether caused her family and friends alarm when she suddenly announced she would marry Henry Picotte, a French-Sioux, on the 30th of June 1894. Despite all objections, they were married as planned. Sometime later, the couple moved to Bancroft and became the parents of two sons, Caryl (b. 1895) and Pierre (b. 1898). Mean-

SUSAN LA FLESCHE—PHYSICIAN, MISSIONARY, TRIBAL LEADER. Susan La Flesche, M.D., was Susette's younger sister. Her future was also promoted by her father, Iron Eye, and, like Susette, after her elementary education in reservation schools, she attended the Elizabeth Institute. But she continued her education, first at the Hampton Normal and Agricultural School in Virginia before going to the Women's Medical College in Philadelphia, where she graduated first in her class. Unlike Susan, who lived away from the reservation and made her career on a larger, national scene, Susette spent her life in the reservation and neighboring communities. There—as the first American Indian woman to practice scientific medicine and as a Presbyterian missionary and tribal leader—her services to the ill and efforts to upgrade health conditions in the region won her high respect from all involved. (Courtesy of the Nebraska State Historical Society. From the La Flesche Family Picture Collection.)

while, Susan resumed her medical practice, but Henry became an alcoholic. In late August 1905, he died of complications from this disease.

The recently widowed physician was appointed missionary to the Omaha by the Presbyterian Board of Home Missions shortly after Henry's death—the first Indian ever appointed to such a post. Although her health worsened in the years following 1905, she ministered to the Omaha at the

Blackbird Hills church. In November 1906, the Omaha woman doctor and missionary purchased a lot in the new town of Walthill, on which to build herself a home. At the same time, she worked toward constructing a hospital in Walthill. In 1908, her house was completed, and Susan, her sons, and her aged mother moved in. Some two years later, in spite of illness, Susan traveled to Washington, D.C., as part of a tribal delegation protesting recent government policies. Around the same time, she became Chairman of the State Health Committee of the Nebraska Federation of Women's Clubs, a position she held for three years.

In January of 1913, Walthill's new, modern medical facility opened, with Dr. Susan La Flesche Picotte as its director. Sadly, she did not enjoy her new responsibilities long, for in 1914, she was diagnosed as suffering from "decay of the bones"—cancer in today's terminology. Following two unsuccessful operations in early 1915, the first female Indian physician died at Walthill on September 18, 1915.

Throughout her life, Susan, like Susette, thought of herself as an Omaha Indian. Even after years of eastern education and medical training, she continued to refer to herself as an Indian. Numerous early letters and her 1910–1911 diary show that she called the Omaha "my people," and she distinguished "white people" from "the Indians." While in the East, this observant young student compared things she saw and people she met with what was most familiar to her—the Omaha. She once described a woman from India as having a "complexion . . . just like an Indian's."[13] In a letter from medical school she joked, "I am going to wield the knife tonight—not the scalping knife though."[14] Her identification with the Omaha was not weakened by her eastern schooling. Indeed, two years after her return to Nebraska, the young doctor declared she felt closer to the Omaha than ever. The man she married, Henry Picotte, was three-quarter Sioux and one-quarter French, and they lived on the Omaha reservation. When Susan began practicing medicine, her fluency in the Omaha language quickly drew patients away from the other Agency physician. Final proof that successful physician and respected tribal leader Susan never abandoned her identification with the Indians is that she left a "farewell message to the Omahas," delivered at her funeral in 1915, and that an Omaha Indian gave the closing prayer in the native language.

While living in the East, the young Omaha student remained close to her family and Indian friends. On arriving in Philadelphia, she was dreadfully homesick. Numerous letters prove Susan intended to return to her family, the reservation, and Omaha society during any break from school, if possible. While she was at Hampton, securing Indian company was not difficult. But when the young Hampton graduate was separated from family members and Indian friends in Philadelphia, she sought the company of Indians. Many of her family and friends were living in the East or attending schools there, and either they visited her or she went to them. There is no question that Susan planned to return to the Omaha reservation after finishing her training.

Even while she was at school in the East, Susan helped her family and other Omahas in any way she could, even if it meant self-sacrifice. This young woman's concern for her family's well-being in her absence prompted her to provide them food, clothing, and other goods. Once, when given a dollar to purchase a pair of evening gloves, she sent it home instead to "get meat or something to eat perhaps chicken" for her ailing mother.[15] She purchased cloth and clothing for her nieces and nephews and sent presents home for Christmas. Moreover, because her goal was to become a "medical missionary" to her people, that is, to provide the Omaha improved health care, she set aside all considerations of romance.

Even before graduating from the Woman's Medical College, Susan doctored her family and other Omaha. Her letters from medical school contain pleas urging her family and tribal members to go to professionally trained physicians when ill. In 1886, Susan asked Rosalie to describe their illnesses to her, so she could prescribe treatment by mail. Sometimes the young medical student even sent medications. When she returned home briefly in 1888, Susan found her parents ill and the Omaha suffering a measles epidemic. As a result, she spent her visit caring for her parents and assisting the local medical doctor.

Throughout her life, Susan's primary concern was helping the Omaha, and she did so in a multitude of ways. One way she sought to help was by improving living conditions on the reservation. Cleanliness and neatness were qualities she especially worked to teach the Omaha, and she commended them when she found them in an Omaha home. She sought to abolish traditional Omaha customs she saw as hazardous to her peoples' health and welfare. A year after her return to the reservation, for example, the young physician stopped the spread of a contagious eye disease by instructing the Omaha in personal hygiene. Around 1910 and 1911, she participated in a campaign that resulted in state legislation abolishing community drinking cups. Unfortunately, many Walthill townspeople believed her advocacy of this sanitary measure was needless; thus, the following article appeared in 1911 in *The Walthill Times*: "Now that Dr. Picotte is away on vacation, some public spirited citizen has provided the town pump with a new cup securely attached by a chain."[16] About the same time, this successful woman doctor and town leader launched another, less controversial campaign to eradicate household flies.

Another way Susan served her people was by providing routine, individual medical care. She dealt with several epidemics on the reservation as well. Recurrent influenza, diphtheria, small pox, and typhoid hit with varying severity. She also raised money to build a hospital to improve the quality of treatment. Along with local Walthill leaders Dr. William Ream, attorney Harry L. Keefe, and her brother-in-law Walter T. Diddock, Susan worked on the project. Funds were secured from sources including a benefit concert held at Carnegie Hall, New York City, in 1910,[17] and from the Society of Friends, the Presbyterian Board of Home Missions, and Diddock. Ground was broken for the hospital in January 1912, and it opened on schedule twelve months later.

This highly educated woman also assisted the Omaha by interpreting and writing letters for persons who could not speak or write English. She often helped tribal members with their business and legal problems in her physician's office at the Agency School. In later years, following her move to Walthill, Susan rendered financial and legal help to her people virtually every day.[18]

Susan also acted as a liaison between the Omaha and various Indian associations and missionary groups. She distributed articles sent to the Omaha reservation by the "King's Daughters," part of the Young Peoples' Department of the WNIA. Reading materials sent by branches of the WNIA were made available to the Omaha in her office at the Agency School. In her position as WNIA and Presbyterian missionary, she functioned as a link between the Omaha and charitable easterners.

In addition, this unusual woman became a role model for Omahas her age or younger. Her letters show that she and her sisters were idolized by younger Omaha Indians at school in the East and that they sought to imitate and please young Susan. Later in life, she became a leader in tribal government and affairs because the Omaha knew she could present their views to non-Indians, negotiate with them, and therefore protect the Omaha. By 1909, Susan had assumed a leadership role in the tribe. During the controversy over consolidating the Omaha and Winnebago Agencies, for instance, she called at least one tribal meeting and published an announcement of the meeting in the local paper. She was also appointed by the tribe to a seven-man, one-woman committee, "a sort of a protective body for the tribe," early in 1910.[19]

Susan participated in the local Omaha economy as well. As a tribal member, she had an allotment of 160 acres near Bancroft and received government annuity payments, even while in school in the East.[20] After returning to Nebraska, the young doctor's land remained a source of income. Additional sources of income—atypical for an Omaha Indian, were the salaries and stipends she received as School and Agency Physician and as WNIA and Presbyterian Board of Home Missions missionary. Around 1894, about the time of her marriage, Susan also received a loan from the Connecticut Indian Association. But, like other Indians the Association assisted, she was slow to pay it back.

Early in her life, Susan endeared herself to the Omaha and her work won their respect. But it is more significant to recognize that this successful woman has held their affection and respect even until the present day. One need only read her obituary and the accompanying memorial articles published in *The Walthill Times* to glimpse the depth of Omaha feeling for her. Moreover, as a living testament, the Omaha tribe dedicated the new wing of their tribal health care facility at Macy, Nebraska, to her in August 1986.

While Susan defined herself as an Omaha and participated in the social and economic life of her people, her education and training, like that of Susette's, made her atypical. Her excellent command of the English language and her education were uncommon among the Omaha. The aspiring young girl followed middle-class eastern, not Indian, female role models, and these models motivated her to seek advanced education. While attending the Agency School, Susan saw educated missionary women teaching and ministering to the Omaha. Alice Fletcher also was a professional female role model for her, and Fletcher continued to be a strong influence in her life even after Susan left the reservation. Fletcher largely engineered the Hampton graduate's admission into medical school, first by advocating the training of Indians to practice medicine and then by suggesting that the Connecticut Indian Association and the Bureau of Indian Affairs cooperatively finance the venture.[21]

Many middle-class women Susan met at Hampton and in Philadelphia had received education beyond the teachers' college level, and she followed their lead. For example, her teacher at Hampton, Miss Patterson, left the Institute to attend nursing school. Of greater importance, perhaps, Hampton's school physician was a woman, Dr. Martha M. Waldron. Thus, Fletcher, Patterson, or Waldron, singly or together, may have implanted in Susan the idea that women could become formally-trained medical professionals, a novel career goal for an Omaha.

Susan accepted Christianity well before she left the reservation. Little is known of her religious activities at Elizabeth; however, she was a member of the church at Hampton and Philadelphia. In Philadelphia, she attended church regularly and participated in many church activities, including Christian Endeavor and YWCA meetings, eventually becoming corresponding secretary of the local YWCA branch. She also attended prayer meetings at the college and held services for hospital patients. The devout young physician continued attending church services, organizing and participating in innumerable church activities after her return to the reservation, particularly in her missionary capacity.

Although the externals of Omaha culture—for example, dress—had changed since the days of her father's "Make Believe White Man's Village," Susan nonetheless lived and dressed in eastern middle-class styles. While in Philadelphia, she was conscious of how different the housing, food, social etiquette, and fashion were from the reservation. Once during her Philadelphia years, the young medical student stayed with a wealthy Mrs. Ogden and was overwhelmed by the luxurious appointments of the Ogden home, particularly finger bowls and a coffee urn. Indeed, like many Indians, Susan became accustomed to the eastern middle-class, urban lifestyle and felt dissatisfied with some aspects of life on the reservation after her return. Later, when successful physician Susan built her home in Walthill, she equipped it with a fireplace and furnace, plenty of windows, and a bathroom with indoor plumbing. These were luxurious, modern features of "civilization" found in a considerable number of eastern urban homes, an occasional Nebraska home, but almost never in an Omaha home on the reservation.

Concerned with dress and personal appearance, Susan did her best to follow eastern fashions. In Philadelphia, she began wearing her hair up because it was fashionable, and she marveled at clothes the Connecticut WNIA chapter bought her. After returning to the reservation, the young woman was so unhappy with the selection of available clothing that she had Frank send her clothes from Washington.

This "civilized" Indian woman's break with Omaha tradition did not stop with her changed beliefs, habits, and preferences; she sought to change the language, beliefs, and ways of life of her Omaha people as well. She especially hoped to spread Christianity among them; thus, she provided Christian education and services. Following Iron Eye's death in 1888, church attendance among the Omaha had plummeted. From 1889 onwards, the determined young physician worked to renew Omaha Christianity by speaking before church groups, interpreting during Sunday church services, encouraging tribal members to marry in Christian ceremonies and to perform Christian funerals for the deceased, and in other ways through her WNIA and Presbyterian missionary work. The year after her move to Walthill, she helped organize a Presbyterian Church there and regularly taught in its Sunday school. She also provided pastoral care to individual Omahas.

Susan furthermore led her fellow Omaha toward eastern, middle-class standards by teaching at Indian schools and by encouraging education when she could not teach them. In 1910, she revealed her philosophy on this subject when she noted that Dan Grant "asked me to help him get Fred who is 17 into school. I talked to Fred and told him an education was necessary so he could make the most of himself."[22] She sent her sons to Nebraska public schools and encouraged them to do well there.

She encouraged other Omaha to adopt eastern middle-class customs, social etiquette, and fashions, and she promoted such change both by setting an example and by sharing her experiences of eastern life. The young medical student filled her letters from Philadelphia with vivid descriptions of architecture, art, music and everyday city life, and she sent magazines such as *Harper's* and the *Century* home to Rosalie. Following her appointment as Agency physician, the optimistic young doctor made reading materials of all sorts available in her office at the school.

Susan also worked to reverse one direction she saw Omaha society taking by staunchly supporting the temperance movement. Her father, Iron Eye, had organized the tribe against alcoholic beverages. Later, during Susan's Philadelphia years, she continued to support temperance. When Iron Eye died, liquor consumption increased dramatically, and after the young medical graduate Susan returned in 1889, she observed its terrible effects. In 1893, she campaigned to enact laws deterring criminal activity perpetrated by drunken Indians. In 1909, her temperance work resulted in the prohibition of the sale of alcohol in any town built on Omaha lands.

By mid-1889, when Susan arrived on the reservation and began doctoring tribal members, her direct involvement in reservation affairs was enormous and unmistakable. On the other hand, she also participated in community, state, and national affairs.

Susan was accepted into these communities partly because of her Christianity and because of her desire to become a medical missionary. In Philadelphia, she attended missionary meetings and lectures and occasionally spoke before missionary groups. Years later, her position as missionary with the WNIA and the Presbyterian Board of Home Missions increased her contact with non-Indian Christians and further facilitated her acceptance by local, state, and national communities.

Susan's advanced education and work as a physician were additional factors that paved the way for her partial acceptance. She treated both Indians and non-Indians, but her practice among the latter was neither regular nor extensive. Although local physicians often asked her to accompany them to see their female patients, for the most part Susan doctored non-Indians only when other physicians were unavailable. The Omaha woman doctor was respected by local physicians; however, Walthill's non-Indian citizenry generally preferred treatment by their own doctors. Furthermore, Susan did not consider routine treatment of non-Indian patients her responsibility. Once in 1910, she instructed one such couple to send for another physician as she "could not spare the time."[23] Another time she noted, "I refused a call to [Dr.] Beckner's white people because I have to save myself for Indian work."[24]

Nonetheless, this energetic Indian physician actively participated in medical organizations and became involved in public health work in Nebraska. She served on Walthill's Board of Health, and she organized and worked in several public health programs there. She campaigned to erect drinking fountains in the Walthill public school and to start school health inspections. She personally conducted physical exams for Walthill school children and made health inspections of other Walthill premises. Susan helped organize the Thurston County Medical Association; she also attained membership in the Nebraska State Medical Society in 1891.[25] As chairman of the state health committee of the NFWC about 1910, she was involved in various public health activities. Among these were public education programs and exhibits, programs aimed at improving public health, especially for children, and the locally infamous abolition of the community drinking cup. Her work building an Indian hospital also benefited all Walthill's citizenry because the hospital served everyone, not just the Omaha.

Her involvement in other local and state organizations further indicates the extent of her acceptance into Nebraska society. On the local level, Susan became a member of the Order of the Eastern Star; she organized Indian exhibits and activities at the Thurston County Fair; and she took part in local

Woman's Clubs activities in Walthill and other Nebraska towns. She was invited to speak to the Omaha and Ashland Woman's Clubs and at the 1910 annual convention of the NFWC third district chapters. All this was in addition to the state office she held in the NFWC.

Susan functioned in the larger society as both an informal and formal Indian representative. She became a spokesperson for the Omaha during her medical school years. From that time on, letters, articles, and reports this Omaha woman wrote about her tribe appeared in Bureau of Indian Affairs records, in numerous Hampton Institute, WNIA, and Presbyterian publications, as well as in Nebraska newspapers like *The Walthill Times* and the *Omaha Bee*.

She often served as a source of information on Omaha life. In Philadelphia, for instance, the Omaha medical student spoke to homeless boys about Indians, and she contributed a "story of a Buffalo Hunt for Prof. Holmes' 3rd Reader."[26] Back at home, she furnished Alice Fletcher with information on Omaha earth lodges. Later in life, Susan also lectured on topics such as "Legends of the Red Americans and Totem Tales," "Omaha Customs and Legends," and "On the Origin of the Corn" to community groups across Nebraska.

Susan's acceptance of eastern middle-class etiquette, dress, and so forth, eased her assimilation into "society," as did her knowledge of their pastimes and popular culture. The young Hampton student learned to skate and to play ten pins and checkers. While in medical school, she watched parades, visited art museums, listened to choral and orchestral concerts, attended operas, heard lectures, and went to teas.

She often socialized informally in eastern society. In Philadelphia, she was frequently invited to attend cultural events, was asked into fine homes on purely social occasions, and repeatedly visited the W. W. Heritage family, with whom she became close. In the East, the articulate young medical student occasionally went to middle- and upper-class homes to discuss Indian issues as well. In early 1887, for example, she was "invited out tonight to tea by Mrs. Unger a lady who is much interested in Indians . . ."[27]

Following her return to Nebraska, the Omaha physician and missionary continued to socialize frequently and comfortably with non-Indians, especially with Harry Keefe—a Walthill attorney and village councilman—and his wife. Mrs. Keefe and Susan were active in Walthill's Woman's Club activities. Even more telling, however, are the multitude of references to activities and visits with the Keefes in Susan's 1910–1911 diary, as well as the fact that on one occasion she even vacationed for two weeks with them.

During her life, this exceptional Omaha woman was given special attention by, formed close relationships with, and was respected and admired by many non-Indians—her teachers, fellow physicians, missionary women, and others. Cora M. Folsom, a Hampton teacher, became so close that Susan referred to her as her "Little Mother." That General Armstrong had great respect for her is evident in his recommendations for her admission to medical school. The respect and appreciation that the entire citizenry of Walthill and Bancroft felt for their prominent townswoman was manifested at her funeral, as well as in the obituaries and memorial articles published soon afterward in *The Walthill Times*. Perhaps even more indicative of the respect accorded her by the larger national community was the appearance of her obituary in such prominent newspapers as the *New York Sun* and the *Washington Post*.

Accepted by non-Indians, and as often as she moved among them, Susan still felt most at home with the Omaha and occasionally felt discomfort in the larger society. When the recent Hampton graduate entered medical school, she initially feared living apart from other Indians in an alien world. During her Philadelphia years, her awareness of the separation of the Indian and non-Indian worlds was reinforced; sometimes her discomfort resurfaced when she was singled out because of her Indian heritage. In 1886, for example, the dean of the medical college welcomed Susan before a large lecture audience and announced she was proud to have an Indian in the medical school. On another occasion, she and Frank created a considerable stir at the Philadelphia New Year's Day parade. As the young medical student described it, "When we got into Independence Hall we attracted so much attention and they all looked at us so, so we concluded it was rather too hot in there & came out."[28] In later years, Susan was singled out, thus separated from the larger society, when attention was called to her as the first female Indian physician and medical missionary to her people.

Susette La Flesche Tibbles and Susan La Flesche Picotte are examples of what late nineteenth century reformers and government policy makers intended to accomplish in transforming "the Indian." Both women took advantage of the educational and civilizing efforts of mission, government, and eastern schools. Their education far surpassed that of the typical contemporary Omaha, whether male or female; indeed, they were among the most highly educated people in the state of Nebraska. Both sisters adopted eastern middle-class etiquette and fashions, as well as the Christian religion. But much of their successful adjustment must be attributed to their father, Joseph La Flesche, who saw to it that his daughters would be able to function in the world outside the reservation. The two La Flesche sisters participated more or less comfortably in non-Indian society, each living a considerable portion of their lives in an urban setting and joining in voluntary and professional organizations and activities. However, Susette and Susan continually identified themselves as Omaha Indians and devoted much of their lives to serving the Omaha population in one fashion or another. For both, that meant helping the Omaha adapt to the dominant society. Both women naively believed that they were no different from other Omaha Indians and that, with education and legal rights of citizenship, their people would aspire to, and could achieve, what they had done and be accepted into the mainstream of American society. Unintentionally, each sister became a public celebrity on both local and national scenes. Susette became an instant star as a result of her involvement in the Ponca case, while Susan's fame grew slowly throughout her life because of her work among the Omaha.

However, these women each played distinctly different parts in Omaha and the larger society. Susette was involved in public reform activities designed to pressure the federal legislature and courts into actions favoring Indians, but she lost contact with the Omaha people. Susan, in contrast, directly participated in the life of her tribe. She became a medical missionary to her people, and as such she worked to improve both their physical and spiritual condition. Much of Susan's work was one-on-one: treating the sick, ministering, teaching, and advising individual Omaha. Susan was thoroughly attuned to and skilled in the niceties of eastern middle-class life, an acculturated Omaha Indian who returned to spread "civilization" among the members of her tribe. Susette, on the other hand, while well-versed in the national culture, wanted others to accept the Indians without eliminating all aspects of their culture. Moreover, Susette harbored a bitterness toward Americans that was rarely expressed by Susan.

On the whole, the two sisters, although springing from the same roots, led different lives. Their views on changing Omaha culture and the extent of their promotion of it varied, as did the roles they played and the reputations they earned in both Omaha and the larger society. Susette's public image was that of a woeful, beautiful Indian maiden who aroused public sympathy for the wrongs and mistreatment perpetrated on her people. Susan, on the other hand, appeared a magnificent, Christian missionary doctor admired by everyone for her work.

NOTES

1. For the sake of clarity, we will refer to these two women by first names alone.
2. Unless noted otherwise, information presented in this chapter has been drawn from the following secondary and primary sources: Norma Kidd Green, *Iron Eye's Family: the Children of Joseph La Flesche* (Lincoln, Neb.: Johnsen Publishing Company, 1969); Dorothy Clarke Wilson, *Bright Eyes: The Story of Susette La Flesche, An Omaha Indian* (New York: McGraw-Hill, 1974); *Historical Sketch of the Connecticut Indian Association from 1881 to 1888* (Hartford, Conn.: Press of the Fowler & Miller Company, 1888); Valerie Sherer Mathes, "Susan La Flesche Picotte: Nebraska's Indian Physician, 1865–1915," *Nebraska History* 63 (1982), pp. 502–30; Laurence M. Hauptman, "Medicine Woman: Susan La Flesche, 1865–1915," *New York State Journal of Medicine* 78 (1979), pp. 1,783–1,788; *The Walthill Times*, *The Omaha World Herald*, *The Independent* (contemporary newspapers); and letters, other manuscripts, and documents contained in the La Flesche Family Papers [LFP] and the Alice Fletcher Papers [AFP] in the Nebraska State Historical Society [NSHS] in Lincoln, Nebraska.
3. Susette La Flesche to Commissioner of Indian Affairs, undated letter, as quoted in Wilson, *Bright Eyes*, pp. 131–32.
4. Joseph La Flesche to Alice Fletcher, March 13, 1886, AFP, NSHS.
5. Frank La Flesche to Rosalie Farley, December 16, 1886, LFP, NSHS.

6. Francis Paul Prucha, *American Indian Policy in Crisis: Christian Reform and the Indian* (Norman, Okla.: University of Oklahoma Press, 1976), p. 115.

7. Alonzo Bell to Carl Schurz, August 5, 1881, as quoted in Prucha, *American Indian Policy*, pp. 119–20.

8. Susette La Flesche Tibbles, "Introduction," in Thomas Henry Tibbles, *The Ponca Chiefs* (Lincoln, Neb., University of Nebraska Press, 1972), p. 3.

9. Stanley Clark, "Ponca Publicity," *The Mississippi Valley Historical Review* 29 (1943), p. 508.

10. Susette La Flesche to *St. Nicholas Magazine*, September 1880, as quoted in Douglas Street, "La Flesche Sisters Write to St. Nicholas Magazine," *Nebraska History* 62 (1981), pp. 517–18.

11. Susette La Flesche Tibbles to *Wide Awake Magazine*, 1883, as quoted in Wilson, *Bright Eyes*, p. 355.

12. National Museum of History and Technology, "Women in Science in Nineteenth-Century America," exhibit catalogue (Washington, D.C.: Smithsonian Institution Press, 1978); Margaret Rossiter, *Women Scientists in America: Struggles and Strategies to 1940* (Baltimore, Md.: The Johns Hopkins University Press, 1982) pp. 89, 327 note 4.

13. Susan La Flesche to Rosalie Farley, October 24, 1886, LFP, NSHS.

14. Susan La Flesche to Rosalie Farley, November 5, 1886, LFP, NSHS.

15. Susan La Flesche to Rosalie Farley, October 29, 1886, LFP, NSHS.

16. *The Walthill Times*, August 11, 1911, p. 4.

17. Charles Wakefield Cadman, *Da-O-Ma*, Concert Program, May 27, 1910, LFP, NSHS.

18. Susan La Flesche Picotte, "Diary, 20 September 1910 to 19 January 1911," LFP, NSHS.

19. *The Walthill Times*, January 21, 1910, p. 1.

20. "Annuity Payroll," Omaha Tribe, 1886, U.S. Bureau of Indian Affairs, NSHS.

21. Rebecca Hancock Welch, "Alice Cunningham Fletcher, Anthropologist and Indian Rights Reformer" (Ph.D. dissertation, George Washington University, 1980), p. 2.

22. Susan, "Diary, 1910–1911," November 5, 1910.

23. Susan, "Diary, 1910–1911," September 28, 1910.

24. Susan, "Diary, 1910–1911," December 21, 1910.

25. H. Winnett Orr, *Select Pages from the History of Medicine in Nebraska* (Lincoln, Nebraska, 1952), p. 79.

26. Susan La Flesche to Rosalie Farley, March 2, 1887, LFP, NSHS.

27. Susan La Flesche to Rosalie Farley, January 26, 1887, LFP, NSHS.

28. Susan La Flesche to Rosalie Farley, January 4, 1888, LFP, NSHS.

CHAPTER 7

Mourning Dove: The Author as Cultural Mediator

Jay Miller[1]

PRESENTING MOURNING DOVE (1888–1936)

Christine Quintasket's career in the turn-of-the-century Pacific Northwest was one of singular extremes. The late nineteenth-century land allotment policies of eastern philanthropists, designed to incorporate Indians into American life as self-supporting yeomen farmers, had effectively impoverished many Indian communities, including that of Christine's own Salish kin. Like many others she truly was <u>assimilated</u>—on the lowest reaches of the American economy. To provide the barest of living standards she and family were forced into seasonal stoop labor, commonly as migrant workers in American-owned farms and orchards of Puget Sound. But while daily "living and eating dust" to feed herself, her creative self flourished when engaged in large literary tasks, for as a young woman she had conceived the ambition of becoming a novelist with the role of building cultural bridges of tolerance, carrying the beauties of Salish traditions to American readers. The core of this chosen identity is perhaps reflected in the mythic figure whose name she selected for her self-as-author, Mourning Dove, the ancient messenger who augured good tidings of a season of plenty. In this respect Christine as Mourning Dove, putting aside her financial poverty, created and enjoyed cultural riches. Three key mentors can be seen in the development of her personality and calling. One was the elder Salish woman who tutored her in the ethos of that people. The second, surprisingly, was an orphaned Irish-American teenager, adopted by her parents, who taught her to read the potboiler prose he was addicted to. The third was a journalist-Indian hobbyist-literary patron who pressed on her an astounding choice between two tracks for her future: one trail leading to dismal obscurity, the other to redemption in a shining tomorrow as literary celebrity. Although full of grandiose promises and autocratic demands, this Samaritan did not subsidize her, freeing her to expend her energies in the perfection of her talents and the completion of her manuscripts. Mourning Dove thus remained an impoverished, struggling artist, regularly reverting to Christine Quintasket, the culler of apple orchards, boarding house washerwoman, and hop picker. Such exhausting labor was enough by itself to guarantee chronic fatigue and periodic illness. Combined with the demands of her calling as author, her life was often overwhelming. It was when driven to exhaustion and despair by such demands that Mourning Dove the authoress cycled into Christine Quintasket the Salish girl, returning to the settings of her childhood to rest her body and replenish her spirit with Salish foods, medicines, and rites. Her finished literary accomplishments were few and in the judgment of later critics perhaps less than preeminent. But as a self-made, self-directed woman, one who overwhelmed the most extreme adversity with her own talents and labor, she created for herself a personal monument of joy in being and becoming. (J. A. Clifton)

Through her adult years, Christine Quintasket, an Interior Salish woman, was careful to have the world outside the Colville Indian Reservation know her by other names.[2] Chief among these was Mourning Dove, her pen name. She also identified herself by the family names of her two husbands, McLeod and Galler, along with various given names: Christal, Catherine, and Christina. In this manner, she managed to compartmentalize herself, partitioning her identity in terms of the major roles she played, segregating one from the other within the several social contexts where she interacted.

Mourning Dove, her expressive pen name, marked a persona appropriate to her life's greatest ambition. As a young woman, she was determined to become a novelist: she would build literary bridges between her natal Indian culture of eastern Washington state and the larger American world that she increasingly moved through. Indeed, because of her 1927 novel, *Co-Ge-We-A*, she became the first Native American woman to publish in this genre.[3] Subsequently, Christine's friends and literary advisors encouraged her to turn to Indian folklore. Reluctant at first, she eventually did so with enthusiasm.

This additional creative enterprise piqued her curiosity in new ways, developing a congruence with her major aspirations. After years of labor, she went on to publish a collection of legends, *Coyote Stories*, in 1933.[4] At the time of her death in 1936, she had made much progress on at least two other book-length manuscripts. One was called *Tipi Life*, the other, *Educating The Indian*. These seem to be alternative versions of the same raw materials, one cast in a personalized vein, the other written impersonally. Disconnected pieces of a third book also survived her passing, fragments for a history of the Okanogan Valley.

While struggling with these three unpublished manuscripts and several articles,[5] together with the hard necessity of supporting herself by common labor, Christine also became increasingly active in reservation and regional politics. She was especially involved in urging local companies to hire Indian labor, particularly when the businesses were located on the reservation. Eventually, during the mid-1930s, she became associated with the efforts of the Bureau of Indian Affairs to carry out its new "Fair Deal for Indians." This activist role put further strains on her energies and strengthened her growing self-confidence, which developed slowly—too late to find full expression in her creative writing.

Mourning Dove's Homeland

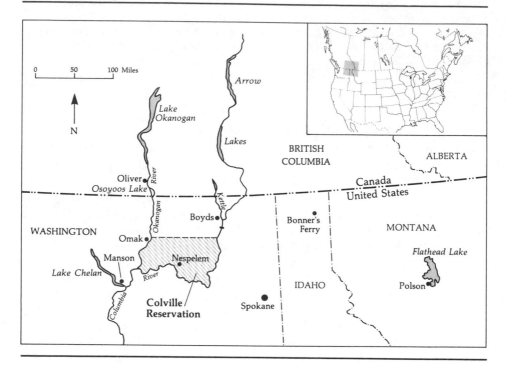

Her autobiography tells of her birth in 1888 under dramatic circumstances. Her mother was in a canoe crossing the Kootenay river near Bonner's Ferry, Idaho. After birth, the newborn Christine was clothed in the only garment available, a man's shirt. Retrospectively, she made these events symbolic of a life of transition, foreshadowing her later life of travel and tomboy behavior. She was the eldest surviving child of Joseph [native name: Skiyu] and Lucy [nee Stuikin or Stuyikin] Quintasket. As each of her succeeding siblings was born, Christine remembered that she felt a withdrawal of love. While remaining emotionally attached to her father, she was wary of her mother, who insisted on the strong standards required of her family, descendants of the chiefly line at Kettle Falls, the prime salmon fishery of the upper Columbia River, and later site of Fort Colville.[6]

Her father, whose ancestry stemmed from the Canadian Okanagan and Nicola, was orphaned at nine when his parents died within two months of each other. Her mother's maternal line was Colvile, while the paternal one was Lakes, a marriage pattern characteristic of chiefly rank throughout the Northwest, where high-ranking families regularly intermarried along dynastic lines. Her mother's mother had taken the family to live among the Kootenay at Windemere because she was opposed to the use of flogging by the chief at Kettle Falls as punishment for crimes. For unclear reasons, Joseph, Lucy, and family are listed on the Lakes portion of the multitribal roll for the Colville reservation.

The Colvile community at Kettle Falls was among the first of the Columbia River Salishan peoples to accept Catholicism. They had been exposed to this new religion by converted New York Iroquois acting as fur-trade voyageurs, who were first to teach Northwest Indians about the Great Prayer (mass) and the Black Robes (Jesuits). Later, in the 1830s, the Flathead and Nez Perce sent delegations to Saint Louis to ask the bishop there for priests. In response, Father Jean Pierre De Smet came to the inland Northwest, establishing a mission among the Flathead in 1841. To this day, Catholic hymns and prayers used on the Salish reservations are in the Flathead-Kalispel-Spokan dialect. Christine's parents, as true of many others, professed both native and Catholic religions, a spiritual dualism tolerated by the Jesuits. The priests repressed or discouraged only the traditional beliefs and customs that conflicted with canon law and Church teachings. Thus, Indian converts continued to use both native and Christian names.

Pacifism and sexual equality were the hallmarks of the Plateau culture area. The first was in accord with Catholic dogma, the second was not. According to Jesuit Father Joset,

> The women were 'viragos' making it very difficult for the missionaries to inculcate a "Christian" sense of female submission. Joset contrasted the Colvile to the Lakes, Okanogan, and others of his "mountain" dwellers. These other tribes had properly submissive women, and men who did their fair share of work by hunting. Joset believed that the salmon economy of the [Colvile] was responsible for the difference.[7]

Among the Plateau Salishans, Catholicism has been most closely associated with the work of Stephen De Rouge, who founded most of their missions. It was at his insistence that Christine, in 1895, was sent to the Goodwin Mission School of Sacred Heart Convent at Ward, Washington. This was near her family's homestead at Piya or Kelly Hill, near Boyds, Washington. Mostly French-Canadians, the Sisters of Providence who were her teachers there were obligated to use a second language, teaching English to children who spoke several languages of the Salish stock. This could only have added to the confusion of young Christine. Her first experience in boarding school lasted but a few months. Lodged in this strange environment, with its alien language, foreign foods, and threatening unfamiliarity, Christine soon fell ill.

She returned to her parents' home to recover, soon thriving on fresh-caught salmon taken at the falls. Ever generous, shortly after Christine's return, her parents took in two lodgers. Both made a profound impression on the development of this soon-to-be aspiring author. The first was an old woman named Teequalt, sometimes called Long Theresa or maybe Ann Theresa. This homeless elder became teacher and chaperone for Christine as she quested for guardian spirits and prepared for puberty. While the family was now housed in a cabin, Teequalt insisted on living by herself in a mat tipi behind the house. A profoundly traditional elder, she had as little to do with Americans and their ways as possible. Teequalt pushed Christine in one cultural direction.

The other guest resident in her home attracted her to a different path. This was Jimmy Ryan, a teenage Irish-American orphan who had encountered Christine's father when they worked together hauling freight. A place was made for Jimmy in the Quintasket household and, eventually, he married into a neighboring native family. In the habit of reading penny-dreadfuls—yellow-backed, dime-store novels—Jimmy taught Christine and her siblings to read from this popular fiction. In later years, Christine recalled how "Kentucky" was among the first printed words she learned because it figured so prominently in one of these thrillers. Jimmy was ever kind and patient, traits that stood him well in a native family. He rarely got angry, even in the face of unexpected adversity. When his adopted mother, Lucy, used an unfinished adventure tale to paper the walls of the cabin, Jimmy avidly continued his reading, with Christine helping by finding the succeeding pages.

In 1898, Christine went back to Goodwin Mission, truly enthused with the wonders of learning and the "mysteries" of books. She ended her career there in 1899, since circumstances prevented her return after she made her first communion. According to the chronicle of the mission, federal funding for native students was cut off in that year. Instead, they were to attend the school at Fort Spokane, where the Colville agency was located. A younger classmate who knew her at the convent school recalled she was a teenager. Since the records at Goodwin Mission listed her as ten years old when she first enrolled in 1895, it is likely that she was born in 1885 or slightly earlier, suggesting she was a few years older than she admitted to later in life. During her time home in 1900, Christine watched as surveyors arrived to plat the reservation, carving out individually owned allotments, breaking down communal ownership, and introducing the "civilizing" virtue—and large risks—of private property. During these trying times, she also experienced the personal stress of puberty. Strictly supervised, instructed to fast and work hard, she was finally sent off by her elders alone into the night to quest for power. Hardly had she reached formal adulthood when, on May 8, 1902, her mother died. Convinced sorcery had been the cause of this tragic loss, the family identified a likely culprit but never sought revenge, for the suspected woman drowned shortly afterward in a shallow puddle. Christine interrupted her schooling, becoming the surrogate for her dead mother and taking on the responsibilities of caring for her father and siblings.

In 1904, her father remarried to a new wife scarcely older than Christine. Whatever friction this may have created at home, Christine was also anxious to continue her education. She found an opportunity near Great Falls, Montana, where she obtained room, board, and permission to attend classes in exchange for her labor as matron at the Fort Shaw Indian School. This move brought her into a closer relationship with Maria, her mother's mother, who had lived some years in Montana. Grandmother and granddaughter remained attached to one another until 1910, when Maria died and the Fort Shaw School closed.

While in Montana, Christine met and married Hector McLeod, a member of the Flathead tribe. For a time, they lived at Polson, near the southern tip of Flathead Lake. There she witnessed the 1908 roundup of the last wild herd of bison, which had been sold to the Canadian government. Evidently, the chaos and pathos of this last bison roundup had a phenomenal effect on her: she decided to make it the subject of a novel.

This event probably also had a profound, more personal dimension— supplying her with a spirit helper after she had ceased active questing for one. Years later, she several times alluded to a supernatural encounter involving a bison skull lying on the earth near her favorite meditation spot. This spirit was particularly responsive to her wishes, dreams, and hopes. A letter of January 15, 1919, includes the postscript, "Did you forget to send me a small picture of the painting of me on the rock with the buffalo skull?" Interestingly, this is exactly the pose taken by the heroine of Christine's novel at her meditation spot overlooking the Montana range.

Christine was not wholly convinced that marriage was for her. She had resisted such entanglements for some time, and had earlier refused to learn love medicine from her grandmother. She feared the loss of her embryonic identity in the demands of being a wife. Thus, the marriage to McLeod, undermined from the start, was never satisfying. For years, the couple was estranged, although they were not divorced until 1917.

During 1912, she lived alone and undisturbed in Portland. It was there, presumably, she sketched out a penciled draft of her first novel. It concerned "a young Indian agent who used an Indian maiden's love lightly." Unsatisfied with her creation, she hid it in the bottom of a trunk. But she remained determined to produce a polished version. Moving to Calgary, Alberta, she enrolled in a business school to learn typing, shorthand, and composition. As the only Indian enrolled in the school, she was ostracized by other students and subjected to racial snubs. Christine responded by displaying a quiet dignity that left her unscathed, on the surface at least. Still, she maintained good grades, mastering technical skills that would later serve her well in her literary endeavors.

During visits home, her friends and relatives began to express suspicions of her motivations, for she did not fit the expected roles for either American or Indian women of her age and time. Alienated from both groups, and at odds with her husband, she filled long journals with her hopes for novels that would help Indians and Americans to understand one another. It was a period of transition for Christine, in which she fashioned the rudiments of the role she would play during her life: an author of novels promoting intercultural tolerance. We do not know exactly when she first fixed on Mourning

CHRISTINE QUINTASKET AS A PUBLIC FIGURE, THE AUTHOR, MOURNING DOVE. As a young woman of much talent and initiative but little education and less means, Christine Quintasket formed the ambition to use her writing ability to interpret and explain Indian cultures to American audiences. Becoming an author under her pen name of Mourning Dove, her life was spent in alternating periods of creative writing and the arduous, low-paid labor that poverty forced on her. Despite her experience of chronic economic deprivation, she completed the first novel published by an American Indian woman and a collection of Salish Indian legends, as well as several book-length manuscripts unpublished at the time of her death. (Unknown.)

Dove as a pen name, but this is the most likely period. In Plateau mythology, this figure is an evocative supernatural prototype, the wife of Salmon, himself symbolic of plentitude. Mourning Dove is the mythic creature who annually greets the spring fish runs with her mournful cry. Christine's intention in the selection of this image for her literary identity is not easily penetrated. She dreamed, perhaps, of welcoming a new time of joy and abundance, while gaining recognition as the messenger.

The most fateful meeting of her life occurred at the Walla Walla Frontier Days celebration, probably in 1915. There, Mourning Dove met Lucullus Virgil McWhorter, a forceful advocate of Indian rights from Yakima, Washington.

McWhorter was impressed by her determination and offered his help and connections. Reluctantly, she allowed him to see the raw draft of her novel. He found it amateurish and melodramatic, but promising. By encouraging her continued efforts, he provided soothing balm for the anxieties of an unpublished and awkward author. Also, on a more practical side, he invited her to live with his family while they worked on a revision. She accepted, and the manuscript took new but unfinished form. Afterward, they continued to discuss further improvements in letters. Over the years, their extensive correspondence filled in what would have been major gaps in the record of her life.

In a letter of November 29, 1915, which would have terrified a less durable soul, McWhorter charged Mrs. Christal McLeod—now sometimes called Mourning Dove—with a choice between two trails. The one to the left was easy and well traveled by generations of Indians, he stressed, but it led to a dark cloud of oblivion. That to the right, in contrast, was winding, precipitous, and rarely taken, but it led to the future light of immortality, a halo reflected from the Indians' sacred bundles lovingly carried there. The left- hand fork, in McWhorter's rich prose, was

> . . . a mingling of beauty and ease, luring to all. I see many on this trail. They are bearing bundles which glow and shine like gold that is washed from the river beds. These bundles are the traditions and history of the tribes. They are bourn by the old people, who look sad and I hear them wailing as they try to leave their bundles by the wayside for others who are to follow, but they cannot rid themselves from the binding cords. They pass with their bundles of light—the history of their people—into the cloud and are seen no more.

> [Along the trail leading to the fork] I see old people open their bundles and take from them many beautiful stories, which glint in the sunshine like silver and gold, and see them give these to the young woman who eagerly places them in her bundle, which daily grows larger. I see the old people take her by the hand and bless her as she passes on. I note the happy look that radiates from the face of the young woman as she receives these gifts from the many old people, and I see her bundle growing larger and more valuable as she travels towards the parting of the trails.

> I see in her vast possibilities. I see a future of renown; a name that will live through the ages, if only she will decide to take the right-hand trail. Helping hands are held out to her, and the trail will not prove so rough as it appears. Your race-blood will be of actual benefit to her in this work. It is a duty she owes to her poor people, whose only history has been written by the destroyers of their race. Let Morning Dove of the Okanogans take cheer and step out from the gloom of ghostly fears, into the golden light of opportunity, exulting in her own strength and show to the world her nobility of purpose to perpetuate the story of her people in their primitive simplicity. Nothing is in the way of your success.

Few young authors have ever had thrust on them such a direct, frightening yet enchanting and ego-enhancing challenge. In the righteous, missionary-like enthusiasm of an age when Americans subscribed to an image of the disappearing Indian, McWhorter pressed on Mourning Dove an awesome prospect: she alone could preserve, protect, and communicate the ancient traditions of her people.

But Christine was a poor, struggling, self-supporting woman. She first had to earn her bread and shelter before she could shoulder the awesome responsibilities McWhorter offered. Nonetheless, during September of 1916, she remained in Polson intent on writing, instead of going to the Yakima Valley as a migrant worker to pick hops. Apparently the revisions of the novel had not gone smoothly, for she wrote McWhorter, apologetically, "If I don't get my temper up sometimes, people will think I am dead." Christine had been at the Spokane Fair, where she met her father and sister. Then, on September 12, she drove thirty-five miles through the country described in her novel, commenting that she saw the exact spot where her heroine committed her heart to Jim, the half-breed ranch foreman who had saved her life. In a postscript, she asked about copyrighting the novel, insisting this be done in the name of Christal McLeod, not in her father's or her own given name, hoping to save her father unwanted attention that he did not understand. It appears that Christine was separating Mourning Dove, her creative self, from her identity as daughter and kinswoman.

Irrespective of her literary ambitions, her finances were never enough to provide much leisure for writing. Hardly a month following this trip, she was forced to seek employment. That October, Christine began work as a housekeeper in Polson, caring for a family with six children and complaining of her poor health. Such concern with her well-being, the high expectations she held for herself, and a desperate need for income are continually revealed in her correspondence. Now she chastised herself for not being a "thoroughbred," and without the sixty-five dollars needed to meet expenses, she expressed fantasies of robbing a bank, stealing a horse, or going to work at the Deer Lodge State School for "crooks." She was never free of financial worries, which caused her great anxiety until the end of her days.

She began 1917 deathly ill at the family homestead in Piya. Local physicians diagnosed potentially fatal pneumonia and inflammatory rheumatism; and during a brief moment of lucidity, she recalled seeing her father and brother weeping at her bedside. Eventually, she was cured—by an aunt possessing traditional medicine power. Despite this recovery, for the next nine days she could swallow only water. Then came a badly needed emotional uplift: at this critical moment she received a contract for her novel.

Such promising news did not, however, end her poverty. Still forced to work before she could write or rewrite, later in the year she obtained a teaching post on the Inkameep Okanagan Reserve, across from Oliver, British Columbia. The teacher before her had been a southern Black man, and Christine later delighted in telling her family and others how he had the children speaking English as though they were raised on a Dixie plantation.

Her role as teacher agreed with her outlook as a literary figure, also providing temporary prosperity and security. Her letters during the

1917–1918 school year are filled with an aura of new beginnings. In November, she was enthused about her new tent with its stove and rockers: she had built its board floor herself. Her wants escalated to include the expense of buying a typewriter to aid her work. But, a sister and her family living nearby proved a mixed blessing. The comfort of kin close by had to be balanced with her need for privacy to work intensively at her writing. As she found more time to devote to these efforts, she allowed herself the luxury of making a cautious admission to McWhorter: she harbored a terrible fear of the dark. This was the first of several phobias she revealed over the years.

When her teaching duties ended that June, she wrote McWhorter full of life, thanking him testily for at last telling her he was "still in the land of the living," reporting she was getting along splendidly, becoming fat and saucy. The weather had been warm, she observed, and she had acquired a dark tan working in her extensive World War I victory garden. But more of her deep, persistent anxieties showed through. Christine admitted to a great apprehension about snakes which, she believed, were becoming a menace that year.

Two bull snakes appeared near her home, but children, helped by a terrier, killed one of them. Later, a huge black and yellow rattler crawled out from under the house; again, it was killed by children aided by a passerby. Its mate was seen in a neighbor's chicken coop, but it escaped. Full of fear, she began each walk with great caution, watching carefully for the reptiles—except when she spied chickens scratching and pecking in her garden. Then, concerned for her vegetables, she chased them, oblivious to dangers. Unlike other tribes, her people had no aversion or taboo about killing snakes, she assured McWhorter. The threat she saw in snakes was personal, and it may have stemmed from the fact that, in mythology, it was Rattlesnake who killed Salmon, the husband of Mourning Dove.[8]

The following August, before her teaching duties resumed, Christine hoped to find work on the coast in a fish cannery, where she could earn three or four dollars a day. She needed extra money because her inflamed tonsils had to be removed, surgery that would cost fifty dollars and deplete her scanty savings. Although complaining of pains in her chest and heart, her outlook remained cheerful. Proud of her new home and responsibilities, she promised McWhorter photos of her tent and "my little Indian chums, a lot of little kids." As always, she tried to save money to finance her novel, "if she [Cogewea] ever makes good." But she planned several weeks' travel, as well, wanting to enjoy the grand Fourth of July celebration at Nespelem, Washington. In the stilted, self-effacing language she sometimes used to express gratitude to her advisers, she assured McWhorter, "Injun never forgets."

Late in the year, Christine embarked on a new literary venture, an article on the good work of the Red Cross among the Colville people during the devastating influenza epidemic of 1918. A draft was sent to McWhorter for editing, together with an apology that it made a poor Christmas present. Proud of herself, she announced the account of the Red Cross accomplishments was written without a dictionary, adding "ain't I getting smart."

This letter was written far into the night, in the chill of her tent, after the fire had died. Her day had been too busy to do any writing. She had risen early to get her sister off to Spokane to pick up her daughter, who would keep Christine company after the mother left. Christine had declined the trip, for she wanted privacy for some days. "I work best when I am practically alone," she observed. Recovered from a bout with the dreaded influenza, during the day, she and her sister rode a hay rack five miles into the countryside to bring in a load of dry wood for fuel, and she "felt fine after the airing." And, she was proud of her creative industry. No slacker she, while everyone else celebrated the year-end holidays, Christine labored over her folklore notes.

Thus, her holidays were uneventful: she had no money for gifts, for the flu had emptied her bank account. But, she had her niece for company. Still concerned about her Red Cross essay, in January 1919, she asked McWhorter to use his best judgment on it, so that it could be published in the Spokane *Spokesman-Review*. Yet, her replies to his queries were not always prompt. She refused to write a response on January 13, for instance, because it is "such a hoodoo number for me." Meanwhile, she received a letter about a woman who wanted to make a movie about "real Indian life"; and so she had "almost left off folklore thinking, and started a movie play, ha, ain't I fickle folklore writer?"

Apparently this was not her first effort to break into script-writing. There had been earlier movie plans, helped by the Yakima, Nipo Strongheart, which left her disappointed and cautious. She would remain wary about such speculations, she noted, "till cash is solid. Their silver tones don't go with this Injun, Injun knows." She went on to explain how she was all set to ship a gun back to McWhorter but there was a mix-up. Then, as it grew darker, she gave up efforts to send it on, because she was "afraid of spooks."

This long letter ended with a revealing comment on the hard conditions of her creative efforts:

> Well I think I will close, everybody is in slumber-land where all decent country folks should be, but I think they think I am looney or have too much company, because I use too much lamp oil. I fill my lamp every night. I write better at night, because my sister is asleep and the kid, and than no one talks to me, to make me nevrous. I do much better, I am my own boss, and home is sweet when you are IT. I am much happier than when living with my sister, where the children worry me so much.

Following this homage to solitude, it is a surprise to learn of her remarriage later in 1919. Her second husband was Fred Galler, member of a large, prominent native family of central Washington. While Galler offered quiet, emotional support of her writing, the marriage brought no improvement in her finances or work conditions. After leaving her teaching position, Christine could find no steady employment. Yet, lacking children of their own, the couple added to their responsibilities by often looking after nieces and nephews.[9]

Then, as is still true of most Indian families of the region, the Gallers partly supported themselves with seasonal migrant labor in the orchards and fields of the Northwest. For people in such circumstances, incapacitating sickness is a grave hazard. Thus, when Fred fell ill for a month in early 1920, Christine had to run a boarding house in Omak, feeding and caring for fourteen roomers. In season, they worked long days thinning, picking, or packing apples. Sometimes she also harvested hops and other field crops. But no matter how long or arduous her days, Mourning Dove devoted her nights to reworking and typing up legends or literary efforts. The woman burned her candle at both ends. Both health and morale suffered as a result.

Christine's hopes and dreams rose and fell. In September of 1921, she planned a theatrical tour of the East with Nipo Strongheart, a Yakima closely associated with Hollywood. Anticipating her absence, she made arrangements for a nephew of eleven and a girl of five to board with another family. Since she had no appropriate traditional clothing, she asked McWhorter and other friends to lend her native dress. Meantime, she worked in local orchards to save expense money for the trip. While traveling to these jobs, she visited a Spokane museum and discovered that her namesake was spelled Mourning Dove. Reporting on this experience December 27, 1921, ever after she spelled her pen name in the same way as the species. Earlier, she referred to herself as "Morning Dove." This is all the more curious because, in her 1933 collection of legends, she does not identify their mythological prototype by name. She merely described the creature as the grieving wife whose cries greeted Salmon every year on his return from the sea.

Apparently, her trip East never materialized. A later letter explained why not. She had again fallen ill, required surgery, and was recovering in a Canadian Okanagan community. The distractions of living with her sister and children had forced her to move. It was, she explained,

> . . . my sister and her children that broke my nevrous [nerves] terrible. I couldn't write, never had time for nothing else but work, work. I began to think that the country was no place to write stories at. I had a good mind to run away long ago, till sister came to stay with me, and I had my place moved across the creek where the wind is not so bad.

She and this sister lived "in style, eat everything imaginable. From bacon and dry meat, and from canned salmon to dried fish and salted steelhead salmon. We even had bear meat last, two weeks ago, I didn't like it very much." Evenings, she visited an elder, Toma (Rocks), who narrated "lovely folklore" for her collection.

At long last, McWhorter made final arrangements with the publisher for the often revamped novel. Mourning Dove's letter to him in January 1922 indicated she was returning the signed contracts, and lamenting a minor calamity—her typewriter's "spring-wire" had broken. But, by February, she was again discouraged, concerned with "getting nothing in return for our efforts." Neighbors were poking fun at her work, making her "terrible nevrous all this winter," and she desperately needed to succeed, "honestly for keeps, and that means hard on the system."

In May of 1922, the wife of the governor of Nebraska mailed to Mourning Dove personal comments on the manuscript. A friend of McWhorter's, this new critic generally approved, but insisted it be written in the best possible English prose. She recommended the heroine be known only by a simplified form of the Okanogan word for chipmunk, but not also as Agnes. Her suggestions were followed. In a more personal vein, Christine expressed sadness about her sister's departure for Canada. On the other hand, husband Fred had delighted her. Waiting for a ride, he had picked up the manuscript and read it straight through, giving up his trip to town. The next morning, she left for Spokane to visit her nephew, who had been under treatment in the tuberculosis sanitarium there for almost a year.

Through the August apple harvest in 1922, Christine earned eight to ten dollars each day picking the ripe fruit. As fall arrived, she harvested her garden and busied herself stocking her larder for the coming winter: she was preparing for a long season of writing. That November, McWhorter made some—hopefully—final changes in the manuscript, which Mourning Dove approved. In her reply, she reported how she had an old Indian woman spotted as a source for more legends. Despite the contract, there were many delays before the book was at last published in 1927.

The intervening years were full of false hopes and alarms. In mid-1925, for example, she was elated with news that the novel would soon be printed. Cogewea, her "little Indian squaw is on her way," she exulted. Then, in August, came a sobering demand: two hundred dollars were needed before the book could be printed. Certainly, Mourning Dove had no such funds, her bank account usually held no more than fifteen carefully saved dollars. Apparently the ever-resourceful McWhorter came to her rescue, using subscriptions for the book to raise the required sum.

But there was another two years of delay. In the meantime, Christine continued her double work life. Since the Gallers again experienced hard times through June 1924, she ran a rooming house for her aunt, while Fred fished the Okanogan River to feed their four cats. Her folklore collecting work also required much energy, as she sought out elders and transcribed their stories. Trips to the mountains provided her only recreation, but even these journeys were devoted to expanding her understanding of nature.

Mourning Dove found relations with her publisher, Four Seas of Boston, increasingly vexatious. Using her typewriter as a weapon, she neatly shrank their acreage, calling them Four Ponds and Four Puddles or—with mounting anger—Four Liars. Christine's immediate personal problem was the audience of neighbors in Omak, who continued smirking at her long-unfulfilled aspirations. Her shame was increased because of a premature 1916 revelation of her aspirations and primary purposes for writing novels, plans publicized in newspaper articles and announcements. "It's all wrong," she had then proclaimed, "this saying that Indians do not feel as deeply as whites. We do feel, and by and by some of us are going to be able to make our feelings appreciated, and then will the true Indian character be revealed." The neighbors, likely envious of the publicity given to her determined drive and unusual ambitions, were even less forgiving as eleven years passed with no material evidence of her success.

By 1926, much of her time was occupied with the collection of legends, which Mourning Dove always called "folklores." McWhorter, trying to spice them up and add authenticity, insisted she add numerous native words and phrases using English spelling. This was impossible because the sounds of Salish are much more complex than allowed for by the English alphabet. However, even as Mourning Dove tried to make Salish conform to the confines of English spelling, she demanded McWhorter print such efforts "without fixings and dashes" (diacritics).

That November, Mourning Dove wanted to see the preface to *Co-Ge-We-A*, carefully explaining,

> . . . what white blood I have is not of Scotch strain. My [first] husband's name was McLeod but I am of Irish decent, I think. That is, my grand father's name was Haynes or Haines, but my father never took his name and went by his step father's name who really raised him. And to save dad's feelings please do not mention any names. it would dig up the past because in the early days many white men never married their Indian wives legally and only cast them aside for white women when thire kind came. And of course my dad was the unfortunate one. So let the past rest for his sake. My grandmother thought no doubt she was correctly married by her Indian tribal ceremonies.

These genealogical claims are noteworthy because all evidence indicates her father had only native ancestry. One suspects Mourning Dove was drawing a fictional family tree, trying to segregate her public literary self from her ancestral Salish identity. Perhaps, also, by claiming partial White ancestry, she sought to present a more appealing image to her middle-class American audience. On other fronts, she mentioned knowing the Indian agent, who was "once at my house and admired our little home very much because it was clean and well taken care off." In this and other ways, she expressed pride that Indians were no longer wards of the government.

The publication of *Co-Ge-We-A* was greeted by many favorable reviews from all over the country. Even the regional papers were laudatory. Mourning Dove's election to the state historical society soon followed. Still, neither her financial nor medical conditions changed: the hard-won literary acclaim did not bring improvement in her life conditions.

The long-delayed appearance of *Co-Ge-We-A* launched Christine on a new set of activities. She became a far more public person than earlier. In February 1928, for instance, she joined with eight other native women to found the Eagle Feather Club, dedicated to programs of social betterment and welfare for natives. Their motto was "One for All, and All for One." That spring, she again suffered serious illness. But, by late April, she was well enough to think of a drive into the country, where she would dig bitter roots (rock rose) to cook with milk, making a medicine to soothe her ailing stomach. By then, her weight had dropped from 174 to 150 pounds. As part of her recovery, she found it restorative to let her bobbed hair grow long.

Early in 1929, McWhorter, at work editing her folklore manuscripts, sought her helpful comments. Her hasty note indicated that she was too busy to respond to his numerous queries about the stories. Fred was again unemployed, and they planned to rent out their nice house in town. She was occupied preparing the cottage for prospective renters; they had already calsamined (whitewashed) its three rooms themselves.

At this moment, McWhorter introduced her to Hester Dean Guie, a Yakima newspaperman who soon agreed to take up the chore of editing the legends for publication. With her conditional approval, Guie also provided illustrations for the new book. This new relationship caused a three-way flow of questions from Guie to McWhorter to Mourning Dove and back again. Dean Guie's concern was, with nagging insistence, to assure both consistency and integrity for the stories. The threesome proved a successful and productive editorial team, for *Coyote Stories* was released in 1933 under the imprint of Caxton Press, McWhorter's usual publisher.

That April, Fred at last found work on a railroad in the woods. Christine, meanwhile, extended her new public role, now actively "battling for the rights of her people." She found a strong issue when a lumber mill on the reservation defaulted on its promise to hire Indians, and she set out forcefully to remind them of their obligations. In the same season, she started speaking in public on a variety of subjects. At the Tonasket Civic League, she spoke of Indian life. She held forth, similarly, before the Women's Christian Temperance Union of Pateros; while at Ellisford, she lectured for an hour and a quarter. But none of this contributed to her finances: to support herself she earned money thinning apples.

She was also active in two Indian women's clubs. Aside from the Eagle Feather Club, the Wild Sunflower (in Salish, *Namtues*) Club encouraged the perpetuation of native crafts and traditions. When a young girl of the Eagle Feather Club got in trouble with the law, Mourning Dove intervened effectively and was pleased when the sheriff released the girl into her custody.

Toward the end of 1929, Christine communicated to McWhorter a new goal. She wanted to master American slang so she could write Wild West stories. When these were sold and published, hubby Fred would not have to spend hard-earned money on pulp magazines—since his wife would have her reprints for him to read. Christine was elated over her developing technical skills: she felt she could write native words better and type faster than ever before. As an indication of such confidence, this letter was composed while waiting for the potatoes to cook for the evening meal. Usually she wrote only in solitude, wary of any distractions. But she was only seemingly relaxed. For all of this was a mere prelude; now came a foreboding outburst of great consequence, leading to the writing of her autobiography. A letter of late 1929 included this significant eruption:

> I'm madder than the dickens today. Do you remember the [agency farmer], the skunk that caused us so much trouble, he's agent here and has been the last year. Well, he is trying to lord it over us Injuns, and he has been going around the white people and telling them that I never wrote the book Cogeawea, to knock me, and I put it up to the club members and we are circulating a petition to oust him out as agent . . . I have my fighting clothes on for him now.

Nonetheless, she took some consolation from the publication of *Co-Ge-We-A*. "After the holidays, I shall be Mourning Dove the AUTHOR," she announced full of pride, presumably because royalties were due then. Yet, that Christmas brought hard times once more. The Gallers were penniless, for Fred had again lost his job.

In this same letter, she promised after New Year's to mail McWhorter an account of what she called "Lake Spiritualism," a Salishan seance ritual with parallels throughout the circumpolar regions. This reference marks a significant change in the fate of her correspondence. From then on, important incidents remarked in the letters also found their way into the text of her autobiography.

One was written from Omak in mid-February 1930. As always, she used a favorite nickname in addressing McWhorter:

> Dear Big Foot
> There are seven legends here inclosed for your eyes to roam on. To me it would be correct to put in all the legends whether interesting or not, for the sake of my people the Indians of this location where I have worked for years to collect for publication, which the "poor dears" did not know I was going to write stories for printing purposes while they told me in every day "talk". Of course, it looks sneaky, but it was the only means I could be able to collect datas, otherwise it would have been hard for me to get the material which should be preserved for the coming generation of Indians.

She then went on to emphasize,

> You will see that in my *recastings* I have purposely ommitted a lot of things, that is an objection to printing and reading, but an Indian knows the story and can read between the lines just the same. So it is best that we save it all You will find that at the ends of these legends when known the location I usually tell it as a forword, and you can dress it up a little to suit yourself. But not too much Shoo-ya-pooh's [white man's] BIG WORDS.
> I shall work on words and will forward same soon as I can. Will enclose what words [Judge William] Brown made too. So you can compare same. Got letters from Washington with application blanks for census taker, maybe will take the job, and can collect some more datas while on the job for US that is providing it is on the Reservation.
> Our love to you. Have been ill this week but better today, have too work, no time for foolery of getting ill.

The next day, Mourning Dove attended a "ceremonial meeting" of the Camp Fire Girls, who had declared 1930 their Indian year and dedicated themselves to the study of native lore. She spoke to them of Okanogan traditions, ever willing to promote mutual understanding by acting as a cultural interpreter.

By the end of February, she had resumed her role as reservation activist, now busy circulating a petition calling for the removal of her critic, an agency farmer. Her folklore writing continued, for now she mailed McWhorter a Wolves and Salmon legend, arguing again that the numeral three was the traditionally correct pattern or sacred number of her people. In over a dozen letters, she insisted on *three* as the sacred number. But McWhorter and Guie remained skeptical, pressing her to check and make certain. Use of the wrong number in the forthcoming book of legends, they believed, would invalidate her work in the eyes of professionals. At last, after consulting the Kootenay texts of the famed anthropologist, Franz Boas, McWhorter and Guie capitulated.[10] In hindsight, today we know both Christine and Boas were misguided. Among these Plateau Salishans, the traditional sacred number was five, although by Christine's generation, Judeo-Christian influence had introduced the magical three, as in the holy trinity, except among a minority of ultra-traditionalists.

During 1930, Christine increased contacts with her various literary advisors, some of them self-styled authorities on local Indian cultures. This fomented a dispute with two local people, Judge Brown and a Mrs. Manning, about whether ravens were indigenous to the area or not. Christine insisted that they were rare. She was still short of money, and her life was disrupted by Fred's friends. Also, the anti-Indian snobbery of her Omak neighbors caused her to leave the house in town, where she was made to feel like an intruder. She returned to the reservation house at East Omak. About her continuing financial indebtedness to McWhorter, she was especially apologetic. The letters from him, often forwarding questions from Guie, asked her to provide nomenclature and spellings for native words. Such "brain fever twisters" caused her much frustration, she complained. In all, Guie was a stickler for needling precision and consistency, so much so that he was an annoyance. "How large was Chickadee's bow?" he would insist. "What was it made of? Elk or deer rib?" After much discussion, Mourning Dove fancied it was elk, since that was more appropriate to the might of this tiny legendary hunter.

During the spring of 1930, she published in *Comfort* magazine a letter describing Omak, netting her a response of four hundred fan letters. Basking in this modest fame, she again became excited about film prospects: this time a production crew was due soon, supposedly. Then, in April, she took up the issue of Indian fishing rights, speaking before the Omak Commercial Club. When the reservation lakes were closed to non-Colvilles, she made herself arbitrator between the Indian Agency and American sportsmen. Furthermore, under the strain of the public pressure, her marital life collapsed. At

Easter mass, she and Fred fell into a bitter quarrel, whereupon Christine left for Canada intending a permanent separation. Her determination lasted but three weeks; she returned to a messy house, dirty clothes, and "no grub." Yet, her heart was glad, she announced, for "Fred and I are trying to fight life together again."

In Canada, Christine had imposed a strict regimen on herself, seeking a guaranteed, traditionally Salish renewal of health and spirits. Each morning before dawn, she prepared a sweat lodge. Thus, starting her days cleansed and refreshed, she found joy in the singing of birds, in admiring the wildflowers. She was resting from the "fuss and fume of Indian work." At last, her "nevres settled," she grew thinner and, she observed of herself, "My brains are clearer too, I think without much thought."

Reunited with Fred, Christine attributed their troubles to sorcery. She was convinced some evildoer had used a whirlwind and a lightning-struck tree to affect their minds and feelings. Seven days in the sweat lodge, however, supplemented by herbs and songs, had conquered these malign influences. Once home again, to increase their new-found strength and gain a more certain cure, she planned an August trip into the mountains when the "flowers of mystery" bloomed. She would use them in preparing a counter spell, using a formula purchased from a Canadian Okanagan woman. Such self-assurance, as often the case for her, alternated with self-doubts. Concerns with her liabilities were expressed in a letter of May 19th: "I am so poor in grammer and writing names that I dread to try, and the more I try the worse I get with those ferneral [infernal] words in Indian . . . My nevres are gone, I need a rest."

At the end of May, she acted as chaperone for a school trip from St. Mary's Mission near Omak, consisting of seventeen children, three nuns, and a priest. The party camped at Kettle Falls; there Christine was reminded of her grandfather's sister, who threw herself off Suicide Rocks because she was forbidden to marry the man she loved. She also found the old quartzite deposit at the falls, a site visited by her people for centuries to make scrapers for the preparation of hides. Mourning Dove chipped out a few of the traditional tools herself, intending them as gifts for her favorite elders. Later, an account of the Kettle Falls fishery and of the "tanning rocks" appeared in her autobiography. Such pleasures were undermined by simultaneous disappointments: her first publisher, Four Seas, decided to end the run of her novel. An ever-anxious author, by scouting around she tallied seventy-five unsold copies in her immediate area.

Soon, she was snapping at Guie about the next book. He had suggested she pose for a photo on horseback wearing a "root hat." She replied angrily—such basketry hats were only worn by the Yakima and Nez Perce! Her Okanogan ancestors wore just a headband! On the other hand, she approved illustrations the excessively meticulous Guie had done for some of the legends, while insisting he delete anything that looked like modern clothing.

In early June 1930, she attended the Salmon Days festival at Keller in the reservation's Sanpoil area. She expanded on this visit in a letter describing the size and distribution of salmon in the Kettle and Okanogan rivers. Later that month, the collaborators elected to include the names of storytellers in the new book, if Mourning Dove could remember who had narrated each tale. In her correspondence, she reminisced about her relative at Kettle Falls, Chief Kinkinawah, and recalled the special Blue Jay Dance of the Lake and Chewelah tribes. During these weeks, she was repeatedly pressed by McWhorter and Guie for even more precise cultural details. Their most frequent query concerned the different Salishan names for the golden and bald eagle. Christine got into a muddle over this, in the end reporting correctly, "I could find the names for them in Indian, but just can't find a white man that could tell me the difference on the two breeds of birds."

During June, she was back in the orchards picking apples, presenting herself as Christine Galler, not Mourning Dove. Indeed, she was pleased her friendly employers did not know that she was an author. She was merely "one of the rest of the Indians there working. Feel better and can work better too." But, she warned her editors, "after working for 10 hours in the blazing sun, and cooking my meals, I know I shall not have the time to look over very much mss., but fire them on, and between sand, grease, campfire, and real apple dirt I hope I can do the work."

A July letter mentions Red Dawn, one of Fred's relatives who had published a series of Colville stories in several issues of the 1930 *Washington Farmer*.[11] Such publicity for a female writer of native legends may have provided further incentive for the completion of Mourning Dove's autobiography. The couple was then living on the shore of Lake Chelan. Fred was employed; Christine was not. Instead, she was swimming every day, taking sweat baths, and flagellating herself with nettles to acquire luck for the July 4 gambling games. "It may bring luck," she complained wryly, "but the blamed things sure sting, and my arms still feel like they were numb with its stingy feeling. Ain't I foolish? But I want to know and prove everything by experience." Apparently, the self-punishment produced a desired consequence, for a letter of July 8 reported she was "indeed lucky at the bone games at Wapato Point."

By the end of July, the Gallers had moved to Pullman, the site of Washington State University, in the midst of vast wheat fields. Fred was earning two dollars a day as a ranch hand. Awake at 4:30 A.M. to feed the mules, he had breakfast at 5:30 A.M., began "work" at 6:30 A.M., and returned that night at 6:30 P.M. for supper. In Omak, Christine noted, Fred could have earned four dollars a day for fewer hours and less toil.

In these letters, Christine arranged to meet McWhorter in Nespelem. From there, Fred would drive them in a car to places pointed out by Yellow Wolf, an ancient veteran of the 1877 Nez Perce War. Together the four would tour Chief Joseph's route and battle sites, so McWhorter could collect notes and recollections for his book on the Nez Perce retreat as recalled by this aged warrior. McWhorter suggested they take along a second woman, but Mourning Dove flatly refused. "I don't [want] no woman bothering me on driving," she grouched. "She would be just in my way, if anything should happen to the car. Women are generally helpless around machinery, and *nix* on them. I hater to travel with them. too sisified and helpless."

By early August, they were in Palouse, Washington. There Fred earned six dollars a day plus his meals by sewing grain sacks. Christine, who had suffered an injured ankle, reported she could now walk on it—another hardship endured. Meanwhile, she was consumed with literary concerns during odd moments of spare time. In mid-August, for example, halting her car on a side street in the town of Colville, she unpacked her typewriter and dashed out an explanation of how camas root is cooked in a pit oven. She had already traveled a hot, exhausting 150 miles that day and had another twenty-five to go for a week's visit with family at Boyds. Later she planned to join Fred in Palouse, when "hubby is through" with his temporary job.

That autumn, the couple was back in the apple orchards, Christine remarking, "We are camping and we live and eat dust." She and Fred earned top wages of four dollars for a ten-hour day. Later, at Naches, Washington, she told of rising at five in the morning, putting in a ten-hour day, six days a week packing apples. On the day of her letter, she had filled 133 boxes of Yellow Newtons. Her Sunday "rest period" was given over to laundry and other personal chores. That season's work in the orchards cost Christine forty pounds of body weight. She spent the holidays at Boyds, attending Christmas service at the mission, lamenting how the children's choir sang in English—not Indian—which "made my heart ache." From McWhorter came a welcome gift, the two-volume set of the *Handbook of North American Indians*.

During 1930, a political party became active in the reservation's Inchelium district. Known as the Colvile Indian Association, it had its origin in a 1901 trip to federal agencies in Washington, D.C., a trip made by three Colviles and a Jesuit priest who were seeking the triple payments of $500 each promised to the Colviles in compensation for the loss of the "North Half" of their reservation.[12] By 1930, when people in Inchelium had become increasingly concerned with alleged misuse of tribal trust monies, they formed a coalition around the men who had made the first trip to the capital, twenty-nine years earlier. Younger tribal members raised in the area, such as Christine, also began to take leading roles. After several years as a spokeswoman, Christine became widely recognized as a concerned advocate of her people's rights.

Through the spring of 1931, Fred was again unemployed and struggling. One happy note was a mention of 600 fan letters, which brightened Christine's spirits. But, living close to nature, fresh threats to her security—not all economic or literary—were never far away. While foraging for berries that August she encountered a silver-tipped grizzly, hungry and dangerous, which scared her off. Ever the recorder of her experiences, she wrote about her precipitous flight with her typewriter propped atop a suitcase inside a tent made of common sheeting. The couple enjoyed life out-of-doors. While she gathered food or pecked away in the flimsy tent, Fred and Christine's brother went "looking for colors," panning for gold in the nearby creek.

In 1933, Mourning Dove again grew hopeful. *Coyote Stories* was at last in print, and new stories kept her at the typewriter. Developments in the nation's capital also provided some uplift: Commissioner John Collier's efforts to reform the Indian Service she found particularly promising. But while she still faced back debts, she could almost see her way clear of them, and her efforts as a political agitator continued. The agent called a meeting for May 8, 1933, at Christine's insistence, to find out why the on-reservation lumber company was not hiring more Indians. By the end of the year, she and Fred were again having difficulties, but her efforts to dislodge the hated agency farmer had, after much work, been effective.

During 1934, she corresponded with Commissioner Collier, offering her support for his efforts to secure adoption of the new Indian Reorganization Act by her reservation. Her enthusiasm for this exercise in "therapeutic democracy," however, was not shared by many other Colvilles. During a sometimes stormy council meeting at Nespelem in April 1935, she struggled long and hard to gain approval for a Colville constitution, but the Indian Reorganization Act was rejected. After years of minor successes, Christine experienced first-hand political failure and rejection. She complained that the Nespelem meeting was a mess, the interpreters unmotivated, and her people ungrateful. Nevertheless, at the next elections in May 1935, Christine was elected to the Tribal Council, the first Colville woman ever to win such office. She was one of four representatives from the Inchelium-Boyds district.

Despite the many increasing demands due to her new political role, Mourning Dove continued her creative writing. She alluded to a new novel about "real" Indian life, one designed for translation into a film script. Ever self-effacing, she chided herself that this was but another "air castle." Much overworked, and always overcommitted, her health continued to deteriorate.

In the morning of August 8, 1936, the woman born Christine Quintasket, later known as Christal McLeod and Christina Galler, familiar to her wider audience as Mourning Dove, died in the hospital at Medical Lake, Washington.[13] Her death certificate gives the cause as "exhaustion from manic depressive psychosis." In death, as in life, the ups and downs of her spirit pursued her, now into the official records. Happily, her occupation was listed as housewife and authoress, for which she would have been grateful. Her body was carried back to Omak for burial in the local citizens' community cemetery, where she had selected and paid for a plot. Her fears that marriage would lessen her identity are borne out by the concrete slab atop the grave. It reads, simply, Mrs. Fred Galler. There is no way of knowing that this simple monument marks the last resting place of Christine Quintasket, the Colville Indian who became the first native woman novelist, Mourning Dove.

Only briefly was she remembered in the region where she lived and labored. On the Saturday following her death, events of her life were featured, complete with a publicity portrait, on the upper center of the obituary page in the Spokane *Spokesman-Review*, the most important newspaper in the Inland Empire. But soon thereafter, her achievements faded from popular memory, save for an occasional revival of interest among scholars, and the lasting regard and admiration of her family.

NOTES

1. Unless otherwise noted, all quotations from and references to Christine's correspondence are from Nelson Ault, The Papers of Lucullus Virgil McWhorter (Pullman, Wash.: Washington State University Library). For additional background on Christine, see Alice P. Fisher, "The Transportation of Tradition: A Study of Zitkala and Mourning Dove, Two Transitional Indian Writers" (City College of New York, Ph.D. dissertation, 1979); and Lois Ryker, Hu-Mi-Shu-Ma: Mourning Dove Was the Sweet Voice of the Indians of Eastern Washington, the *Seattle Times*, Sunday, February 18, 1963. For cultural background on the Salish peoples, see Verne Ray, *Cultural Relations in the Plateau of Northwestern America* (Los Angeles: The Southwest Museum, 1939).

2. To avoid unnecessary confusion, I have followed certain spelling conventions of the region. Thus, the reservation settled by many Salish and a few Sahaptian groups is known as Colville, while the member tribe formerly resident at Kettle Falls is here spelled Colvile, after the family name of Andrew Colvile, for whom the famous trading post there was named. Using phonemic spellings of native names would only add to the potential for confusion. For example, the native Okanogan word for chipmunk is *qwqwcwiya*, which is vastly simplified and anglicized for the novel's heroine and title, CO-GE-WE-A. Among the Okanogan, two divisions are commonly recognized. These are the River, American, or Southern Okanogan of Washington State, and the Lake, Canadian, or Northern Okanagan of British Columbia. The middle vowel changes at the international border.

3. *Co-Ge-We-A, The Half-Blood. A Depiction of the Great Montana Cattle Range* (Boston: The Four Seas Company, 1927); reprinted as *Cogewea* (Lincoln, Neb.: University of Nebraska Press, 1981).

4. Edited and illustrated by Heister Dean Guie, with notes by Lucullus V. McWhorter (Old Wolf), and a foreword by Chief Standing Bear (Caldwell, Idaho: The Caxton Printers).

5. Donald M. Hines, ed., *Tales of the Okanogans* (Fairfield, Wash.: Ye Galleon Press, 1976).

6. See David Chance, *The Influence of the Hudson's Bay Company on the Native Cultures of the Colville District*. Northwest Anthropological Research Notes, Memoir no. 2 (1973).

7. Chance, *Influence of the Hudson's Bay Company*, p.100.

8. This fear of rattlers is more perplexing than it may seem, for the Colvilles traditionally had special individuals who talked to snakes and kept people from harm. Other tribes had similar precautionary measures. Yet, for example, the Commanche medicine woman, Sanapia, had a "morbid fear" of rattlesnakes. These reptiles were sometimes seen as instruments of supernatural punishment, or as agents acting for sorcerers. See David Jones, *Sanapia: Commanche Medicine Woman* (New York: Holt, Rinehart, and Winston, 1972), p. 54.

9. While the Gallers had no children, Christine had at least one miscarriage, so she had reason to hope for children of her own.

10. *Kutenai Tales*, Bureau of American Ethnology Bulletin no. 5 (1918).

11. Red Dawn (Emily Williams), Indian Stories, *Washington Farmer* (June 12 and 26; July 3, 10, 17, 24, and 31; August 7, 14, 21, and 28; September 4, 11, and 18, 1930).

12. See John A. Ross, Political Conflict on the Colville Reservation, *Northwest Anthropological Research Notes* 2, no. 1 (1968), pp. 29–91.

13. It is a poignant coincidence that Mourning Dove died the same year that D'Arcy McNickle, the most famous Salish writer, published his first novel, *The Surrounded* (New York: Dodd and Mead, 1936).

CHAPTER 8

From Sylvester Long to Chief Buffalo Child Long Lance

Donald B. Smith[1]

PRESENTING BUFFALO CHILD LONG LANCE (1890–1932)

Born the last decade of the nineteenth century to a North Carolina household defined locally as "colored," with a family tradition of Indian ancestry, Sylvester Long escaped the burden of his ascribed racial identity by moving across the color line. But when many others of his place and time "passed" as Whites, he sought an Indian identity, asserting Eastern Cherokee ancestry. Admitted to Carlisle Indian School as such, he overcame the bigotry expressed by Oklahoma Cherokee at his negroid features and flourished, his large motivation and considerable talents allowing him to graduate with honors, next securing admission to an elite preparatory school on his merits. But he then turned down a presidential appointment to West Point, instead traveling north to enlist in the Canadian Army for World War I service in the trenches in France. Severely wounded, he took his discharge in Calgary, Alberta, where he embarked on a career as a journalist and *bon vivant*, still posing as Cherokee. In this profession, he displayed a huge capacity for empathizing with Canadian Indians, whose doleful conditions he exposed as an investigative reporter. But the core and borders of his own personal identity were unstable. Socially and geographically he had moved far from his roots in North Carolina, and he was constantly on the run, pushing the limits of his fragile public self beyond the tolerance of those closest to him, constantly altering and embellishing his life story. An experience with the Canadian Blood (a division of the Blackfeet) led him to don the title and name of Chief Buffalo Child Long Lance, then to publish a fanciful account of Custer's Last Stand and his own autobiography—as a Blood Chief. The ensuing fame carried him to Manhattan's high literary society, a starring role (as a noble Indian chief) in a film, even greater celebrity and popularity, and a final, emotionally wrenching confrontation with his brothers. They reminded him how far he had come from the restricted opportunities open to his southern Black family. Learning of the fatal illness of his father and unable to abandon the prestige he had won, Chief Buffalo Child then had to face himself as an aging Sylvester Long, the growing possibility of public exposure of his early identity, and the—for him—impossible quandary of being drawn to family responsibilities when threatened with loss of the prestige he had achieved. Within a year, after toying with life-threatening new hobbies such as flying and parachuting, he moved to Los Angeles as a wealthy woman's companion. There, his inner conflicts quickly proved too much, and he died as he had lived—alone, in a place he did not belong, by his own hand. It is impossible not to see the enormous tragedy and the great anger in Sylvester Long's lonely career, one lived in self-imposed exile. Had this talented man been born a generation later, he might have marched pridefully with Martin Luther King, or served the resurgent Lumbee Indians of North Carolina in a leadership capacity, his large personal assets enriched by the esteem of creative association with and contributions to a meaningful community. As it was, Sylvester Long became a sham to escape the socially imposed limits and handicaps of being a southern Black boy. His misfortune, then, was a life of surface images, spent with many idolizing acquaintances but no friend in whom he could fully confide. (J. A Clifton)

The handsome, dark-skinned man and the city editor of the *Vancouver Sun* talked earnestly on that day in late April 1922. Sylvester Long Lance had brought with him his *Calgary Herald* articles on the Plains Indians. Would the *Sun* like a similar series on the Indians of British Columbia?

As Long Lance, in his soft, cultured voice explained his background—as a "Cherokee Indian," the newspaper reporter scribbled down the details. He glanced over his stories on the Blackfoot, Sarcee, and Bloods, then finally broke his silence. Yes, they wanted the series for the Sunday *Sun*. Yes, he could use as his byline the name that the Bloods had given him in Alberta: Chief Buffalo Child.

The story first appeared on May 7th introduced by the *Sun's* city editor:

> Here's a regular story from a regular Indian. It was written by Chief Buffalo Long Lance of Calgary. He is one of the few outstanding figures of his race. He is a graduate of Carlisle Indian School and of St. John's Military Academy of Manlius, New York. He is the only Indian to be appointed to West Point, the United States Military Academy, by a president of the United States. Relinquished this appointment one year later to go overseas with the Canadian troops. Went overseas as a private, was commissioned and rose to the rank of captain. Twice wounded and decorated with the Croix de Guerre.

As suggested by the editor's phrase, "He is one of the few outstanding figures of his race," Indians faced much prejudice in British Columbia in the 1920s. Diamond Jenness, one of Canada's foremost anthropologists, traveled through the province at that time. Frequently he found people who spoke of the native population insultingly, as "Siwashes," and everywhere he heard "shiftless and unreliable" attributed to Indians.

The *Sun's* city editor knew little about the local Indians, who numbered less than a thousand out of the roughly 200,000 people in the immediate Vancouver area. They lived on the tiny Squamish reserves on the north shore of Burrard inlet opposite Vancouver's city center, and on the Musqueam reserve on the north arm of the Fraser River to the south. At best, only two Squamish Indians' names would roll off the editor's tongue: Andy Paull, the young and energetic secretary of the Squamish Council, and Chief Mathias

Sylvester Long's Travels and Transformations

1. 1890. born, Winston-Salem NC, as "Colored Boy," Sylvester Long

2. 1903: travels south & west (Perhaps as far as Oklahoma) w/Wild West Show

3. 1909: enters Carlisle Indian School (Carlisle PA) as Cherokee lad

4. 1912: enters St. John Military Academy (Syracuse, NY) as Cherokee, Sylvester Long Lance

5. 1916: To Montreal, Canadian Army, to trenches in France as Sergeant Long Lance.

6. 1918: Discharged for wounds, travels to Calgary AB as Captain Long Lance.

7. 1922: To Vancouver BC as newspaper reporter, becomes Blackfoot chief, Buffalo Child Long Lance

8. 1927: To New York as celebrity-playboy-author, Chief Buffalo Child

9. 1931: Exposed as ethnic poseur, to Los Angeles as ladies' man

10. 1932: End of trail in Los Angeles, death by suicide.

Capilano, the son of the late Chief Joe Capilano, who once presented a petition to King Edward VII in London, pleading for justice for the Indians of British Columbia. The editor directed Long Lance to see both men: Capilano at the reserve of the same name, opposite Vancouver's Stanley Park, and Paull at the Mission reserve, smack in the center of North Vancouver.

Chief Mathias proved most cooperative. Over a decade earlier, he and his father had helped another Indian writer from the east, Iroquois author Pauline Johnson, from Ontario. Just before her death in 1913, she adopted some of Joe Capilano's stories in her last book, *Legends of Vancouver*.

From Chief Mathias, Long Lance learned the story of the Squamishs' first sighting of an European ship.[2] At dawn, the scouts at the lookout point were startled to see a floating island before them, only a hundred yards or so from the shore. They raced back to the village to give the alarm. As they advanced toward it in their war canoes, the chief saw beings with the same grotesque faces as dead corpses. "Keep away, keep away—there are ghosts on it—I can see their pale faces sticking out of coffins!" He thought the overcoats worn by the pallid-looking men were their coffins.

For a long time, the warriors hesitated about boarding the schooner, until, with great misgivings, the bravest climbed the rope ladder onto the deck. The captain, on greeting them, advanced toward the foremost Indian with outstretched hand. The chief, never having heard of the handshake, thought they were being challenged to a showdown in Indian finger wrestling. He therefore waved away the man with whom the captain was trying to shake hands, and called for the Squamish strongman to accept the challenge. Now, seeing he was misunderstood, the captain shrugged, and approached the chief with outstretched hand. The chief then said to the strongman, "He doesn't want you. He thinks you are not strong enough," and with that, the chief refused to consider the captain's "challenge."

The strangers' gifts also greatly puzzled Mathias' ancestors. They gave the Indians what they believed was snow in a sack (flour), tree cankers (hard tack or sea biscuits), and finally buttons (coins). Long Lance loved this account, and included the full story on May 21st in his article on the Squamish.

On his first visit to meet Andy Paull, Long Lance took the ferry across to North Vancouver, where the Mission reserve was clearly marked by the tall, silver-painted towers of the Roman Catholic Church. Long Lance immediately liked the short but powerfully built man, who at thirty-six was only four years older than he. Paull had attended the local Catholic school and was further educated by Squamish elders, who selected him to become their future tribal spokesman. Only a few years before Long Lance's visit, Andy had visited practically every coastal village enlisting support for a new political organization, the "Allied Tribes of British Columbia," formed by the Indians to fight for their land rights.

Paull explained to his visitor the predicament confronting the British Columbian Indians. James Douglas, an early governor, had followed in the 1850s the practice of purchasing their lands, but after his retirement that policy ended. On much of the mainland and Vancouver Island, the miners, farmers, fishermen, and railway men began taking the Indians' forests, their rivers and lakes, their mountains—offering no payment. Only in the extreme northeastern corner of the province, in 1899, was a treaty signed, one that gave the Indians the same reserves, treaty money, and schools provided by the federal government in Ontario and on the prairies. British Columbia Indians, the provincial government contended, had no claim to the land. Automatically, on discovery by Britain, it belonged to the Crown. The government argued the small tracts of land already "given" the Indian bands as reserves sufficed.

Andy Paull was amazed that Long Lance, just arrived in British Columbia, immediately grasped their problems: the theft of their land, the strange customs forced on them, the constant pressure on them, until they could no longer breathe. In his series for the *Sun*, this amazing man, touted as a World War I hero, presented the Indians' side of the story. He defended their customs, and their right to hold to their traditions. Why, he asked, did the Department of Indian Affairs and the Christian missionaries try to destroy Indian society, to do away with totem poles and traditional carvings, to end important native ceremonies like the Potlatch? To a non-Indian audience, he also explained the Indians' requests for "full title to their reserve lands, as enjoyed by the other tribes of the Dominion, and for better education facilities and medical attention . . . instead of asking for financial remuneration for the reserve lands that have been taken over and sold by the province in the past, they are asking for extensions where they are most needed."

Following his accounts of the Squamish and Musqueam in Vancouver, Long Lance visited and wrote about the Nootka and Kwakiutl on Vancouver Island, and then the Lillooets, the Shuswap, and the Kootenays in the interior. Andy Paull, who kept abreast of everything written about the British Columbia Indians, must have been one of his readers during the summer of 1922. No doubt he admired the smooth prose of the likable "Cherokee" journalist who communicated his ideas so easily and forcefully in English.

One passage, which appeared in the *Sun* on May 19th, came directly from Paull. As Long Lance wrote:

> "Work and pray, pray and work, and then work and pray some more." This is the heart-breaking dictum that has for several generations been thrust upon the Indians, declare some of the prominent Indians of this province. With this ascetic regime he has been urged, if not compelled, to throw aside every native custom that formerly gave him self-respect and the strength of character to face the battles of his isolated existence. And in the same breath he was commanded to adopt a new set of rules totally foreign to his native outlook. All this in spite of the fact that the world has not yet recovered from the most prodigious war in its history—waged to subdue a nation whose avowed intention was to conquer all other nations and to impose upon them their way of "looking at things."

Perhaps Paull saw the "Indian" writer on his next visit to Vancouver in the summer of 1926. Invited to speak at the annual meeting of the American Railway Development Association, Long Lance addressed railroad men from across Canada and the United States in late June. Meanwhile, the "Chief" who had first introduced himself to Andy as an "Oklahoma Cherokee,"[3] now intimated he was a Blackfoot Indian from Alberta. He told his Hotel Vancouver audience:

> The first white man we saw was long before the Mounted Police came out, at the Hudson Bay Trading Post, Rocky Mountain House. It may be of interest to get an

Indian's first impression of the white man. The first thing he did was to go up to the white man and smell him. He said he smelled just like the cattle which we see today.[4]

Two years later, the Chief told the full story in his autobiography, *Long Lance*, published in New York. What a tale it was—the narrative could not have been more dramatic. He explained how he had been born in a Blackfoot tipi on the Great Plains. His first recollection as a child, he went on, was the aftermath of a Blackfoot skirmish with the Crows. "Women and horses were everywhere," he wrote, "but I remember only two women: my mother and my aunt." His mother's hand was bleeding. That scene haunted him, leaving "such a startling impression that all during my growing years it kept coming back to me. I wondered what it was and when I had seen that strange panorama, or whether I had ever seen it at all or not—whether it was just a dream." Only when he had "grown into boyhood" did his aunt confirm the details. After he told her his tale she exclaimed: "Can you remember that? You were only 14 months old then! It was when your uncle, Iron Blanket, was killed in a fight with the Crows—and your mother had cut off one of her fingers in mourning for him, as the women used to do in those days."

Actually, Long Lance's deception was greater than anything Andy Paull might have suspected. He had lived a lie since the age of eighteen, from the time he had entered Carlisle Indian School in 1909. His true life story has to do with the inequities of racial segregation, and flight from a community that stigmatized him as a Negro. Chief Buffalo Child Long Lance was one Sylvester Long. His father was of mixed Native American and probably of European and African ancestry as well. His mother was one-quarter Croatan (Lumbee) Indian and three-quarters White. And, in the climate of the times when Sylvester grew up, he was considered no different from any other "colored" person in Winston-Salem. More significantly, he considered *himself* no different. As far as he was concerned, his life held no more promise than that of any Black on the other side of the rope at segregated picnics, who said "Sir" and stepped into the gutter whenever a White man approached him.

Sylvester had grown up at the turn of the century, when the system of Jim Crow racial exclusion flourished. Like all those viewed as "colored," he underwent daily humiliations. It was not just sitting at the back of the streetcar that shamed him, or the fact that Blacks had to drink out of separate water fountains; it was knowing that the most inadequate White would always be considered superior to the most talented Black. His people were sternly reminded of this even in shoe stores. While others could try on as many pairs of shoes as they wanted, Blacks had just one chance. They had to go in knowing their exact size and style. But for Sylvester, there was one possible escape from the straight jacket of segregation: he looked like an Indian, as Americans, with their stereotypes, believed Indians should appear.

Sallie Long, Sylvester's mother, was part white, part Indian. In North Carolina, her mother, Adeline Carson, was classified as "Croatan," the name given at the turn of the century to people of mixed Indian, English, and African ancestry, who since have achieved the legal status of a federally recognized Indian group—the Lumbee.[5] Adeline's mother was an Indian from South Carolina and her own father was a White, Robert Carson. Sylvester would have known his maternal grandmother, for she lived into the 1920s. Sallie's natural father, that is, Sylvester's maternal grandfather, was Andrew Cowles, a local politician, who became a state senator. He died in 1881.

Joe Long's antecedents are not so easily identified. Probably partially Afro-American in ancestry, since he had grown up in slavery, he never knew his parents. His obituary in the Winston-Salem *Journal* of November 16, 1932, says he was born in 1853, a "member of the Catawba tribe of Indians," and, it continues, "as a boy he was taken into the family of the late Rev. Miles Long, serving his young master as a slave."

Whatever the full racial-ethnic background of his parents, Sylvester Long was born in Winston-Salem, North Carolina, on December 1, 1890. On reaching school age in 1897, Sylvester learned what it meant to be labeled "colored." Although there was a White elementary school only three blocks from his home, he had to attend the Black school two miles away. By 1904, he had enough of this. After finishing sixth grade, he left home and joined a traveling Wild West show. He was thirteen years old.

Little is known of his first five years away from home. On the road with other Wild West roustabouts, he undoubtedly passed as an Indian, capitalizing on his high cheek bones, straight, jet black hair, and coppery skin. Gradually he begun to think of and identify himself as an Indian. When he returned home in 1909, on August 10, he and his father applied for the boy's admission to the Carlisle Indian School in Pennsylvania. The school had been teaching Indians since a former Indian fighter, General R. H. Pratt, opened it in 1879. Carlisle, in the thinking of American philanthropists, was to inculcate Indian youth with the skills and virtues of Christian civilization. For Sylvester, it served other purposes.

Joe Long honestly could not say from which Indian society he was descended. Thus, in his son's application, he identified him with the best known in North Carolina: the Cherokees. Already, Sylvester spoke some of the language. While on the road with the Wild West show, a Cherokee named Whipporwill began teaching him. Although Carlisle preferred applicants listed as full bloods, all those claiming one-quarter or more Indian ancestry could apply. Sylvester enrolled as a Cherokee.

His early days at Carlisle were painful. The Cherokees were a proud, color sensitive, prejudiced people. Only recently slave holders, they had fought for the Confederacy in the Civil War. Generally speaking, the Cherokee students were anti-Black. So, from the first, they refused to accept Sylvester Long as one of them. The youth might pass as Indian among less sensitive whites; the young Cherokees proved a much tougher audience.

A teacher, James Henderson, later recalled in a confidential letter to the Commissioner of Indian Affairs: "The legitimate Cherokees were indignant at his posing as an Eastern Cherokee and a delegation of their number went to the Superintendent and protested his enrollment. I remember well that one of

SYLVESTER LONG AS ADOLESCENT (c. 1905). Born in Winston-Salem, North Carolina, both parents were born into slavery and he grew up in the "colored" community. He knew his parents claimed some Indian ancestry, but could not prove this. Capitalizing on his appearance, he joined a Wild West show, and later entered the Carlisle Indian School, where he built a new identity as Sylvester Long Lance, a Cherokee Indian. (Photograph by Newman Dalton, Courtesy of Glenbow Archives, Calgary, Alberta.)

"SYLVESTER CHAHUSKA LONG-LANCE—'CHIEF,' " was the caption beside this photograph in the St. John's Yearbook, 1915. *By now firmly identified as a Cherokee, Long Lance had demonstrated much talent and leadership ability and graduated from Carlisle before entering St. John's Military Academy. Soon he was awarded entry into West Point by President Woodrow Wilson as an Indian, an opportunity he did not take. (Glenbow Archives, Calgary, Alberta.)*

CHIEF BUFFALO CHILD ON EXHIBIT.
After service in the Canadian Army in World
War I, this "Oklahoma Cherokee" asked for his
discharge in Calgary, where he worked as a
reporter for three years. There, he developed a
great concern for the conditions of the Canadian
Indians. Ceremonially adopted as Buffalo Child
by the Blood Indians of the Blackfoot
Confederacy, he changed his name and identity
to Buffalo Child Long Lance, Blackfoot Chief.
While working as a journalist in Vancouver, he
returned several times to Calgary, where, in
1923, he appeared at the Calgary Stampede in
his pan-Indian costume. (Glenbow Archives,
Calgary, Alberta.)

THE BEAU BRUMMELL OF BROADWAY. Much in the public eye as a successful
magazine writer and author of his acclaimed autobiography as a Blackfoot Indian Chief, in
the late 1920s, Buffalo Child Long Lance moved to New York City. One of his first purchases
was a tuxedo and top hat, and he was quickly dubbed the Beau Brummell of Broadway by
fellow literary celebrity Irvin S. Cobb. Here,
he appears in his Broadway tribal costume, in
a sketch drawn by a close friend, the Princess
Alexandra (Kaiser Wilhelm's
daughter-in-law), who was then working as
an artist in New York and who presented
Long Lance to others of Manhattan's
community of exiled European nobility. But
his threatened exposure as an impostor forced
him to leave New York for Los Angeles in
1930, where he soon ended his career by
suicide. (Glenbow Archives, Calgary,
Alberta.)

their number indignantly exclaimed, 'Cherokee nigger!' " One of Sylvester's classmates at Carlisle was Emma Newashe, an Indian from Oklahoma. In a memoir about him published in 1933, she recalled how Henderson gave him the name Sylvester Long Lance. Presumably this was to help "Indianize" his identity and to ease his adjustment among his peers in school. At Carlisle, Sylvester found his claim to Indian status being legitimized.

Faced by criticism from his peers, Sylvester refused to back down. He knew that this was his one chance to escape the racial stigmas and the restricted opportunities of rigidly segregated life. He adopted the tactic known as *racial passing*, not uncommon in this era. What distinguished Sylvester Long Lance was that he assumed an Indian identity. For an individual alone to succeed in such a transformation requires an extraordinary demonstration of achievement, and personally securing the acceptance of others. At this, the young man worked hard. *The Carlisle Arrow* magazine noted on October 28, 1910: "Sylvester is interested in everything he does and he knows how to apply himself."

Carlisle provided a combined elementry and trade-school education. Boys were trained as carpenters, shoemakers, tailors, and printers. A bright, cooperative achiever, Sylvester won high marks in the shops and excelled in the classroom, particularly in English and history. His teachers quickly recognized his ability and he, in turn, found a new self-confidence.

As Long Lance, he went out for football, but his best sport was long-distance running, at which he was superb. In his second year at Carlisle, he made the track team. He later claimed that in three successive races he had defeated the famous Jim Thorpe, a Sac Indian, in the three-mile run. In 1912, Thorpe was selected to represent the United States at the Stockholm Olympics: he picked Long Lance, two years his junior, as his training partner, and they remained good friends until Long Lance died. When Thorpe played baseball with the New York Giants after World War I, he gave Long Lance a picture of himself in his baseball uniform, and wrote at the bottom: "High Chief—Remember the mile runs, was great training for the Olympics."

Carlisle's teachers helped Long Lance develop his appreciation of literature and encouraged him to write. From the other students, he learned much about their tribes' customs and legends. An unusually talented, skilled, good-natured storyteller himself, as Chief Buffalo Long Lance he would later use much of this material to enhance his public image and to achieve success.

Sylvester Long Lance, then twenty-one, graduated at the head of Carlisle's 1912 senior class. The school immediately enrolled him at Conway Hall, the preparatory school for Dickinson, a neighboring liberal-arts college. The following year, he won a scholarship to St. John's Military Academy, near Syracuse, New York, where he studied military history, organization, and tactics. In his senior year, he won high marks and played on both the school's track and football teams. In June 1915, President Woodrow Wilson selected him as one of his six presidential appointments to West Point. Long Lance was to report to Fort Slocum for the qualifying examinations the following March. All this recognition marks unusually high academic achievement and displays of Sylvester's considerable talents.

Long Lance corresponded with his family reporting his successes. The Longs also heard of his appointment from their daily paper. Like hundreds of other newspapers across the United States, the Winston-Salem *Daily Sentinel* carried the story in late June 1915, on page one with the headline: "Full Blooded Cherokee to Enter West Point."

The Longs quietly kept their pride to themselves. After Sylvester had left for Carlisle, not much had changed for them. Joe continued working as a janitor in the local school system. Though the fair-skinned Abe and Walter might have been able to "pass" as white in a northern city, they stayed in Winston. Their friends and family were all there. Abe had married a dark-complexioned girl, and so would Walter after World War I. In the city, Abe ran a smoke shop and Walter worked at a newsstand. Walter wanted to become a policeman, but coloreds were automatically denied this opportunity.

Long Lance knew that if he really wanted to get ahead, he would have to dissociate himself completely from family. West Point would not admit him if the president discovered his parents were known as colored. It was Woodrow Wilson, after all, who had introduced into Congress the greatest flood of discriminatory legislation in American history. He had proposed twenty bills advocating the segregation of the races in all areas. Although most of the legislation failed to pass, by executive order, Wilson made Negro federal employees eat their lunches in separate rooms and use separate washrooms. A colored could never succeed in Wilson's part of a racially segregated America. As an Indian, it was still difficult. But Long Lance knew that with "a dash of initiative, grit and determination" (as he put it once in an address to some Indian students), he could make it.

As it turned out, Long Lance never went to West Point. The bloodiest war in history was raging in Europe, and he decided to prove himself immediately in combat. It was 1916, and the United States had not yet entered the war, so he traveled north to Canada and enlisted in Montreal. As he wrote in *Maclean's* in 1926:

> Three weeks after I had 'coughed' and said 'Ah-h' for the medical officer, I was on my way to France on the Olympic, as Sergeant B. C. Long Lance, C. Company, 97th Battalion, Canadian Expeditionary force.

At the front, he saw "men gutted and lacerated day in and day out." He fought and escaped injury in the terrible battle of Vimy Ridge. But one month later, his luck gave out. As he wrote to a friend in New York:

> I am in a field hospital convalescing from a wound in the head received a couple of weeks ago. Nothing serious; only a piece of shrapnel in the back of the head and a broken nose—the latter sustained in falling on my face, I presume. I came through the April 9 scrap [Vimy Ridge] without a scratch . . . only to get hit a month later on one of the quietest days we have had lately. Such is war!

Shortly after his release, he was wounded in the legs during another attack. He credited the fact that he was an athlete and in excellent physical condition for his escape from double amputation. Invalided to England, there he served with the British Army for a year. Asked where he would prefer his discharge, he chose the last Canadian province to be settled, distant Alberta, by the Rocky Mountains of Western Canada.

After demobilization, Long Lance joined the *Calgary Herald* as a cub reporter, and during the next three years, he covered every beat: police to sports to city hall. To enhance his image in town, he told those who inquired that he had won the *Croix de Guerre*, and he promoted himself from sergeant to captain. With customary enthusiasm, he became involved in the community around him. He refereed boxing matches at the YMCA, coached football, and helped at the Calgary Stampede. Then, in the summer of 1921, he began to visit the Indians on reserves around the city.

As a rule, Indians were treated despicably in the 1920s. In 1921, farmers around Calgary were paying European immigrants $4 a day for harvest work, but Indians only $2.50. The federal government regarded them as a dying race and did little for their welfare. All too often, proper health services were denied them. Their average life span was less than half that of the national norm.[6] In school history texts, the Indians were portrayed as filthy, childlike, cruel, and constantly at war. Looking around him, Long Lance felt it was time the true conditions of modern Indians were revealed.

On June 11, 1921 his first article on the Blackfoot appeared in the *Herald*. The title of the piece left no doubt about his convictions and determination: "Blackfoot Indians of this District have in the last Fifty Years Evolved from Savage Hunters into an Industrious People. Struck like a Thunderbolt with White Man's Civilization, These Indians were Forced Overnight into a Complete Change of Perspective—Have They Benefited by the Civilization?— White Man's Evils Caused Them No Little Handicap."

Long Lance mentioned he obtained much of his information about modern conditions on the Blackfoot reserve from the Indian agent, George Gooderham. Their first meeting proved embarrassing. Long Lance handed Gooderham his card, but the agent was too preoccupied to read it. From his visitor's dark complexion, Gooderham assumed he was a *West* Indian. When Long Lance said he wanted to write an article on the Blackfoot, Gooderham showed him around the reserve, explaining everything simply, thinking Long Lance had never seen an Indian before. There was a long, polite silence; finally Long Lance identified himself. Despite this awkward beginning, they became close friends.

As Gooderham later recalled, Long Lance had "a wonderful ability to write imaginative stories from what he had known and seen, something that would appeal to the whites." As far as the Blackfoot were concerned, the agent frankly felt Long Lance "didn't know much about Indian life, but he did in many, many of his writings go to the very rock bottom and get the correct story of the life of whatever Indians he was writing about. He was a fantastic man. He could do anything."

During the summer of 1921, Long Lance visited other reserves. In July, he called on the Sarcees near Calgary. He found them in horrible condition. As the headline read, the tribe was "Gradually Dying Off Owing to Ravages of Tubercular Trouble." The Sarcee population had fallen from 300 in 1877 to 155 in 1921. He wrote in the *Herald* of July 23, 1921:

> The plight of the Sarcee is a real tragedy. Little do the people of Calgary realize that they are daily witnessing the passing of a nation as dramatically as any that have been depicted by the pen of J. Fenimore Cooper.

In August, he traveled south to the Cardston to visit the Bloods, where he met Rev. S. H. Middleton, principal of St. Paul's, the Anglican school on the reserve. The two men became friends. Indeed, Long Lance came to consider the priest as his closest friend and named him sole executor in the will he signed on March 30, 1929. At Middleton's suggestion, the Bloods, in February 1923, adopted the Indian newspaperman, giving him a new name—Buffalo Child.

Howard Kelly was a Calgary friend who, at the age of nineteen, was sports editor of the *Herald*. Years later, Kelly remembered his Indian colleague:

> Long Lance used to come to our home a lot, and have meals at our place. In any social get-together he always became the focal point in conversation because of his laughter, his merriment.

There was much anti-Indian prejudice in the Canadian West in those days, but what riled Long Lance most was being seen as Black, as occasionally happened. One such incident was recorded by veteran journalist Fred Kennedy, who worked with Long Lance on the *Herald*. In his book, *Alberta Was My Beat*, Kennedy recalls the time when he was assigned to cover a regimental reunion dinner at the Pallister Hotel. There he found himself at the same table as Long Lance, who held the rank of militia captain in the 50th Battalion.

After dinner, Kennedy, Long Lance, and two others walked across the street to McCrohan's restaurant. They sat down at the horseshoe counter. About ten minutes later, two men entered. Kennedy wrote: "The waitress motioned them to stools alongside our group. They moved forward, stopped and then I heard one of them exclaim, 'I am not sitting alongside any nigger.' The remark was obviously directed at Long Lance."

The target of these slurs paid no attention, so the man repeated it—louder.

> Long Lance excused himself and then, turning to the man who stood there glowering at him, he said, 'Were you addressing me, Sir?' 'I sure as hell was.' Long Lance's left didn't seem to travel anymore than eight inches but when it connected with the man's jaw, he went out like a light.

In spring 1922, Long Lance became restless. For months, he had covered city hall; since the previous fall, he had been given no more Indian assignments. So he decided to liven up the municipal meetings with a mock terrorist attack. Donning a mask, he slipped into the council chamber and placed inside the door of the mayor's office a gas inspector's bag that looked suspiciously like a bomb, the fuse attached sputtering sparks. City commissioners and the mayor ran for their lives, the mayor colliding with his secretary in a jammed exit door. One commissioner dived under a table. Another leaped through layers of storm window glass, then jumped ten feet to the ground. Over the next several days, the rival newspaper, the *Albertan*, played this prankster story for its laugh value. But the *Herald* was not amused: Long Lance was summarily fired.

That proved a blessing in disguise: it forced him into what became a profitable freelance career. In May, he left for the Pacific Coast, where he convinced the *Vancouver Sun* to let him write a series on the Indians of British Columbia. He visited tribes throughout the province and his several articles attracted the attention of editors of both the *Regina Leader* and the *Winnipeg Tribune*. After four months in British Columbia, and several months in Saskatchewan, he joined the *Tribune*, writing about the Indians of Manitoba. Buffalo Child Long Lance, a Blood Indian, was now his byline. On the Assiniboine reserve at Sintaluta, just east of Indian Head, Saskatchewan, Long Lance met Chief Carry-the-Kettle, one of the few noted war chiefs still living in 1922. This aged warrior was then 107 years old. He had led his people to war when Sitting Bull, Crowfoot, and Big Bear were still in their infancy.[7]

Although ill and enfeebled, Carry-the-Kettle insisted on walking a hundred yards unsupported so he might greet Long Lance in the manner becoming an Assiniboine chief of his fame and standing. "He was being visited by a chief of a former enemy tribe," Long Lance later wrote, "and—as his people told me later—he would have walked that hundred yards had he known that it would have cost him his life." "Chief" Buffalo Child Long Lance continued:

> Though Chief Carry-the-Kettle had killed more than one hundred men on the war path, there was something in his face that was truly spiritual—a remarkable gleam of human goodness that made him bigger in my eyes than any man I have seen. When he had to refer to his killings on the warpath he did it with a whimsical air of apology which made it evident that it was distasteful to him. In spite of his destructive record, Chief Carry-the-Kettle was one of those men in whose fearless hands a person would gladly place his life, if it depended on a matter of fair judgment and the kindness of human nature.

On February 16, 1923, four months after their visit, the old Assiniboine chief died. In his memory, Long Lance wrote: "If there is a Heaven and Chief Carry-the-Kettle did not go to it, then I want to go where he went."

During the fall of 1923, in what Long Lance described as "a beautiful stretch of bush-dotted prairieland," twenty miles northeast of Duck Lake,

Saskatchewan, he visited Sounding Sky and Spotted Calf, parents of the Indian martyr Almighty Voice. They still lived only four miles from the bluff where, twenty-six years earlier, their son made his last stand against the Mounties. Long Lance reported how he spent a week with them. Within two days, the old people, who had refused since 1897 to talk about their son's death, started to discuss the tragedy. They told him about their son's arrest for killing a government range steer, and his imprisonment in the Duck Lake guardhouse. As Long Lance explained in *Maclean's* on January 1, 1924: "I had not been there two days when the old mother asked me to exchange names with her and become her adopted son. Under these friendly relations, the old people, without my asking, volunteered to tell me the whole story of their son's career."

Long Lance continually felt impelled to embellish his stories. Almighty Voice apparently escaped from the jail at Duck Lake after a police officer, by mistake, left the key in the prison door when leaving one evening. Long Lance, though, improved on these events, claiming the corporal in charge, through an interpreter, jokingly told Almighty Voice they were "going to hang him for killing that steer." In Long Lance's words, "hardly did the corporal realize the terrible effect which this innocent little joke was going to have on this untutored young Indian." The young Cree escaped and shot dead the first Mountie to track him down.

Then began the greatest manhunt in the history of the Canadian West. For two years, Almighty Voice, "famed throughout the region as a runner, hunter, a man of indomitable courage and independence," evaded pursuit. When finally tracked down, it was because he wanted to be found. Joined by two relatives, he had decided that he would die in one last defiant stand. The determined trio chose a thicket in a half-mile clump of bush lying on rolling, open prairie land.

The large force of police and volunteers charged twice, Long Lance reported. One of Almighty Voice's comrades was hit and died, but he and the other Indian shot down the postmaster of Duck Lake and two more Mounties. The police and their deputies called for reinforcements. Mounties came from Duck Lake, Prince Albert, and Regina, and hundreds of volunteers rode to the scene. That night, Almighty Voice, still unconquerable, shouted off the bluff to the troops: "We have had a good fight today. I have worked hard and I am hungry. You have plenty of food; send me some, and tomorrow we'll finish the fight." All night his mother chanted to him from a nearby hill, urging him "to die the brave that he had shown himself to be." Now and then Almighty Voice would yell back through the darkness: "I am almost starving. I am eating the bark off the trees. I have dug into the ground as far as my arm will reach, but can get no water. But have no fear—I'll hold out to the end."

By the next evening, "the field guns were in place—a nine-pounder and a seven-pounder—and at 6 o'clock the first shells were sent thundering into the thicket." For three days, the Indians had not eaten, drank, or slept. The besieging force kept up the barrage for hours. When they stopped shooting, they heard Almighty Voice: "You have done well, but you will have to do better." That night, sensing the inevitable, Almighty Voice's mother changed her chant to a proud lament: a death song for her son.

"At 6 o'clock the next morning," Long Lance wrote, "the big guns began belching forth their devastating storm of lead and iron in deadly earnestness. It was obvious that no living things could long endure their steady beat. At noon the pelting ceased." Almighty Voice was dead. The bluff where he and his two companions died, concluded Long Lance, "marks the spot where the North American Indian made his last stand against the white man."

Long Lance had a tremendous vitality and zest for life; his prose moves along at the same rapid pace of his own life. How he loved it! In the early 1920s, he covered the world heavyweight boxing matches, traveling across the continent for a number of Western Canadian newspapers. Life was exciting, significant, fully dimensioned, especially at ringside, "where crushing blows are swishing through the air like nine-pounders, where bulky frames are tottering like giant buildings in an earthquake."

These were his salad days and he knew it. His friends in Calgary and Winnipeg remember him as a manly, happy-go-lucky fellow, full of fun. He would dare anything. When challenged by a fellow reporter to duplicate a feat of the "Human Fly," a successful stuntman of the day, Long Lance stood on his head on the parapet of a Winnipeg skyscraper. He boxed, played lacrosse, snowshoed, and everywhere he went succeeded with women—married or otherwise.

One woman, at the Banff resort, almost caused his downfall. Long Lance was at the Banff Springs Hotel in the summer of 1926, working as the Canadian Pacific Railroad's press representative for Western Canada. At the hotel, he met a rich Chicago lawyer's wife. She, her husband, and their houseman were spending the summer in a rented home nearby. The lawyer went to bed early, the wife late.

The couple's houseman took violent exception to his employer's wife having an affair with an Indian. One night he rushed at Long Lance with a razor. The Chief saw him in time and with all his great strength smashed an iron poker over the servant's skull, almost killing him. For days, it appeared the assailant might die and Long Lance would face a murder charge. The man survived, but the Chief was out of a job again.

But this time, Chief Buffalo Child Long Lance had no cause for worry. He had already acquired a name through his articles in major Canadian periodicals and newspapers such as *Maclean's* and the *Toronto Star Weekly*, as well as in equally prominent American magazines like *Mentor* and *Cosmopolitan*, even *Good Housekeeping*. And he had an ace in the hole—a story so sensational he knew he could sell it for almost any price. *Cosmopolitan*, then a general-interest magazine, swallowed his latest fanciful tale whole and published it.

In July 1927, "The Secret of the Sioux" hit the newsstands. After interviewing several old Sioux warriors living in Canadian exile, Long Lance claimed General George Armstrong Custer was not killed by Indians at the Battle of Little Big Horn. He did not die with a revolver in each hand, his golden locks bravely waving in the wind, besieged by thousands of Sioux—as portrayed in the famous Budweiser tavern lithograph. He made no courageous "last stand." Instead, Custer's was a coward's exit—at the height of the battle, the man popularly portrayed as one of America's great military heroes committed suicide.

The protests of American patriotic groups did Long Lance no harm. Thanks to the publicity, he became an overnight celebrity. *Cosmopolitan* asked him to write a book for boys, so he stayed in New York to round it out. First, he reworked several of his published articles on the Blackfoot—even slipping in Carry-the-Kettle and Almighty Voice, then drafted new material on growing up among the Blackfoot. Much of his raw material was gathered from Mike Eagle Speaker, a young Blood student, then studying at the agricultural college at Claresholm, south of Calgary. Long Lance met Mike earlier through the Rev. S. H. Middleton. By late 1927, he completed the book, all 72,000 words, and he presented *Cosmopolitan* with his fictionalized account of Blackfoot life before the Indians settled on reserves. Later, Long Lance told a friend, "They thought it was too good for a boy's book, and forthwith decided to run it as my autobiography." *Long Lance* appeared in the fall of 1928, brazenly described as his life story.

The celebrity status brought by publication of *Long Lance* made him the target of many journalists' interviews. The acid test for the Chief came in early October when he was interviewed by Gladys Baker, New York correspondent for a daily paper that proclaimed itself "the South's Greatest Newspaper," the *News-Age-Herald* of Birmingham, Alabama. Now, the Sylvester Long behind the public Long Lance had to be especially cautious. He certainly had not forgotten the scars of his childhood in Winston-Salem. One slip on his part could lead to exposure.

Gladys Baker and Long Lance met in a small French restaurant on Eighth Avenue. It proved a "no contest" engagement. The Chief impressed her on all counts—first because of appearance. In her article for her southern readers, she described him as "distinguished" looking, making what she considered the supreme compliment, "were it not for his straight black hair, which is cut close to his head, and his skin, which is not red but more the color of ivory-toned parchment, he might be taken for a Wall Street broker." She loved his conversation and his manners. "His voice is low, harmonious and dramatic. He speaks without a trace of an accent. His words attest a wide and tastefully acquired vocabulary. His gestures are broad and simple, his manner one of ease and gallantry."

Not just Miss Baker, but all New York celebrated the Blackfoot Chief. At first, Long Lance loved the attention and excitement. On June 8, 1928, he wrote his Calgary friend Howard Kelly about house parties on Long Island: "You know the kind we've often seen in the movies, but never in practice. Well, I can tell you now that they exist." While in New York, he became a close friend of the Kaiser's former daughter-in-law, Princess Alexandra. After the war, this noblewoman left the Kaiser's son to become an artist in New York. In the Crystal Room of the Ritz Hotel, he danced with Rudolph Valentino's exotic ex-wife, Natasha Rambova (born Winifred Shaughnessy).

> A social lion of the season is an Indian—Buffalo Child Long Lance—who has been invited everywhere (wrote one New York columnist).

The New York society gossip writer Walter Winchell once encountered him at play. In his syndicated column, Winchell observed, "Chief Long Lance, the Indian lecturer, and the first Mrs. Guy Bolton are uh-huh. . ."

For "the Beau Brummell of Broadway," as his friend and writer Irvin S. Cobb called him, there was only one more world to conquer: Hollywood. Soon, he signed a contract for a leading role in a film titled *The Silent Enemy*, to be made in Canada by Douglas Burden, a producer associated with the American Museum of Natural History. Paramount distributed the film. About Indian life in North America before Columbus, the "Silent Enemy" in this movie was hunger. Long Lance played the lead, Baluk, who saves his people. When released in 1930, *Variety* warned: "*The Silent Enemy* is interesting, educational, and a fine study anywhere, but it has not the commercial draw exhibitors look for." *The Silent Enemy* suffered at the box office also, because it was a silent film just when the talkies were capturing the market. But Long Lance received praise for his screen performance. *Variety* endorsed him: "Chief Long Lance is an ideal picture Indian, because he is a full-blooded one . . . an author of Indian lore, and now an actor in fact." And the public loved him. *Screenland* reported in its issue for October 1930, that "ever since the picture was released, Long Lance, one of the few real one hundred-per-cent Americans, has had New York right in his pocket."

But success would not stay sweet, for in 1930, Long Lance's past caught up with him. Unknown to him, his father had been dangerously ill all year. He was in the hospital more than once and needed a major operation. How could the family possibly pay for it? His brother, Abe, was then working as the manager of the colored section of a Winston-Salem movie theater. His other brother, Walter, thwarted in his attempts to join the police force, had opened a detective agency in the Black community. But in that second year of the Depression, business for both was terrible. Pushed to the wall, they had only one option left. One of them would have to ask Sylvester for help. They had followed his career, with what mixture of pride, perhaps resentment, we can only guess. They knew where he was. On December 31, 1930, Walter left for New York.

The brothers met in Manhattan during the first week of January. Sylvester had not seen Walter for twenty-two years, since the morning he left home for the Carlisle Indian School. After the meeting, Sylvester lay awake most of the night. "I have never," he later wrote Walter, "been torn like this before." Then he promised: "I am going to try to make some money now, so that I can help lift the burden." From then until shortly before his own death, Long Lance regularly sent home hundreds of dollars. At the same time, he forwarded money to his old friend, Jim Thorpe, who was also going through hard times.

The forty-first and last year of his life was unhappy. Long Lance took up flying and performed the extraordinary feat of soloing after only five hours and twenty minutes of instruction in the air (and then made three loops for good measure). He began parachuting, and even earned his commercial flying license. But his old zest for life had gone. He had spent twenty years building himself into a superhuman, not simply a successful, accomplished Indian, but a walking, talking image of the Noble Savage. Then, he saw Walter again and was pulled back by his roots, the troubles of his family. Suddenly, an agonizing lesson was driven into his thoughts. While he had achieved phenomenal public success in two countries—as athlete, soldier, author, bon vivant, and actor, his brothers and family still experienced the degrading absurdities of racial segregation.

All Long Lance had wanted was to fulfill himself as a human being, to achieve personal goals blocked by the social accidents and circumstances of his birth. To do that, he had to become more of an Indian than he really was; but he paid his dues. By his own demonstrated achievement, in his successful career, in his book and articles, he had tried to strike down many of the ridiculous notions prevailing about Indians. But now, what could he do? If he went home, the world would discover his parents were identified as "coloreds," and his public identity and writing might be discredited. At the same time, knowing how badly his family needed him, he could not endure the guilt of staying away.

Finally, Long Lance decided in May 1931 to leave New York for Los Angeles, where his friend Jim Thorpe lived. There, he found employment as the secretary and bodyguard of Anita Baldwin, daughter of a rich mining magnate, for her forthcoming European tour. For years, this wealthy woman had been interested in North American Indians; she owned a large collection of books on the subject. Much impressed by this extraordinary Plains Indian, following their return from Europe, she paid for his additional flying lessons at the neighboring Glendale airport. She also allowed Long Lance, whenever he wished, to use the library at her mansion at Arcadia outside Los Angeles. He often did so.

But these fresh adventures did not still his anguish. On Saturday, March 19, 1932, he talked to his dentist of suicide. That night he went to a movie, then returned to the Glendale Hotel and began drinking. When he came down into the lobby from his room, the desk clerk noticed he carried a pistol. Then he was seen entering a taxi, which carried him to Anita Baldwin's estate, arriving about midnight.

Anita Baldwin, reading in her library, heard him arrive and greeted Long Lance at the door. His behavior startled her, as she later testified in a written statement read at the coroner's inquest: "He acted in a manner that I had never seen before, being quite abrupt, very depressed and non-communicative." She left him on his own in the library.

Alone with his thoughts for nearly two hours, Long Lance at last placed the muzzle of the new .45 caliber Colt against his right temple and pulled the trigger. When the police arrived, they found his body slumped on a leather settee at the end of the library, the revolver clutched in both hands.

So much of his earnings, royalties, and fees he had given away; after his death he left almost nothing. Once his personal effects were sold and bank accounts closed, there was only about $700 left. He was buried in the British Empire veterans' section of the Inglewood cemetery, Los Angeles.

Andy Paull, who read everything he could about Indians, must have noticed the *Vancouver Sun* article captioned, "Long Lance is Suicide. Former Vancouver News Writer Ends Life in L.A." The story appeared with a photo of the Chief in his Plains Indian regalia on March 21, 1932—almost ten years exactly after Andy and he had met. What would the Squamish Indian leader have said of Long Lance had he discovered his original identity? Would Paull's judgment have changed?

Probably not. For on anyone's terms, Long Lance was a survivor and an achiever, in an era when it was difficult for non-Whites merely to exist with dignity. And he had employed his newly adopted identities, his position, and his skills to advocate the rights of Canadian Indians during the troubled 1920s. While the assumed persona of Chief Buffalo Child Long Lance certainly nourished the wants of the man born Sylvester Long, the man beneath the image used it as an instrument to serve the needs of others.

Whatever name he bore—Sylvester Long, Long Lance, Chief Buffalo Child, the person was friend to many, Indian or otherwise, Canadian or American. While expressing and perfecting his own talents, he warmed many spirits, informed a multitude of readers, aroused public awareness of problems long ignored. Long Lance's friends were shocked and incredulous when they heard that he had taken his life. Jim Thorpe, who had received a letter from his old Carlisle friend only a week earlier, later said that Long Lance had given "no indication of worry or despondency." Yet, the imposter's friends knew little about the complex and introspective Long Lance, a man tortured by his own lies and deceptions.

To lead a full life, Sylvester Long was forced by a vicious racial system to conceal his true background. But his various assumed identities were more than simple instruments for his passage from a context where inequality would be forced on him, to one where he could be measured by his deeds. In his public life, he became an effective civil rights activist, employing his earned prestige to serve others. In the end, the terrible personal cost proved too much for the inner man to bear. He chose to leave his life as he had built it: of his own volition, by his own hands. Of his life and its ending, what can we say, except, *Tout comprendre c'est tout pardonner*—To understand all is to pardon all.

NOTES

1. Much of the material in this essay originally appeared in my two-part article on Long Lance in *The Canadian Magazine*, February 7 and 14, 1976; (my thanks to Alan Walker and David Cobb for their assistance with its presentation); and in a short essay in *Horizon Canada* 4, no. 47 (1985), pp. 1,124–1,128. The fullest treatment of the "Chief" is given in my biography, *Long Lance: The True Story of an Impostor* (Toronto: Macmillan, 1982). The University of Nebraska Press published an American edition of the work in 1983. I have footnoted in this essay several additional references not cited in *Long Lance*. The National Film Board of Canada has produced a one-hour documentary-drama about his life, *Long Lance*, which was released in January 1987.

2. Chief Mathias Capilano's version of the arrival of the Europeans also appears in "Strangers Appear on English Bay," *Romance of Vancouver*. Compiled by Native Sons of British Columbia, 2 (1926), pp. 5–6.

3. The obituary in the *Vancouver Sun*, March 20, 1932, recalls that he was Cherokee.

4. Long Lance quoted in *American Railway Development Association. Proceedings of the Eighteenth Annual Meeting. Hotel Vancouver, Vancouver, B.C., Canada, June 23, 24, and 25, 1926* (St. Paul, Minn.: Riverside Press, 1926), p. 26.

5. Karen I. Blu provides an up-to-date review of the Lumbees and their history in her study, *The Lumbee Problem: The Making of an American Indian People* (Cambridge: Cambridge University Press, 1980).

6. Hugh A. Dempsey, "The Blackfoot Indians," in *Native Peoples: The Canadian Experience*, ed., R. Bruce Morrison and C. Roderick Wilson (Toronto: McClelland and Stewart, 1986), p. 432.

7. Edmund Morris, *The Diaries of Edmund Montegue Morris. Western Journeys 1907–1910. Transcribed by Mary Fitz-Gibbon* (Toronto: Royal Ontario Museum, 1985), p. 74. Entry in his diary for the summer of 1908. Frank Dumont, nephew of Gabriel Dumont, the great Métis leader, told Edmund Morris the story of Almighty Voice.

CHAPTER 9

"A Place in Your Mind for Them All": Chief William Berens

Jennifer S. H. Brown[1]

PRESENTING WILLIAM BERENS (1865–1947)

Much of what we know of Saulteaux (Manitoba Ojibwa) culture, social institutions, and psychology came out of a long relationship between anthropologist A. Irving Hallowell and Chief William Berens. Owing to the methods of anthropology at that time, Berens never appeared in the published record as a whole, understandable person. He was a man of many secular parts—hunter, trapper, commercial fisherman, guide, anthropologist's key informant, surveyor's assistant, carpenter, farmer, stockman, and—like his father—band chief. Also, Berens was a marginal person of much experience in the larger Canadian world, whose antecedents lay in the northern fur trade, both Indian and European. Unlike some others of the region, however, his paternal line was Ojibwa, for his family ties to Anglo-European life and culture were through his mother. The great-grandson of a Great Lakes-area Ojibwa who pioneered Ojibwa occupation of Manitoba, his life was spent on an ethnic crossroads. From his father and his father's father, he drew the core of his identity and knowledge, notwithstanding the dual heritages to which he was exposed. A member of a converted Methodist family, in his early life he elected not to seek and take traditional Ojibwa sacred power as his paternal ancestors had done, but such knowledge was an inescapable part of his being and experience. Encouraged and directed by his father to welcome and cope with social and technological change, Berens saw and later used the first steamboats on the region's waterways, witnessed the first treaty negotiated with his community, and—as band chief—insisted that his young men not fight with the Canadian Army during World War II. Clearly, Chief William Berens was not a pristine aboriginal Ojibwa from a static, unchanged Saulteaux community. He was the product of several centuries of cultural change and adaptation. Yet, despite his life-long involvement with things and ways Anglo-Canadian, he lived largely with an inner Ojibwa world view, sensitized to Ojibwa views of sacred power and well-being, committed to fundamental Ojibwa norms and styles in personal relations and interaction. Born to and socialized in a dual cultural heritage, Berens was master of the delicate art of accommodating pressures for change to a persistent Ojibwa personal and group identity. His skill in these respects was amply displayed in his adult career as band chief, being neither the first nor the last in his line, a man whose person was marked by historical continuity combined with creative adaptation to the altered circumstances of himself, his family, and his community. (J. A. Clifton)

In the summer of 1940, William Berens, chief of the Berens River band of Saulteaux Indians* on the east shore of Lake Winnipeg, Manitoba, recounted his reminiscences to anthropologist A. Irving Hallowell, who was completing the last of several summers of fieldwork in the area.[2] We have no first-hand descriptions of that occasion. But the two men must have spent many hours together while Berens talked and Hallowell wrote, to set down the closely written fifty-six-page manuscript that resulted. And at that, the text covered only the first forty of Berens's seventy-five years, ending abruptly as of about 1905.

From this document, however, as through Hallowell's other fieldnotes and writings and a variety of additional sources, we attain a rather close view of several sides of this complex and versatile personage, who was so important both to his people and, through Hallowell's writings, to a host of scholars and students in anthropology and psychology. He was a community leader for thirty years, from the death of his father, Chief Jacob Berens, in 1916, until his own demise in 1947. And as Hallowell's friend and collaborator, he mediated the transmission and interpretation of his people's history, religion, and world view to communities extending far beyond his own.

Aside from these roles, he lived a life of many intersecting circles. He was born in the mid-1860s, shortly before Canada's confederation as a dominion in 1867, and before that new nation acquired title to Rupert's Land, as the Hudson's Bay Company [HBC] territories west and north of the Great Lakes were known. He vividly remembered his father's signing of Treaty No. 5 in 1875 and the beginnings of the reserve and mission phase of his people's existence. Besides being chief, his occupations later ranged from hunting, trapping, fur trading, and commercial fishing to guiding and interpreting for surveyors, Indian agents, and anthropologists. Near the end of his life, he occasioned some controversy for the way that he led his community through the World War II years.

Through A. I. Hallowell's agency as scribe, questioner, and listener between 1930 and 1940, William Berens generated close to 200 pages of manuscript text, set down in English in Hallowell's hand. These rich materials (stories, myths, anecdotes, accounts of dreams, and the reminiscences noted earlier) might be considered easy grist for the biographer's mill. Yet, their use to reconstruct a life history in our search for William Berens presents problems, as does the biographical enterprise itself for any North American Indian. Biography, and particularly autobiography, are historically recent European literary inventions, celebrating the progressive and cumulative careers of individuals. Like the disciplines of history and anthropology

---

*Saulteaux is an older French name for the widely dispersed peoples later called Ojibwa or Chippewa, and is still used for these bands in Manitoba. Ojibwa and Chippewa are alternate spellings of one word. The former is preferred by the people themselves and is standard in Canada, while Chippewa is commonly used in the United States. The Saulteaux are among the groups known as Northern Algonquian.

Chief William Berens's Territory

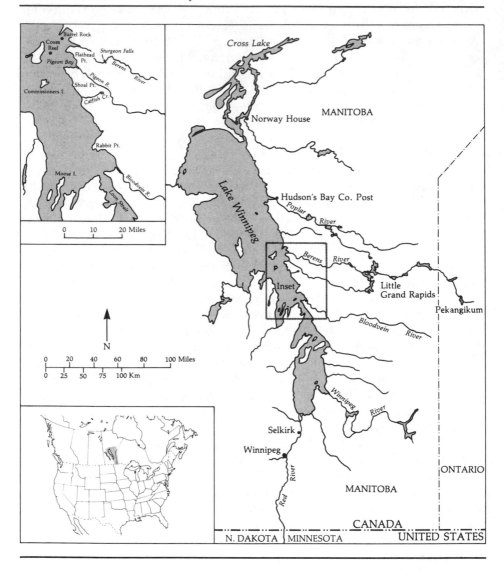

themselves, they are built on sets of cultural conventions, assumptions, and values foreign to native North America. We need not go so far as Calvin Martin's postulate of the gulf between native North Americans and Europeans as being a virtually unbridgeable abyss between "the people of myth and the people of history," for the dark dualism of his analysis echoes, at times, the old and problematic dichotomy between Civilization and the Noble Savage. But we can take seriously his expression of caution long standard in anthropology, that in much scholarly writing "the Indian is usually shoehorned into the dominant culture's paradigm of reason and logic, its calculus of viewing the world and manipulating its parts."[3]

On a more technical level, it is important also to keep in mind the collaborations through which William Berens's story has passed. Indian autobiography, as Arnold Krupat observes, is typically a "contradiction in terms," given the cultural frontiers that it crosses. The genre usually arises from "bicultural composite authorship," as a text passes from its Indian "subject" or "author" through a process of translation, transcription, interpreting, and editing by an outside agent who shapes its final form.[4] William Berens would not have "written" his reminiscences or given them the form that they took without the impulse, opportunity, and motivation (material and nonmaterial?) that Hallowell provided. This point by no means invalidates their content or "accuracy." But it does remind us that Berens was not the sole creator of this manner of organizing and presenting his experiences.

We are not without clues, however, on the question of how Berens or other Northern Algonquians would conceive of and recount the stories of their lives on their terms. The key organizing principle governing Northern Algonquian oral narratives is the distinction between secular stories grounded in personal human experience and myths involving other-than-human beings, or between *təbatcəmoin* and *atsokan*, to use the terms that Hallowell recorded at Berens River in 1932. The *təbatəmoin* class comprises "('true') stor[ies], personal experiences of actual human beings, whether contemporary or not." *Atsokan* stories, in contrast, tell of:

> what happened 'long ago' when things were 'different' than they are today—a mythopoeic era [although their personages still manifest themselves to the Ojibwa in dreams and in the conjuring tent] . . . Both are believed to be 'true' but the characters in the *atsokan* stories represent types of human beings or animals that behave in a manner not met with in everyday [waking] life and are superior in 'power' to people who live today.[5]

The term *atsokan* has further referents that show the power and distinctiveness of these narratives. It can also refer to the major mythic characters themselves, such as *Wisekedjak*, the Trickster-Transformer, and *Mikinak*, the Great Turtle. Since such personages as these are the ones who appear in the dream quests of individuals at puberty, the *atsokanak* (plural) are also *pawaganak* (dream visitors), who may confer help and power. Recipients of such dream visitors are forbidden to talk freely about their experience or their *pawagan*. Similarly, *atsokanak* as a class of narratives are related only in proper ritual conditions—at night, in late fall, or in winter, "when the lakes and rivers are frozen, when there are no leaves on the trees and when hunting and trapping are at their height."[6]

The Northern Algonquian opposition between mythic and secular narrative has implications for doing biography. Ideal biographers not only get their dates exact and chronological sequences straight, in accord with a non-Algonquian frame of reference;[7] they also plumb their subject's deepest and most formative experiences to link motivation with behavior and action.

In doing so, they seek to blend domains that most Berens River Ojibwa kept separate. The revealing of a special dream relationship with a *pawagan* risked the destruction of that tie and the loss of power and protection. So, discussion of this fundamental aspect of Ojibwa autobiography would have been strongly taboo.

For William Berens, biography breaks no such prohibition. His family had been at least nominally Methodist for two generations, and he spoke openly to Hallowell about how he, in his youth, had rejected the privilege of a *pawagan* tie when it was offered.[8] Yet, he was close enough to the experience of these sacred domains to feel the consequences of breaking rules of conduct enjoined by the *atsokanak*, as when he was plagued by toads for having told certain myths in summer, out of season.[9] His strongly Ojibwa frame of reference guided and surely constrained the reminiscences that he gave to Hallowell in 1940. For these are simply *tɔbatcɔmoin*, personal stories that do not plumb too deeply into religious experience and dream encounters. Hallowell gave him the format for stringing these stories together in a connected chronological discourse and, no doubt, the opportunity for being introspective. But Berens, in this setting, kept the discourse on a secular level. He did not blend the genres of narrative.

This essay on William Berens is also of the *tɔbatcɔmoin* class. Tellers of these stories are not subject to seasonal taboos. Nor are they excluded from mentioning or telling some kinds of stories about the *atsokanak*, insofar as some such nonhuman beings (e.g., the *memengwesiwak* who live in rocky cliffs beside lakes, the *windigo* or cannibalistic monster, and the *pinesiwak* or thunderbirds) may be encountered in everyday waking life.[10] They observe certain boundaries with respect, however, and this account attempts to do likewise.

The family of William Berens, or *Tabɔsigizikweas* (Sailing Low In The Air After Thunder), to give his Saulteaux name, epitomized, as Hallowell put it, "the broader sweep of historical events in the Lake Winnipeg area and the consequences of the acculturation process." Through his paternal line, Berens was a member of the Moose "sib" (Hallowell's term for Ojibwa descent groups) at Berens River. Hallowell's genealogies of the 1930s identified three distinct Moose patrilineages with different regional origins. The Berens line traced its ancestry back to Yellow Legs, *Uzauwɔskugat*, who was living on the west side of Lake Winnipeg in the late 1700s and died before 1830. Berens family tradition places Yellow Legs's origins in the Lake Superior area. If this is correct, he was one of the first Ojibwa (or Saulteaux as they are usually known in Manitoba) to grow up west of Lake Winnipeg; most sources place their first major movements into this area in the 1780s and 1790s as they and their Montreal-based fur trade associates extended their ranges westward.[11]

Yellow Legs was remembered as a great leader of the Midewiwin or Grand Medicine Society, and possibly was the first to introduce its curing rituals into central Manitoba. His wife, Mistamut, who lived long enough to know some of her great-grandchildren around Berens River, told of his achievements. As a *manao* or curer who received medicines from the *memeng-weciwak*, he once walked on water to a small island in Lake Winnipeg to obtain a special remedy. Another time, he sent two men to an island to bring him a certain stone he had described; it later exhibited its magical properties in the Midewiwin lodge.[12]

Yellow Legs's eldest son, *Maskwa* (Bear), who was William Berens's paternal grandfather, was born about 1790. Bear married a woman named *Amo* (Bee), or Victoria in her burial record of 1890, of the Pelican sib; she was from the Cumberland House (Saskatchewan) area. They and Bear's younger brother, *Cauwanas* (The One Who Travels With The South Wind), later moved to the east side of Lake Winnipeg. Bear brought with him his father's sacred stone, and he and Cauwanas, in the 1860s and early 1870s, conducted the last Midewiwin ceremonies recorded at the mouth of the Berens River, while William was a small boy. William's paternal grandparents and his great uncle, Cauwanas, were strongly influential in bringing the boy up within Ojibwa culture and traditions.[13]

Berens River, in William's youth and before, however, was not a static or homogeneous community; nor was his family. Hallowell remarked on the considerable mobility of the Ojibwa lineages whose genealogies he traced; various founders had reached the area from distant communities in every direction. Ojibwa subgroups along the river had met and mingled with one another, and to a lesser extent, with Crees and with fur traders of British, French, and Algonquian ancestry. Indeed, William's immediate kin exemplified such mingling, perhaps the best of any group that Hallowell recorded. Correspondingly, they exhibited much diversity in the ways that they adapted to life in a community that was both changing and diversifying.

William's grandfather, Bear, died at Berens River around 1873–74 without converting to Christianity, just before the Methodists opened a mission there. He did, however, eventually adopt a European-style surname, Berens (borrowed ultimately from that of two HBC governors), which his son Jacob carried on. Bear's brother, Cauwanas, was converted late in life and was baptized Roderick Ross. The flexibility of Northern Ojibwa surname adoption patterns in this period is illustrated by the options chosen by the offspring of Cauwanas: one kept the name Ross, while a second chose MacDonald and a third took the surname of Felix. The name Cauwanas also persisted as a surname around Berens River. These surname developments suggest that, to a degree, identities were also changing or diversifying in response to new situational needs.[14]

Jacob Berens or *Nauwigizigweas* (Center Sky), William's father, was born about 1832 by Hallowell's account. Other sources place his birth in 1834 and translate his name as "Something Going Across The Sky," referring to Halley's comet, which appeared that year. About 1861, he became the first Berens River Saulteaux to convert to Christianity, during a visit to the Methodist mission at Norway House at the north end of Lake Winnipeg. There, Jacob learned the Cree syllabic system that the Methodists were using to transcribe the scriptures and was baptized by the Reverend George McDougall.[15]

Possibly, Jacob's crossing of this bridge to an alien religion was a quest for new powers comparable to those of his father and uncle. Or, it may have been related to a development in his personal life—his marriage to Mary McKay, whom the Berens River Ojibwa identified as "White." Mary (1836–1908) was the daughter of William McKay, HBC trader at Trout Lake post in Ontario's Severn River drainage. Although there is uncertainty about some of her grandparents' identities, they, as well as her parents, may have been of mixed European-Algonquian descent. The Berens River Ojibwas' classification of her as "White" would have been influenced by her evidently fair complexion, by the fact that the Berens River people (to judge by Hallowell's data) used no intermediate racial term such as "halfbreed" or *métis*, by the fact that they classified people by patrilineal descent, and finally, by her linguistic and cultural attributes (speaking English, drinking tea). In the 1930s, William Berens recalled that tea drinking was uncommon before his father's time. When his mother's parents settled late in life at Berens River, a subject of notice that his maternal grandmother "made her weekly cup a part of the Sabbath ritual."[16]

In one significant respect, William Berens's mixed parentage reversed a pattern usual in such families. Intermarriage had long been commonplace in the fur-trade setting of northern Canada.[17] But typically, the European social and cultural influences and the fair complexions came to these families' offspring through the paternal line, while native mothers transmitted to their children the Algonquian values, knowledge, and linguistic usages that they themselves had maintained. Ties with Indian kin and communities were usually maternal ties. As Euro-Canadian cultural and political forces gained strength in the later nineteenth century, the European-descended fathers of mixed families were commonly identified in one way or another with these forces. In such settings, Indian cultural influences were in a sense "feminized" and weakened, given the male-dominated social order that prevailed.

William Berens, however, received his Ojibwa heritage through a line of strong male leaders whose influence seemed little reduced by his father's Methodism, while his main exposure to Euro-Canadian values came through his mother. As he remarked about his family, "I learned the white ways from my mother and the Indian ways from my grandparents on my father's side so I know what both are like."[18] William's relatives offered a reversal of the usual pattern linking an increasingly powerful Euro-Canadian culture to males, and Indian culture to females. Possibly, as an Ojibwa boy growing up in this setting, William was able to achieve a balance between the two worlds that was not usually attained—while "tilting" somewhat toward the Ojibwa side, at least in his later years, and in his conversations with Hallowell, although that anthropologist postulated the presence of greater psychological conflict than is suggested here.

The first decade of William's life saw increases in cultural mingling both in his family and on a broader scale, as Berens River became a crossroads not only for Ojibwas and fur traders, but also for missionaries, treaty commissioners, and other outsiders. His father, Jacob Berens, was a force for some of these changes, in encouraging the first missionary to come to Berens River and in signing Treaty No. 5 as chief. And he evidently fostered an openness to change in his son. "Don't think you know everything," he advised him. "You will see lots of new things and you will find a place in your mind for them all."[19]

Possibly this attitude helped William to grow up without experiencing severe religious conflicts. Since his parents did not allow their Christianity to cut them off from unconverted relatives, William participated both in Methodist observances and in Ojibwa religious events that left lasting impressions. Besides attending the Midewiwin, he saw his grandfather, Bear, cure people with his medicines and conduct shaking tent performances. Since Bear had lost all the fingers of his left hand except the thumb, William concluded from the shaking of the tent and other evidences that Bear and his rituals could tap powers that Christianity could not:

> I used to see [Bear] go into the conjuring tent but the voices I heard coming out from it did not seem like his voice . . . I had reason to believe that my grandfather knew what he was doing and that his beliefs were true. I used to hear my mother talk about God but I did not see anything that my mother did that proved to me that what happened was through the help of God. I saw no power comparable to what I had seen my grandfather use.[20]

In the summer of 1874, William helped in building a church and house for the first missionary, the Reverend Egerton R. Young, who arrived that fall. "I wanted to understand what this man was talking about," William recalled. "Finally, I got enough sense to believe in Christianity."[21] The Young family resided at Berens River for two years. Their departure was precipitated by Mrs. Young's ill health and also, almost certainly, by concern at the extent to which their eldest boy, born at Norway House in 1869, was becoming Algonquianized. These influences came both from his Cree nurse, brought from Norway House, and from the Berens River Saulteaux, who welcomed him into their wigwams and ceremonies. A reminiscence by their son, E. Ryerson Young, late in life, makes no specific reference to the Berens family, but vividly describes his attraction to the local people and his virtual adoption into their warm and culturally vigorous community, shedding sidelights on the quality of William Berens's childhood experiences.[22]

In September 1875 came an event more momentous than the establishment of the mission. People had been talking about "the great Queen who was buying the country"; Indians had been arriving from all over for council meetings; and traders were converging on Berens River to sell goods for "treaty debt." On September 19 (the 20th according to a published account),[23] William was awakened by a frightful noise like a *windigo*—the whistling of the first steamboat to arrive at Berens River. Lieutenant Governor Alexander Morris and his party had come to negotiate Treaty No. 5. Jacob Berens was at meetings all day and got home late that night after signing the treaty. When William awoke the next morning, he was struck by the sight of new clothing lying beside his father: "a red fancy coat and dark blue pants, socks, and boots. There was also a flag and a medal!"[24]

The terms of Treaty 5 specified that the Berens River reserve was to be surveyed and subdivided, with 160 acres assigned each family of five. The Indians kept, however, "the right to pursue their avocations of hunting and fishing throughout the tract surrendered . . . subject to such regulations as

CHIEF JACOB BERENS AND HIS WIFE, MARY MCKAY, THE PARENTS OF WILLIAM BERENS. Although the photographer and date are unknown, this image must have been captured before 1909, since a copy of it is in the lantern slide collection of the Reverend Egerton R. Young, who died that year. Jacob Berens is wearing his official "chief's coat," marking his rank and recognition by Canadian authorities, and his government medals, recalling his role in the negotiation and signing of Canadian Treaty Number 5. (Courtesy of the Archives of Ontario, Toronto, Canada.)

may from time to time be made." These "avocations" also received support from the provision of an annual grant of $500 to purchase ammunition and twine for fish nets.[25] Thus, access to customary resources and occupations was not then closed down. Indeed, the Berens River people were evidently not exclusively using guns; William's grandfather used the bow and arrow in hunting moose, and his father used them for partridges, muskrats, and rabbits.[26]

In the short term, the visible consequences of the mission founding and the treaty were localized and specific. Jacob Berens, already something of an innovator, had a new elected political role that brought him some standing among a network of native leaders and in the context of a federal governmental department. With church and governmental support, Berens River acquired a school, although its results were thoroughly mixed in the early decades.[27] Annual treaty payments from this cession brought a flurry of free traders each summer as "treaty time" approached, and for better or worse, these men offered a greater diversity of small goods than the HBC post.

Of greater importance than local mission, school, or treaty, however, were the broadening interconnections that in this period began to link Lake Winnipeg communities with an increasingly complex economic and political universe. Through his already extensive family ties, and presumably through inclination, William Berens was drawn into the new and rapidly evolving regional social-economic order in a variety of ways.

Between 1876 and the mid-1880s, William had a total of about two years of schooling with a succession of three different missionary teachers who followed the Reverend Young at Berens River. He never achieved comfort at writing, as shown by the help he sought when drafting letters to Hallowell. But he quickly acquired other skills. He traveled by dog team with his father when Jacob Berens carried mail from Berens River to Winnipeg and visited the Indian Affairs office there. He fished, trapped, hunted, and helped harvest the family's potato crop in the fall. One summer, he worked building houses at Selkirk, the town just south of Lake Winnipeg; and there he had his first experience with brandy.

In 1886, William had the first of several jobs assisting government agents in their travels. He joined the Lake Winnipeg survey party of Frederick Wilkins and carried the "target" on which the surveyors trained their sights. He also began to work around the HBC post at Berens River, haymaking, digging potatoes, and rowing the skiff.

The early 1880s saw the start of a new era on Lake Winnipeg—the opening of the first commercial fisheries. Many Icelandic immigrants who settled on the lake in the mid-1870s were fishermen, and they soon began shipping fish to Winnipeg on the new steam schooners that were also used in the lumber trade. Transport innovations and growing access to American markets propelled a quantum leap in the fishing industry: from two sailboats harvesting 72,867 pounds of whitefish for one firm in 1883, it expanded to seven tugs and sixty-five sailboats producing 1,400,000 pounds for several companies in 1886.[28]

William, like many other people around Lake Winnipeg, was soon drawn into the labor opportunities that resulted: "this was the first time I started to earn big money—$2.50 a day, grub on top of that, and a drink of whiskey before supper." A fish buyer hired him to set nets and to smoke and haul fish. In the winter, he continued to go out on the trap lines with his father. And the local Hudson's Bay Company post, evidently facing some competition for labor in the changing conditions, offered him more permanent employment for the first time. About 1887, he signed a two- or three-year contract at one-hundred twenty-five dollars a year to serve as an interpreter and do other jobs at the Berens River post.[29]

In the summer of 1888, he almost lost the HBC job when he took advantage of another work opportunity without notifying his employer. A survey party arrived at Berens River to start an upriver journey to lay out the new inland reserves for the Ojibwa under the terms of the treaty. William was offered one-hundred dollars to help on a 260-mile trip to Grand Rapids and Pekangikum. This two-month inland experience evidently enlivened his interest in the up-river communities—an interest that again found an outlet when Hallowell accepted his offer to conduct him up the river over four decades later.

Aside from this trip, another event at some time during these years kept William vividly in touch with his Ojibwa universe. Being a member of the Methodist church, he had never gone on a dream fast. But the *pawaganak* sometimes visit without being sought; and on one occasion, William had a dream experience with the same personages—the *memengwesiwak*—who had favored Yellow Legs, his great grandfather. He visited them in their rocky cliff abode on a branch of the Berens River (at a site he later recognized when he saw it for the first time in waking life). As a Christian, he did not take up their offer of blessings and medicines, and since no bond was established, he felt no restriction on recounting the dream. He felt, however, that at any future time he could have revisited the spot and accepted their gifts of power. Faced with a traditional choice he did not take, William confidently expected that option remained open to him in later years.[30]

Berens spent the next years partly in HBC work, but more in occupations of several sorts for the fish companies. His account of the next decade mentions dozens of places he visited along the 300-mile length of the lake, and dozens of people he met, both native and White.

About 1896, he became engaged to Nancy Everett, daughter of William Everett and Nancy Boucher of Berens River; they were married in January 1899. Both Nancy's parents were of mixed descent. Her paternal grandfather, Joseph Everett, was a Saulteaux Indian who was adopted by the Métis leader, Cuthbert Grant. Joseph had married the daughter of a Scots trader and an Indian (both unidentified), who had been raised by the wife of William McKay at Trout Lake. On her mother's side, Nancy's grandfather was Joseph Boucher, said to be a French Canadian from Montreal, who had married a Norway House Cree woman and settled at Berens River.[31] Hallowell said little about Nancy, and her husband's reminiscences covered few of their forty-eight years together (she was still living when Berens died in 1947). But her background had similarities to her husband's; strongly Saulteaux in her community ties, she also had a diverse ancestry comparable to his.

During these years, Berens had two experiences working for and traveling with agents of the federal Department of Indian Affairs. His recollections of them and their conduct furnish a rarely found record of work experiences narrated from the native side. While working on a tugboat for a fishing company at $35 a month, Berens was approached by Inspector Ebenezer McColl, who offered $45 a month if William would help him on his rounds. They traveled to ten of the Indian reserves around the lake, and a council was held at each. Berens was impressed with the way that McColl spent time "talking to people, inquiring whether they had first class articles—everything—rations—any crooked work?" And he felt McColl was "the best

CHIEF WILLIAM BERENS IN HIS LAST YEARS, DURING THE 1940s. In this period, Berens opposed the participation of men from his community in the armed services during World War II. (Courtesy of Maurice Berens.)

inspector the Indians ever had since treaty was signed." He was struck, too, by the fact that on their return to Winnipeg, McColl insisted that Berens and another Ojibwa employee have "dinner at his own table," and then paid them promptly, adding "a suit of clothes as a present on top of that."[32]

Berens's other experience working with an Indian agent left him less impressed. When he and Agent W. J. Short were preparing to leave Selkirk on a trip around Lake Winnipeg, Berens "got in along with my chums—started drinking," while staying at a Selkirk hotel. When he recovered, he hurried over to where Agent Short was staying and was told he was "not well." Berens went to his room and found him in bed: "He was worse than me." So while the agent recovered from his overindulgence, Berens finished the preparations for the trip—by dog team, in winter. The agent rode in the cariole, and drew on Berens's liquor supply when his own flask ran dry.[33]

As indicated, William Berens's reminiscences are largely an account of secular events, without much overt Saulteaux cultural or religious content. Two incidents, however, one before his marriage and one after, demonstrated that he still lived very much in an Ojibwa cultural universe—one in which sickness and other mishaps were often attributed to animate agents, human or nonhuman, whom their victim had offended.

While Berens was in Selkirk, following his job with Inspector McColl, he bought a bottle of gin to be shared with a few of the other native men working on the lake boats there. One man in the party was overlooked, although not by his intent. The next day, Berens was suddenly hit by "a pain as if somebody was stabbing me with a needle in the knee," and could not move his leg. He was taken to hospital in great agony, and his knee swelled up enormously. It was operated on, and the surgeon found in it two grains of shot and two pieces of metal. He questioned his patient at length about whether he had ever been shot, even while in his mother's womb; Berens knew of no such thing ever happening.

After twenty-two days in hospital, Berens asked the superintendent to be released. It was October, and he was anxious to get back to Berens River before freeze-up. Also, as he told the superintendent, he was confident that his father, Jacob Berens, could accomplish a cure and that in ten days' time he would be walking. The hospital let him go, and he moved gratefully home from an alien framework of medical treatment to his own. Jacob Berens's diagnosis, one he knew "white people don't believe," was that the shot fragments had entered the knee "through an Indian's magic powers." Jacob and his brother boiled medicines in a big kettle, then poulticed the leg twice a day. In ten days, William was able to walk, though the leg was stiff for another two months.[34]

Soon after he was married, Berens and his wife were camped on an island in Lake Winnipeg near the mouth of the Poplar River, while he was buying fish for the Dominion Fish Company. One afternoon, Berens "began to feel scared—even my body was quivering." He could not eat, and tried unsuccessfully to get his wife to leave the spot: "If you're alive you can tell what happened but if we both die then no one will know." Then, at sunset,

> I could see a cloud rising in the west. It was calm, sun shining bright, there was not a cloud all day; this was the first. Then I could hear the thunder—just as something striking my body . . . I thought I was going to get killed by the thunder that night . . . you could see the lightning when it struck that rocky island—running all over like snakes—fearful. We hid our heads under the blankets.

After a while, a voice seemed to speak to Berens, saying, "If you can see daylight coming—big dark clouds and light between on the north side, have no fear then—you will be safe." Finally the storm passed, and the sky appeared as the voice described. "I jumped up and walked out then," Berens recalled. "I said, 'This old fellow did not kill us yet.' "[35]

Berens's reminiscences explained his view of this event and its cause. Some time before, when he was working in the HBC store, an old Indian man had asked him for tobacco and a pipe, and he had refused the request. He vividly recalled the scene in the store: "Everybody was scared of this old man . . . Everybody was quiet when I talked back. One old fellow told me I had made a mistake. 'I'm sorry for you,' he said. But I did not give a damn. I did not think he could hurt me." The thunderstorm was caused by this man (who was camped near the Berenses when it happened); he was trying "to do something to me by his magic power."[36] Both this and the Selkirk incident illustrated Berens's strong sensitivity about following Ojibwa norms of social interaction—sharing, giving, and respecting the requests (and potential powers) of one's elders.

Although Ojibwa modes of explanation and values about sharing and obligation guided Berens's thought patterns and personal relationships, they by no means kept him from functioning in an economic universe that was increasingly dominated by entrepreneurship, wage labor, money transactions, and new and more specialized occupations. Early in his history of intermittent contract work for the Hudson's Bay Company, he negotiated a raise when his duties were increased. Later, when buying fish for a buyer, Sandy Vance, who had advanced him nets and supplies, Berens found his middleman position threatened by a visiting buyer who offered the Berens River fishermen higher prices; he quickly contacted Vance who agreed to match the visitor's offers. One other summer, Berens bought a twenty-six-foot sailboat and used it to buy and haul sturgeon for the Hudson's Bay Company.[37]

In 1899–1901, Berens was in charge of the HBC Poplar River post north of Berens River, at twenty-five dollars a month. As he recalled, the post "was in bad shape before I took hold. I pulled the post out of the hole and I asked for a raise." When the Berens River manager refused, Berens left to work as a buyer for the fish companies that summer. "I was doing well. In about eight days I made $300 . . . sturgeon and caviar." During the next three winters, Berens had mail-carrying contracts to points around Lake Winnipeg. He also began buying fish and furs for a free trader, making the rounds of the Indian camps ahead of the HBC agent. Because of him, the Berens River post manager, Frederick A. Disbrow, "was worrying a lot—I was a pretty hard proposition for him. He was watching me just like a cat watches a mouse. He did not want me to get ahead of him into the camps."[38] Berens clearly enjoyed the tactical challenges of outwitting the Hudson's Bay Company at the time, though he periodically returned to its employ in later years.

Berens's reminiscences break off as of about 1904 or 1905. Other sources, however, including the recollections of family members, help to continue the story. In the decade following 1905, he again worked at least intermittently for the Hudson's Bay Company at one-hundred fifty dollars a year. His son John recalled that William was allowed to set out traps when carrying supplies to the Indian camps, and thus supplemented his income with his own furs while picking up those of others for the company. Berens also worked for a while at Norway House, and then had charge of the HBC outpost at the Bloodvein River, south of Berens River.[39]

When William's father, Chief Jacob Berens, died in 1916, William succeeded him, serving as chief of the Poplar River, Bloodvein, and Little Grand Rapids reserves and of his own band. In 1921–22, however, the other bands began to elect their own chiefs, relieving Berens of the pressure of both trying to visit these reserves several times a year and continuing to work for the Hudson's Bay Company.

As chief, Berens was assisted by three councillors. As payment for his services, he received twenty-five dollars annually from the Canadian government, and his councillors received fifteen dollars, plus a new outfit of clothes every two years. The chief's jacket had "brass buttons and a one inch wide gold braid around the collar and cuffs; the pants had a two inch wide red stripe on each leg." Twice yearly, Chief Berens traveled to Selkirk and Winnipeg to check on rations and other matters; he also had charge of distributing monthly food supplies (flour, tea, lard, rolled oats, bulk beans, salt pork, and molasses) to the old people on the reserve.[40]

His descendants also remember that he placed much emphasis on agriculture. He had two large gardens that each yielded up to a hundred bushels of potatoes. He kept livestock, too, and at one point he had as many as thirteen cows. While his family used the potatoes and milk, a large portion was also given to families on the reserve. The Berenses and some other families would cut and stack hay for two or three weeks each summer on hay land six or eight miles from Berens River; in winter, it would be hauled in by wagon. Several horses were also kept for hauling hay and firewood. William Berens's influence and example led Berens River to be "the only reserve on Lake Winnipeg to practice agriculture to such an extent," according to family recollection; after his death, "the practice went into decline."[41]

In the 1930s, Chief Berens was instrumental in opening the commercial fishing on Lake Winnipeg to Indians. Previously, Indian fishermen were not licensed to operate; their fish-selling activities were clandestine (although Berens's reminiscences mention no encounters with enforcement agencies). Berens worked with Roxy Hamilton, his Liberal member of the legislative assembly in Manitoba, and with representatives of the Catholic church, to remove the restriction. He also negotiated contracts for the Berens River band to cut and haul wood for the HBC post and for the lake ships that visited Berens River. The HBC woodcutting employed thirty men, and the company also paid fifty cents a cord as stumpage fee to the band's account.[42]

During these busy years, William Berens also found time and "a place in his mind" for A. Irving Hallowell, the visiting anthropologist. The man of history (deeply enmeshed in the secular activities of chief and entrepreneur) became, at intervals, a man of myths, reaching back to his religious traditions, and most of the time he welcomed the opportunity. Berens was in his mid-sixties in 1930 when he first met Hallowell (who was then in his late thirties). It would have been natural enough for him, at that age, to start thinking more about his Ojibwa heritage and his ancestors. But other factors, too, may have made him responsive to Hallowell's questions and interests. Berens had seen more than six decades of change and diversification in the Lake Winnipeg area; and while he had benefited from some of those developments, he was certainly aware of losses—of customs and ceremonies that no longer flourished.

Additionally, one particular incident, although not mentioned explicitly by him or Hallowell, may also have helped trigger a sympathetic response to the anthropologist. In the summer of 1926, one of Berens's sons, aged seventeen, who had been attending the local Methodist-run day school, became one of its first two students eligible to take the high school entrance examination. He apparently overslept and missed the examination, and then was not allowed another chance because of "a serious misdemeanor," its nature unspecified. Chief Berens, angered at his son's treatment, withdrew his other children from the school, and there was bad feeling between him and the teacher for at least two years.[43] This falling out may have caused Berens at least to reassess (though not reject) his church connection.

During the summer months, Chief Berens made a practice of meeting the lake ships that stopped at Berens River on their way between Selkirk and Norway House (at the north end of the lake) and talking to acquaintances and visitors. On July 1, 1930, Hallowell was aboard the S.S. Keenora when it stopped for about an hour at Berens River. Traveling up to Norway House on his first venture into Manitoba, Hallowell felt himself launching into the unknown: "I had only the vaguest notions about the physiography and history of the region I was entering, or the location and ethnography of the Indian population." His fortuitous meeting with Chief Berens on that trip north shaped the course of his next decade of studies, for in Berens, he found an "interpreter, guide, and virtual collaborator," knowledgeable, intelligent, and experienced.[44]

In mid-August 1930, Hallowell returned from his brief visits to Norway House, Cross Lake, and Island Lake, staying for a week at Berens River. He spent a good many hours with Chief Berens. They walked to the cemetery to see Jacob Berens's grave, and Berens sold him some artifacts.[45] And, Hallowell later recollected,

> as a result of long conversations, my interest in the Ojibwa people began to crystallize. . . . I was particularly impressed by the fact that there were still unchristianized Indians 250 miles up the river in the Pekangikum Band. Besides this, Chief Berens said he would go with me if I wished to arrange a trip to Lake Pekangikum.[46]

Two years later, they made that upriver trip together for the first of several times, leaving "what my friend Chief Berens called 'civilization' at the mouth of the river," to visit communities far less touched by Lake Winnipeg traffic, immigration, missions, and fisheries.

The beginning of this essay raised the question of how William Berens's recollections may have been filtered and structured through Hallowell's recording of his reminiscences in 1940. A reverse question arises, too: how did Berens's perceptions help to guide and shape Hallowell's outlooks and syntheses of data? We cannot fully answer either question. But it seems that Berens and Hallowell agreed on one matter; the upriver communities were still a world of the primitive and traditional where the old ways survived almost untouched. To visit Pekangikum was to visit "the living past in the Canadian wilderness," as Hallowell put it, for here one could still observe the ceremonies and lifestyle that William Berens's father and grandfather had experienced.

Writing sometime in the 1960s, Hallowell was explicit about how Berens had influenced his own intellectual framework and orientation: "from the beginning of my association with him, I became historically oriented as a matter of course because we made constant reference to the persons of past generations in the genealogical material we had collected together." Hallowell's richest genealogical materials came, naturally enough, from Berens himself. As a consequence, Berens's own four-generation family history came to stand, in a sense, as an implicit prototype of Hallowell's explicit model for the Berens River Saulteaux. Hallowell's abstract "cultural gradient" across space, from pagan and aboriginal Pekangikum down the river to Pauingassi, Little Grand Rapids, and Lake Winnipeg, had its temporal analogue in the generations from Yellow Legs to Bear to Jacob and William Berens.[47]

The correspondence between the two gradients—historical and cultural-geographic—was powerful and convincing. It excluded, however, various data and questions that were beyond Hallowell's reach at the time of his fieldwork. More specifically, neither Hallowell nor Berens had any accurate idea of how much Ojibwa-Euro-Canadian interaction had occurred along the Berens River from the mid-1700s to 1821. Only recently has detailed archival research revealed the extent of early fur-trade activity, both HBC and Montreal-based, in the upland regions known as the Little North, east of Lake Winnipeg.[48] It is much clearer now than in the 1930s that Pekangikum cannot be taken as an unchanged "aboriginal baseline." While still pagan and relatively "unacculturated" compared to the downriver communities, its people, too, would have experienced the coming of outsiders, and also the region-wide fur shortages that occurred during the intensive trade competition before the Hudson's Bay and North West companies merged in 1821.

Although Berens and Hallowell may have agreed on cultural gradients, and although they got along well enough to collaborate during several summers of intensive fieldwork in the 1930s, they did not always maintain complete harmony. At times, Hallowell asked much of their relationship. In 1935, a year in which he did not visit Berens River, the anthropologist sent Berens nine pages of detailed queries on Saulteaux names and genealogies, leaving spaces for answers to be written in. After one attempt to sort out some confusion, Berens added, "I am not want to say things to spoil your work. You Better stay with your own notes. I know we are trying to do our best to get everything correct about those people."[49]

An incident that probably occurred in the summer of 1936 led Hallowell to admit that Berens sometimes must have found his work for and with him taxing. On a deeper level, it suggested that in some areas such as dream interpretation, the two were unlikely to reach any fundamental accord. One morning, while they were traveling upriver to Grand Rapids, Hallowell asked Berens if he had had any dreams the night before. Berens related that he had dreamed he was out traveling with a boy, on snowshoes:

> I sighted a camp but there was no one in sight. Then I heard the sound of chopping in the bush. As we came closer a man [a stranger] appeared. This man handed me some money, over one hundred dollars in bills. I could see an X on some of them. But the bills were the color of that [pointing to Hallowell's yellow-brown sleeping bag]. This man also gave me some silver and I gave some of it to the boy. I asked whether this was all right and the man said 'yes.'

Hallowell then asked what Berens thought the dream meant. Berens believed "it might indicate that he would catch a fox the next winter," inferring this from the color of the bills which he thought very curious, and linking the fox to the money it might bring him. This interpretation, as Hallowell knew, reflected the customary Ojibwa outlook on dreams as prefiguring what might or could happen. But, for his own part, Hallowell took it differently: "The Freudian symbolism in this dream [feces = money] is so transparent that it needs no further comment. On account of the color of my sleeping bag it could hardly have been more forcibly emphasized." He added that the dreamer's seizing on the color of the bills demonstrated the centrality of that element. Hallowell then attempted to explain the Freudian symbolism of the dream to Berens who, he thought, "seemed in no way resistant to the idea."[50]

One cannot, of course, read this response as acceptance; Berens was undoubtedly skilled at the Ojibwa custom of showing respect to an important outsider, no matter what curious things he might be saying.[51] And Hallowell's own flat acceptance of Freudian interpretation in this instance is striking. Two entirely different frames of reference for dream interpretation confronted one another on this occasion. But, to use more recent terms, while Hallowell accepted Berens's interpretation as emic—representing an intrinsic Ojibwa mode of interpretation, and his own as etic—the application of an objective frame of analysis, readers fifty years later may be struck by how emic both of them were, with Hallowell's reflecting the mechanical application of strong cultural currents in neo-Freudian anthropology of the 1930s.[52]

In the next paragraph of his discussion of Berens's dream, Hallowell revealed more about his conception of their relationship and Berens's attitude towards him than in any of his other writings so far discovered. As he noted, Berens, then aged about seventy, had been "his interpreter and mentor" for several summers:

> He has become rather tired of the work, however, and rationalizes this by telling me that I have already written down all I need to know. Here he was then starting off on another trip . . . This dream is probably the expression of repressed aggression towards me. I was the man he failed to recognize . . . I gave him the money, which approximated the amount he would earn, but the money was also faeces, metaphorically speaking . . . At the same time, since we have been close friends, he could not turn me down, and he needed the money as well. But . . . internally he very much resisted going. Besides, the journey up the river is not an easy one. There are 50 portages . . . and W. B. has been accustomed to do his share of the carrying, besides the cooking. Then when we are encamped there are (to him) the endless inquiries and hours of translating what other people have to say.[53]

Hallowell and Berens worked together for two more summers after this event, in 1938 and 1940. In light of Hallowell's observations on their relationship, the attention that he gave to Berens himself in 1940 is of some interest. He probably had a mixture of motives in taking down Berens's reminiscences at that point; he may have realized that Berens might not be around much longer to record his life story, and that he himself might not be able to continue fieldwork during the war years (indeed, he did not return after 1940). But he may also have decided that in using Berens as his bridge to the upriver Saulteaux, he had too much overlooked the aging chief—the man who made it all possible. No doubt the reminiscence-recording became tedious at times, and indeed the task never got finished. But at least for Berens, this time, the "endless hours" were for a change not spent on "what other people have to say."

The World War II years, which followed Hallowell's last season of field research, brought some new challenges to Berens and his community. Warfare was not something Berens personally feared; indeed, in his youth, he had had a dream that gave him an assurance that in battle, bullets would never hit him.[54] But he did not want to involve his people in the war, and since band members required his permission to enlist, he had the means to uphold his position. His grandson explained his controversial stand and its results:

> William's attitude was that he would not send men overseas to kill people that he did not know; in this he was supported by the other Chiefs around Lake Winnipeg and there were no enlistments from Poplar River, Little Grand Rapids or Bloodvein.[55]

He did, however, aid the war effort through peaceful means, recruiting both treaty and nontreaty Indians to help harvest crops on farms in Manitoba and Saskatchewan, to make up for wartime manpower shortages. The local HBC manager would receive word about how many men were needed, and Chief Berens would gather them, accompany them to Winnipeg, and bring them back after the harvest; for this, he received five dollars a day.[56]

Chief Berens died at Berens River on August 23, 1947. A *Winnipeg Tribune* obituary praised him as "a fluent and gifted speaker and an energetic leader of his people."[57] Closer to home, one of his old Indian friends described the funeral and paid a personal tribute in his own reminiscence:

> When the body was took to the church the people were walking. They started singing . . . a beautiful song . . . I was feeling in my heart that it's very kind. I think that was what they felt too. That was the last of Old Billy Berens. I knew he was a very honest man and he was a nice speaking man when he lived in this world.[58]

A. I. Hallowell had evidently hoped to return to Berens River that summer but he did not make it. William Berens's final letter to him, dated January 3, 1947, suggested they were still on good terms: "I was very glad when I receive the Christmas card from you . . . You might think we forget you. But we don't forget you yet at all . . . I am the oldest here now. But will be very glad to meet you again. I will tell you lots of things when I meet you this summer."[59]

The story of William Berens might be amplified in numbers of different directions, and as noted earlier, it could be told in many different ways. One theme, however, remains central. Intersecting with many facets of a changing world, Berens maintained his personal self-identification as an Indian even though his mother, according to family tradition, was categorized as "White" (being classified, as was William, with primary reference to her paternal roots). Just as William "identified with his father, Jacob," so his sons in turn "considered themselves Indians,"[60] despite having a mother and three grandparents of mixed descent.

The extent to which William Berens remained Saulteaux in identity, culture, and personal ties while functioning in a diversity of occupations and social settings presents a challenge to A. I. Hallowell's limited dual contrast between the "acculturated" lakeside Ojibwa (such as Berens) and the upriver "pagan aboriginals." Closer examination through the magnifying glass of biography reveals far more texture and complexity in this remarkable individual than emerged in Hallowell's published references to him.

In a sense, however, the Berens-Hallowell collaboration itself continues to bear fruit. Each man, through his recorded interactions and responses, helps to bring the other, as well as himself, into clearer focus.[61] It must be said, too, Hallowell himself provided the first impulse for this study. His published works, referring repeatedly as they did to "Chief Berens," "W. B.," and "my most valuable informant," pointed to a need to bring this man out of the shadows and to place him center-stage, speaking with his own voice to the extent that he and other sources would allow. Finally, the time seemed right. By chance and good fortune, Hallowell's papers, Berens's reminiscences, his descendants' recollections, and the chance to include this study of Chief William Berens in a volume of biographic studies of similar figures all conjoined to provide an opportunity that, if not guided by a *pawakan*, has seemed at the least providential.

NOTES

1. I am indebted to Beth Carroll-Horrocks, manuscripts librarian of the American Philosophical Society, Philadelphia [APS], and other staff members, for assistance in using the Hallowell papers, acquired in 1983. My research there was supported by a small grant from the Canadian Social Science and Humanities Research Council Aid to Small Universities grant program. Much invaluable information on Chief Berens's life came from his grandson, Maurice Berens, who during his undergraduate and graduate studies at the University of Winnipeg, carried out considerable oral and documentary research on Berens River. My thanks also to Mary Black-Rogers for her generous sharing of her notes and files on Berens River families and history.

2. Except where otherwise indicated, the source for information about the first forty years of William Berens's life is in his "Reminiscences," recorded by A. Irving Hallowell. TS. (prepared by M. Berens and J. Brown) of manuscript in Hallowell Papers, Col. 26, APS. The Berens River fur trade post journals (B.16/a) in the

Hudson's Bay Company Archives, Provincial Archives of Manitoba, Winnepeg, are also rich sources on the activities of Berens family members, along with other HBC documents.

3. Calvin Martin, ed., *The American Indian and the Problem of History* (New York: Oxford University Press, 1987), pp. 195, 96.

4. Arnold Krupat, The Indian Autobiography: Origins, Type, and Function. In *Smoothing the Ground: Essays on Native American Oral Literature*, ed. Brian Swann (Berkeley, Calif.: University of California Press, 1983), p. 262.

5. A. Irving Hallowell, Folklore: Berens River, Ms., 1932–33, Hallowell Papers, Col. 26, APS.

6. A. Irving Hallowell, n.d. Untitled ms. labeled "III. Introduction," on oral narrative and behavioral world, pp.15–17, Hallowell Papers, Col. 26, APS.

7. See Hallowell, *Culture and Experience* (New York: Schocken Books, 1967), chapter 11.

8. A. Irving Hallowell, *Contributions to Anthropology: Selected Papers of A. Irving Hallowell* (Chicago: University of Chicago Press, 1976), p. 98.

9. Hallowell, *Culture and Experience*, pp. 253–54.

10. Hallowell, *Culture and Experience*, p. 98.

11. A. Irving Hallowell, "Berens River," Ms. chapter 1, pp. 13–14, Hallowell Papers, Col. 26, APS; Hallowell, *Culture and Experience*, p. 118; Charles A. Bishop, "Territorial Groups before 1821: Cree and Ojibwa" In *Subarctic*, 6, ed. June Helm *Handbook of North American Indians* (Washington, D.C.: Smithsonian Institution, 1981), p. 160.

12. Hallowell, "Berens River," Ms. chapter 1, pp.14–15.

13. Hallowell, *Culture and Experience*, p. 260.

14. Edward S. Rogers and Mary Black-Rogers, Method for Reconstructing Patterns of Change: Surname Adoption by the Weagamow Ojibwa, 1870–1950, *Ethnohistory*, 25 (1978), pp. 319–45.

15. Mary Black-Rogers, personal communication; John Maclean, *Vanguards of Canada*, (Toronto: Missionary Society of the Methodist Church, 1918), pp. 124–25.

16. Hallowell, "Berens River," Ms., chapter 2, p.17.

17. Jennifer S. H. Brown, *Strangers in Blood: Fur Trade Company Families in Indian Country* (Vancouver: University of British Columbia Press, 1980).

18. Berens, "Reminiscences," p. 8; see also Hallowell, *Culture and Experience*, p. 260.

19. Berens, "Reminiscences," p. 1.

20. Berens, "Reminiscences," p. 7.

21. Berens, "Reminiscences," p. 7.

22. Jennifer S. H. Brown, A Cree Nurse in a Cradle of Methodism: Little Mary and the E. R. Youngs at Norway House and Berens River. In *First Days, Fighting Days: Women in Manitoba History*, ed. Mary Kinnear (Regina: Canadian Plains Research Center, 1987).

23. Alexander Morris, *The Treaties of Canada with the Indians* (Toronto, 1880), p. 147.

24. Berens, "Reminiscences," pp. 9–10.

25. Morris, *The Treaties of Canada*, p. 346.

26. Hallowell, "Berens River," Ms., chapter 3, p. 9.

27. Susan E. Dueck, Methodist Indian Day Schools and Indian Communities in Northern Manitoba, 1890–1925. Unpublished M.A. thesis in history, University of Manitoba, 1986.

28. L. C. Hewson, "A History of the Lake Winnipeg Fishery for Whitefish, *Coregonus clupeaformis*, with Some Reference to Its Economics," *Journal of the Fisheries Research Board of Canada*, 17 (1960), pp. 625–39.

29. Berens, "Reminiscences," pp. 21, 24.
30. Hallowell, *Culture and Experience*, pp. 97–98.
31. A. Irving Hallowell, Ms., "Berens: Boucher and Everett genealogies," Hallowell Papers, Col. 26, APS.
32. Berens, "Reminiscences," pp. 40–41.
33. Berens, "Reminiscences," pp. 48–49.
34. Berens, "Reminiscences," pp. 42–46.
35. Berens, "Reminiscences," pp. 55–56.
36. Berens, "Reminiscences," pp. 54–55.
37. Berens, "Reminiscences," p. 49.
38. Berens, "Reminiscences," pp. 51–53.
39. Maurice Berens, "Chief William Berens," Unpublished paper, University of Winnipeg, pp. 3–4.
40. Berens, "Chief William Berens," pp. 7–9.
41. Berens, "Chief William Berens," pp. 10–11.
42. Berens, "Chief William Berens," pp. 13–14.
43. Dueck, Methodist Indian Day Schools and Indian Communities, pp. 94–96.
44. Hallowell, "Berens River," Ms. chapter 1, pp. 2, 9.
45. A. Irving Hallowell, Field Notebooks, Aug. 16–21, 1930, APS.
46. Hallowell, "Berens River," Ms. chapter 1, p. 10.
47. Hallowell, "Berens River," Ms. chapter 1, pp. 11, 13–14.
48. Victor P. Lytwyn, *The Fur Trade of the Little North: Indians, Pedlars, and Englishmen East of Lake Winnipeg, 1760–1821* (Winnipeg: Rupert's Land Research Centre, University of Winnipeg, 1986).
49. Berens, 1935.
50. A. Irving Hallowell, "Freudian Symbolism in the Dream of a Saulteaux Indian," *Man*, 38 (1938), pp. 47–48.
51. Mary Black-Rogers, "Ojibwa Power Interactions: Creating Contexts for 'Respectful Talk,'" in *Proceedings of Conference on Native North American Interaction Patterns*, ed. Regna Darnell (Ottawa: National Museums, in press).
52. William C. Manson, "Abram Kardiner and the Neo-Freudian Alternative in Culture and Personality," in *Malinowski, Rivers, Benedict and Others: Essays on Culture and Personality*, ed. G. W. Stocking, Jr., *History of Anthropology*, 4 (Madison, Wis.: University of Wisconsin Press, 1986), pp. 78–79.
53. Hallowell, "Freudian Symbolism in the Dream of a Saulteaux Indian," p. 48.
54. Hallowell, *Contributions to Anthropology*, p. 467.
55. Berens, "Chief William Berens," p. 15.
56. Berens, "Chief William Berens," pp. 16–17.
57. *Winnipeg Tribune*, Obituary of Chief William Berens, September 2, 1947.
58. Tom Boulanger, *An Indian Remembers: My Life as a Trapper in Northern Manitoba* (Winnipeg: Peguis Publishers, 1971), p. 39.
59. William Berens, Letter to A.I. Hallowell, January 3, 1947. Hallowell Papers, Col. 26, APS.
60. Berens, "Chief William Berens," p. 18.
61. Jennifer S. H. Brown, "A. I. Hallowell and William Berens Revisited," in *Papers of the Eighteenth Algonquian Conference*, ed. William Cowan (Ottawa: Carleton University, 1987), pp. 17–27.

CHAPTER 10

Dan Raincloud: "Keeping Our Indian Way"

Mary Black-Rogers[1]

PRESENTING DAN RAINCLOUD (1903–1974)

Although not the first of the last of the Great Lakes Algonquian shamans and *Midewiwin* (Grand Medicine Lodge) priests, Dan Raincloud's twentieth century career as a Minnesota Ojibwa religious-medical specialist illustrates the difficulties faced and the tactics used by those who work to perpetuate old forms of religious thinking and ways of coping in radically altered social settings. In many respects, the styles of this hard-pressed ritualist express the thoughts of Claude Levi-Strauss about the techniques of the *bricoleur*, the religious jack-of-all-trades who has to confront a wide variety of problems in his clients and patients with a limited and heterogeneous repertoire of mystical knowledge. Dan Raincloud, however, faced an array of difficulties unknown to his eighteenth century predecessors. Then, practitioners of the several Ojibwa religious specialties were many, the *Midewiwin* priests especially abundant and organized, arrayed in ranks of novices to seniors, with systematic, formal instruction available to beginners, and corrective commentary a constant feature of the professional's practice, both from fellow adepts and from whole communities of true believers. Raincloud, with few exemplars available in his time and reservation community, had great difficulty in even securing enough instruction for him to sense and project a confident mastery of a large enough array of mystical knowledge to be of effective service. And, in his often solo practice, he often faced skepticism, disinterest, and competing forms of religion and curing unknown to earlier generations of practitioners, in a community where commitment to the traditional culture was constantly threatening to slip away. He was therefore to a degree deviant, in that he was one of the few of his generation who decided early on a life dedicated to sustaining the heart of the Ojibwa way, by seeking and mastering traditional sources of power and transcendental knowledge. This decision, which was recurrent and not once-and-for-all-time, often oppressed him, when his strong sense of personal duty and heavy burden of responsibilities weighed on his limited time, energy, and skills. This decision he visualized as a persistent option point, a forking between radically opposed cultural roads, a larger alien one promising wealth and plenty, and a smaller familiar one leading to risk and an unknown future. The later forks differed from the earlier bald White-versus-Indian alternatives. Afterward, he had to face choices between secular political-administrative powers and exclusively religious ones, between practicing on the local or a regional level, between the privacy of ministering to the needs of Ojibwa clients or making presentations before American medical audiences, between seeming ordinary while becoming extraordinary, between the lures of national-level political activists seeking alliances with traditional power-figures or hewing to his community's preferences. How Dan Raincloud coped with such stresses when sustaining and developing the core of his identity and perfecting his knowledge and skills provides an object lesson in the individual techniques of cultural persistence and change. As the author shows, Dan Raincloud certainly was a man of acquired, polished charisma, as well as one ready with a self-effacing and self-protecting wit. (J. A. Clifton)

Mary, I have to work on my Indian way very hard. Some of it I will have teach so we keep going. I always too much on my hands. I'm wishing some one does the things I am ask to do. Maybe I should not know all I know. God must be the one who had me to be like this.

Dan Raincloud to author, June 24, 1968

Historians read words in documents written by persons now gone, seeking interpretations of the past. The words anthropologists heed are spoken by the living, known personally. Such words, out of context, may not communicate much. Interpreting an alien culture—whether separated by time, tradition, or both—is always a risky business. For anthropologists, it requires much observation, and interaction, and intricate communicating.

My friend and teacher, Dan Raincloud, Sr., had his own knack at communicating, whether using his English or his Ojibwa language ("Chippewa" locally), or through his interactional routines. While in many ways not typical of elders among the Minnesota Chippewa during the 1960s, he was not marked as isolated or deviant by them. On the contrary, Dan always operated from the true center of "his Indian way," whether dealing with his own people or with outsiders. His distinctiveness emanated from the very centrality of the role he sustained, central to what remained of the traditional culture. This was the essence of the complex identity he imparted.

Dan's words above are from a letter written nearly four years after our meeting. If I interpret correctly the meanings he intended, his words can reveal a good deal about the stresses his people were experiencing during the final decade of his life. He died in 1974, not having resolved the tensions of his time, which he had taken on as a kind of personal responsibility, and which became for him a painful dilemma. As spiritual leader, his focus was on the precarious continuance of the Indian religion, although secular matters also concerned him. I shall maintain that a person in his position necessarily had his finger on the pulse of local change, and could therefore be consulted as a barometer of the prevailing cultural climate. For many of his contemporaries, Dan Raincloud was inevitably a personage to be reckoned with on this twentieth century Indian frontier.

We met during my first field research year at Red Lake Indian Reservation in northern Minnesota, 1964–1965. Born in 1903, he was then nearing

Dan Raincloud's Dominion

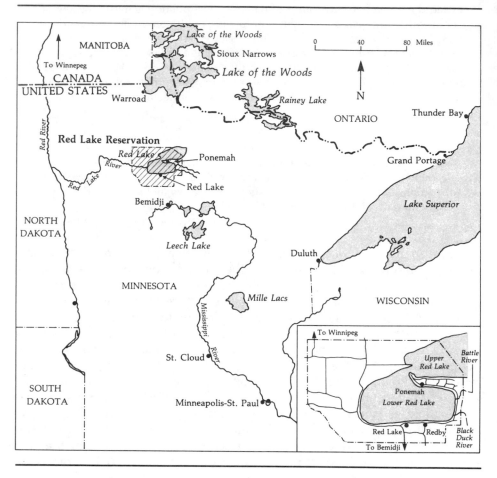

sixty-two years. A tall, spare man with quick movements, especially of the eyes, his was an almost pixie face—noteworthy in a person so important. But he rarely *acted* important, at least as outsiders might understand the posturings of power and prestige. Nonetheless, even strangers took him seriously after first acquaintance.

He was not heavy of girth, as were many men in his community. He once had been, he told me—until 1960—when he lost a grown son in a boating accident. "I nearly died when I lost my boy, I just barely got over it . . . that's why I'm thin, lost twenty pounds." He never regained the weight, although he did regain his prestige, which was at risk from this omen of weakness. Another Ojibwa elder explained how Dan "probably lost out some when his son died," alluding to signs that spell spiritual disfavor. Where Dan lived, a man's prestige suffered if he was beset with misfortunes, for such events were not accepted as accidental. They were caused—by those with superior power. That was the only major misfortune I know of in Dan's adult life. But he started his career handicapped, for his father died before he was ten—before he fasted and got knowledge about his "powers."

Through that first year, I started learning about traditional Ojibwa beliefs from a half-dozen elders, lifelong residents of the community of Ponemah. Among these mentors was Dan Raincloud. English was for them a second language, if used at all. They helped me understand their Indian Way by explaining how they classified all the *bema.diziwa.d* ("living things") of the world, as named and spoken of in Ojibwa by the *gete anishina.beg* ("people who lived the old ways").[2] They called themselves my "teachers." Ranging in age from sixty to eighty-five, all had been born before Christian missionaries settled in Ponemah. The two women, when in their teens, were among the first Christian converts and the first to start learning English.

Dan also began learning English at that time but never converted to Christianity. For from early youth he *knew* that one day he would be a spiritual leader in the Indian Way, serving those who still believed as the *gete anishina.beg* had. He learned this through the customary boyhood "fasting" (*gi.?igoshimowin*), a time when a personal "spirit" (*a.diso.ka.n*) might appear in a "vision-dream" (*ina.bandamowin*), to establish a permanent relationship with the supplicant. A gift of power bestowed at this time is spoken of as a "blessing" (*gashki?ewiziwin*).

Dan chose to reveal something about his own fasting experience shortly before I left the reservation in late 1965. One day he announced his readiness to tape record an account of his life, in his language. Two days before, he had hesitated, saying,"it could be told just a little, but not too much," insisting some parts could not be "explained" in English. He demurred despite the fact that we had just visited the site of his fast, where he had described the building of his *wasisawan* ("nest"), and the signs telling him he had been visited by an *a.diso.ka.n*. As it turned out, his life story, recorded that day, consisted of a sentence or two in Ojibwa, then his own translation, more Ojibwa, then translation, and so on. Some of his English was like this:

> I was a poor boy, when I was a little boy. My father was a sickly man, so my mother raised me. Why I did the fasting was to try to find some other way that I can live longer, and have strange powers. I did get what I wanted, when I fasted there at Sand Hill, then. I noticed there were some *manido.g* ("spirits") in that place. I sometimes used to hear humming, that is, talking, by themselves. I was scared of them.
>
> Before I was born, I think I was a Thunderbird. I used to come with the Thunderbirds, and now I know just exactly where we went by, through here. When I was a boy, that's when I learned that I was to become a Grand Medicine man [of the *Midewiwin*]. Everything I know [i.e., learned] came true, every bit of that. There were two things that I was given [a choice of] at the time of my fasting: one, to be rich, and the other one, to have many powers, strange powers that I could have.

So I chose the strange powers instead of being rich. At every reservation, afar, they talked about me, the way I had powers. [But that was later,] I didn't bother what I had learned until 1932—the doctoring, and Grand Medicine singing.

Today is forty-seven years [since] I was at the Wahpeton Indian School [North Dakota] . . . At that time I used to work at shocking [harvesting grain]. That was before the days of these combines. This is where I found a woman that I could have married—a white woman. I did not want the offer, due to the woman being too beautiful . . . and here I was, I don't know who I might call myself. . . . The old man gave me, if I stayed with the girl, eighty acres, a kind of car of that time [called] an Overland, some pigs, cows, chickens, farm equipment, horses. I did not accept.

After that I went back to Wahpeton, back to singing more . . . I never thought about this girl, while I was there . . . I was a real good singer, when I was a young man. I sang songs any time of the night those songs came to me. The Indians know that I own the songs, not stealing from somebody else's songs. They like the songs that I sing to them.

After that time, when I left Wahpeton and came here to the reservation, I forgot that I had been to school. Didn't even talk English either. Then in 1932 I started to be friends with lawyers and representatives and also I read newspapers, and right from there I started back. And that's where I got to learn to talk English again . . . I'd almost forgotten that a white person, uh . . . he had a way of living, or anything. I'd just simply thought I was just an Indian.

And now I began to walk out and sing, on account of this old man who was having this Grand Medicine dance, to help him out. [But] there was nobody that I can sat with [learn from] who knows something about this Grand Medicine . . . At that time I could not even accept [all] the offers, [when] I was invited to be with the Grand Medicine man. At times [now] I don't like to use the Grand Medicine, due to the fact that I'm too busy working.

Before examining the events he chose to tell in this rather fragmented retrospective recital, it is necessary to consider an important aspect of any of Dan's communications: the things he left unsaid. From the start, Dan had made a stipulation that on some matters he must remain silent. As the work developed, the demarcation of his no-talk territory became one of the more important findings of my study. My other Ojibwa teachers were also bound by talk taboos. But the areas and executions of Dan's reticence, I discovered, differed markedly from those of the others. And, unlike Dan, they had not made this an explicit condition of our work. Each, however, had his or her own means for protecting the privacy built into the Indian Way. Contrasting their performances was valuable both in reaching an appreciation of the basic system, and in understanding Dan's special role in it.

A word about terminology and about Dan's many hats. When he used the phrase "Grand Medicine" he was referring to the *Midewiwin* society (in English, "Grand Medicine Lodge"). He also spoke of a "Grand Medicine man" (*Mide?iwewinini*), a functionary of that society. In English, this is often shortened to "medicine man," and used ambiguously, to refer to the use of powers not necessarily connected with the Medicine Lodge. For example, a second powerful role is that of "curer/healer" (*nana.ndawi?iwewinini*), and another is the "conjurer" (*ji.saki.winini*, the "shaking tent" man). These three were said to be distinct from one another, acquired in different ways, and used for different purposes. Yet another such role is the "singer-drummer" (*ni.mi?-iwewinini*), for songs themselves can be "medicine" (*mashkiki*). Indeed, almost all practice of powers is accompanied by appropriate songs. This Ojibwa word *mashkiki* defies English translation. When I write "medicine" here, I mean the Ojibwa concept. And when they appended "man," they included the women who sometimes acquired and acted out these influential roles.

Dan Raincloud had been blessed with all of these "strange powers." When he later recorded a history of his curings, he explained that while he had also received *ji.saki.* powers, he had never "bothered that." It would make his life stronger, he observed, to keep some powers without using them. He was, in addition, a singer-drummer, a name-giver who had named over one hundred people, a hunter, a fisherman—and also a dancer, carpenter, politician, and spokesman-orator. One who donned many hats from time-to-time, Dan Raincloud was, in his own words, "an all-around man."

Dan's versatility may in part reflect the contemporary condition, when there were few left who were able or willing to assume the various specialty roles. However, it also appears to have been characteristic of the kind of men who had been leaders in the past. For my part, it caused some perplexity, for it was not always clear to me what hat Dan was wearing at any given moment. Indeed, perhaps his special influence among his people was aided by this fact: the multiple roles he played could result in confusion, and wariness of a man so gifted. One suspects that the power of such leaders has always rested partly on their capability of creating this very type of confusion.

Although in his 1965 account Dan highlighted the *Midewiwin,* he revealed little of this secret society. The Grand Medicine Lodge formed a large part of his no-talk territory. He intimated more than once the difficulties of speaking of it in English. This was one of Dan's ploys in shutting off a subject.

Another way he had for indicating our approach to that forbidden zone was to point out the particular settings required for speaking of the topic at hand. "That's 'way out of line for us, Mary," he would say, "We don't usually talk about that . . . [That talk] is what we use when we do it." The last phrase is crucial. Dan's response to a query regarding the learning of *Mide?iwe* was just: "I wish you had watched that—you should have been there when I told you . . . [to come]." He meant his invitation to a recent initiation ceremony at his house, which I had missed. His lesson was clear: a person speaks of his or her powers and their acquisition *only while using them.* The telling is part of the doing. When asked to give a ritual name in the naming ceremony, for example, the name-giver tells of his dream in which the name was significant, and this telling is the active ingredient in the giving. At any other time, speaking of the dream or other spiritual encounter robs it of its power.

How, then, did Dan Raincloud bring himself to relate so much of his spiritual history in the 1965 life sketch? For one thing, he brought into play one of his unique and creative skills. He used his power to convert our interaction, then and there, into an appropriate, ritual setting. This he accomplished by presenting me with some medicine and singing a song, legitimizing entry into what was otherwise the no-talk zone. Others used various tactics to avoid speaking of something when the time and setting were wrong. Dan alone altered the context to fit his speech.

The discussion so far has served to introduce Dan Raincloud, and the "research encounter" whence I first came to know him. Over the decade that followed, I was to see this genuinely traditional Ojibwa man operating on a shifting cultural boundary in changing times. His lifelong role tension and alternating identities were exacerbated, peaking in the 1968 lament, "too much on my hands" and "maybe I should not know all I know." If he was so well endowed with special powers and success, so well equipped to deal with both the Indian Way and the modern world, what accounts for his wish at that time to be unburdened of his accumulated load of knowledge and responsibility?

The attempt to understand and to answer that question can take the form, first, of reviewing the pertinent facts of his life up to 1965—and then beyond, to his death in 1974—while examining closely the recurring themes in his own testimony. Then, his life must be viewed in the context of the larger, outside events of his day, and how these affected Dan's people and their Indian Way.

The salient message in his 1965 recollections concerned a fork-in-the-road choice he faced when but ten years old, while fasting. In one way or another this theme—being rich or having "strange powers"—is woven through subsequent remembered decision points. Never again did he speak directly of that choice, which renders its explicit, volunteered revelation here of great value in understanding later remarks and behavior.

Dan's father—"a sickly man"—died when he was small. So, "to find some other way that I can live longer," he sought powers in a vision quest. During this encounter, a generous benefactor promised that the strongest of traditional powers would be his, in the future. Or, if he preferred, he could elect success and riches of a purely secular nature in the White man's world. His statement, "I chose the strange powers instead of being rich," sounds final and decisive, yet as his life unfolded, he made that decision over and over again. The fork kept reappearing, alternatives constantly tempting him.

At fifteen, he was sent away to an Indian school, and during this period, a nearby farmer offered him riches and a too beautiful daughter. He refused, because "here I was, not knowing who I might call myself." Clearly, as Dan understood it, the choice concerned personal identity. This "White-wife" reference was a persistent minor theme in Dan's accounts of his life, and in his relations with me and others. It could be mistaken for a personal overture in his habit of "teasing" women. However, he told of another dream-vision, when a female spirit appeared. She instructed him to expect to marry a White woman. This, Dan explained, he tried to reject; but he was "forced" to listen to the female spirit. Later, at serious points in our discussions, he was apt to interject this theme laughingly as a subject-changer. It took me quite awhile to recognize Dan's romantic behavior and reputation as part of the power role; whether he invented this extension of it to suit certain settings will always remain unclear. Dan had a greater-than-average Ojibwa talent for creating ambiguities.

Turning away from the promise of riches on a father-in-law's farm, Dan recalled a period of success at Indian singing, of quitting school, returning to the reservation, and forgetting to speak English. Indeed, so he recalled, he forgot that White people "had a way of living, or anything. . . . I just simply thought I was just an Indian." Another critical decision was made; again it had to do with being "just an Indian." This self-identity theme, and the social contexts where it was a factor, absorbed him for years.

Then came 1932, which we know heralded the Great Depression, extraordinary poverty in reservation communities, and the "Indian New Deal" of President Franklin Roosevelt and Commissioner of Indian Affairs John Collier. Suddenly, both roads opened before him. In the following years, Dan acquired friends and influence among non-Indian Americans, again speaking English and reading newspapers. Later, he told me he had spent this decade in political activity "to save the tribe." But at the same time, he also "began to walk out and sing" at Grand Medicine sessions. Curiously, the 1965 text, which at the beginning had presented these as alternative roads, suddenly turns them into concurrent activities.

And then Dan's last sentence leaps to the present, when his problem has become one of insufficient time to carry on the Grand Medicine "due to the fact that I'm too busy working." "Work" here refers to his everyday economic and political activities, which at the time of speaking Dan seemed to consider the more important road to follow, according to this rather abrupt ending of his life account.[3]

On the modern, secular side of Dan's life, there is supporting evidence. A published history of Red Lake Reservation lists him among representatives from Ponemah in the 1957 General Council meetings. During 1965 and 1966, he spearheaded a winning political campaign; his son, Dan Jr., became the new Council member from Ponemah. The following year, he appeared as spokesman for the local Indians' boycott of merchants in the nearby town of Bemidji, a successful protest against racially derogatory remarks broadcast from the town's radio station.[4]

Why was Dan Raincloud called on to speak for others in these causes? His speech did not exhibit a superior or even standard command of English, unlike his more elegant Ojibwa. Other Red Lake Indians reported they turned to him because he was not "put-down as a stupid Indian" when he dealt with outsiders, the way most felt they were. I, too, experienced the power of his expressive voice. Despite the sometimes tangled English syntax, his messages came through forcefully. So Dan's two roads started running parallel, and by 1965 he was finding himself uncomfortably running with a foot on each.

The old Indian road was providing its own internal stresses. On the one hand, others were recognizing his eminence in the realm of "strange powers," indeed perceived him as one about whom the people would now say *gota.nenda.gozi a?awe* ("that person is dangerous" because of knowing medicine)—a lesson volunteered by my teacher, Madge Downfeather. For her part, Cora Jones regularly referred me to Dan as the expert on matters of the old religion, which she claimed to have abandoned when young, adding that people who still believed those things looked to Dan to make the offerings and contact the spirits in the old way.

To his contemporaries in 1965, the observable facts would add up to an image of more than ordinary power. They could see what Dan had accomplished: curings; diagnosing; a significant level of the *Midewiwin* knowledge; success in games and in love; good gardening, fishing, and carpentry; political effectiveness; and persuasive talk. Of equal importance to them was a different manifestation of his power: he had not been struck down or enfeebled by phenomena beyond his control. The last evidence alone pointed to a respectable level of power and strong protective blessings in the eyes of those who believed the old Way.

On the other hand, some old-timers still questioned Dan's adequacy to fulfill all the functions that were now devolving to him. Such concerns came to a head when the senior Ponemah medicine man, Old Nodin, was unavailable for the performance of a *Midewiwin* funeral rite. While admitting that "this old man here, named Nodin" could still "preach a sermon for the dead people," my teacher, Alec Everwind, was pessimistic that any man now living could carry out these rites properly and exactly, as the old people had done in the past. This was especially so for funerals—the hardest to learn, the most important to perform correctly. Alec's father had performed them authentically; he classified such funerals as "good *Mide?iwe.*"

Alec was asked to fill in and try to conduct this funeral, although he himself had never taken instruction from his father. But he modestly refused. Cora said flatly, "nobody don't dare do it—*I* wouldn't!" Eventually, Dan did accept the responsibility, whereupon both Alec and Cora were critical of his performance. Alec complained, "he missed part of it . . . You can't do that. Some of the old people . . . they come back and say, 'Well it sure is too bad we can't have anybody that can say the whole works . . . that's what they claim, he missed a lot of it, what he's supposed to learn."

The funeral ceremony was surely the most exacting and sensitive of all. Furthermore, it was becoming critical to the viability of the Indian religion. For there were those of the older generation in Ponemah who now advocated joining the Christian church on grounds that otherwise there would be no one to bury them. Cora Jones was one, by her own report. She said *she* would have a Christian burial.

Dan privately questioned his own adequacy, especially for conducting funerals, and knew the risks of doing them improperly, before he was ready. If he was the person most qualified to be called in, when Nodin could not come, was it not the beginning of the end for the Indian Way? This led to other, often-expressed worries. Each year, Dan had seen fewer believers, and sensed less interest among younger men in taking up medicine careers "so we keep going" in the future. The old ways were dying, so Dan thought in 1965. What, then, should he do with his knowledge?

Men of power such as Dan felt a special responsibility toward the knowledge they held. This was peculiarly acute for the *Midewiwin* formulas and rites, which could only pass from elder master to younger initiates within the order. In 1965, Dan was asking himself: would the knowledge die with him? Indeed, his own instruction was incomplete and threatened to stay that way: Old Nodin, with whom he had been "sitting" as novitiate, was now in hospital. The prospect of becoming the sole repository of the remaining knowledge of the Indian Way was beginning to disturb him. His alone might be the decision whether or when to cease Grand Medicine rites altogether. He also would have to decide alone whether to reveal and record the Indian Way for posterity. For such decisions there was no traditional precedent, and there would be no one of comparable power to consult.

Still, in 1965, there was Old Nodin. For me, Nodin was an enigmatic backstage presence. I never caught more than a glimpse of him. This aged medicine man, said to be near ninety and almost unable to work, enjoyed a staunch reputation for consistently refusing to talk to outsiders at all about his life or work. As 1965 ended, when even the Red Lake Tribal Council expressed a desire to record and preserve his knowledge of the funeral ceremony, Nodin refused. On the reservation, there was general concern that when Nodin went, the Grand Medicine would go with him. Dan Raincloud, like others, held his old master in great respect. But Dan was working out his own interpretation of the impasse and his personal need to resolve it.

All of this was background to Dan's late 1965 decision to record his life story, a decision made after nearly a year's pondering as to which things he could safely tell in such a setting. Although then convinced the old beliefs were dying, and with them the need to preserve his powers by silence, his actions continued to show traditional caution. Yet, he had been moved to put on record some particularly sensitive highlights of his life's path, finding an ingenious way to legitimize the setting. In view of what happened after 1965, it will be of interest that this recording took place at a low tide of the Indian Way. Dan was reviewing the past and where his life had led him, but with all his powers he did not prognosticate the events of his remaining years.

By summer 1967, when I "sat" with Dan again, his horizons had undergone some alteration. In part, this came from the outside world's rapidly growing interest in Indian ways, a development that was to turn around his priorities, whether he wished it or not. Between 1965 and the early 1970s, Dan was astride a dilemma, a particularly acute and painful one. For one thing, he and his constituency were nearly overwhelmed by the modern world. The rest of his story will be a record of what he did about it. From his fluctuating behavior, and seemingly contradictory statements during these

THE RITUAL FACE OF DAN RAINCLOUD, SR. Displaying his serious exterior as leading ritualist, Raincloud appears in his dancing costume at the Old Ponemah sacred ground in August 1967. (Photograph by author.)

years, I came to see him as a kind of barometer that registered the level of traditional belief as it rose and fell in his constituency. For while he did not predict the future, he had his finger on the pulse of change. A spiritual leader whose position depends upon his people's belief would be the first to notice their wavering.

First, his fame as an Indian doctor had spread, bringing an increase in his curing work. On July 12, 1966, his photograph had appeared in a *Minneapolis Tribune* series about Indian health. Dubbing him "medicine man," it showed him with his curing instruments. After a brief reference to his "sucking the germs" with the tube-like *okanag*, the story ended: "Then he turned his back, refusing to discuss these secrets any further."

In August of 1967, he again received recognition from outsiders for his healing profession. The United States Public Health Service invited him to speak before a conference in nearby Bemidji, Minnesota. On my arrival two

DAN RAINCLOUD'S JOKING IMAGE. With a comic grin, wearing a pun-fun sweatshirt next to his house in Ponemah in 1965, Raincloud here presents a different aspect of his self. The play on words, "All I Want Is to Be Left A Loan," communicates a dual message. These portraits show two typical stances of those Ojibwa who functioned in the medicine man role. (Photograph by author.)

weeks before this scheduled event, I found Dan and others absorbed preparing "The Role of the Medicine Man," the title of his invited paper. Tom Cain, another of my teachers, was to share the spotlight as coauthor and interpreter, since Dan elected to address the government doctors in Ojibwa. Tom was truly bilingual and bicultural. His father was Irish, his mother Ojibwa; they had raised their family in his mother's home community, Ponemah. In 1967, Tom was teaching courses on Ojibwa language and culture, both in the school and in a government adult education program. Unlike Dan Raincloud, when Tom Cain taught about the Indian Way, it was usually in third person, at that time.

While helping Dan gather herbs and roots for his speech, I found him more protective than before of his no-talk zone, troubled with decisions about what part to tell and what to withhold. The pooling of medical knowledge across cultures he found an alluring new idea, and his contribution was being accorded the respect it deserved. The Red Lake Tribal Chairman, Roger Jourdain, also favored Dan's participation, and was scheduled to introduce the presentation. They knew, though, that only parts of Dan's knowledge would be of benefit to non-Indians.

But Dan's double road now brought new dilemmas: he was representing his people in yet another modern context, but this time it was as a specialist in traditional Indian ways. How would this affect his efforts to cure? Would such a public revelation not jeopardize the strength of his powers? His Indian Way was enjoying greater interest from both Indians and non-Indians. Yet, for him to meet the demands of both involved logical contradictions: the latter required talking about it, the former demanded silence. The two roads had not been envisaged as merging into one. Difficult new decisions added psychological stress to the load of "too much to do." He worried about his own health.

The Public Health speech went well; Dan chose to limit the material chiefly to herbal remedies, and his adeptness at dodging sensitive subjects was never in better form. For example, queries about medicines for love, for gambling, and for hunting—and the *Midewiwin* songs that went with them—were parried with an apparent jest (in English): "I can't tell all my secrets, with our Chief here—he'll take away my business."

The continued effectiveness of his medicines following the conference left believers content that Dan had not said too much. Nevertheless, he now started exhibiting serious ambivalence about continuing his medicine work—just when his roles in both arenas depended on it. His accounts of how well the Indian Way was faring began to be interspersed with strong reiterations about wanting to quit. This new theme will bear watching.

Dan's "doctoring" was much on his mind that summer of 1967. He asked me to tape the history of his *nana.ndawi?iwe* curings. Always he had spoken more freely of these than of *Mide?iwe*, but the tape finds him hedging here and there. At one point, he asserted, "I hate to do it," explaining "if I fail they'll say 'doctor's no good'." However, he "could not refuse," for he did not want his patients dissatisfied. In essence, *they would not let him stop.* He was never explicit about whether it was doctoring or *Mide?iwe* he wished to stop, but could not. Sometimes it seemed to be both.

From 1966 through 1969, Dan's letters to me reported the size and success of a growing number of "Grand Medicine Dances"—some thirteen meetings were mentioned. "There were 40 of us at one of them but this is not largest. I been singing a lot," he wrote in February 1966. By December 1969: "We been having Grand Medicine Dances for five weekends, this is the longest we ever had for some time." But success brought problems, as he indicated in his letter of June 1968 heading this essay: "I always too much on my hands." A month later, he went further, informing me "I tried to quit but the people says no," adding soon thereafter, "I now refuse the dance . . . I have to get away from the old place they will hate me for this." And, in January 1969, after a trying and traumatic year: "hope they won't bother me any more . . . they were two men tried [to get] me to teach them I told them I don't want to do that any more."

The last accompanied news of Cora Jones's death the previous fall. She had requested an Indian funeral after all, and Dan conducted it, reluctantly, for he wrote of her husband Bill, "took him long time [to get] me to go and talk, since I say no." Community doubts about his qualifications for performing the funeral ceremony seemed to have disappeared. At least twenty Grand Medicine funerals were counted during 1966–1969, with Dan conducting most, if not all. During this time, Old Nodin was available only occasionally for consultation. By 1969, that aged ritualist seemed to have delegated his position as spiritual leader to Dan Raincloud.

Coping with so much death was part of Dan's agony, a state of mind that peaked in summer 1968. He wrote on July 23, "Have your letter for a cheer up a little as has been on hard go. . . . The hardest I face yet on R.M. Cloud who was killed in the [Viet Nam] War. . . . I just barely made it never was shakey before. Johnson was buried on 4th of July, and 2 men drowned at Red Lake about the same time as our bad luck. . . . I can't keep my mind off how we are here at Ponemah." That August, he expressed his depression, suggesting that he did not want to live to be old but would rather die soon, that he was probably a weak man.

Because of the many deaths and accidents that summer, Dan was not sleeping well, nor was his wife, Madeline. He said the troubles were due to the drinking, and the paving of the Ponemah Point road. He did not mean that the accidents occurred on this road. From the start of its construction, he and Madeline were worried that bad luck would come of it, for the bulldozers had dug up old Indian ground. In July 1969, nearly a year later, there had been no fewer than eleven recent burials with Dan officiating; and he was still busy with these dismal rites. The many deaths at Ponemah were again described as "very bad luck around here." Since the concept of "luck" was all but absent from traditional Ojibwa belief, it is likely that this was something of a euphemism for other suspected causes of the community's load of misfortunes. Events did not occur accidentally, remember; they were caused.

For emerging at Ponemah was its deeper layer of traditional commitment. It is of interest that only two Christian funerals were mentioned. The fact that when her end neared Cora asked to be buried in the Indian Way speaks for the strong roots and enduring viability of the supposedly "dying out" religion. This nascent resurgence was not confined to Ponemah and did not go unnoted by an increasingly interested outside world; it caught the attention of the *Minneapolis Tribune* in a December 11, 1968, news story written by Gerald Vizenor. Dan's role was prominent in this account, which reported an Indian funeral he had conducted at Warroad, Minnesota, on

December 10th, identifying him as "Daniel Raincloud, the Midewiwin medicine man from the nearby Red Lake Reservation." This occurred scarcely a month before Dan wrote to me, "I don't want to do that any more."

His ambivalence and stress were not relieved by any slackening of demand for his ministrations. On the contrary, calls for his services were coming from ever more distant places, through Northern Minnesota into Ontario and as far east as Niagara Falls.

If Dan Raincloud was a barometer of community commitment to the Indian Way, his greater involvement in ritual activities measured a substantial rise in barometric pressure during this period. Hence, the danger of talking should have been on the rise too. Was Dan then showing less readiness to discuss forbidden subjects? Was his internal conflict partly a consequence of feeling he had told too much already? The increased pressure on him, whether it came from without or within, at its peak produced a state of near trauma. And indeed, discussions did become more truncated.

I was present during parts of the summers of 1967 through 1969. The first summer fresh plans were made to tape record the funeral ceremony for the Tribal archives—this time with Dan performing, not Nodin. I was nominated to do the recording, but the plan somehow got lost, whether by neglect or design is not clear. Instead, I accompanied Dan while he visited patients. The following summer, when I inquired about these patients, he preferred not to discuss them. Instead, he invited me to attend a funeral. Once again, *doing* won out over *discussing*.

In August of 1968, as he entered the time of his deepest pain and ambivalence, he spoke of his attempts to quit. But after refusing two would-be patients, he feared "they will be mad at me." At the time, I attributed his lack of interest in recording his knowledge for posterity to his general depression and lowered self-confidence. I later realized that this new silence came not only from his worry about perhaps being "a weak man" after all, but also from his sensing the renewed power of this kind of knowledge in the living present. Its preservation (and his) lay in not "telling too much." His barometer was working.

My brief visit in 1969 turned up another new believer. Tom Cain, who had usually separated himself from traditional people by third-person usages, speaking of "their religion" in his courses on Indian culture, had gone to Dan in quest of some medicine for himself. Tom showed it to me, but then silenced my questions with a strong command to be quiet, adding "Don't desecrate that medicine."

Dan volunteered a corroboration when I stopped at his house that day, but said only that it was the first time for Cain, and that it must have worked since Tom had not returned. I asked no questions. Dan seemed less disturbed or depressed than when I last saw him, despite a fall in May when he fractured several ribs. His spirit was elevated, perhaps, because he had professional company. Old Nodin had been in Ponemah the previous week, helping with a Grand Medicine curing rite, and would appear at another, soon. Moreover, Dan's invitation to Alec Everwind to aid in funerals the past year had apparently been accepted.

During these several trying years following 1965, Dan himself experienced a few misfortunes and illnesses, but he came through strong. Deaths of young people were especially ominous, and he worried much over those who lost sons in Viet Nam and children in automobile accidents. His own record was relatively happy: he "nearly lost" his grown daughter in 1969, but she recovered. He reported his own health as up and down. The extra pressures of 1968 had put him into the hospital for a short stay, of which he wrote that the reservation doctors "couldn't cure" him. But each time I saw him, he did not seem ill. Even in August of 1968, while he spoke of being depressed, he looked and acted much like the vigorous old Dan.

Vigorous enough, indeed, to be sounding out two fresh candidates for his fantasy "White wife" companion. These two young women, anthropology students doing their duty, were interviewing him.[5] They confided to me their reactions to his overtures: he was an egoist and a silly old man. He had informed them that one of them was "the woman" fated for him. His persistent seeking for this dream-prophesy was likely to get him into trouble, I thought. At the least, he would be sadly misunderstood. While I had puzzled over his fantasizing a "romance" with me—he sometimes went so far as to address me as "wife" in letters—I now became apprehensive, fearing he would be marked as a comic character.

With a new sense that this dream-vision was very real to Dan, I began to recognize it as a contributing factor to his dilemma. It seems to have been increasingly difficult, as his senior years approached, for Dan to reconcile the failure of this particular blessing. Yet to me, as well as to the students, his teasing and none-too-subtle hints did seem silly and inappropriate. Nonetheless, he persisted. To do otherwise, to have forsaken this blessing, would have undermined his faith in the Indian Way. All else promised so many years earlier had come to him; the image of the White wife must lie yet in the future.

My understanding of Dan's faith was improving, and especially its relation to his role as a leader, a person who affected the lives of others. He necessarily differed from them, both in the mainsprings of his faith and in the visibility of his influence. Recognized power-holders like Dan were entrusted with special responsibility in Ojibwa society, for their powers gave them greater control over others than was normally acceptable. As a rule, coercive behavior was frowned upon; even talk or thoughts of this nature should be suppressed. The appropriate stance was one of powerlessness. Alec once expressed it perfectly, with just the right note of ambiguity: "I haven't got no power or anything. I just live." Nevertheless, Alec rarely missed an opportunity to point out that he had lived for seventy years without succumbing to illness or other forms of helplessness. This fact spoke far more than words of a person's power.

Such a humble stance could not, however, be maintained in the same manner by those whose powers were used on behalf of the people. Their position was generally spoken of as "responsibility for others," rather than control, and they were expected to use, not abuse, the powers of leadership. It should be apparent by now that the Indian Way did not separate "sacred" from "secular" areas of life. Only the modern path did that. On the old path, "religious" beliefs entered into all of life's activities and goals, triumphs and disasters, weaknesses and strengths. "Powers" referred to the whole range of abilities necessary to get through life, starting with the most mundane, and every living creature possessed some. Those with the strongest powers, in any given circumstance or need, would lead, so long as success marked their decisions and actions.

I do not believe Dan's inner faith ever wavered. Even when assessing the falling off of his constituency as some turned their backs on the Indian Way, he never dismissed it as meaningless or false. But his position of influence, and indeed his confidence in his own powers, depended heavily on the faith of others—their faith in the Way, their faith in his continued rapport with his spiritual guides. In this, his faith differed from theirs; he was, in a sense, more dependent on them than they on him.

To summarize the painful pregnant years from 1965 to 1970, which finally saw the birth of new directions and horizons for the old ways, three elements of that creative struggle can be noted. First, the entangling of Dan's two paths, when events in the world were upsetting his expectations, and the dying out was transforming into a rebirth. This presented him with disturbing contradictions. Decisions about speaking or remaining quiet on traditionally sensitive subjects were pressured from opposing directions. These he weathered, and attained acceptance as a leading man of power, both from his people and from the outside world. But not without the sense, for a time, that his contexts were going out-of-control.

Being out-of-control, in the Ojibwa view, was a sign ushering in the second element. His fears that he was losing his powers were based on dual facts: traditional belief was growing in his community, but so was "bad luck." Surely these believers must soon lose their faith in his protection, or blame him in one sense or another for failing his responsibility. His self-doubts grew; he wanted to quit, but others would not let him.

The third element is the charting of the prevailing cultural climate by watching Dan as barometer. Each of his decisions and actions, as they hewed to one or the other of the two still separate paths, should represent to us his weighing of the old ways versus the modern. Up to 1970, the balance seems to have been precarious and indecisive. The old path was not becoming a mere trail; in fact the Indian Way was seen to be widening, and Dan was still with it. Was that road fated to end abruptly at the chasm sharply separating the two cultures? Or could that gap be spanned? Perhaps the bridge then building between the old and the new was partly the fruit of Dan's painful labors. Having traveled this far, determined to arrive somewhere, Dan could not escape the responsibility for design and construction of a way to connect the two.

After 1970, I began to view Dan's life-story text as a symbolic representation of the dilemma of his people, a kind of modern legend. His recurring
fork-in-the-road identity choice stood for the perpetual riddle of our time,
"What is an Indian?" and his tangled paths were the various Indian struggles
to survive with dignity and integrity. Dan's life-legend, recorded in 1965, was
a creative effort to grasp larger events by personal metaphor, although not
necessarily a self-conscious process.

In his last years, although he did not entirely resolve either his own or the
larger paradox, his creative side showed itself ever more clearly. And the way
in which he lived out his legend suggests a broader conclusion: modern
Indians are far from immobilized by the perpetual riddle.

Dan continued to be active and effective on both life paths, and
increasingly in control of their tendency to merge. At Christmas 1970, when
I stopped to see him again, he was noncommittal about the state of the Indian
Way. Its revival since 1965, and his undoubted place within it, he simply
accepted. He did not seem to consider its future assured, however; perhaps
he still liked to think of himself as "the last of the greats"—a phrase that had
once revealed the element of vanity in his impulse toward recording for
posterity. Nonetheless, he rode with me to Minneapolis that Christmas to
visit a daughter for purposes that became apparent only afterward. Three
years later he declared of her, she was "catching on quite a bit," meaning she
was mastering knowledge of Ojibwa medicine.

His letter of March 1971 was full of news about his far-ranging activities.
He had traveled to a meeting in Phoenix, Arizona, where he served as
consultant on setting up a tribal credit union patterned on the successful one
for the Red Lake community. On local commitments, he added, "I have to be
a teacher at Red Lake High School starting next week and am ask to St. Cloud
and St. Paul." Of Ojibwa herbal medicine, he commented, "I don't think I will
make the medicine any more I will [send] someone for it . . . I won't pay for
it as others will."

This did not, however, represent a neglect of curing work. Indeed, all signs
indicated that his private practice was, if anything, increasing. While in Minneapolis in fall 1972, he was busy caring for patients and clients. Those who
saw him there reported he was still worried about lack of younger people to
carry on this work, for he was now fully dedicated to promoting its continuance.

Dan Raincloud's 1972 visit to the Twin Cities represented another
unanticipated convergence of his two roads, and another shuffling of the
social contexts that usually guided his choice of actions. He was there at the
invitation of the American Indian Movement—to deliver prayers at a gathering of this recently organized national Indian organization. Indians from thirteen states were present, preparing for a march on Washington, D.C., to
protest the policies of the Bureau of Indian Affairs. AIM leaders paid Dan $200
plus expenses, which impressed him; but he did not join the march.

He spoke with mixed feelings of this appearance. That his hosts had not
translated his Ojibwa prayers into other Indian languages disturbed him,

since many could not understand what he had said. He also questioned the marchers' behavior in Washington, destroying property and causing trouble. He was expressing sentiments shared by others in his community, Ponemah, where AIM's militancy was not much favored: it was not doing things in the Indian Way. Dan's assessment of his participation was expressed enigmatically, saying he had done it "just for the money."

If this signified that he placed his prayers at the AIM meeting on the side of the modern rather than the Indian Way, was his dilemma compounded or resolved? Were his two roads not converging, his commitment to using "strange powers" now paying off in both traditional and modern spheres? Or was this the death knell for the authentic use of his Ojibwa heritage? If his life-legend had stood for a prolonged identity crisis of his people, what did the involvement with AIM say of their future?

Visiting Dan in Ponemah during March of 1973, I found him absorbed creatively, sorting his various demands, getting his shifting contexts under control. Where once he created a context to fit his performance, as when he first told of his life-legend, he was now about to create a performance to fit newly emerging contexts.

Busy and productive on both roads, no longer dismayed when they crossed over or converged, Dan mixed talk of all in sequence. "Politics" was one example—his tribe's Credit Union committee was lobbying for government help, with Dan acting as its chairman. Another example was his assessment of the previous autumn's AIM affair. Several AIM members had later visited him, but their presence in Ponemah had not brought the feared disturbance. He also recounted his travels to medical and university groups, where he spoke publicly about Indian medicine, for which he was generously reimbursed. I judged his health must have improved, too, permitting all this running about. But he did not care to remain away from home long, he said, since Madeline was not well.

He believed his "medicine" had made "money come in" these last few years "without working" (see note 3). The amounts paid him for his various appearances was something that greatly impressed him, judging by his frequent references to them. That his position as "medicine man" was thus yielding a substantial improvement in his economic state still did not strike him as a contradiction of his life-legend.

However, in 1973, Dan spoke at greatest length of his doctoring practice and the current status of the *Midewiwin* (now using the Ojibwa term for Grand Medicine). Several developments stood out. No longer was he alone, for two younger men were "sitting with" him, taking instruction. Another man was available also, who had learned his Grand Medicine elsewhere; Dan said of him, "he doesn't really know it." And Nodin himself was still only semiretired. When forgetful of details, particularly of songs, Dan consulted this elder practitioner at a nearby rest home. The songs were hardest to remember and teach, Dan observed. On the other hand, sometimes Dan had to correct Old Nodin, who, now approaching ninety-nine years, was slipping somewhat.

A large *Midewiwin* event was soon to take place, he told me. For this occasion, Old Nodin would be fetched from the rest home, to cure a chronically ill woman whose previous treatments had not succeeded. Three other recent *Midewiwin* curings had been successful. Dan's descriptions indicated strictly traditional procedures. No longer did he speak of quitting outright. Now he mentioned not wanting "to do it so much." At one point, he complained of his many chores, "I hate being somebody."

The final bit of news was the most surprising: he was at this moment in the midst of tape recording the Ojibwa "marriage ceremony" for an outsider. I knew of no such tradition. "Was there an Indian marriage ceremony in the past?" I asked. "No," replied Dan, shaking his head. But he had been asked to perform a few recently, adding that he had told the couples they might get the signature of a Justice of the Peace as well. If Dan knew no traditional Ojibwa marriage ceremony, what was he using? His answer: he was delivering the first half of the funeral rite. So this was finally being recorded for posterity.

But Dan was holding back on that. It was very important, he said, that only the first half of the funeral rite be told. Recording the whole would be too dangerous. He added, "I've got grannies. God might think 'he wants to get rid of one of his grannies' if I told the second half."[6]

So there was Dan, monkeying around with contexts again, marrying the old with the new—as if he himself had willed the coming together of his two roads. In one creative act, he enhanced the mystique of the funeral ceremony and resolved the paradox of how to preserve it, by transmuting part of this ritual into an Indian marriage ceremony. This rendered it both less dangerous and more useful, while preserving the sanctity of the "dangerous" core for perpetuating his Indian Way. True to his formula, he had found a way to tell "just a little but not too much."[7]

Dan had previously dubbed me with an Ojibwa nickname that he said meant "I wonder why." But, at this time, he also decided to bestow on me an official Indian name, a strong one "that you will remember the rest of your life . . . the best bird that I used to dream of." He again spoke in both Ojibwa and English. I tape recorded this short ritual—except for the part where he asked to stop recording.

The last time I saw Dan and Madeline, in autumn of 1973, they were still cautiously protecting the Indian Way. I arrived early that September with a man unknown to them. When Madeline saw this stranger, she immediately withdrew Dan's invitation for me to attend a ceremony he was off performing, just down the road. Instead, we were invited in, to await Dan's return. Their news that day showed a further widening of the Indian Way, both for Dan and for the Ponemah community. He had conducted four recent funerals, one at Leech Lake for which he was paid sixty dollars. Patients were coming from nearby and from places further away than ever before. And Dan was still traveling, recently into Canada, where he helped with a shaking tent rite. As earlier, it was Madeline's health that worried him now more than his own.

But within a year Dan was gone; he died in summer 1974, after being hospitalized the previous December, when a leg was amputated. Back home in March, he was again discouraged about there being no one to attend to his patients or his *Midewiwin* functions, for the younger apprentices were not yet adequately trained. When someone approached him asking for a cure, he indicated he might try it—just this one more time, but he would never practice thereafter. I know little of Dan's last days, even now, nor about his funeral. But it seems his personal horizons, and those of his Indian Way, kept expanding until near the end. He continued to act out his life-legend, playing his part in closing the gap between the two roads of life faced by his people, employing his "strange powers" to give more meaning to their travels.

The several themes running through Dan Raincloud's legend and his life have been shown to represent, first, the identity struggles of many of his people, then the normal vicissitudes of his traditional role of Ojibwa man of power and, finally, the potential of that role and of this man as a bridge to the new. It remains to explore further the last idea, the qualities of his life that "made a difference" on the Indian frontier of the 1960s and 1970s, despite his long-ago choice to take the path of the *gete anishina.beg*—the old Indian Way, as he called it.

To have chosen the hard and dangerous road could only mean, really, that he was ambitious to make a difference in the world around him. It took a certain amount of ego and vanity and self-advertising to be an Ojibwa medicine man. Persons of power could not assume the humble stance, the safe position, that was characteristic of the ordinary man. A comprehensive comparison of the words and actions of Dan Raincloud, with those of Alec Everwind as prototype of those professing no public powers, yielded that very fact. The findings indicated that the sharpest difference between these two men lay in their respective attitudes toward taking risks. It was hazardous to hold strong powers, as Alec said more than once, for "you might misuse them."

When Dan elected the path of "strange powers," he knew it was hazardous. But he could not then have anticipated the multiple conflicting demands that he would later face. Yet, the chosen role, by its nature, gave him an uncommon sense of where his people were heading. In stressing that he sensed change, however, it should not be overlooked that this role helped him to influence the course of events as well.

Dan's expressed commitment to "saving the tribe" was real, I believe. It was not just an excess of ego that told him it was up to him. He was not special because he was a medicine man; he was a medicine man because all along he had been a specially talented, creative, and daring individual. On both paths, he reached across frontiers.

The powers and leeways of the traditional role were just what the new demanded, including the courage to innovate "just a little" and risk the consequences of trailblazing. On the Indian frontier were novel challenges during the decade that ended in 1974. In fighting to protect his Indian Way, to keep it going, Dan was finding novel means for building a bridge to the future, while yet staying within the old structures. For him, at least, the two roads that had once seemed so distinct thus came together. And for many more, the Indian Way triumphed over extinction, remaining a well-tended path through the wilderness of human existence, one that does not draw a boundary between the secular and the sacred.

The life-legend that Dan Raincloud wove for me in November of 1965 seems to have encapsulated with almost uncanny insight the significance and the place on the Indian frontier of the role he was ever choosing, and the plight of his people during this period. He probably was not aware of its prophetic, as well as historical, accuracy. However, even in everyday language, and quite explicitly, he knew he was right. Here is a private little sermon he reported delivering to a new missionary in Ponemah, back in 1965. He was telling me that he had never joined a Christian church, and he added:[8]

> I was telling Mr. Hayes, even a 4th grader or a 5th grader knows that Christ was born across the ocean, not in America. So therefore Christ taught the white people, not the Indians. We should all know that, I said. And God he taught us what to use. We know God just as well as anybody else, I said . . . Mr. Hayes said, "You're right, you're right." I know I'm right. I just told him that, not to think I don't know nothing.

NOTES

1. My thanks go to Dan himself, who trusted me with the telling of his story, and to my other Ponemah teachers, Ray Cloud, Alec Everwind, Madge Downfeather, Cora Jones, and Tom Cain, as well as many other Red Lake Chippewa people, notably Mr. Roger Jourdain, then Tribal Chairman. Colleagues consulted, in the field and elsewhere, were Frank Miller and his students Lucia Agaard and Katie Salter, Walter Bateman, Nancy Lienke, Tony Paredes, and June Checklund—all of Minnesota—and Algonquian scholars Edward S. Rogers, James G. E. Smith, Ruth Landes, and Janet Chute. Over a period of twenty-two years, it is hard to include all mentors and supporters; of the latter can be named the U.S. National Institutes of Health for a predoctoral field research award, the U.S. National Science Foundation and Department of Public Health for research grants; also Canada's A.R.D.A. Project, and the Royal Ontario Museum in Toronto.

2. Mary B. Black, "An Ethnoscience Investigation of Ojibwa Ontology and World View," Ph.D. dissertation, Stanford University, 1967. The Ojibwa orthography of that study is used in this essay. Other writings of the author that bear on the present subject include: "Ojibwa Medicine Man as Barometer of Change," Algonquian Conference, 1973; "Ojibwa Questioning Etiquette and Use of Ambiguity," *Studies in Linguistics* 23 (1973), 13–29; "Ojibwa Power Belief System," in *The Anthropology of Power*, eds. R. Fogelson and R. Adams (New York: Academic Press, 1977); "Ojibwa Taxonomy and Percept Ambiguity," *Ethos* 5 (1977), pp. 90–118; "Ojibwa Power Interactions: Creating Contexts for 'Respectful Talk,'" in *Papers of the Conference on Native North American Interaction Patterns, Edmonton 1982* ed. R. Darnell (Ottawa: in press).

3. At other times, Dan used "work" in English to refer to his efforts toward the Indian Way. This inconsistent usage probably reflects a cultural conflict faced by his people, for whom cash remuneration for tasks performed was replacing older forms of payment such as a reciprocal exchange. In 1965, another Ponemah elder said of Dan, he "only started working the last few years," implying that earlier Dan lived on the gift-payments received from patients and clients. Dan's 1973 comments on cash remuneration for "medicine" services again underline changes in the conceptualization of "work."

4. E. F. Mittelholtz, *Historical Review of the Red Lake Indian Reservation, 1858–1958* (Bemidji, Minn.: Beltrami County Historical Society, 1957), p. 87; J. A. Paredes, "The Passive Chippewa, No More," Ms., personal communication.

5. Tape recordings of interviews at Red Lake Reservation in 1968 by K. Salter and L. Agaard are deposited in the tape archives of the American Indian Research Project, University of South Dakota, Vermillion, S.D. See Ruth Landes, *Ojibwa Religion* (Madison, Wis.: University of Wisconsin Press, 1968), pp. 16–20, on similar behavior of a nearby shaman in the 1930s, and her further depiction of this informant.

6. See Charles Brill, *Indian and Free: A Contemporary Portrait of Life on a Chippewa Reservation* (Minneapolis, Minn.: University of Minnesota Press, 1974), pp. 102–03, for an English version of the recording made by Dan at that time. This book also has photographer Brill's excellent portraits of Dan, Madeline, and Old Nodin, and reservation scenes during the period of my residence there.

7. This was Dan's phrasing of the rule that telling a part, but not the whole, does not constitute a violation. A. I. Hallowell described "a general taboo . . . which forbids him [an Ojibwa] to recount his dream experience in full detail, except under certain circumstances," in his "Ojibwa Ontology, Behavior and World View," in *Culture in History*, ed. S. Diamond (New York: Columbia University Press, 1960), p. 46. In the present essay, as elsewhere, I have striven to follow this important rule; there can be no other way, when presuming to submit Dan's story for public perusal.

8. Another view of Dan's ideas about "God" and "Christ" can be found in S. Steiner's chapter, "The Christ Who Never Came" in *The New Indians* (New York: Harper & Row, 1968), pp. 96–100. Steiner recounts incisively his 1966 visit to the "old priest" in Ponemah, a visit Dan mentioned, but about which he had little to say.

CHAPTER 11

Maud L. Clairmont: Artist, Entrepreneur, and Cultural Mediator

Thomas H. Johnson[1]

PRESENTING MAUD L. CLAIRMONT (1902—)

As the middle nineteenth century's Rocky Mountain fur-trade society declined with the expansion of sedentary American communities, and as the nomadic high plains Indian tribes were finally settled on reservations, the whole ethnically composite mass of individuals and groups of this transitory occupational subculture who had flourished under earlier economic conditions were forced into hard choices. Some elected to affiliate themselves with and as Indians, others continued living on the margins of reservation Indian communities, and still more passed into the larger American population. Many were attracted to identification as legal Indians owing to the numerous incentives available, which ranged from sentimental attachments to economics lures. Maud Clairmont's several ancestral lines and her multiform ethnic heritages illustrates such ethnic passages. Born at the turn of this century to a kin group of composite Euro-American nationalities and varied Indian tribal relations, her direct ancestors associated themselves with the Wind River reservation Shoshone and neighboring peoples. Her own early experience was in a family of Catholic ranchers and entrepreneurs, a family whose members were severally identified variously as Shoshones, Breeds, or Whites; a family that had long operated on the margins between the Shoshone and the outside world. Her life and career illustrate how such processes continue into the present day. Along with being wife and mother, she assumed the role of a cultural gatekeeper, welcoming and advising strangers who arrived with various interests in Shoshone reservation affairs, managing communications and impressions as cultural interpreter and mediator. In sequence, her responsibilities were formalized as she won political offices and acted as reformer, leader, and teacher. As a mature adult and a successful businesswoman, she embraced the Indian Reorganization Act's reforms of the middle 1930s, aiding in the development of formal governmental institutions and economic development for the Shoshone. In this respect she was a path-breaker, and given her heritage and experience, she understandably remained a woman dedicated to intergroup tolerance and accommodation. In her later years, however, following the dramatic rise of the Red Power movement in the late 1960s, young local adherents of ethnic separatism saw her and her generation of leaders as a conservative Old Guard, to be deposed and replaced. In her later years, Maud Clairmont has had to face unanticipated ramifications of her own ancestors' tolerant ethos, which she modeled for her children, and of the new formal corporate institution that today manages Shoshone affairs. Modern tribal governments like that of the Shoshone have membership restrictions, commonly defined in racial terms by minimal "blood-quantum" percentages. Maud Clairmont's children, continuing in an old family tradition accepting of out-marriage, produce grandchildren who do not meet the minimal requirements for legal identification as Shoshone. As the boundaries of ethnic membership have been thus rigidly legalized, she and others of her background are faced with a continuing dilemma, how to transmit their ethnic identities and traditions onto their posterity while sustaining their place as members of Indian corporate organizations. In her later years, Maud Clairmont thereby experienced a conflict between two opposed forms of social life, the ethos of family and community versus that of bureaucracy, a controversy whose outcome is still in doubt. (J. A. Clifton)

Born in 1902 and still alive, Maud L. Clairmont is a woman noted for her distinctive personal identity, together with her social identity as an enrolled member of the Wind River or Eastern band of Shoshone. For several generations before her birth, her ancestors were leaders among these Indians. They were of multiethnic, multilingual antecedents, and were closely associated with Washakie, chief of the Shoshone during the last century. However, their composite tribal-Euro-American heritage, their use of English as well as native languages, and their Roman Catholic religious background distinguished and distanced them from most Shoshone. Moreover, some members of her kin group became ranchers during the General Allotment Act era late in the nineteenth century, thereby gaining private ownership of land in areas that later proved to contain oil. Later, Maud aided the tribe in obtaining a greater share of its oil and gas revenue in the 1940s and 1950s.

Although their homes were within Wyoming's Wind River Shoshone reservation, Maud and other members of her extended family grew up in what was, fundamentally, a regional variant of the American rural ranching subculture. While accepting the values and aspirations of that subculture, they nevertheless recognized kin ties and acted out relationships with Shoshone "fullbloods." Nonetheless, their values and activities were and still are oriented toward the individual, combining—especially for men—a rugged, outdoor-oriented existence with subsistence work based on ranching and a money economy. Locally labeled "breeds," or "mixed bloods" by scholars, they were a mixture of several Indian and European ethnic groups. Depending on the situation or person, they might assume an "Indian," "White," or "Breed" identity, reflecting the society's penchant for racial classification.

This dual ethnic association posed numerous problems for the construction of satisfying personal identities. In innumerable contexts, they were

The Wind River Reservation Setting

characterized as "Indians" by others, hence placed in a separate and—in this region—a less prestigious ethnic category. More tolerant Americans intermarried with some of the "mixed-bloods" who were anxious to move out of a stigmatized category, of being "Indian." Shoshone "full-bloods" contributed to the strains of this social identity, for they often looked down on the "breeds" as not genuinely Indian. Seen analytically, this "breed" class was a catchall, a useful way of categorizing and treating people not firmly identified with any one group, particularly at times when ethnicity or race were important sorting factors in social activities.

Maud told of people who were legally affiliated with the tribe, or who were Indian in ancestry, but had so firmly chosen the American lifestyle and social attributes that they asked that their names be removed from tribal rolls. They wanted to be recognized and accepted as "White." But there were also individuals in her family, such as her great aunt Mary Rabbittail, who elected to live like the "full-bloods." In the early 1900s, when Maud was a child, the latter were still the majority in the Shoshone reservation community. Thus, some Shoshone "breeds," those of composite ethnic-racial antecedents, rejected the ascribed identity of Indian and were close to being assimilated into the American ranching subculture, while others identified themselves with and were assimilated among the traditionalist Shoshone. However, most people marginal to Shoshone communities created a separate identity that was reasonably logical and consistent, if at times somewhat contradictory. Maud L. Clairmont's life experiences and her efforts at constructing a satisfying personal identity in this complicated multiethnic community are detailed in this essay.

Maud described some of the ways these identity complications arose. When the Shoshone obtained court-claims money from the United States in 1938, for instance, many strangers who had never lived in the reservation community asserted membership because of their "Shoshone blood."[2] Moreover, the Wind River Shoshone, in voting not to accept the Indian Reorganization Act of 1934, have liberally interpreted the customary Bureau of Indian Affairs (BIA) criterion of a minimum of one-quarter "Indian blood" as a basis for enrollment, so as to include the non-Shoshone Indian ancestry of a nonenrolled parent in the child's declared "Shoshone blood-quantum." This inclusion perpetuates the social identity of being Shoshone Indian, even if slight Shoshone ancestry is inherited from but one parent. The total ancestry of the child must add up to at least one-quarter "Shoshone," and the child can only be enrolled if ineligible for enrollment in another tribe. This has been a creative way of maintaining the size of the tribe's population and of perpetuating a tribal social identity. On a group level, it accomplished the same end that Maud and other marginal people had achieved individually in earlier years. This corporate decision and policy legitimized a broadening of the definition of Indianness, of being Shoshone.[3]

Throughout her life, in many ways, Maud L. Clairmont played the role of cultural mediator or broker between the Shoshone and people outside the reservation, often acting as a cultural gatekeeper for visitors. Her natal language was English, she was socialized in the local ranching subculture, and she was informally affiliated with the Catholic Church early, becoming a regularly communing member in later life. Some of her ancestors, notably her grandmother LeClair and great grandfather, John Enos, were descended from a line of Iroquois converts to Catholicism from Quebec. These were some of the Mohawk who, early in the nineteenth century as employees of the Northwest Fur Company, made their homes in the northern Plateau region where they married Flathead women.[4] Her grandparents were polyglots, speaking Flathead (a Salishan language) and Shoshone (Uto-Aztecan), as well as English (Germanic), and French and Spanish (Romance languages). Her other ancestral lines displayed similar histories of social migrations and ethnic-linguistic diversity.

In her part as entrepreneur, Maud followed the tradition of her Euro-Iroquoian ancestors, but she broadened this role to include occupations that a woman could fulfill—owning and managing a grocery store and a motel-trailer court. Both businesses established additional contexts where she could act as a cultural mediator for customers, visitors, and the general public. Her position on the six-member Shoshone Business Council, almost continuously from 1942 until the late 1960s, provided a much wider array of relationships with outsiders. In her capacity as council member, Maud traveled to the nation's capital, where she met congressmen and dealt with representatives of oil companies. In the local community, she negotiated with business leaders and professional people such as medical practitioners in the local clinic, BIA personnel, writers, artists—and novice anthropologists who solicited her aid and support when first visiting the Wind River reservation. Because of her facility for dealing with people and her ability to persuade congressmen and attorneys to listen to the needs of the tribe, Maud was reelected to the council many times, winning the largest or the second-highest number of votes on several occasions.

Educationally, Maud L. Clairmont also achieved well beyond the average for her time and region. She completed about two years of college and taught in a country school on the reservation for several years. With an unusually effective speaking ability, and a well-developed capacity for presenting her ideas forcefully, she consistently advocated reforms on the Business Council, particularly improved health facilities, educational programs, and economic development. Since most of the Shoshone corporate income came from oil and natural gas royalties, Maud promoted greater exploitation of this resource, which brought in a higher income for the Wind River community. Because of their extreme poverty until the 1940s, when oil and gas income first became significant, her proposals were widely supported. However, by the late 1960s and anxious to retire from public life, Maud became increasingly despondent about the Shoshones' future. Inevitably oil, gas, and other mineral resources would be depleted, she foresaw. Without a stable economic base and other more reliable kinds of job opportunities, she worried that the tribe would someday again be reduced to the poverty of the 1930s.

In her third major public role, that of artist, Maud Clairmont interacted with others similarly engaged, and with American art teachers and craft specialists. Her works have won many prizes and awards, indicating her high standing among local patrons of the arts. She would probably most like to be remembered as an artist, but because she also played a significant part in local political and economic life, Maud is an uncommon person in the Wind River reservation community for excelling in so many areas.

Yet, there are others like her, of composite Indian-Euro-American heritage and ancestry, who have grown up in the reservation community and have gone to school there or in boarding schools as she did. Many of these marginal people continue to live in the area, if not directly on the reservation, and they play important, sometimes decisive, roles in the tribal government. However, the position of this long-influential elite was challenged in the 1970s by younger leaders, individuals and coalitions inspired by the American Indian Movement (AIM). To them, Maud and others like her represented the "establishment," a gentry who accepted the forms and values of American society and who advocated the acceptance of these by other Shoshone.

These emergent, younger leaders were much less willing to compromise or to negotiate than Maud's generation. Once they won control of the Wind River Business Council, they adopted a separatist position and passed an ordinance banning all Americans from the reservation, other than on the public roads and those who owned private homes, an exclusionist policy the older council members would never have accepted. When they discovered that much oil had been siphoned off by employees of the oil companies, without reporting and payment of royalties to the Shoshone, and that the BIA had not been managing their resources adequately, the militant younger leaders sought and obtained reforms. One such was administrative: when the old BIA superintendent retired, he was replaced by a young Cheyenne, Al Spang.

By the mid-1970s, the goals Maud and leaders associated with her had fought for were won. But as an outgrowth of the nationwide War on Poverty and the Civil Rights movement, Indian Rights were being asserted in fresh ways by a new type of leadership. Yet, elders like Maud had long played successful parts in the political drama that led to the improved health and education experienced by this younger generation of leaders. Without the paths they had broken during the New Deal and after, things might have been much different. Maud would like to be remembered as a capable, effective Shoshone leader who provided an example of what young Shoshone might aspire to if they put forth the effort.

I first met Maud L. Clairmont on a warm, bright June day in 1966. Accompanied by two other graduate students, I found her hanging out the wash alongside the motel she operated, just south of the Wind River Agency at Fort Washakie, Wyoming. Only a month earlier, we had written the Shoshone Business Council, of which she was a member, asking permission to conduct research on the reservation. Our acceptance was helped by the fact that our professor, Demitri Shimkin, had researched the Wind River Shoshone during the 1930s.

Before leaving Illinois, I had learned through newspaper accounts that the 1966 Shoshone Sun Dance was being arranged by Tom Wesaw. This was the same sponsor as in 1937, when Shimkin observed this striking, important ritual. The news accounts indicated that the purpose of the dance would be to pray for the welfare of servicemen in Viet Nam and an end to the war in that country. At Shimkin's suggestion, we three apprentice anthropologists decided to spend the summer among the Wind River Shoshone. Shimkin had written a monograph on the Sun Dance that compared earlier nineteenth-century versions to that of the 1930s, so my tentative plan was to study the evolving 1966 dance and compare it to earlier versions.[5]

We three anthropological fieldwork novices were apprehensive, nervously anticipating a hostile reception. But, the foot hills of the Wind River range were magnificently inviting. And as we continued our first conversation with Maud, she described how she had studied one summer at the University of Wyoming, where her favorite subject had been psychology. Thus, placed more at ease, we counted ourselves fortunate to have encountered such a friendly Shoshone, someone we could identify with and who could understand our predicament.

Later in the afternoon after Harold, Maud's husband, returned from a visit to relatives, and after we were settled in our rooms, our preliminary discussions continued. Harold launched an account of how the Shoshone had been forced to give up half their reservation when the government moved the Arapaho onto their Wind River reservation in 1878. This imposition brought legal action by the Shoshone, who sought payment for the lost lands, a suit not resolved until 1938. However, by accepting the terms of this settlement, the Shoshone had to agree to give up half the assets of their original reservation to the Northern Arapaho. This and other matters still rankled, with blame fixed on both the government and the Arapaho. As we now learned, the older generation, especially, still felt strongly about this issue. When Maud and Harold continued their discussion of related issues, they gradually included us to such an extent that we began to feel involved in the problems of the Shoshone community. Shortly, news of who was leading the Sun Dance that year and brief descriptions of this ritual were introduced into our conversation. Maud and Harold had begun our advanced training in anthropological field research.

When I reflected on the events of that first meeting, I was struck by how Maud failed to fit my naive image of an American Indian. I began to wonder about her history and relationships to the Shoshone. What amazed me was her total ease in the presence of strangers, and her absolute frankness. Was she that different from other Shoshone? She reminded me a bit of some of my neighbors in Illinois or Iowa. She was, as she later stated, "only half-Shoshone," meaning half-Indian (i.e., Shoshone-Bannock-Flathead-Blackfeet-Sioux), but she also called to mind the strong, assertive frontier women depicted by Willa Cather. What had produced Maud's opinionated, frank, warm, sensitive, yet businesslike style? I had never met anyone like her.

During the next few days, we ventured into the county seat of Lander, which the Shoshone consider "their town," and arranged for a visit with the Shoshone Business Council, which met jointly with the Northern Arapaho council at the "Fort" (Fort Washakie, the agency headquarters). Most of the players in the ongoing drama of life on the Wind River reservation had changed since Skimkin's time during the New Deal years; of the council of thirty years earlier, only Gilbert Day remained, while the titular "chief" of the Shoshone, Charles Washakie, youngest son of the old chief, had died in the 1950s. His son-in-law, Bob Harris, now chaired the council.

Maud must have sensed our anxiety, for the day after we arrived, she and Harold insisted on taking us on a tour of the reservation. She now told us that from the time she was a small child she had always been interested in knowing as much as she could about people, but her grandparents had told her that such information was only for adults. It seemed to us that as an observer and commentator on the Shoshone, her interests were similar to ours. Half consciously, we began thinking of her as a fellow anthropologist, albeit far more knowledgeable of Shoshone ways than we.

During this exploratory trip, we visited several inspiring locations in the foothills of the Wind River mountains, including Bull Lake and Dinwoody Canyon with its petroglyphs, which were sacred places. Maud's comments indicated how much Wyoming and especially this reservation meant to her spirit. Her love for the beauty and space of Wyoming was something I could not match, for only some sixty-three years of living in this country could have produced the aesthetic sensitivity to the region she so vividly imparted. She spoke of the Wind River valley as if her roots there reached back to the beginning of time.

The following week, the council members, including Maud, questioned us intently about whether we had come to "dig" in Dinwoody Canyon—archaeologists from the University of Wyoming had extracted artifacts from that sacred area without the permission of the council in the 1930s. We denied any such intentions, and without more delay, chairman Gilbert Day, having read our letter of introduction, concluded by turning to the others and saying, "they're all right." Maud moved that we be allowed to talk to the people and study the modern Shoshone: with a simple show of hands, the council accepted our presence.

Maud's open acceptance of three young strangers was characteristic of many Shoshone. But when Maud told me that her grandmother LeClair had always entertained strangers in their log home on Big Wind River when she was a child, I knew that hospitality was a special family tradition as well. When she was growing up, no stranger was ever turned away from the table, and her grandparents had hosted some of the Democratic dignitaries of the day. Her grandmother, she said, always acted like a "lady," though she had little formal education.

Maud was telling us of her pride regarding the hospitable ambience in which she was raised. This gracious candor would not have surprised me so, had I then known the history of her ancestors, the LeClair and Lajeunesse Franco-Indian families. In both ancestral lines, as I was later to discover, Maud's kin included some of the earliest traders and trappers in the Rocky

Mountains, whether of exclusively European or composite ancestry. They had come some 150 years earlier, and they were among the first to explore and to introduce European trade goods to the Northern Rockies. Because these people had lived and intermarried among various tribes for so long—as traders, translators, economic and political mediators, affinal kin, and even leaders among some native communities—being cordial and generous to strangers, and presenting an "open door," was an important strategy if they were to maintain their position.

Of greater importance, the culturally marginal Shoshone, represented by Maud in word and deed, had long repudiated racial or ethnic exclusiveness. Indeed, the success of her ancestors had depended on tolerance for and the capacity to accommodate themselves to cultural differences. These values were becoming more broadly fashionable in the 1960s. Maud and her kindred, therefore, were the products of generations of intermarriage and cultural mingling.

Later research added greater time-depth to and understanding of the ancestral and contemporary group Maud and Harold Clairmont represented. As early as the 1820s, I discovered, many Anglo-American and Franco-American trappers and traders began marrying among the Shoshone bands of Wyoming, which are sometimes called the Eastern Shoshone. Near the close of the fur-trading rendezvous period in 1840, for example, at least sixteen Shoshone women had married such men, including Jack Robertson, the first one to make his home in Wyoming, and Jim Bridger, the famous trapper, whose Green River trading post in the 1840s became a meeting place for Shoshone and other mountain men, as well as immigrants on the Oregon Trail.[6] But many others of varied ethnic and racial background settled among and intermarried with the Shoshone. These cannot properly be called "Métis" (i.e., Franco-Indian), for they were not exclusively of French, or for that matter, British antecedents. Indeed, they included immigrants with Spanish surnames.

Maud's composite ancestry perfectly illustrates the complex antecedents of the marginal Shoshone. She herself, while a member of the Wyoming State Historical Association during the 1950s, traced the ancestry of her mother's father Edmo (Edmond) LeClair to his father, who was a French "doctor" with the same surname. Grandfather Edmo was born in 1847 and died 1929. His father had married a Bannock woman, and Edmo LeClair was born near Lewiston, Idaho, growing to adulthood near Fort Hall.[7] His father was employed by the American Fur Company and he often set broken bones, hence his reputation as a physician. About 1863, grandfather Edmo's parents moved to Fort Bridger from Montana.[8]

At Fort Bridger, Edmo LeClair became well acquainted with the Shoshone; he watched the 1868 signing of the treaty that established their reservation, for example. By that date, he may have settled among them, for the Shoshone camped near the Green River in those years. There he may also have met the Enos family, another of Maud's ancestral lines.[9] Maud suggested that Edmo's father may have come from St. Louis, but there is no documentary evidence of this. Maud's great grandfather Edmo had several other children. One son, Louis, was reported on the 1885 Shoshone Indian Census as "deceased" in 1880, having been married to an "Indian" named Chesmet. Three of Louis LeClair's children were listed in the 1890 Shoshone census. These and others with French, English, or Spanish surnames were listed separately, at the end of the Shoshone Indian census roll.[10]

Others of Maud's lineal, collateral, and affinal kin had their names similarly appended at the end, as a category separate from the "full blood" Shoshone in this census. These included numerous people with Spanish or Mexican surnames such as Guerero, Alijo, and Aragon, the Enos family, into which the LeClairs had married, and other Anglo-Indians with whom these families later married, such as the Jones, Harris, and Boyd families. Altogether, by 1890, about eighty-six (10 percent) of the Eastern Shoshone, whose total enrollment had declined to about 800, were people of composite ancestry.[11] This separate category also included the "squaw men," such as Speed Stagner, those American men recently married to Shoshone women. Such males, together with their families, in those years were legally enrolled as "Shoshone Indians," with whatever benefits accrued to that status.

Sometime after 1871, when the Shoshone began to settle their reservation at Wind River, Maud's grandfather LeClair married Phillesette Enos. Because Maud was raised by her maternal grandparents, and lived in the same ranch house with her great grandfather, John Enos, her cultural background reflects theirs rather than that of her father, George Lajeunesse. George was a Franco-Dakota; and soon after the 1906 death of Maud's mother, Ellen, he remarried. Maud and her brother Herman, thus, were exposed to the values and styles of their maternal grandparents, who were Franco-Shoshone-Bannock and Flathead-Iroquois. She never learned to speak Dakota, nor to think of herself as related to them culturally. In 1904, grandmother Phillesete bore her last child, Edmo, Jr., generally known as Bud. There were several older sisters in the Enos household, Maud's maternal aunts. Her Uncle Bud subsequently inherited his father's ranch and material assets, later running a small ranch on the reservation and marrying an American woman, Esther Stephens.

Her great grandfather, John Enos, was by far the most prominent member of this extended family when Maud was a child. Family tradition claims that he had passed 100 years at the time of his death in 1915, although census records indicate he was somewhat younger, as born about 1825.[12] Maud, Herman, and Bud all told similar stories about "grandpa" Enos. He was Flathead and Iroquois, and was also related to Chief Washakie, who became a leader of the Shoshone about 1840. Enos claimed that Washakie's mother and his mother, identified as Mary, were sisters. We know that Washakie was Flathead on his mother's side, his father being a Northern Shoshone.[13]

MAUD CLAIRMONT AND MARY CORNELIUS. In 1970, Mary Cornelius (right), a Métis woman from Turtle Mountain, North Dakota, visited Maud Clairmont while working for the National Welfare Rights Association. On Easter Sunday that year, the two women had their picture taken in their Easter finery. Cornelius is attired in the ceremonial buckskin dress made by Maud for herself, decorated in her own beadwork, an example of her expertise in arts and crafts. (Courtesy of Thomas H. Johnson.)

If John Enos (or Eneas) was born about 1825, his father was probably Ignace, pronounced Eneas in the Salish language. This was a common name among the Christianized Mohawk from near Montreal, who arrived in Flathead country around 1810 with the Northwest Fur Company. There they married into the tribe and introduced their version of Catholicism, which so impressed Flathead leaders that in the 1830s they dispatched several emissaries on a mission to St. Louis seeking to obtain the services of a "blackrobe."[14] John Enos may also have traveled extensively throughout the Rockies; and family tradition indicates that he spoke French, Spanish, and several distant Indian languages. Other family accounts tell of jaunts south into Mexico, as well as westward to the mouth of the Columbia River, and long employment by the Hudson's Bay Company. He was certainly close to Washakie, and because of his command of languages, he was valuable as a political aide and cultural mediator.

In any event, Maud's Franco-Indian ancestry is certainly traceable to the Iroquois, and her traditions derived from that side of her family accord more closely with the immigrant Iroquois fur trappers of the Northwest, not the Métis proper of the Great Lakes region or the Dakotas. John Enos had several sisters who lived to advanced ages among the Flathead; and his wife, Julia

LeBoeuf, Maud's great grandmother (died 1900), was Franco-Blackfoot, according to Maud's cousin, May Posey. Family traditions record that, at Washakie's invitation, John Enos with his wife and children—there were eleven by the time the family was completed around 1872—migrated from Montana to Wyoming shortly after the Shoshone reservation was established, encountering a Crow war party along the way.[15]

Both the Shoshone and the Crow were allies of the United States in the 1870s, and Maud's grandfather LeClair served as an Army scout, later identifying the burial places of Custer's soldiers at the site of the battle of the Little Big Horn. At Wind River, the six Enos daughters and two surviving sons married—one to a Shoshone, one to a Shoshone-Potawatomi, one to a Crow, two to Flatheads or Salish, one to a Mormon descended from the first Mormon missionary to the Shoshone at Green River and his Shoshone wife, and two to LeClairs. Two other sons were killed in battles with the Sioux.[16]

The 1870s and 1880s were difficult decades for the Shoshone, who were in transition from being a politically autonomous people with ample buffalo for the hunt, to a life confined on a reservation and based on family agriculture and ranching—in a region dominated by American pioneers and their institutions. By the time Maud was growing up in the early 1900s, she and her brother Herman were surrounded by several generations of Franco-Flathead-Shoshone kin on their mother's side, and Franco-Sioux on their father's side. The unusual geographic and social mobility and the flexible adaptability of these kin groups is an indication of the effects that the farming-ranching frontier had on both Americans and native people. One important effect was the consolidation of ethnically composite, multilingual groups on Indian reservations, where they assumed the identities of one or another of the tribes. Yet, the families that Maud and Harold Clairmont represent were just as much pioneers as the Mormons, fur traders, miners, or farmers and ranchers who entered Wyoming and other Rocky Mountain states. Moreover, these multicultural "Indians" were eager to adapt to the American agriculture economy.

These families' awareness of their role as pioneers is truly carved in stone. The LeClairs, Lajeunesses, and Lamoureauxs are listed as founding members of the Fremont County Pioneer Association. In 1904, the association passed a motion to make a twenty-five-year residence the criterion for such membership, and the names of these pioneers, plus several other Americans who married Indian women, were included in the charter list, then engraved on a large boulder that stands in front of the Pioneer Museum in Lander, the Fremont County seat.[17] Thus, Maud's ancestors have their names commemorated along with founders of Lander, agents and employees of the BIA and the military garrison at Fort Washakie, who settled permanently in the area.

George Lajeunesse was the son of a Franco-Dakota (-Sioux) couple, Michel and Elizabeth. In 1870, with Michel's brother and his family, they lived at Fort Fetterman, Wyoming Territory. Michel was supposedly born in Dakota Territory, but his more distant ancestry in Quebec is obscure.[18] Elizabeth, his wife, was said to be "half Sioux," and the specifics of her Euro-American ancestry is also uncertain. She died about the same time as her husband.

During the 1870s, the Lajeunesse family immigrated to the Wind River Reservation at the suggestion of B. B. Brooks, later governor of Wyoming, who informed them they would be able to obtain land there.[19] Ethnically, this family did not consider themselves anything but Sioux, or Franco-Sioux, and Elizabeth was said to be monolingual in that (the Lakota) language, her children acting as translators. The Lajeunesses became enterprising ranchers on the Shoshone reservation.

Maud's childhood and adolescence were spent at the LeClair homestead. This large, two-story log house was built by her maternal grandparents on Big Wind River, about twenty miles from Fort Washakie, some fifteen miles from the site that became the town of Riverton, Wyoming. After years of negotiation, in 1904, the land north of the Big Wind was ceded by the Shoshone and Arapaho to the United States, and soon homesteaders from states farther east moved into the area. The reduced reservation was subdivided and allotted under the Dawes Act, and under the terms of that legislation many marginal families associated with the Shoshone eagerly accepted allotments in the fertile valley of the Big Wind, together with numerous "full-bloods," the authentic Shoshone. The ceded portion, 1,346,320 acres north of Big Wind River, constituted about two-thirds of the original reservation.[20] Anxious to develop a reclamation project in this region, during the next several decades, the government constructed several dams impounding mountain streams running south from the crest of the Owl Creek Mountains.

The main body of Shoshone, however, clustered around Fort Washakie, and Maud's contacts with the tribe came when her grandparents visited relatives in that area. Her grandmother had two sisters who married Shoshone; one of them, Aunt Mary, had married a man named Weed about 1872, but later married a well-known Shoshone named Rabbittail. Aunt Mary Rabbittail lived until 1923, and Maud described her ways as much like those of the traditional Shoshone. On these visits, Maud watched the Sun Dance, learned to understand much of the Shoshone language (not spoken in her home), and formed ties to cousins. The Sun Dance always fascinated her, and she recalled seeing Shoshone gamble during the period of feasting that accompanied this important ritual.

Before Riverton was founded in 1907, the main centers of social life for rural people were the Fort and the town of Lander. Travel was difficult and trips outside the Wind River basin were infrequent. As the only girl near her age in the family, and motherless after the age of three, Maud mainly associated and identified with the males in her family, becoming something of a tomboy, learning to ride horses and to play boys' games with her brother Herman and Uncle Bud (Edmo, Jr.), who were about her age. Great grandfather, John Enos, held in special awe because of his great age, had a private room in the log house where he lived until being stricken with a heart attack in 1915 while on a hunting trip into the Wind River mountains. Grandpa John had been a featured "exhibit" at the Panama-Pacific Exposition in San Francisco in 1915—as a "century old" Indian.[21] The youngsters remembered him wearing a tall Stetson hat and washing his stash of gold coins in a stream, as well as praying regularly as a faithful Catholic.

Maud's early education was in a country school. Her family lived in a rural neighborhood of small ranches, and among them lived several Mexican families who had married Shoshone, such as the Aragons and Hurtados. Like Maud's kin, these people were also marginal to the main group of Shoshone; and when her father remarried, it was to Rosie Aragon, while one of her paternal uncles had married Emma Van Dusen, who after his death married an Aragon. Similarly, one of her mother's cousins, Lucy Enos, married Sequiel Hurtado. Thus, Maud had numerous kin ties to the Mexican-Shoshone contingent of the ethnically composite neighborhood on the reservation.

Besides her LeClair grandparents, the relatives closest to her were maternal aunts. Three of these, Minnie, Nora, and Josephine, married three brothers of a ranching family, William, Charles, and John Boyd. This firm, extended-family alliance was further solidified by the fact that their mother, Louisa (Mrs. William Boyd, Sr.), was a daughter of Charles Lajeunesse (or Seminoe), thus possibly a relative of Maud's father. Two other aunts successively married sons of ethnically distinctive kin groups, the American Jones family, the large Anglo-Afro-American Harris family, and the German-American-Cheyenne Stagner family. In these ways, Maud is related to several of the largest extended kin groups on the Shoshone reservation today. Moreover, such intermarriages were common in the later nineteenth century, indicating a long-established pattern of alliances between such culturally marginal kin groups, increasing their influence in tribal affairs, since they tend to participate in reservation politics as allies.[22] The Harris family, in particular, has provided important political leadership for the Shoshone in recent years, particularly so with the rise of Robert (Bob) Harris to the position of chairman of the Shoshone Business Council.

The multiple intermarriages between such few kin groups during the period 1870–1920 indicates geographic and social isolation from the traditional Shoshone, and from main-line Americans. But as communications became easier with the coming of automobiles and an improved transportation network, such isolation and separateness declined. Maud's generation seems to have been the first to break away from this semi-isolation, as when she went off to Haskell Indian Institute and Sherman Indian School in the late 1910s and early 1920s. At both Haskell and Sherman, she met Indians from many tribes, and became close friends with a Navajo girl who explained some of her people's ceremonies. At these institutions, she was exposed to the early development of what has since become known as pan-Indian culture.

When she returned to the reservation, Maud taught elementary grades in the county-financed Countryman rural school near Fort Washakie. About this time, Harold Clairmont, of Franco-Flathead ancestry, with whom she had corresponded since they both left Haskell, visited her from his home in Montana. A woman he had planned to marry there decided against him, and soon a romance between Harold and Maud blossomed. After Maud and Harold's marriage in the early 1920s, they moved to Montana. But this was only temporary, for Maud disliked it there and was always begging him to move back to Wyoming, which they eventually did. He was a congenial, talkative fellow who could spin a tall Western tale with the best of them. Maud always took the initiative in this marriage, insisting on more room to experiment, while Harold contributed stability to their family life.

During the first decades of the twentieth century, the main Shoshone groups were clustered on allotments around Fort Washakie, in Burris to the north, at Sage Creek, and at Mill Creek to the south. East of Fort Washakie were two groups of Northern Arapaho, the one centered around an Episcopal mission at Ethete, the other—twenty miles farther east on the Popo Agie River—around the Jesuit Roman Catholic mission at Saint Stephens. In time, Maud, Harold, and others succeeded in establishing a separate Catholic church at Fort Washakie. The Episcopal mission had been the sole Christian influence since 1883, when the Welsh missionary, John Roberts, arrived and with his wife established a school for Shoshone girls. By 1900, most Shoshone had been baptized by the Reverend Roberts, who also performed marriages for those who wished them. Indeed, he officiated at the wedding of Maud's parents.

However, by the 1950s, when the Blessed Sacrament Catholic Church's new building was completed and in operation, Catholicism had become the focus of religious and social life for most of those members of the Wind River reservation community who were of partial French ancestry. Meanwhile, the Native American Church (or Peyote Religion, first introduced about 1900), the sweat lodge, and the Sun Dance held the loyalty of the traditional Shoshone majority. Except a small core of active Episcopalians, most of these traditional Shoshones' affiliation with that denomination has been nominal, especially after the death of Reverend Roberts in 1949.

Thus, Maud and Harold Clairmont's lives have spanned Wyoming's transformation from a sparsely settled ranching frontier to the modern era of electronic communications and energy resource development. Earlier, her grandparents and parents witnessed the end of the Indian wars and the inauguration of reservations, just as an earlier generation of Métis and Indian ancestors had participated in the beginning and end of the fur trade, and hence, the coming of American power in the region. During the twentieth century, the marginal Shoshone—those of composite ethnic antecedents— have had to face the same adaptive stresses experienced by surrounding Americans. New technologies, social and political developments, and economic realities have thrust disturbing choices on them. With the decline of family-managed agriculture, for example, new strategies had to be pursued if they were to survive in Wyoming. This first became evident during the agricultural depression in the 1920s and 1930s, when many marginals turned to sheep raising only to "lose their shirts," as Maud put it. Maud's children, starting with Marie, born in 1926, have been raised to confront and to cope with these dramatic changes. With her own children she has worked, not to replicate the past, but to prepare them to meet the shocks of the future.

In 1927, when she was pregnant for the second time, Maud took her grandmother, Phillesete Enos LeClair—then suffering from cancer—to the Mayo Clinic in Rochester, Minnesota. The train trip there was long, exhausting, and expensive. It was also unsuccessful, for the physicians discovered the old woman's illness had progressed too far for effective treatment. But Maud took satisfaction from knowing she had sought the best medical attention for Grandmother Phillesete, the elder woman she felt closest to. Nonetheless, the trauma of knowing her grandmother could not live much longer was too much for Maud. To this day, she believes the worry and strain caused the stillbirth of the girl child she was then carrying. The care she expressed for her past brought a terrible price for her future.

The following year brought more tragedy, when she gave birth to another daughter, Nadine, who also soon died. These losses affected Maud deeply. She longed for more children; and she was rewarded in 1930 with the birth of her second daughter, Vivian, followed the next year by her son, Vernon. By this time, through a friend, Harold obtained employment with the Wind River reservation's irrigation department, and the Clairmonts then moved to Wyoming. The Clairmonts rented a house that had been part of the original Fort Washakie. Since Harold was a BIA employee, they were eligible to rent these government-owned houses. For forty years, he worked for the Wind River reservation irrigation department, and his headquarters was only two miles away from their home. During the 1930s, Maud was busy raising her family; then her closest social ties were with other government employees who lived in the same area. Before 1930, her father and all her grandparents had died.

It was during Maud's middle years, in 1938, when the Shoshone finally received payment of over four million dollars for a claim against the United States for illegally settling the Northern Arapaho in 1878 on the reservation intended, according to the Treaty of 1868, for the Eastern Shoshone. This "judgment fund" was welcomed by the tribe, although in accepting the settlement they had to agree, once and for all, to share equally with the Arapaho the future assets of the reservation. But when World War II began and the demand for petroleum increased, the substantial oil fields on the reservation, which first yielded revenues during the 1920s, were expanded. Some members of the Enos family had begun to receive oil royalties by this time. So Shoshone tribal income increased. Despite widespread sentiment among the Shoshone to have the oil revenues entirely distributed as per capita payments, the Secretary of the Interior would not allow this. Since the United States, as trustee for its Shoshone "wards," was legally obligated to invest part of the proceeds for long-term development, these wishes were not satisfied. Following the dictates of this policy, sometimes seen as "paternalistic," the Secretary of the Interior permitted payment of only half the oil revenues as cash dividends to individual tribal members. The balance was held in the U.S. Treasury in an interest-bearing account for future investment.

Soon after the government's position on per capita payment became known, Maud began speaking out for persons who wanted a larger proportion of the money paid out to individuals as disposable income. Recognition of her leadership ability and this commitment in 1942 led to her first election to the Shoshone Business Council, the second woman ever so selected. Her children were growing up, so she could take on such time- and energy-consuming public responsibilities. Years later, she claimed her strongest supporters in this fight were often the full-bloods, frequently women. During these years, the business council had to make major decisions regarding the allocation of both judgment funds and earnings from oil leases. Another issue was created by the fact that, in addition to holding the line at fifty per cent on per capita payments, the government did not want to make such distributions more than twice yearly. However, the Shoshone proved able lobbyists, and in 1947, they persuaded their congressman to sponsor hearings and a bill to authorize the "segregation and expenditure of trust funds held in joint ownership by the Shoshone and Arapaho tribes."[23]

While lobbying for their goals, business council officers made several trips to Washington, D.C., in 1950, at last successfully obtaining authorization for larger capita payments, claiming that as individuals they were capable of managing their affairs. Maud and other marginals on the Council achieved considerable success and popularity among other Shoshone during this period. In effect, as their ancestors had done, they were acting as intercultural brokers. Then, in 1953, after three years of effort, the tribe received payment for the construction of the Boysen dam and reservoir, which had been built without tribal authorization. Over the years, Maud and other Shoshone lobbyists succeeded in obtaining federal legislation authorizing the distribution of 85 percent of the tribal income as per capita payments, holding back only the small balance as a permanent trust fund. These gains were won in the same period that Congress was moving toward a nationwide termination policy, and so was content to concur in such proposals, which provided for the individualization of jointly held or "tribal" assets.

Significantly, about 1945, Maud decided to move into private enterprise. She had clerked for Matt Maguire in his general store near the Fort for several years, giving her a chance to broaden her social contacts. Matt, she explained, was reluctant to collect many unpaid bills, but Maud took the initiative to secure their payment, easier to accomplish now that the Shoshone were receiving regular per capita dividends from oil and gas royalties. When Matt saw how successful she was in running the business, he persuaded her to purchase the store. She did this by selling a piece of range land near the Owl Creek mountains that she had inherited. With this money as down payment, she bought the store and operated it until 1955. When she sold the business that year, she could proudly say that no accounts were left outstanding.

After the tragic death of her son Vernon by carbon monoxide poisoning, the Clairmonts received his life insurance. They decided to build a home together with a motel and gas station, and bought more than twenty acres on both sides of the highway to Yellowstone and the Tetons. The purchase was from the allotment of an Idaho Shoshone woman. Since Maud was convinced the BIA's assessment of the tract's value was too low, she paid over to the government the required sum, but she also paid an additional amount to the Idaho woman privately, the total amounting to what she considered a fair price for the land. The motel's units were completed in 1955 and it was named "Vernon's" to honor their son. The Clairmonts then moved into their apartment, which was connected to their new business establishment.

With two incomes during these years, the Clairmonts were able to send Marie to nursing school in Portland, Oregon. Maud had taken additional work in psychology at the University of Wyoming, and Vivian completed a degree in education there. In the late 1940s, they purchased a new Lincoln and toured the Pacific coast states.

During the 1950s, Maud, her uncle Bud LeClair, and brother Herman all took art lessons from Mary Back, a native of Evanston, Illinois, who had married a nearby rancher. Joe Back was a great Western-style raconteur, so he and Harold often swapped tall tales. Maud's artistic skills progressed under Mary Back's tutelage, and she proudly displayed several oils and acrylics depicting mountain scenery and local people. Several of her portraits, of well-known Shoshone, showed a good feeling for line and color. She also was known for her highly individualistic taste in clothing, most of which she designed and fashioned. During these years, Maud also learned to knit, and she made numerous large items including a dress, afghans, and hats.

Many people considered her a talented woman. Although she never sold her creative work, she did win prizes for her art at the local Wind River Art Fair, and her knitting was exhibited at the local reservation and county fairs, also winning prizes. She was especially proud of the ceremonial white buckskin dress she made, decorated with elk's teeth. When Mary Cornelius, a Turtle Mountain, North Dakota, Métis, came to Wind River in 1970 to create a series of "actions" for the National Welfare Rights Organization, she stayed with Maud, and the women found that design motifs in the beadwork of their ceremonial dresses were similar. As culturally marginal political leaders, the two women had much in common. Both were public figures, cultural brokers who combined aspects of Indian and Euro-American ways of life in an attempt to construct a significant place for themselves and to adapt to the rapid pace of change. Of more importance, both declared their dedication to protection of their respective Indian communities and the cultural and spiritual traditions esteemed by both.[24]

During the late 1950s and 1960s, Maud continued to operate Vernon's Motel, to serve on the Shoshone Business Council, and to meet and counsel strangers who came to the reservation. Aside from young anthropologists, among them were various authors and researchers.[25] As a political leader, observer of things Shoshone, and member of the Fremont County chapter of the Wyoming State Historical Association, Maud could give the special needs of such visitors much attention and help. She also provided congenial surroundings and lodgings on the reservation, which was fifteen miles from the nearest establishment with rooms for rent.

By 1960, the composition of the Clairmont family was altered. Her oldest daughter, Marie Clairmont Beck, had left to work as a nurse in the Portland, Oregon, area. There, early in the 1950s, she married an American. Since they were unable to have children, she asked to adopt a Shoshone, and during the late 1950s, she became the mother of James (Jimmy) Beck, a Shoshone boy classed as a "full-blood," whose parents were from Ft. Hall, Idaho. Marie later divorced her first husband and remarried an Ohioan, Don Rofkar, whom she met in Oregon. By him she had two children, and by 1966, they moved to the reservation to open a campground for tourists on the route to Yellowstone Park. This enterprise, named the "Teepee Village," did not succeed, and eventually Marie obtained a divorce, supporting herself and the children through nursing, first on the Navajo reservation, and later in the 1970s at the Public Health clinic in Fort Washakie.

Marie then purchased a trailer home, which she parked adjacent to her mother's motel, hooked up to one of the trailer rental spaces Maud had astutely added to the facility. Marie continued living there through the 1970s, but Jim Beck had joined the Navy, and her daughter, Robin, married an Arapaho. Don, her son, attended high school in Lander. Marie has displayed exceptional understanding of Indian health and social problems, and contributes significantly to the welfare of the reservation community. However, she and Maud often disagree on the present state of Shoshone and Arapaho affairs. Maud was more inclined to blame the Indians for their failure to conform to American values and standards, and for their desire to be treated as a special people. Marie, on the other hand, more often places blame for unrest on social conditions, unemployment, poverty, and minority-group status.

Maud, too, could be sensitive to limitations to development set by social and economic structures, but she also seemed to feel the Indians showed too much resistance to social change and that they were insufficiently ambitious. She certainly was aware of the problems caused by persistent poverty and poor health, but she was particularly critical of the absence of tribal planning for future economic security and was now fully convinced that the oil and gas resources would not last forever. In this respect, Maud's views seem to have matured over the years, for in the 1940s, she seemed preoccupied with pressing problems such as the alleviation of poverty and infectious diseases among the Shoshone. Although she had worked hard for higher per capita payments and increased oil production to fund them, she later expressed the view that eventually this source of income would also disappear, and the Shoshone would then have to make other adaptations. She had raised her children to adjust to rapid change, and was convinced that others would have to follow her example in time.

Soon after graduating from high school, Maud's younger daughter, Vivian, married Earl Anson, an American whose family's roots were in Kansas. The Ansons both became elementary school teachers, obtaining degrees from the University of Wyoming. While attending school and teaching, the Ansons somehow raised a family of seven children in Las Vegas, Nevada. But each summer, they returned to Wyoming for an extended vacation at Maud's. When, in 1980, Earl's health deteriorated, and because both could retire early, the Ansons decided to move back to Wyoming to be closer to Maud. They told me often that they did not like living in Las Vegas, and considered it a poor environment in which to raise children. However, because there were few job opportunities in Wyoming, they could not do this and—much to Maud's disappointment—as late as 1987, the Anson children had to remain in Nevada. With oil prices low and Wyoming's agriculture in decline, the area's economy affected more than the fortunes of Maud's grandchildren. All residents of the Wind River area then found fewer opportunities than they had known in the 1960s.

In 1969, Harold Clairmont—the steady, gentle teller of tall tales—died suddenly. He had become grossly overweight, and he had moved into private quarters, a small Airstream trailer behind the motel. During his last years, it sometimes seemed the motel was not large enough for both Clairmonts, since much of the space was taken up with Maud's numerous paintings and her extensive personal collection of clothing and furniture.

When I arrived in the fall of 1969, I found Maud still grieving for Harold. As a coping mechanism, perhaps, she had bought a new Toyota "Land Cruiser," and was planning many excursions into the country, fiercely asserting her independence and determination to start a new life. I knew that in spite of their sometimes strident differences, she missed Harold immensely. She spoke of him constantly, as if she could not yet believe he was gone, then consoled herself with their priest's assurances that Harold had died in a state of grace. But her grief had an angry dimension to it as well: she was convinced his compulsive eating caused the debilitating weight problem that had really killed him, speaking as if his death was an act of volition. He had "eaten himself into the grave," she then complained. In truth, Harold's problem was that, following a lifetime of heavy work responsibilities, after retiring in 1965 he found little to do that was satisfying, except to pump gas occasionally and to help Bud LeClair with ranch work intermittently in summers. But winter days hung heavy on his hands, for Harold was a man who had to be around people. He was, indeed, comfortable being with almost anyone, but had never sought public office and so carried no major role responsibilities with him into his retirement years. Undoubtedly, he also missed the beautiful Flathead Lake country in Montana and his own kinfolk.

When I again returned to Wind River in 1975, little seemed the same. Tom Wesaw, the Sun Dance leader and Maud's Shoshone cousin, died in 1972. His death left another gap in Maud's life, and so she had sought out new relationships. One of these involved a younger man, John Price, or "Indian John" as he was known locally. About forty and recently divorced, he was living with Maud. This new direction in her life caused a considerable stir; and as a result of the ensuing gossip Maud ceased attending the local Catholic Church, instead traveling to Lander for services.

One Shoshone Business Council member, a distant male cousin born out of wedlock, had the audacity to inform Maud pointedly that "cohabitation" was prohibited on the reservation. This inventive moralizing Maud found humorous. She retorted: her association with Indian John was no illicit affair, merely close friendship and cooperation. Besides, she continued, Indians had often lived together out of wedlock, in customary "Indian style" marriage without the sanction of church or state. Maud's daughters came to accept this new relationship, as did most in the community familiar with Shoshone mourning traditions, which tolerated even greater excesses in a widow's behavior during her bereavement than those expressed by Maud.

Forever adamantly independent, Maud refused to end the caring relationship she had with John, who suffered from gout and emphysema and could do little work. He was a man of little education, who was—as he said of himself—"just a cowboy." In the eyes of an interested observer, Maud had found a younger version of Harold Clairmont. There were many resemblances between the two men, for like Harold, John was an amiable, even-tempered man who enjoyed spinning yarns and being with people. Maud obviously cared for him. When I received a Christmas card from her in 1986, it was signed "Maud and John," just as in previous years she had enscribed them "Maud and Harold." In Maud's devotion to her man, there was a substantial convergence of the Shoshone relationship known as *hainch* (friendship) and the American "partner" or "buddy" linkage. The difference was that, in both cultures, these bonded pairs always involved males. Maud's disposition in this respect is yet another expression of her distinctive personal identity.

Following Harold's death, Maud rented motel rooms only to selected people, to visiting anthropologists and their guests, for example; and in 1975, then seventy-three, she decided to close it entirely. Thus, when I and a friend visited Wind River in 1980, she indicated it would be best if we stayed in a bunkhouse on a ranch rented by a niece and her husband. If her daughter Vivian could return to live there, Maud entertained hopes the motel might be remodeled and reopened, but this was not to be.

Maud, artist and free spirit, was both adventurous and religious at the same time. She did not conform to a common stereotype about devoutly religious people: that they are timid, reserved, and highly circumspect in their behavior. Her own religious values were deeply personal and, although she never missed mass, she was careful not to condemn others for not regularly observing the surface trappings of institutional religion or, for that matter, not being outwardly religious at all. On the other hand, in part likely reflecting common American prejudices about chemically induced altered states of consciousness, she had nothing good to say about the use of peyote in Native American Church services. The "Peyote Religion," in the experience of her early life, was a controversial, nontraditional Shoshone ritual, for it had been first introduced to this community only when she was a child. Her Grandmother LeClair disapproved of the use of peyote by a nephew, Tom Wesaw, but the Native American Church gained many adherents during the first decades of this century, and was ably led by Charles Washakie, son of the old chief. Maud did find other Shoshone rituals stirring and beautiful, notwithstanding her ardent Catholicism. Perhaps Grandpa Enos had provided her an effective, open-minded, syncretic model of religiosity, for although a firm Catholic, he took regular sweat baths even in the coldest days of winter. Maud's generally tolerant attitudes were widely shared in the Shoshone reservation community, where there was limited pressure to conform to any one faith, an acceptance of a variety of religions, and an emphasis on personal choice.

In 1966, for example, when she and Harold first described the Sun Dance for me, they went out of their way to discuss its aesthetic features and to emphasize the healing aspects of this ceremony. Harold talked about the men he knew who regularly led it, those like Johnny Trehero and Tom Wesaw, who "really believed in it." Since they knew I needed a sponsor before I could be accepted as a participant-observer in this closely managed ritual, the Clairmonts directed me to Herman St. Clair, a religious leader from a well-to-do, traditional Shoshone family, who was also a member of the business council.

The last half of the summer of 1966, I spent time with Maud's uncle—Bud LeClair and his wife—at their rustic ranch house on Little Wind River, where I had a chance to reflect on Maud and Harold Clairmont's place in the Shoshone community. Bud LeClair provided the perspective of a close relative who was raised with Maud, helping me to appreciate that what she had accomplished had not been easy. The BIA's policies at the time, for instance, were not supportive of many Indian business efforts. Bud LeClair, for example, had tried unsuccessfully to get Bureau financing for a drive-in theater.

Maud had displayed shrewd judgment when she took over Matt Maguire's store at the time when the Shoshone gained income from oil leases. She invested capital from inherited land for which she had no use and placed it into a profitable venture—the store. Again, with Vernon's insurance benefit, she made a wise investment in a home and motel-gas station. She dealt fairly with the Idaho Shoshone woman, when she could have had the land cheaply, simply by paying the BIA's low assessment of its value. With all these efforts, Maud became well-known locally in the Lander business community, and she gained increased influence among the Shoshone, who continued to trust her leadership in the council.

During the 1950s, Maud's political ties shifted to the Republicans who, as she claimed, helped the Shoshone more than had the Democrats in securing a larger share of the oil and gas revenues paid as dividends to Shoshone individuals. Unfortunately, the Wind River reservation was also considered ripe for termination during these years, but the joint Shoshone-Arapaho Business Councils strongly and successfully opposed this development.[26] Nonetheless, Maud has remained a strong Republican to this date, insisting that individual efforts should be rewarded, and that Indians should be treated "the same as everyone else," opinions she often expresses. Her ancestors, however, were staunch Democrats.

When, with the help of probate records, a complete genealogy of the descendants of John and Julia Enos was compiled, I saw that their lineal and collateral descendants, plus their affinal kin, included over 400 people—about one-fifth of the Shoshone tribal membership in 1970. This kinship network—Maud L. Clairmont's kindred—also extended to people not enrolled as Shoshone, Americans resident in Lander and Riverton. Those within Maud's kindred classed as Shoshone Indians included some who were traditional people associated with the Sun Dance, for example, and others closer to Catholic Franco-Indian traditions. In all social and cultural dimensions, whether language, values, social-economic class, or religion, her kin were an exceedingly heterogeneous human aggregate.

In effect, the composition of Maud's kindred reflects the past century or more of the history of the Shoshone and marginal frontier folk associated with them. In this period, the Shoshone have changed dramatically. Once they were composed of clusters of tiny bands of self-sufficient foragers, in which extended families were typically the largest unit of social and political integration. They once displayed little internal differentiation or formal political organization. Formerly, they consisted of people much alike in language and culture, perhaps even with a substantially shared genetic heritage. With the introduction of the horse, during the eighteenth and nineteenth centuries, in ways similar to their southern kinfolk, the Comanche, the Eastern Shoshone developed the institution of powerful chieftains. Leadership coalesced around important individuals such as Washakie (1804–1900), and the Eastern Shoshone became known as Washakie's band of Shoshone, or sometimes the Green River "Snakes."[27]

As replacement for the former social-political organization came a reservation-based community with a formal political structure, institutionalized as the Shoshone "tribe" and governed by the elected business council. This emergent modern Shoshone "tribe" was defined in American folk-legal terms. In the people who compose its membership, its basic organization and functioning, and its economic dimensions, the modern tribe bears little resemblance to the historic Shoshone bands. Thus, while perpetuating a Shoshone group identity, the modern "tribal" organization and ethnically composite reservation community represent massive transformations. Formerly an independent, culturally distinctive people, the surviving Shoshone have been incorporated into one of the numerous local multiethnic groups categorized as Indian by Americans. Among popular beliefs about their identity are convictions about an exclusively shared, common social and cultural heritage. Certainly this population has a distinctive heritage but it is by no means exclusively Shoshone.

Maud Clairmont's heterogeneous ancestry fully demonstrates this point. The descendants of her focal ancestors, John and Julia Enos, comprise an aggregate that displays great variation in social identity and cultural style, whether counted as allotted Shoshone or not. Rather than being exclusively-Shoshone, their heritage represents a sequence of interlocked cultural frontiers, in which peoples of widely different backgrounds mingled and interbred, some of them eventually joining as members of the modern Shoshone tribal organization.

Maud's personal style reflected the complexities of, not only her own, but the entire contemporary Shoshone heritage. Her position as a kind of gatekeeper, where at her motel she welcomed and briefed strangers, displayed both an openness to change and a concern with managing first impressions of the Shoshone. In her lifetime, she matured as a distinctive person, one sustaining her identity as Indian while always willing to consider new ways. Because of her composite ancestry, and that of other marginal Shoshone like her, she has perhaps run somewhat ahead of the flock. Her striking economic and political successes, for example, mark her as representative of the reservation's new middle class, not of the Shoshone in general. However, if her lifetime of distinctive adaptations does not in microcosm exactly mirror all Shoshone, a close inspection of her emerging identity provides important clues to understanding how the modern Shoshone have become who they are.

For the whole Shoshone population, too, is of increasingly composite ancestry, both culturally and biologically. If Maud Clairmont and others close to her are seen as individual forerunners of an evolving Shoshone identity, the value of inspecting her career and person will be clear. In truth, while perpetuating an old identity—and such symbols as Sacajawea, Washakie, and Horse and Buffalo days—the modern Shoshone have become a new people; adapted to life in a rapidly changing social and political environment. Certainly, a core of traditions from the last century have been preserved, but even during the days of Chief Washakie, the Shoshone understood the necessity of change. Indeed, they have made adaptive responses to sequential political-economic transformations part of their cultural inventory. This dynamic tradition is particularly evident among Maud's Franco-Indian forebears, who had lived between the Indian and European worlds so successfully for generations. The critical role they played has obviously been perpetuated by Maud, standing at her motel facing outward and coping with strangers visiting the Shoshone.

A minority in the modernized "tribe" are descended exclusively from Shoshone ancestors. Indeed, the Arapaho, who share the same reservation, often characterize their neighbors as "mostly breeds," which, as expressed, carries a connotation of contempt, of being less than genuinely Indian. The same sentiment is not widely shared among the Shoshone, however. Nor is any such attitude expressed in practice. While their tribal enrollment regulations specify a "one-quarter Shoshone blood quantum" for legitimate enrollment as members, they have bent this regulation to accommodate children of less than the requisite ancestry. In this manner, the formal tribal organization insures the perpetuation of its membership, and reduces conflicts with enrolled parents whose children by Indians of other communities would otherwise be disinherited. But, at the same time, this practice contributes to the growing cultural heterogeneity of the Shoshone population.

The Wyoming Shoshone have been ingenious about admitting new, ever more marginal members. If a Shoshone man or woman enrolled as "one-quarter blood" marries an Indian of different tribal affiliation, the generic Indian "blood-quantum" is added to that of the Shoshone parent in fixing the identity of their child as Eastern Shoshone. The one effective limitation comes into play when the outside spouse has no identifiable Indian ancestry. In such cases, the children of Shoshone with less than the minimum one-quarter "blood-quantum" are not eligible for legal enrollment, since to be enrolled the child must have inherited a combined total of one-quarter Indian ancestry, including some known Shoshone ancestry, from one or both parents.

This peculiarity of Shoshone membership qualifications causes numerous problems. Maud has faced such issues both as a grandmother and as a leader in tribal political affairs. With one exception, because her children have commonly married non-Indians, all her grandchildren are "three-sixteenths Eastern Shoshone blood," hence, not accepted as members of the tribe. When one Shoshone illegally tried to enroll his grandchildren, in an open meeting of the tribe's adults (the General Council) Maud attempted to get the tribe to broaden its membership criteria. She moved that all grandchildren of tribal members of one-half or more "Shoshone" ancestry be made eligible for enrollment. As this would have allowed grandchildren with as little as one-eighth blood to be enrolled, greatly increasing the recognized Shoshone population, her motion was defeated. But the purpose of her action—to prevent the tribal chairman from illegally enrolling his grandchildren—was accomplished. Recently, her one granddaughter—not eligible for enrollment as a Shoshone, married an Anglo-Arapaho from the same reservation. Their children will be enrolled as Arapaho, hence, part of an emerging, joint Wind River Shoshone-Arapaho identity group. As old intergroup enmities fade, intermarriages between the two populations are increasing. However, in contrast to the Shoshone, the Arapaho remain a much more exclusive, closed community. Thus, there is little likelihood of a formal merger of the two organizations soon.

Over the years, some Shoshone have criticized Maud for her individualism, but few denied that during the period when the tribe most needed flexible and creative leadership, she helped provide it. During the 1930s, she was about as nontraditional as a Shoshone woman could be: her nickname translated as "red lips," for instance, referring to her shocking use of lipstick. Such negative attitudes, however, could not deflect this woman from her chosen course, and few could question her loyalty to the tribe and its best interests.

Overall, Maud's personal identity has reflected the intersection of the many old ethnic strands which, joined on the Wyoming frontier, have produced the modern multicultural Shoshone reservation community. The development and the persistence of this new cultural identity has demanded much creative manipulation of symbols, great tolerance for ethnic differences, and regular self-examination. Maud Clairmont, through her adult life, placed herself between the Shoshone community and the outside world. She shunned neither and, in significant ways as entrepreneur, artist, and business council leader, has conquered both. Together with other leaders who guided the Shoshone past the demands of the Indian Reorganization Act (when they rejected a BIA sponsored constitution), and who successfully obtained land claims settlements and lobbied for larger per capita payments, she has contributed her share to Shoshone political victories. These have been won without the forfeiture of Shoshone rights to manage their own resources. Some of her grandchildren still live in the area. Although now not eligible for enrollment as legal Shoshone Indians, some may marry back into the tribe, making her great grandchildren legitimate participants in this modernized, ethnically composite Shoshone community. Perhaps they will carry into the twenty-first century the traditions of leadership established by Maud L. Clairmont and earlier generations of culturally marginal people associated with the once self-sufficient, culturally distinctive Shoshone bands.

NOTES

1. His essay is based on field research conducted between 1966 and 1987. I owe an enormous debt to all the institutions that have supported my work with the Shoshone, including: The University of Illinois, Champaign-Urbana, the Doris Duke Foundation, the University of Wisconsin-Stevens Point, and the D'Arcy McNickle Center for American Indian History at the Newberry Library, Chicago. Maud Lajeunesse Clairmont graciously granted me permission to write her biography, which I now, in 1987, the beginning of her 85th year, dedicate to her. Any distortions or inaccuracies are unintended, and are the responsibility of the author. For additional information on the Shoshone, see Thomas H. Johnson, *The Enos Family and Wind River Shoshone Society: A Historical Analysis*, Ph.D. dissertation, University of Illinois, Champaign-Urbana, 1975 (Ann Arbor, Mich.: University Microfilms International, 1979); Demitri B. Shimkin, "Eastern Shoshone," in *Great Basin* 11, ed. Warren L. D'Azevedo, *Handbook of North American Indians* (Washington, D.C.: Smithsonian Institution, 1986), pp. 308–35; and Virginia C. Trenholm and Maurine Carley, *The Shoshonis: Sentinels of the Rockies* (Norman, Okla.: University of Oklahoma Press, 1964).
2. Maud L. Clairmont, personal communication.
3. Johnson, *The Enos Family*, pp. 317–20.
4. John C. Ewers, "The Iroquois in the Far West," *Montana, The Magazine of Western History* 13 (1963), pp. 1–10; and Jack A. Frisch, "Iroquois in the West," in ed. Bruce G. Trigger, *Handbook of North American Indians, Northeast*, 15, pp. 544–46.
5. See Demitri B. Shimkin, "The Wind River Shoshone Sun Dance," *Bulletin of the Bureau of American Ethnology*, 151, pp. 397–484 (Washington, D.C.: Smithsonian Institution, 1953). More recent accounts include Thomas H. Johnson, *The Wind River Shoshone Dance: 1966 and 1967*, Ms., Doris Duke Archives, Department of Anthropology, University of Illinois, Champaign-Urbana; for a more extensive treatment, Joseph G. Jorgensen, *The Sun Dance Religion: Power for the Powerless* (Chicago, Ill.: University of Chicago Press, 1972); and Fred W. Voget, *The Shoshone—Crow Sun Dance* (Norman, Okla.: University of Oklahoma Press, 1984).

6. Leroy R. Hafen, ed., *The Mountain Men and the Fur Trade*, 1 (Glendale, Calif.: Arthur H. Clark, 1965). William Swagerty (personal communication) counted sixteen trappers with Shoshone wives.

7. Grace R. Hebard, n.d., untitled interview of Edmo LeClair, Sr., Hebard Collection, Western History Archives, University of Wyoming, Laramie.

8. Hebard, LeClair interview.

9. Johnson, *The Enos Family*, pp. 113–163.

10. *Shoshoni Census, 1890*. Bureau of Indian Affairs Census Records, Record Group 75, National Archives, Washington,D.C.

11. *Shoshone Census, 1980*.

12. *Shoshone Census, 1885, 1890–1895*.

13. Grace R. Hebard, *Washakie* (Glendale, Calif.: Arthur H. Clark, 1930), p. 51.

14. John C. Ewers, "Gustavus Sohon's Portraits of Flatheads and Pend d'Oreille Indiana, 1854," in *Smithsonian Miscellaneous Collections* 10, No. 7, 1948.

15. A photograph of the Enos sisters, some wearing Indian attire, some "citizens' " dress, including Bat Weed (born 1874) as a child with his mother, Mary, is a prized possession of several descendants. The photograph was probably taken in 1876 at Fort Washakie.

16. Johnson, *The Enos Family*, pp. 164–285.

17. The Fremont County Historical Society, in *Annals of Wyoming* 26, no. 1, 1928, pp. 54–64.

18. *United States Census, 1870, Wyoming Territory*, lists Michel and Elizabeth Lajeunesse and children, as well as Newel or Noel Lajeunesse, at Fort Fetterman.

19. Information supplied by Alfred Ward, a great-grandson. No explanation is given for why a Franco-Sioux family would settle among the Shoshone.

20. The ceded portion was restored by an Act of Congress in 1939, and land previously sold gradually reacquired. See Paul B. Wilson, *Farming and Ranching on the Wind River Reservation, Wyoming*, Ph.D. dissertation, University of Nebraska, 1972.

21. Johnson, *The Enos Family*, p. 163.

22. This complex web of kinship is detailed in Johnson, *The Enos Family*, chapters 4 and 5.

23. See *Hearings before the Subcommittee on Indian Affairs of the Committee on Public Lands, House of Representatives, 80th Congress, 1st Session, on H.R. 1098, March 15, 1947, a bill to authorize the segregation and expenditure of trust funds held in joint ownership by the Shoshone and Arapho tribes of the Wind River Reservation*.

24. See Plate, p. 259.

25. Among these were Robert and Yolanda Murphy, of Columbia University's Anthropology department; Mrs. Virginia Trenholm of Wheatland, Wyoming, coauthor of *The Shoshonis: Sentinels of the Rockies;* myself, Michelle De Riso, Betsey Conklin, Joseph Hemphill; and Demitri Shimkin, of the Department of Anthropology, University of Illinois, Champaign-Urbana.

26. See Joseph Hemphill, *Development of Tribal Government on the Wind River Indian Reservation*. Paper in lieu of master's thesis, Doris Duke Archives, Department of Anthropology, University of Illinois, 1971.

27. Grace R. Hebard, *Washakie*. See also Demitri B. Shimkin, "Dynamics of Recent Wind River Shoshone History," *American Anthropologist* 44, 1942, pp. 451–62.

CHAPTER 12

Joe True: Convergent Needs and Assumed Identity

Robert Stahl

PRESENTING JOE TRUE (1949—)

A first reaction to the story of this young Texan might be that it is a modern captivity narrative, but it is not. Instead, it is a tale of mutual captivation, between some modern Kiowa and a young American long convinced that Indian ways, particularly Indian religion, formed a desirable alternative lifestyle for himself. In this respect, Joe True's experience with and as a converted Kiowa resemble the seekings of many American youth who experiment with new religions and communal groups of various kinds. From the perspective of his Kiowa hosts and family, they were following an ancient social strategy, that of recruiting and socializing new members who displayed a willingness to affiliate with them and to serve their interests. Although the details of Joe's first dramatic meeting with the Kiowa—when he acted the part of the brave warrior guarding them at risk of his own life—was happenstance, he was on the scene because of his own volition, and he certainly would have found some other way of making contact with this or a different Indian community. The most significant element in this sensational encounter was that it provided him rapid entrée and an open opportunity to display a sincere interest in Kiowa ways, especially their rituals. His conversion thereafter was neither sudden, emotionally wrenching, total, nor permanent. And, it was not a once-in-a-lifetime event. On the contrary, Joe True's temporary affiliation with the Kiowa was an important episode in a career of such searching for meaningful group membership, social contexts where he could find personal rewards—esteem, recognition, and affection—in belonging and contributing, and where he could grow and develop as a person. His later disaffiliation reflects an important fact. Such conversions are not necessarily fully accepted by all involved. Joe True later experienced much stress and anxiety from the negative reactions of both some Kiowa and the Americans to whom he presented himself as an advocate of Kiowa ritualism. The former found themselves thwarted by Joe, displaying jealousy at what they saw as a competitor for the affections of their kin; the latter reacted to him as a vulnerable anomaly and an impediment to their practice of treating Indian practices as a diverting pastime. Joe True's temporary identification and behavior as a Kiowa ritualist, thereby, reflects the freedom of contemporary American self-process, the mutability of social identity, as many young people sequentially experiment with one group affiliation after another. Like many other Americans, Joe was trying on an alternative mode of being, reflecting the common weakness of lasting individual commitment to groups and institutions, and the multiple alternative subcultures available for inspection, testing, and at least temporary affiliation. The experience of this young man must be contrasted with those young Americans of an earlier frontier era who were forcibly abducted and subject to coercive induction into Indian families and communities. Joe was a man acting of his own volition, making choices, actively exploring new cultural opportunities. He was and is not alone in these respects. (J. A. Clifton)

Ideally, anthropological inquiry follows a premeditated course. Working from a carefully drawn research plan, we deliberately collect relevant data in face-to-face encounters with people in their communities. Normally, we are taught, such field research inquiries proceed to formal analysis of this raw material, and then a write-up of findings. But like other social scientists, anthropologists appreciate that life does not always follow ideal courses. Sometimes our encounters force us to engage the unexpected. Such a possibility is dignified with a name, the surprising observation or serendipitous discovery.

Rarely, however, does the problem in cultural understanding deliberately search out and tantalize us, provoking puzzlement, confusion, and finally, disciplined inquiry. While teaching at a university in Southeast Texas some years ago, I experienced such an unanticipated encounter. The cultural puzzle actually strode unannounced through the door into my office and introduced himself. To safeguard his privacy, we can identify him as Joe True.

At first glance, Joe, in most ways, was indistinguishable from other young oil refinery workers in the area. In general appearance somewhat neater and better groomed than many, there was little to set him apart. About six feet tall, of medium build, he was blue-eyed and had a slightly ruddy complexion. His sandy hair was trimmed neatly to a length that exposed his ears and he was clean shaven. Dressed casually in a colorful blue print sport shirt and slightly faded jeans, he presented himself with confidence, without seeming boastful or arrogant. On closer inspection, I spied one incongruity: he was wearing traditional Kiowa moccasins. But it was his manner and his agenda that first startled, then annoyed me, for he announced himself as an Indian with a mission.

This first encounter left me with feelings of strong ambivalence toward Joe. He was not only a walking contradiction, he was an irritating and challenging one as well. After introducing himself, he quickly revealed he had come to test me. Was I sympathetic toward Indians? Did I know enough to be teaching courses about Indian culture? He also volunteered his services as a guest speaker on Kiowa tradition in my classes. Both from what he said and from his attitude and manner, he seemed to present himself as a young Kiowa concerned that his people, and Indians in general, receive fair treatment in college courses dealing with Native American life. He spoke of his relatives, especially his grandparents, in conversational contexts that

Joe True's Landscapes

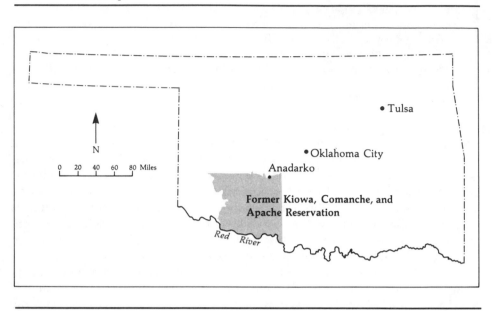

N

0   20   40   60   80 Miles

• Tulsa

• Oklahoma City

Anadarko

Former Kiowa, Comanche, and Apache Reservation

Red River

identified them as Kiowa living in Western Oklahoma. But he didn't "look Indian." Phenotypically—in physical appearance, he was obviously Caucasian. Moreover, except for his Kiowa moccasins, in dress and language, he was nothing but Euro-American in cultural heritage—an east Texas refinery worker.

I was left with serious misgivings about who Joe "really" was and what his self-asserted Kiowa identity meant; but from the start, I found him fascinating. I had recently moved to southeast Texas from Oklahoma for my first university teaching position, and was busy writing my dissertation on Indian farming in Southwestern Oklahoma. During the previous year, I had interviewed many elderly Kiowa, and was now immersed in relevant historical sources. Then Joe walked in. This young refinery worker was being presumptuous, I believed. He was irritating, indeed, threatening to a young professional just embarked on his career.

I had enough experience with Indians to be convinced I understood something of "genuine" Indianness. Working for a year and a half at a small Indian college where I was on close terms with many students, together with numerous trips to Western Oklahoma to visit Kiowa friends and to attend pow-wows, left me comfortable with this conviction. True, I was still conscious of my ignorance, particularly when around or interviewing traditional elderly people. I was fully aware I had much to learn. Yet, when this young, blue-collar Texan challenged me, boldly stating he had something to teach me, I was indignant. Nonetheless, teach me Joe True did. During the five years following our first uncomfortable encounter, he helped me gain insights into aspects of Kiowa life I had known only superficially. He was, in addition, a one-person phenomenon, a bundle of surprising observations in his own right, and it was my responsibility as a scholar to understand him and what he represented, as well as to learn from him of Kiowa ways. In the end, his anomalous identity forced me to reexamine my understanding of ethnicity, and to address my own ethnocentrism.

Although my initial irritation and confusion dissipated, in one way, my first impression of him never changed. Joe True was invariably sincere and natural, comfortably unself-conscious in the presentation of his Kiowa identity. This was true not only in our private encounters, but in all the varied public settings where I observed him. These included many social events where the Kiowa accepted him as one of themselves. More than anything else, his forthright, guileless manner prompted me to seek understanding, both in personal terms—Joe True as an intriguing friend—and in anthropological terms as well. I had to resolve what I saw as a contradiction between Joe's biological ancestry and his original cultural heritage and social identity, and his apparent, new ethnic identity. How had this young Texan become ethnically Kiowa?

Joe's existence as Kiowa, I realized finally, violated my unexamined assumptions about cultural boundaries and ethnic identity. In retrospect, I can see my first reactions to Joe were entangled with the commonly accepted notion that so-called "blood quantum" is a useful, if rough, index of cultural traditionality among Indians. A common unstated assumption is that "full-bloods" are culturally more traditional than "mixed-bloods." By extension, therefore, the quality of a person's authentic cultural performance is necessarily somehow connected with the quantity of biological ancestry. But here was Joe True, accepted by Kiowa as genuinely Kiowa, yet of no Indian ancestry at all.

Consciously, as a professional anthropologist, I believed and professed an opposite idea: culture was not biologically inherited at all, but was the product of learning, in essence, the symbols and meanings shared by a group and acquired by individuals from that group. Despite formal training as an anthropologist, I realized, my thinking still harbored some of the conventions of American racial thinking. According to these ethnocentric racial conventions, Joe True could not be authentically Kiowa because he was not biologically "Indian."

Confronted with surprising observations and intellectual confusion, scholars are forced back onto their sources, in this instance, accumulated thinking about ethnicity.[1] The attributes most often used to define an ethnic group are two: first, cultural distinctiveness, which marks the group as different from others; second, common biological ancestry. Such thinking, applied to the Kiowa themselves, works well enough. Clearly, they were a people with common culture and shared ancestry. But Joe had no Kiowa ancestors: how then had he acquired the language, knowledge, mannerisms, and values—the cultural distinctiveness, which made him acceptable to these Indians?

In other ethnically mobile individuals, we know, this involves a series of complex psychological and social processes. The first of these is self-identification with a particular ethnic group, followed by acquisition of an active social role in that group. Next, must come acceptance of the asserted identity by others, and the personal incorporation of the group's world view and behavioral norms. The identification of an individual with particular ethnic groups, we also know, often develops "directly and rapidly, arising out of involvements in particular situations rather than as the outcome of slow, continuous psychological development."[2] Such processes, we will see, were certainly involved in Joe True's transformation from Texan to Kiowa.

But of even greater value in understanding Joe True and other ethnically mobile individuals like him are the thoughts of A. Irving Hallowell, who confronted the issue of "Indianization" specifically. Hallowell borrowed the phrasing "transculturation" for this process and applied it systematically to many examples like that of Joe True. He defined transculturation as: "the process whereby individuals under a variety of circumstances are temporarily or permanently detached from one group, enter the web of social relations that constitute another society, and come under the influence of its customs, ideas, and values to a greater or lesser degree."[3]

Transculturation, as Hallowell understood the process, and as we can appreciate, is not restricted to "Indianization." It is a worldwide phenomenon including, for example, "Americanization" and "Arabization" as well. Moreover, in its effects on individuals, it is not an all-or-none process. Indeed, the degree and persistence of change in content and strength of the ethnic identity of individuals varies considerably. The person's age when the process begins is particularly significant, as are prior attitudes toward the new host group. Length of association with or residence among members of the new ethnic group plays an important part in mastery of their views and values, as does the motivation of cultural migrants, and the specific roles made available to them. Above all else, the receptivity of the host group critically affects what happens to individuals in the process of ethnic identity transformation.

Hallowell had in mind the many persons who, over the course of American history, have abandoned their natal ethnic identities in favor of becoming Indian. Among these were numerous English and French captives taken during frontier wars, as well as those otherwise sought out by various Indian societies and enticed into switching their identities, and the volunteers who went in search of a more satisfying way of life for themselves. Looking at Joe True in the context of such ideas, I came to see that he represented a contemporary example of a centuries-old process. An account of his experiences among the Kiowa is, I at last recognized, something of a late twentieth-century captivity narrative.

Joe and I first were acquaintances; we became friends. In the process, I learned more of his life story. Joe's father was a blue-collar, forty-year veteran of the same oil refinery where Joe worked. Of Scotch-Irish descent, his father's family had resided near Austin, Texas, for generations. Joe's mother came from an old Mississippi family of mixed French and English origins. Though Joe's family was actively involved in the Baptist church, he recalled no exaggerated emphasis on piety or worship. Joe experienced what he termed "a normal, happy childhood," although he was always somewhat of a loner.

More introspective than his peers, he recalled being vaguely dissatisfied. He had friends and playmates, but his early devotion to long-distance running (with Billy Mills as an idol) and his avid interest in Indians set him apart. Since boyhood, Joe explained, he had always been interested in Indian culture. An automobile trip through the Southwest brought his first actual observations of Indians; thereafter, he devoured books about them. By the time he was a boy scout in the Order of the Arrow, he knew enough to be dissatisfied with the scoutmaster's's version of "Indian craft and lore." Later, he joined an Indian hobbyist organization and was again disappointed by the shoddy representations of Indian culture he encountered. Such hobbyists, dressed in their versions of Indian costumes, were enthusiastic and sometimes excellent mimics of pow-wow dance forms, but they had little or no personal experience or involvement with Indians, Joe discovered. Theirs was a glamorized, superficial reconstruction of Indian cultures, he learned, one reflecting their stereotypes.

Thus motivated and concerned, Joe was long displeased with what he could learn about Indians through conventional American sources and representations. Then, during the summer of 1972, when in his early twenties, Joe took vacation time from the oil refinery where he worked and drove to Oklahoma for the Annual American Indian Exposition. Arriving in Anadarko, he asked directions to the fairground from a group of Kiowa teenagers standing in front of a market. As it happened, they were camped with their families at the exposition and were happy to give Joe directions. Noticing from the license-plate frame on his car that he was from Port Arthur, Texas, they asked eagerly if he knew the rock music star, Janis Joplin. Joe admitted that he did not but told them he had gone to high school with that celebrity's cousin. This reply brought an invitation to their family camp, where Joe could elaborate on his description of Port Arthur and what he knew of Janis Joplin.

Within a few hours, Joe's visit to the Kiowa camp involved him in a situation that created a durable welcome for the young Texan. One of the teenage Kiowa girls he met was off drinking, while Joe visited with her grandparents. Wandering into another tribe's campground, she was surrounded by a dozen young men who threatened to rape her. Her sister ran back to the Kiowa camp, crying for help, discovering that Joe and the girl's twelve-year-old brother were the only ones present capable of rescuing her. The two ran to the scene, and immediately found themselves in gread danger. But just as the girl's attackers turned their attention to Joe and the brother, a group of adult Kiowa walked by and quickly took charge, defusing a life-threatening confrontation.

KIOWA GOURD DANCE GROUP. Once adopted and assimilated into a Kiowa family and community, Joe True was assigned a role in promoting the expansion of the Gourd Dance society. Here, on July 4, 1976, the Kiowa Gourd clan—a chapter other than the one to which Joe belonged—assembled at Carnegie, Oklahoma for their "Annual." (Photograph by the author.)

Because of his courageous interference, the attackers threatened Joe: he would not leave the fair grounds alive, they boasted. Back in the Kiowa camp, he was invited to stay the night, so the family could protect him. Although they had just met, the girl's grandparents spontaneously began speaking to Joe as "grandson." Not until much later did he understand the significance of being addressed in that way. His loyalty in defending a family member had created a debt, he discovered, one that could not be discharged in any quick, simple way. So the elders adopted him.

Informal, temporary adoption by a Kiowa family is often done to honor someone. By themselves, such displays of esteem are not rare occurrences. What was unusual in this instance was the family's recognition of the importance of Joe's wholehearted response, when he disregarded his personal safety and responded as their defender in a dangerous crisis. Thus, their commitment to him was immediate, compelling, and durable. By the close of the fair, Joe felt thoroughly comfortable with his new kinfolk, and had been invited to visit them at their home. Because of his keen interest in Indian culture and the warm reception he received, he began making frequent trips to Oklahoma and was soon publicly and formally adopted. In this way, his new family proclaimed their acceptance of Joe True before the community at large.

Joe's Kiowa family was actively involved in one of the *Tai'peh* (Gourd Dance) groups. Originally, the Tai'peh was a Kiowa warriors' association, of the kind typical of horse nomads of the Great Plains. After several decades of dormancy, in 1956, the Tai'peh was revitalized. Since then, this institution has experienced phenomenal growth, accompanied by several factional schisms disrupting the original membership.

Several reasons for the broad appeal of the Gourd Dance are easily recognizable. The Gourd Dance has become linked with the popular pantribal Pow Wow, and came to represent a distinctively Kiowa contribution to these large celebrations of Indianness. In the years shortly after its revival, the Gourd Dance was most frequently restricted to the afternoon "filler" spot before the evening meal and the evening "social dance" program at many Oklahoma Pow Wows. But as their membership grew, the Gourd Dance group began holding more dances of its own and soon won wider acceptance and more prestige. Eventually, Gourd Dance performances were scheduled in the prime early evening time slot.

Although Gourd Dance performances exhibited much of the general form of other Pow Wow enactments, they differed in two important ways. Gourd Dance outfits were inexpensive by comparison with War Dance costumes, and the actual Gourd Dance steps were much simpler and less physically demanding than the gymnastic feats required of war dancers. Both of these facts make Gourd Dance participation easy and attractive to many Kiowa. Additionally, although only men are inducted as members and manage the affairs of the association, thus preserving the older form of an exclusive warriors' society, today whole families participate in Gourd Dance activities.

During the public performances entire family groups, with men and boys in front and women and girls behind, dance slowly from their positions on the perimeter toward the center of the arena. At the end of each set of four songs, the dancers return to their places. "Give aways," honoring songs, and "specials" (fund-raising songs) are interspersed between sequences of specifically Gourd Dance songs. Although prescribed etiquette is not complex or burdensome, dancers must and do behave with respect and decorum in the presence of the Gourd Dance drum.

Today there are four separate formally organized Gourd Dance groups. Together, they occupy an important position in Kiowa life. Through their popular year-round activities, they promote ethnic identification and closer ties between urban and rural Kiowa than might otherwise exist. By joining a rural Gourd Dance group and through participating in its periodic dances, Kiowa living and working in nearby cities can reinforce and enrich their understanding of who they are and where they belong culturally, and they are able to maintain relationships with numerous other Kiowa.

Soon after the formal adoption ceremony, Joe's family encouraged him to begin Gourd Dancing with them. In Joe, his adoptive grandparents saw an opportunity to fill a social void. Although both his new grandfather and grandmother were descendants of prominent tribal leaders, neither had always fully cherished their Kiowa identities. Indeed, until only a few years before meeting Joe, they—like many other twentieth-century Indians—had downplayed their ethnicity in an attempt to better cope with the non-Indian world.

While both the grandparents and their children had renewed their Kiowa identities through involvement in the Gourd Dance society, their grandchildren—Joe's peers—had displayed little interest beyond the peripheral socializing involved. These were the same youngsters who first invited Joe True to their camp—to seek through him some faint personal contact with the American celebrity Janis Joplin. In Joe, the grandparents saw a surrogate, perhaps a guide for these disaffected Kiowa youth, one who might redirect their attention and interests. Joe had displayed personal courage in protecting their granddaughter, like a proper Kiowa warrior. Immediately thereafter he exhibited respect and unwavering interest in their ways. Responding, they saw him as an instrument who might help fill their needs. His new grandfather was deeply touched when Joe offered him a hand-rolled cigarette and asked to be taught traditional Kiowa "ways," especially those connected with the Tai'peh.

Before long, he was inducted into that organization, widening his circle of Kiowa relationships and accelerating a broader acceptance of him as Kiowa. From his Kiowa kin, Joe continued to receive the personal support he needed; but participation in the Gourd Dance society provided him a broader set of Kiowa social contacts, and contexts where his emerging ethnic identity could be enlarged, reinforced, and legitimized. By 1976, so trusted had Joe become by the Gourd Dance membership, they asked him to help form a daughter chapter in southeast Texas, for Indians—and for other sincerely interested recruits. Similar chapters had already been established in widely separated places: Dallas, Texas; Macy, Nebraska; and Columbus, Georgia. By this time, Joe had been formally adopted into several additional Kiowa families associated with the Gourd Dance, further increasing the network of kin, friends, and associates who accepted him as one of themselves.

Joe, newly converted, set about his assigned missionary responsibilities with enthusiasm and, at first, with good effects. He gradually drew together a group of some thirty people interested in Gourd dancing, including fifteen Indians and as many other Texans. Initially, Joe was to merely help establish the chapter. However, when three local Indians tried to gain control and subvert the parent society's original intent by barring non-Indians from membership or even marginal participation, the Oklahoma organization, which did not want a racially segregated membership, placed Joe in charge of forming the chapter.

In 1977, this new chapter was officially chartered by the Gourd Dance society as an affiliate, whereupon Joe was elected to a two-year term as one of its head men. Unfortunately, Joe was unable to restrict recruitment to neophytes seriously interested in learning Kiowa ways. Many more individuals seeking amusement—the Indian hobbyists—joined than he had hoped for. Yet, still convinced that familiarity with an authentic Kiowa organization would both benefit the hobbyists and promote intergroup understanding (a major aim of the Gourd Dance sponsors), he accepted their entry into the new chapter. So at both the charter meeting in Oklahoma and the first local membership meeting in Texas, many Indian hobbyists were inducted, too many to allow the chapter to develop in a way consistent with the intentions of its original organizers.

The recently converted Kiowa—the new officer of the Gourd Dance society—soon learned his tolerance was backdrop for an organizational disaster. Full of his own sincere zeal, Joe had assumed these hobbyists would respond to contact with Kiowa models and his coaching by mastering proper Gourd Dance etiquette and by accepting Kiowa values. This was not to be. Instead, the original hobbyists quickly recruited others like themselves, introducing into the Gourd Dance group a form of competitive power-seeking alien to the ethos of this Kiowa institution. What amused them most, it happened, was not simply play-acting Indian. For while Joe was trying to lead by example, in traditional Kiowa fashion, the hobbyists were maneuvering for a corporate takeover. Restricted by his understanding of the ideals of traditional Kiowa leadership, which stressed harmony and altruism, Joe failed to quell this revolt. Moreover, as the balance of power noticeably shifted, the small number of Indian members stopped attending chapter functions. Joe True was now head of a racially segregated Gourd Dance chapter, whose membership had little genuine interest in Kiowa ways or aims.

In their turn, the hobbyists interpreted Joe's Kiowa leadership style as a sign of personal weakness. His careful avoidance of any personal confrontations and his calm speeches to the membership exhorting them to pursue the society's ideals did nothing to correct that conviction. The hobbyists had never adopted the traditional Kiowa values that molded Joe's behavior and style, which he cited as guides for their activities, values that still exerted a moral force in Kiowa life. At first, the hobbyists were content with informal, private sanctions—taunting him with dead owls (potent symbols of death to the Kiowa) deposited on his doorstep at night, and blatantly neglecting financial obligations to the parent society, leaving Joe and a few friends with the full burden, and similar insults.

Seeing that Joe True was not much moved by such private insults, the dissident hobbyists soon escalated the level of conflict and went public. Joe was then subjected to a variety of obvious indignities before the Gourd Dance chapter, all designed to reduce his standing and effectiveness in the group. One device much favored by the hobbyists was to create mock honors, displaying not their support or esteem but their contempt for the elected head man. Under this unrelenting attack, Joe was deserted by all but his closest friends. They, too, had been made targets of such insults, and were unwillingly dragged into compromising, open confrontations. Eventually, they resigned from the Gourd Dance chapter, leaving Joe in an impossible position. With the tide running so heavily against him, Joe was forced to acknowledge the reality of the takeover. Instead of waiting for the upcoming election and its inevitable result, he resigned his position in the daughter chapter his Kiowa kin had asked him to form.

This conflict within the affiliated chapter was paralleled by a power struggle between two factions of the parent organization. When election time came, Joe's party lost the leadership positions held for many years. Then, as if his reputation had not already suffered enough, Joe's adoptive grandparents gave credence to some of the vicious rumors about him spread by the hobbyists. These rumors were transmitted and reinforced by a member of his adoptive family who had come to resent Joe. She felt he was occupying the "favorite grandson" position that was her own son's birthright. She also harbored hostile feelings because Joe had married a non-Indian girl in Texas instead of her daughter, the girl that Joe had once helped rescue. When the grandparents became noticeably cool toward him, Joe's self-esteem was so wounded that he recoiled, gradually withdrawing from contact with his Kiowa kin. He still cared deeply for them but was forced to recognize his powerlessness under the circumstances. Six months after the elections in Oklahoma, he was no longer in close contact with his adoptive family and had stopped attending Gourd Dances.

The wounds to his person cut deep. Not content in believing he had failed only in the public arena, or with blaming the hobbyists for unscrupulous tactics, he became convinced these were but symptoms of a greater personal problem. While pursuing Kiowa ideals, however lofty, he had somehow neglected his personal relationship with the Almighty. This thought came to him when he began reading the Bible for solace while depressed. Ever introspective and in search of a large revealed truth to embrace, Joe recognized discrepancies between conventional Christianity as practiced around him and what he read in the New Testament. Just as he had been dissatisfied with unauthentic versions of Indian culture, he was similarly dissatisfied with the pronouncements of Christian ministers from their pulpits and in the mass media. Thus, he began searching anew, looking for the authentic or "original" Christianity. Through conversations with his Jewish brother-in-law, Joe learned that he was not alone in his quest, that Messianic Jews and some Christians shared the same concerns and viewpoint. From that moment on, the study and interpretation of the Bible became the central focus in his life, ultimately leading to formal religious training for the ministry.

While engaged in this renewed spiritual odyssey, Joe maintained only the most tenuous communication with his Kiowa family. Only recently, while attending his Kiowa "grandpa's" funeral, did he find a basis for rapprochement with his adoptive family. As a result of this recently renewed contact, Joe may start visiting Oklahoma again, and possibly even resume Gourd Dancing. But for now, Joe has quit his job at the refinery and is putting all his energies into ministering to a small congregation of Christians and Messianic Jews. His time is devoted to conducting Bible study groups, formally observing the Sabbath, preparing for his weekly religious radio program, and running the embryonic church school. He is energized by his new calling and responsibilities and is at peace with himself.

In the five years before his unhappy disengagement from the Kiowa, I witnessed Joe in a wide variety of social settings, both in Oklahoma and Texas. Whatever the social context—among Kiowa or others, both in casual social exchanges and in formally structured activities, he consistently and unpretentiously behaved in a manner appropriate to a Kiowa of his age, sex, and family background. At the refinery, he was frequently harassed by Texan coworkers for his Indian involvement. At Gourd Dances, I observed him closely, as he interacted with other Kiowa. He was welcomed when he approached the drum, as strangers are not, and could sing many of the traditional Tai'peh songs. His accomplished, frank, authentic style of communicating was most impressive, as was the Kiowas' obvious acceptance of him in his new role. There could be no doubt about the depth, extent, and authenticity of his identity transformation. Inwardly, he had become Kiowa, and the Kiowa accepted him as such, validating the conversion. Joe had, at least for the time, among receptive Kiowa, assumed a new ethnic identity.

The Joe I first reacted to seemed strange because of a conceptual dissonance, a conflict between two incompatible sets of ideas. At the start of our relationship, one way of thinking—everyday, common-sense, American folk ideas about Indian identity—overrode the rational way of thought demanded of a professional anthropologist. In the former way of thinking— resting on deeply embedded American convictions about social race—Indian identity is based on supposed biological ancestry, expressed by the metaphor of "Indian blood." Since Joe True, in his physical appearance, did not seem to have American Indian biological ancestry, he could not be properly Indian. Yet his manner, style, thinking, values, and professed ethnicity marked him as Kiowa. It was this apparent contradiction that demanded systematic thought and empathetic understanding.

Thinking and observing as an anthropologist forced a different conclusion, one reinforced by the responses of Joe's Kiowa kin and community. Whatever his biological ancestry, socially and psychologically he had become Kiowa. It happens that these culturally conservative Kiowa, like other traditional Indians, do not much concern themselves with an individual's biological ancestry. Instead, they respond to the merits and strengths of a person, looking for attributes that are worthy and valuable. Initially, Joe, a stranger to them, stood and countered a threat to one of their young women. The girls' grandparents immediately responded by embracing him socially, drawing him into a web of kin relations. This process, begun accidentally, continued as Joe's wants increasingly converged with the expressed needs of this Indian community. The Gourd Dance society soon employed him as a missionary advocate, sending him out to organize and serve their purposes. Among these was their desire to build new ways of communicating across the boundaries between themselves, as Indians, and other Americans.

Joe had much to offer the Gourd Dance society. An energetic worker full of enthusiasm for serving his new people, he cheerfully undertook the most menial and inconvenient tasks for the organization without considering his public image or comfort. His earned income was based on the union scale for petroleum workers, which exceeded that of all but a few of the association's members; and Joe was generous with his support. He was also a capable and trustworthy representative living at some distance from Oklahoma, situated where he could help in the formation of an expansion chapter of the parent society. But beyond his practical worth to the Gourd Dance organization, Joe was valued by Kiowa for his personal integrity, his dependability, his reverence for their traditions, and his obvious though muted desire to be one of them. In the end, Joe was considerably resocialized, his private and public identities transformed. The Kiowa had, in important ways, assimilated him as one of their young men. Knowing him better, they later gave him important tasks to accomplish, carrying out goals important to their welfare. This was not an uncommon event for the Kiowa. Through their recorded history, they are known to have recruited and assimilated a variety of strangers. What is especially interesting is that it is a contemporary event, one that an anthropologist could stand next to and watch develop.

The relative merits of these dissonant ideas, the American myth of race and "blood" and conflicting social science knowledge of culture and social learning, are not ordinarily, easily, or readily tested in everyday activities. The former manner of thinking is older, more pervasive, and compelling. The doctrine of "racial blood," indeed, is embraced by influential vested interests that defend its validity. As applied to Indians and other "racial" minorities, even highly educated social scientists and scholars in the humanities are not always immune to its lure. Moreover, ordinary observation among contemporary Indian communities seems to confirm its truth. In these communities, we can witness a systematic coincidence of biological ancestry and ethnic identity. Because many modern Indians have acquired this way of thinking through their experiences with other Americans, their pronouncements also seem to underscore the truth of this racial doctrine. Nonetheless, for a late twentieth-century professional anthropologist unwittingly to think in such terms is no less a contradiction than for a modern American geneticist to argue that cousins should not marry because they will produce defective offspring, or for a trained physician to believe that illness is caused by an imbalance in bodily humors.

However, physical appearances and the seeming association of biological ancestry, cultural heritage, and ethnic identity are deceiving. Looking behind appearances into the histories of Indian communities we can find many Joes—aliens incorporated into Kiowa and other Indian communities because of a convergence of individual and community needs. Joe's experiences, seen objectively, show the falsity of the American racial doctrine, expressed metaphorically in the "myth of blood."

Later, as Joe's relationship with the Kiowa developed, and as he was given new and heavy responsibilities, rifts developed. They employed him as a go-between, assigning him the responsibility of carrying the message of the

Gourd Dance into new fields. In this different setting, Joe's Kiowa identity was tested and his failure to convert an unsympathetic and hostile American audience to an acceptance of Kiowa ways precipitated fresh conflicts and jealousies. When his adoptive Kiowa kin looked on him with disapproval, Joe responded by withdrawing, seeking understanding within himself. Then another identity shift occurred, as Joe worked to surmount these disturbing experiences and rise above them, pursuing a new and more meaningful integration of self and community. While the particulars of the story of Joe True's association with the Kiowa may be uncommon, his example as a young American on a twentieth-century spiritual odyssey is by no means unique.

NOTES

1. Ronald Cohen, "Ethnicity: Problem and Focus in Anthropology," *Annual Reviews in Anthropology* 7, 1978, pp. 379–403; George De Vos and Lola Romanucci-Ross, eds., *Ethnic Identity: Cultural Continuities and Change* (Chicago: University of Chicago Press, 1982); and Anya Royce, *Ethnic Identity: Strategies of Diversity* (Bloomington, Ind.: Indiana University Press, 1982).
2. George L. Hicks and Philip E. Leis, eds., *Ethnic Encounters: Identities and Contexts* (North Scituate, Mass.: Duxbury Press, 1977).
3. A. Irving Hallowell, "American Indians, White and Black: The Phenomenon of Transculturalization," *Current Anthropology* 4, 1963, pp. 519–31. Hallowell borrowed this term from Fernando Ortiz, who coined the word to emphasize that acculturation was a reciprocal or two-way process influencing, for example, European cultures as well as those of native peoples. See his *Contrapunteo del Tobaco y el Azucar* (Havana, Cuba: J. Montero, 1940). Bronislaw Malinowski embraced this phrasing and the idea of two-way or transcultural change idea with enthusiasm, but this research lead was not effectively pursued for some years.

CHAPTER 13

Ooleepeeka and Mina: Contrasting Responses to the Modernization of Two Baffin Island Inuit Women

Ann McElroy

PRESENTING OOLEEPEEKA (1949—) AND MINA (1944—)

An important insight is given by the experiences of these two young Baffin Island Inuit women, whose people prefer not to be called by the demeaning word Eskimo: the forces of rapid social change do not fall equally on all members of any community. In a period when these Inuit were actively participating in a social and political transformation, increasingly taking hold of their development and affairs in the modern world, some individuals flourished, participating actively and productively, enriching their identities and the status of their families. But, in the same period, others remained passive, ineffective and seemingly victimized by developments over which they could exert little control. As the author explains in this close study of two contrasting Inuit women, the early family situations and experiences of individuals helps us understand how such pronounced variation comes about. Ooleepeeka, for instance, was raised in an intact family headed by an important leader, one with a steady income, whose members provide effective guides to the future for growing children. Mastering English early, and developing confidence in meeting and dealing with Anglo-Canadians through formal education and travel, Ooleepeeka remained close to her natal family, assumed a leadership role in her community, and grew into a flexible, bicultural adult, effectively in command of her life. Her career displays the possibility of sustaining a cohesive and meaningful continuity with older cultural forms while coping creatively with the pressing issues of the present and future. Mina, in profound contrast, came from a family broken by the deaths of her mother, several stepmothers, and father, and she lacked the stable support of capable elders when growing to adulthood. Mina's fractured socialization experiences are reflected in her problems as an adolescent and an adult woman. Instead of maturing into a person confident in herself, one who could commit herself to her marriage and children with full satisfaction and reward, one able to assume a satisfying work role and participate effectively in the transformation affecting the Inuit, she remained frozen as a disgruntled adolescent. Ooleepeeka's family, on the one hand, buffered and protected her from disabling experiences, preparing her for full adulthood; Mina's family life, on the other, disabled her, sharply limiting her ability to grow into a person who could deal with the stresses that would face her in later life. Continuity of living in family, with kin, and of community gave Ooleepeeka a firm grip on her identity and a significant place in the future of the Inuit. The absence of such continuity weakened Mina's life chances. Therefore, in Ooleepeeka we see a cohesive, satisfying, growing identity, a core of psychological well-being as a modern Inuit surrounded by a periphery of various cultural alternatives between which this woman picks and chooses. In Mina, sadly, we can see the sometimes damaging consequences of rapid social change, where the accident of birth churned family disorder into seemingly perpetual personal disrepair and dissatisfaction. But as the author cautions, these are only two of a variety of personal styles of adaptation in contexts like that of the Baffin Island Inuit, who must cope endlessly with social and technological transformations. (J. A. Clifton)

Ooleepeeka and Mina are two young Inuit women of southern Baffin Island in northern Canada.[1] I encountered them almost twenty years ago, while doing research on the psychological adaptation of Inuit to modernization in two arctic settlements.[2] Living in Frobisher Bay and Pangnirtung for fifteen months between 1967 and 1974 (over several summers and one complete winter, October 1969 to May 1970), I was witness to an impressive cultural and political transformation. Inuit were affirming pride in their language and history, developing legal and political sophistication in land claims negotiations, and working to influence the future of their homeland, which they considered a separate political entity called *Nunavut*, "our land."[3] I learned much about this transformation from Ooleepeeka, an activist whose special upbringing and unique talents made her an outstanding model for native women. I could frame my relationship with Ooleepeeka as that of psychological anthropologist and key informant, but somehow these stiff academic role descriptions miss the reality of our relationship. She was teacher and storyteller, and I, learner. She was critic, I supportive sounding board. Learning, communicating, and articulating the political parameters of her situation: these were the dimensions of our interaction.

During these field trips, another young woman taught me much about northern realities. I call her Mina and remember her as a contrast to Ooleepeeka in many ways. Far from being an activist, she seemed to be swept along passively by pressures of change and family instability. Her understanding of the economic and political forces underlying her situation was less informed, less sophisticated than Ooleepeeka's, yet, I could still sense in our conversations her need to understand, to develop a cognitive grasp of what it meant to be an *Inuk* in Frobisher Bay in 1970 and not a *Kadlunat* (literally "eyebrow," the term for Europeans used by Inuit, who were far more impressed with the bushy eyebrows of the whalers and explorers who first contacted them than with their light skin color).

Baffin Island Inuit Landscape

Mina, born in 1944, came to Frobisher Bay in 1956 from Lake Harbour, a nearby village, with her father, siblings, and a stepmother. Ooleepeeka was born in 1949 and lived most of her life in Pangnirtung, a Hudson's Bay Company post and Anglican mission hospital center about a hundred miles to the northeast of Frobisher Bay. The period of Ooleepeeka and Mina's childhood was an important point in Inuit history, a time of gradual shifts from a hunting and gathering, nomadic pattern to a new, settled lifestyle in small settlements.[4] Men still hunted, but jet airplanes and construction were believed to have disturbed and diminished the game, so they also drove taxis, swept floors, and carved stone sculptures for a living. While many women continued to process animal skins, the younger ones were learning to be store clerks, secretaries, dental hygienists, and teachers' aides. Schoolchildren studied in English, a language many of their mothers and grandparents did not understand. The jigs and reels learned from whalers in the nineteenth century were still being danced in church halls, but competing with this entertainment were bingo games, cowboy movies, and pool halls. There was hesitant but increasingly urgent talk about native land rights and increased representation in northern development. Above all, there was change in the political and cultural awareness of the Inuit as a people.

I call this era a "quiet revolution" because change in awareness involved no violent demonstrations, prolonged boycotts, or claims of victimization and oppression. Rather, the changes in which Ooleepeeka, Mina, and their peers participated involved gradual, strategic turns toward a more assertive stance vis-a-vis southern Canadian society. The 1970s was a decade in which young northerners said, "we choose to be called Inuit, 'the People' or 'Human Beings,' as did our ancestors. We no longer answer to *Esquimaux*, 'eaters of raw flesh' in the language of our traditional enemies, the Algonquians." The 1970s decade was a time to share ideas and coordinate art festivals and sports events with Greenlanders, Alaskans, and other related Canadian groups, rediscovering a common heritage and shared goals and learning political strategies for directed change. In 1971, young Inuit formed a national organization, Inuit Tapirisat of Canada, or ITC, to document land claims, to regulate the extraction of minerals and other resources from the north, to increase native employment, and to promote bicultural education.[5]

Readers familiar with traditional Inuit culture[6] will recognize how dramatic the change in the arctic biocultural environment has been. Before extensive contact, the people of Baffin Island were enmeshed in an ecological system of extreme cold, a short growing season, little edible vegetation, and a small number of species of marine and land animals, mostly migratory. While some northern groups specialized in hunting either sea mammals or land animals such as caribou, the *Nugumiut* and *Oqomiut* maintained a mixed, seasonal subsistence of primarily seal, whale, fish, birds and caribou. They were selective and energy efficient in exploiting resources, rarely eating fox, wolves, dogs, bear, or lemmings, and maintaining a high protein, high fat, low carbohydrate diet.[7]

The nomadic groups were quite small, often fifteen to thirty consanguineously and affinally related individuals. Larger groups camped, fished, and hunted together in seasons of abundance, and several families shared each dwelling. In winter, snowhouses were used, especially when the group traveled. Semisubterranean stone or sod houses were also used, at least up to the first encounter with the British explorer Sir Martin Frobisher in the sixteenth century.[8] The people lived in skin tents in warmer weather. Some marriages were polygynous, although serial monogamy and wife-exchange partnerships were more typical. Even by the beginning of the twentieth century, after contact with Anglican missionaries, the ratio of eighty-nine females to one hundred males under the age of nineteen reflected continued practice of female infanticide, while the ratio of one hundred twenty-seven females to one hundred males over nineteen reflected the high mortality of hunting accidents.[9]

Political structure was linked to hunting relationships and kinship. Leaders or camp bosses were the most skillful in hunting, knew the geography intimately, and could mobilize the greatest number of kin and trading partners. Feuds occurred at times, but there was no organized warfare, and formal political or territorial structures were not needed. Religion was shamanistic and based on a natural cosmology of powerful, animistic forces inhabiting the seas, skies, mountains, and inanimate objects. Religious rituals focused on hunting, illness, and psychotherapy.

Famine was an ever-present threat, but life was not unremitting harshness or continual food shortage. In good times, when arctic char came upstream to spawn and the caribou followed the expected migration routes, Inuit ate well, stayed healthy, and celebrated life with great exuberance. But the ecological system was in delicate balance. Each lifetime included some experience of famine, of having to eat animal skins, tree bark, sled dogs, or in the most extreme and rare cases, having to eat other human beings to survive. Almost every mother gently laid at least one dead baby under a rock grave and could not protest when her husband decided that a newborn daughter should not be allowed to live. Every elderly person, at one time or another, considered suicide to benefit the group.

After Frobisher's initial contact, other explorers, whalers, and traders came in the seventeenth and eighteenth centuries. These contact agents employed, traded with, and sometimes married native peoples. They introduced white flour, sugar, tea, tobacco, and alcohol. By 1883, Franz Boas[10] noted that the Oqomiut and Kingnaitmiut of the Pangnirtung region depended heavily on trading relationships and employment with the Scots, English, and American whalers. By 1905, some species of whales were nearing extinction, and most whaling stations had closed. Many people returned to year-round hunting, but epidemics among the dogs, a variety of contact diseases (tuberculosis, diphtheria, syphilis, malnutrition), and a credit and debt system with trading posts supporting trapping efforts undercut their independence. They desired material goods, especially firearms, cloth, and metal tools, and thus hunting gave way to trapping for the market and purchase of imported foods. The need for goods, medical care, and emergency rations led to a general receptivity to mission influence, government authority enforced by the Royal Canadian Mounted Police, and schools.

Thus, from about 1880 to 1950, the people of Baffin Island faced a new set of environmental challenges, not from natural forces but from cultural intrusions by strangers seeking opportunity and profit in the north, bringing with them new ideas and technology. Survival was no longer just a question of coping with the physical environment. It also became a matter of developing advantageous relationships with Europeans and southern Canadians, of coping with new diseases and nutritional patterns, and learning to live in settlements. It meant decisions about whether to become Christian, to send one's children to school, to seek medical care, to accumulate household goods. Each time a decision was made by a family to accept these elements of the outside world, something was lost in terms of autonomy and traditional identity, while something was gained in terms of opportunity and advantage in the changing contexts of multicultural flux and intrusions.

Frobisher Bay was an Air Force Base during World War II and a DEW line construction site after the war. In 1959, it became an administrative center with a small native population of about three hundred, mostly wage laborers and their families. Increasingly, people came looking for wage employment, medical care, and emergency food rations, and by 1963, the population included nine hundred native people, with more than half the population economically dependent on the wages earned by eighty-eight married and forty-eight single men. The seven hundred nonnatives, mostly from southern Canada and from other Commonwealth nations, including India, Africa, Scotland, the Caribbean, Australia, and New Zealand, held most of the professional and administrative positions in Frobisher Bay. This affluent group had great influence on young Inuits' notions of a desirable mode of living.

In 1970, Frobisher Bay was the most modern settlement on Baffin Island. Jet planes landed and departed several times a day, transporting government employees and construction workers, teachers and nurses, tourists, hospital patients, and students. Residents used a heated swimming pool and bowling alley, played hockey and baseball, attended movies, dances, and bingo games. The bars were full; the churches were full; and the streets were usually crowded with snowmobiles, taxis, buses, and trucks. The local radio broadcast in English, French, and *Inuktitut*. The grocery and department stores carried a large inventory of merchandise brought in by ship and plane, including TV dinners, diver's watches, miniskirts, bathing suits, and birdcages. A dozen eggs cost $2.50, a quart of fresh milk $2, and one night at the hotel $70.

Materialism and economic development were pervasive themes in the ethos of Frobisher Bay in 1970. Eighty-seven percent of Inuit males and 31 percent of Inuit females aged sixteen to sixty-five were wage employed, mostly by the federal and territorial governments. The average household income was $6,500, the range from under $1,000 (9 percent) to over $13,000 (1 percent) and the average household size was 6.5 people. Housing was subsidized, taxes minimal, and medical care free. A number of families were enjoying considerable cash income from jobs as well as government payments of family allowance, old-age pensions, and sale of furs and handicrafts. They spent this cash on automobiles, televisions, stereos, children's toys, snowmobiles, plane trips, plumbing, and carpeting. Unmarried construction workers and airport workers, who had even more cash to spend in summer when employment rates were highest, purchased large amounts of liquor and beer, expensive watches and tape decks, boating equipment, and motorcycles.

The community of Pangnirtung, which also figures in the narrative sketches of Ooleepeeka and Mina, is a smaller settlement, with around 600 Inuit and 50 Euro-Canadians in 1970. Pangnirtung was settled in the 1920s, when a Hudson's Bay Company trading post, a Royal Canadian Mounted Police station, and a church hospital were established in Cumberland Sound, some 150 miles northeast of Frobisher Bay. It was only after 1966, when an epidemic reduced the dog population and deprived hunters of transportation, that large numbers of families were permanently relocated to Pangnirtung.

There one saw less affluence. The average annual income in 1971 was $3,366, the per capita income was $587 (half the Frobisher Bay figure), and 83 percent of the families had an annual income of less than $3,000. Only eleven out of 103 households had an income in 1969 of over $5,000, but those high incomes went up to $10,000. Twenty-seven percent of all males between sixteen and sixty-five were employed, and 40 percent of all households had one or more individuals employed. Thus, the majority of residents did not have a job and depended still on hunting and fishing, as well as carving, sewing, and other crafts, and government assistance.

My account of Ooleepeeka is not a biography in a strict sense, but rather a portrait of an individual during one segment of her life. In many ways, the narrative reflects the way Ooleepeeka presented herself to me, a social scientist and outsider to the community, and the way the relationship developed over several years. I would not say we were friends, but we were cognizant of one another, took each other into account. For me, Ooleepeeka was living out history, enacting decisions that I found momentous. I can only speculate on how she viewed me. Inuit sometimes refer to southerners as "mosquitoes" (kittoriat). Like mosquitoes, Europeans come in pesky swarms in the summer and annoy you with their bites and buzzing, but they leave before winter and really are not important in the overall scheme of things. Perhaps it was because I stayed through the winter, actually thriving as I shifted to a primarily seal, caribou, and fish diet, that Ooleepeeka did not call me kittorriak. Euro-Canadians were also said to talk in loud voices, just as they might to the deaf, believing that increased volume would help overcome linguistic or cultural barriers. Since I talked quietly, listened well, and learned some of the language, perhaps this counted for something.

The format for the biographical sketches of Ooleepeeka and Mina will be a case-study approach, combining narrative from field notes with ethnographic commentary. Biographic details are presented not in strictly chronological order, but rather in the sequence of self-disclosure as rapport developed over the years. A final summary contrasting the adaptive styles of the two women will follow the presentation of Mina.

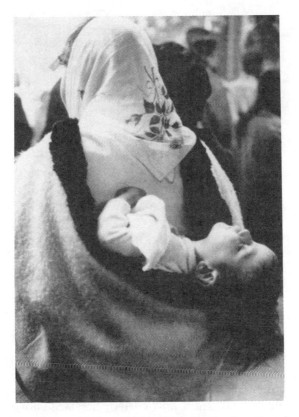

INUIT INFANT SLEEPING IN AN AMAUT. *While this Inuit mother shops at the Hudson's Bay Company store, her infant sleeps in the* amaut *(mother's parka), a warm and secure infant carrier used from birth to three years old. (Photograph by Ann McElroy.)*

I first encountered Ooleepeeka in 1969 in Pangnirtung, shortly after she returned from art school in Montreal and announced her engagement to a southern Canadian. Her cousin, Ooloosie, told me that Ooleepeeka's picture had been in a national newspaper recently, in an account of an exhibit of Eskimo art in Montreal. Ooleepeeka was regarded locally as a celebrity, for she had come to know several important political leaders while working as an interpreter. It was said that nothing daunted her. Once Ooleepeeka walked right up to an elderly statesman touring the North, I was told, and asked him to be her partner in the square dance at the community house; the community talked about this unusually bold behavior for years after.

Ooleepeeka and her fiance first met the previous summer on a flight from Montreal. The young man, of Scots-Canadian background, was flying north to teach school in Cape Dorset. They kept in touch, and shortly after Christmas, they decided to marry and informed her parents of the decision.

ANTHROPOLOGIST ANN MCELROY CARRIES A TWO YEAR OLD IN A SUMMER AMAUT. Carrying toddlers is usually the responsibility of preteen girls, which frees adult women for work with seal and caribou skins. (Photograph by Christina Tikivik, courtesy of Ann McElroy.)

I first met Ooleepeeka at the Hudson's Bay Company Store, a daily gathering place for many of the settlement's residents. Ooleepeeka detached herself from a group of friends, came over, and introduced herself in a warm and confident manner. She was about twenty-one years old and exceptionally beautiful. Her hair was cut short and curled; her face showed little sign of makeup. She was dressed, like her girlfriends, in stretch slacks, stylish high leather boots, and a knitted turtleneck sweater. Her homemade parka was fringed with soft, white fox fur and intricately embroidered with the floral designs characteristic of Pangnirtung seamstresses.

The warmth of her introduction surprised me. I had become accustomed to Inuit shyly extending a hand, eyes kept down, while murmuring a few soft words of welcome. Ooleepeeka's style of self-presentation definitely departed from the expected pattern. She did not shake my hand, and she stood closer to me than expected. She made eye contact and held it steadily.

As we talked, I noticed how quickly the conversation shifted to my concerns. She had evidently heard much about me. How was I getting along in Pangnirtung? Was I given enough to eat? Was I finding the language difficult? Did I like the family who had taken me as a boarder? Her concern for my welfare was striking, although her nurturant attitude was not dissimilar to that of older women in the village.

When I asked about her engagement, she said that a group of young women—teachers, nurses, and her former schoolmates—had given her a surprise bridal shower the day before. The wedding was scheduled to coincide with the visit of a minister the following month, since Pangnirtung had no resident minister with the authority to conduct a marriage ceremony.

The timing was tight. As in most settlements, the housing shortage in Cape Dorset was acute, and as yet they had no house arranged. Her bridal gown had been mail-ordered, and she wondered if it would arrive in time. Some friends who planned to be away from Pangnirtung had offered the use of their house for the couple's "honeymoon" (Ooleepeeka's word). The conversation ended with an invitation to attend the wedding.

In the aboriginal culture, all adults were expected to be married, and most women first married in adolescence, but Ooleepeeka's decision to marry in her twenties fit the current norm of delaying marriage. According to the 1969 census figures, 90 percent of the girls and all of the young men aged nineteen and under in both Frobisher Bay and Pangnirtung were *not* married. By the age of twenty-four, 56 percent of the women had married, while 83 percent of Frobisher Bay males and 76 percent of Pangnirtung males aged twenty-four and under were not married. Between 1958 and 1969, there was a definite trend toward delaying marriage at Frobisher Bay, including recognized common-law marriages. In 1958, 23 percent of the girls in the fifteen to nineteen age group were married, while in 1969, only 9 percent were married. Similarly, in 1958, 48 percent of the males in the twenty to twenty-four age group were married, while in 1969, only 17 percent of males in this age group were married.

Delay in marriage was due to several factors, notably an increased preference for residence separate from the families of either bride or groom, and a severe housing shortage. Many young men did not have steady jobs. Young women who had traveled or studied in southern Canada often did not consider Inuit youths to be desirable marriage partners. There was a disproportionate sex ratio in the community in 1967, as well: seventy-four single males and fifty-two single females between the ages of fifteen and twenty-four. This inbalance was due, in part, to the influx of young men from other settlements looking for work.

Of the sixty-seven single males in Frobisher Bay between the ages of seventeen and twenty-four in 1967, only twelve (18 percent) had married by 1971, and two of these marriages were to Euro-Canadian women. Of the thirty-three single females in the same age group in 1967, by 1971, ten (30 percent) had married Inuit men, twelve (35 percent) had married Euro-Canadians, and eleven remained single. Thus, Ooleepeeka's upcoming marriage to a southern Canadian was not an unusual choice.

I did not see Ooleepeeka again until she walked down the aisle of the church with her father and one attendant, her sister. The bridal gown had arrived only the day before, a full-length lace dress with a veil. Her father wore a dark blue suit and tie, a trim, straight figure looking younger than his sixty years. The bride's sister, who had also married a Euro-Canadian several years before, wore a brocade dress and fresh flowers in her hair.

The church was brightly lit, the altar decorated with plastic flowers. There was no organ music. The rumbling of the oil furnace, the wailing infants, and the sharp, whining wind beating against the small frame building created a stark mood. The wedding party walked quickly to the front of the church, where the minister, groom, and best man were waiting. With the exception of the bride's family and close relatives, most of the Inuit sat near the back of the church, while Euro-Canadian guests sat in the front.

The ceremony was brief and subdued. As it became obvious to the congregation that the entire service, including the visiting clergyman's sermon, would be completely in English, a soft murmur of surprise arose in the back. "It's not right . . . her mother doesn't understand English," whispered an Inuit woman next to me.

A few minutes after the ceremony finished, the church was empty. It was cold and windy outside, too dark for photographs, and no one had taken pictures inside the church. The strident sputtering of snowmobiles prevented prolonged congratulations, and the wedding party sped away to the reception in a "bombardier," a peculiar, enclosed snow vehicle resembling a small, streamlined tank.

I stopped at the home of the Inuit friends who had accompanied me to the wedding to have tea and *palowak* (bannock, a thick panbread) before going to the reception. My friends appeared to be depressed. They tried to communicate to me, in Inuktitut, that the whole service hadn't seemed quite proper—no hymns, nothing said in the native language to make the girl's family seem part of it all. They knew the clergyman could speak Inuktitut and felt that he should have arranged a bilingual service and some music.

Later, my hosts said, "Aren't you going to the party?" I said I was planning to go, but I hoped they would come with me. There was a moment of indecision, then with a slight laugh—"Too many 'mosquitoes' there. But you go ahead. They will have good food, and everyone will be 'happy,'" using the native euphemism for "high" on alcohol.

When I arrived at the party, given in a teacher's house, the party was in full swing. About twenty Inuit and twenty-five Euro-Canadians were enjoying a twenty-five pound turkey, salad, jello, sheet cake, and spiked fruit punch. As my friends had predicted, all the guests were "happy," but none was intoxicated.

The bride's father embraced me warmly and said in English that he was proud to have me at the party, that it was a great day for him and he was proud of his daughter. He introduced me to his new son-in-law saying, "and I'm proud of this boy, too. He's gonna be good to my little girl. He's a good man. I'm gonna teach him about hunting, all the things I know." The father repeated this speech to me and to several other guests throughout the evening. The old man was the center of attention; people were embracing him and joking with him, trying to persuade him and his wife to do an old-style jig, and resisting his efforts to control the consumption of liquor. The bantering and horseplay increased through the evening, much of it involving young Inuit and Euro-Canadian men teasing and flirting with the older Inuit women, while their husbands "defended" them with comically exaggerated ferocity. The bride and groom left the party quietly, and the festivities continued for another hour and a half.

Similar to many parties I attended in the course of field work, it was not surprising that the reception was given at a teacher's house. Euro-Canadian houses, rented at subsidized rates, were much larger and more elegantly furnished than the native prefabricated houses. Visiting and parties were major forms of entertainment, and the homes of young teachers and craft center administrators were especially popular places for Inuit youths to gather. They walked in without feeling constrained to knock, and they left when they felt like it without formalities. Sometimes older Inuit came to these houses as well, and those who knew little English sat quietly, reading a magazine or joining a card game. Interaction was warm and relaxed, with much joking and horseplay. Physical contact between young Inuit and Kadlunat involved much wrestling, good-natured pummeling, leaning on each other's shoulders, tickling, and poking. People played guitars while others sang, beat bongo drums, banged with spoons, pots and pans, and washboards. With no liquor outlet in the settlement, very little beer and hard liquor were available, and drugs (that is, marijuana and hashish) were not shared with Inuit guests. Large quantities of soda, coffee, tea, and chips were consumed at these parties, as well as occasionally popcorn and homemade ice cream.

When liquor was available, at wedding and holiday parties, and when men returning from work in other settlements brought several bottles of scotch or rum, few native people abstained from drinking despite the church's attempts to encourage sobriety. Older women often wrinkled their noses when offered a drink, but they could be persuaded to take a little alcohol in tea, and they might drink enough "tea" in the course of an evening to join freely in the sexual teasing and horseplay typical of many parties.

Frobisher Bay parties were rather different, largely because liquor was readily available to both natives and Europeans through a government outlet, with the qualification that people recently arrested for public drunkenness or other violations would not be allowed to purchase alcoholic beverages. Consequently, more parties involved steady drinking, with a fairly predictable series of events. There was an initial period of singing, guitar playing, and dancing. People quickly became "happy," in local terms, after three or four beers or two glasses of whiskey. They were initially affectionate and demonstrative, hugging and hanging on each other, expressing their loyalty and good will toward others, but after a few hours, drinkers became morose. Then men and women cried freely, recalling deaths of family members and expressing feelings of guilt and pleading with others (especially spouses) for forgiveness. A third stage, rarely seen in Pangnirtung, was incipient violence. People began shoving one another, throwing beer cans around, accusing others of molesting their spouses, and bringing up past conflicts and resentments. Actual violence and injury sometimes occurred, although belligerent people were often kicked out of the house and then walked around the settlement, talking loudly and disturbing sleeping people until they were taken into "protective custody" by the police.

I again met Ooleepeeka fifteen months after the wedding, in a store in Frobisher Bay. Her husband had taken a job at the new high school, and they had just moved to the settlement. They had a four-month-old baby boy. Ooleepeeka described an easy birth in the Frobisher Bay hospital. "The nurses wanted me to take medicine for the pain, or even to put me out, but I wanted to be completely awake to see my baby born and I wouldn't take anything, not even an aspirin." Had the first months been difficult? "No, not really. He's in good health because I'm nursing him. Lots of babies have terrible ear infections or diarrhea because of the canned milk, but he's doing fine. Also, my mother gave me an *amaut* (a mother's parka) to carry the baby. When he's fussy, I just put him in and go for a walk or bounce up and down. What a difference it makes!"

Although Ooleepeeka wasn't employed, she was involved in organizing a program called Eskimo University. I asked if we could meet to discuss the project, and she invited me to her house. One of her friends, an Inuit woman who was the local representative of the Western Arctic organization COPE— Committee for Original People's Entitlement, had interested her in joining a group concerned with preservation of traditional native materials. She winced at the term Eskimo University, stating that was "a bad translation of an idea we never really named, just something like *Inuit Iliniavik* [Eskimo school] or *Inutitut ilitsiyuut* [they are learning Eskimo ways]. But somebody called it Eskimo University instead, and some people liked that name, but some people thought we were just acting big."

I had heard that the group was organized to protest exploitation of interpreters and translators, but Ooleepeeka presented a different view of the group's goals. "Well, you know, the children aren't learning the old ways. They're forgetting everything, it's not being passed on. Nobody is writing it down so the kids can learn it in school. So we are talking to the old people, and we are going to write it all down or put it on tape, like on those radio programs. The kids don't know our history. My father is going to tell us about how it was in the old days, and he's going to tell us the names for all those things. You know, each part of a seal and a caribou and a whale had a special name, and each part went to a special person; you cut them up in a special way. And we have to write that down, because the children don't know it. And the name for the plants, and the places where you can hunt, and the old stories and songs. We're going to get all that down, and put it in a place where the people can read it. It's going to be in syllabics, and even that, well we have to teach the kids how to read syllabics, so they can read those stories, and so they can write letters to their folks."

The four local leaders of Eskimo University included three Inuit women married to Euro-Canadian men. When I commented on this, Ooleepeeka laughed and said, "Well, yes, you know we want our children to learn both ways. Kadlunat are not better than Inuit, and we are not better than Kadlunat. They are different. The kids can learn both ways. My father told me that."

During several visits over the next few months, I got to know Ooleepee-ka's husband, Paul. He was a quiet, reticent person; we usually talked about the baby, sports, the new school, the weather, and local events. Ooleepeeka and Paul found that fresh seal and caribou meat and arctic char were hard to get in Frobisher unless one was part of a sharing network. Her mother occasionally sent them frozen char, and in return, Ooleepeeka was planning to take some bakery bread on their trip home. She urged me to take flour and sugar to Pangnirtung the following week, for ice had delayed the Hudson's Bay Company supply ship and supplies were critically low.

Ooleepeeka and Paul both liked to tease, and my attempts to speak Inuktitut during that period often gave rise to gentle teasing. More than once I was dependent on Ooleepeeka to translate for me. Once I tried to leave a message by phone to arrange a ride back to the house where I was boarding. Ooleepeeka suggested I call Symonee, the catechist, who would probably be driving over to the Apex Hill neighborhood. I dialed his number and, when told that Symonee wasn't home, began to leave a message in Inuktitut for him. The party hung up. I turned to Ooleepeeka, who was suppressing a smile, and asked, "didn't I say it the right way?" She answered, "well, not really. Don't feel bad. Now you know what it is like for people who have to learn to speak English." She dialed the number and left a message for the catechist to pick me up.

I learned from Ooleepeeka and Paul that Inuit like to tell stories that parody distinctive traits of Kadlunat, pointing up their incompetence in using the language and in coping with the arctic. The stories also reflect the unpredictability of dealing with Euro-Canadian administrators. The pro-longed subordination of Inuit has required defenses against disparagement of identity and loss of a sense of autonomy, and humor is one such mechanism. These stories are often told to children, and children in turn make up similar but less structured jokes and riddles. Here are four examples:

> An Inuk came home from work one day and could not find his house. He went to the *Inuliriji* (administrator) and asked where his house was. Inuliriji said, "Oh, Ottawa said we had to move houses today."

To "move house" in Canadian English means to move one's belongings from one dwelling to another, a frequent experience for Inuit who are shifted from house to house by administrative order. The joke here is that Inuliriji took Ottawa's (i.e., the federal government's) orders literally and somehow managed to move the man's entire house.

The following joke reflects the imperfect use of the language by admin-istrators, as well as their stubbornness in communicating:

> There was a terrible storm, and when an Inuk returned from hunting, his house was gone. He went to the Inuliriji and asked where his house was. This Inuliriji spoke a little Inuktitut and said, "your house has walked away (pushualupok)." "Do you mean it flipped over (pishilaupok) in the storm?" asked the Inuk. "No, pishualupok," (it walked away), replied the administrator.

The next story suggests that Europeans talk far too much and lack decisiveness in a crisis.

> Three Kadlunat were out in the hills and a blizzard began. One man said, "let's drive back to town." The second said, "let's find an Eskimo to help us." The third man said, "let's build a snow house." They talked a long time and the blizzard got worse and they died.

The final story pokes fun at "eyebrows" who try to speak Inuktitut without knowing the proper pronunciation of words. We also sense here the hostility felt toward those Euro-Canadian males who solicit sexual favors from Inuit women; here such a man is made to appear foolish in his clumsy pronunciation:

> There was a man who spoke a little Inuktitut. He came to a tent and asked for a woman. The people inside gave him a pot. He asked again for a woman. They gave him some paper. He asked again, and ningeok (old lady) came out to show him where to go. He ran away.

The point of the joke is that the word for "woman" in Inuktitut and the basic root for "defecation" or "feces" are very difficult for English speakers to distinguish.

When I returned for a visit the following week, Ooleepeeka had a visitor, a young Inuit woman married to a Euro-Canadian. It was a sunny day and we decided to go shopping. The visitor carried her baby in an amaut, while Ooleepeeka put her baby in a stroller, commenting that she hoped to get an amaut from her mother before winter. She added that amautit were hard to borrow these days and expensive to make; besides, some people thought that a baby's legs would not grow straight if carried too frequently in an amaut. There are no paved roads or sidewalks in Frobisher Bay, and the baby had quite a bumpy ride in the stroller.

At the Hudson's Bay Company store, Ooleepeeka left the sleeping baby in the stroller outside while she went in to shop. I asked whether she would like me to watch the baby. She said no, it would be all right. "If he cries, someone will come in and tell us. Nothing will hurt him." The other woman smiled at me and said, "It's okay. This is not Montreal."

When we returned to the house, we had tea and talked a while. Although both women were fluent in English, they conversed almost completely in Eskimo, with just enough English phrases to keep me fully oriented. They talked about keeping house, the current movies, their husbands' food preferences, and how they wished their mothers were with them to help care for the babies. Relaxed moments of silence were frequent, too, and I realized how adaptable Ooleepeeka was to different styles of communication. With me or with her husband she kept up a steady conversation, while with an Inuit friend she fell into the less verbal mode of interaction characteristic of Inuit visiting patterns.

During one visit, Ooleepeeka's father had just returned from a tour of Greenland, and we spent several hours discussing his postcards, travel brochures, and photographs. He enthusiastically commented on the high standards of cleanliness and order of the towns and villages he had visited. He was particularly impressed by the fact that many of the schools, shops, radio stations, churches, and fishing industries were managed and staffed by native Greenlanders. He repeatedly expressed surprise that young children were first taught in Greenlandic and that the curricula were geared toward northern skills and subjects. "That's the way it should be here," he stated emphatically. We should have nice houses like they do—big houses, two stories. We should get the town fixed up real nice. And there's jobs for all the people there. And I never saw anybody drunk, and no trouble. We have to get it like that here."

It was only after we had known each other for almost two years that Ooleepeeka gave me details of her childhood. She had been born after the war, before Pangnirtung was a real settlement. Her father was an important man; he had worked for the mission for a long time, since the 1920s, and he had assisted traders and doctors, explorers and military personnel. Her father and uncles were active hunters as well. She remembered seeing old photographs taken in the 1930s in which they posed with wide grins, standing on *komatit* (sleds) or in *kayat* (one-man boats), wearing the warm and durable *attigit* (scraped skin garments). In summers, her mother had worked for "the Company," joining many other women in butchering and scraping whales for the oil-rendering vats, which now stand unused and rusty in Pangnirtung.

Ooleepeeka's childhood was unique in several ways. Her father had a steady cash income, and although the family went to hunting camps in certain seasons, she considered her home to be in the tiny settlement, where she lived with her family in a frame house. Although her mother never learned much English, Ooleepeeka and her siblings learned English in early childhood from missionaries, traders, and doctors. She was one of the first to attend school in the settlement and to go away to the Churchill Vocational Centre in northern Manitoba. When the opportunity arose to study in Ottawa, her parents agreed. She recalled her father giving this advice:

> "You've had all this school and you don't know much about Eskimo ways. If you were a boy, I would try to teach you. But a woman's work is hard, the Eskimo way of life is hard. So the best way is for you to get more school and learn the new ways. But don't forget the language, and don't forget your family. You should always help your family."

Her first year in Ottawa was difficult. She lived with a southern family who was kind to her, but they didn't really understand how terribly lonely she was. She had a large room of her own, and it was the first time she had slept alone in a room. Her hosts were generous and gave her nice clothes, "but they were cold people. The man was almost never home, and he just thought about his work all the time. They didn't talk to me very much. They just thought about getting money and buying things."[11]

Ooleepeeka had to take the bus to school. Sometimes she got lost, and it was hard to ask directions. She missed her family and wanted to return home, but she stuck it out and eventually learned to talk to people. Her best memories were those of traveling by bus during vacations. After a year, she gained enough confidence and knew enough English to travel on her own. It was during these trips that she learned not to be afraid of strangers and new places. The fear, she thought, was mostly caused by language problems, not knowing the words, not knowing how to say things the right way. After she felt more sure of herself, she was able to talk to anyone, and she found out that many southern people were not cold, just a little bit afraid, too.

During her second year in Ottawa, she started to help other students adjust to living in the city. She worked part-time as a translator for the government. She worked with a native government consultant from the Baffin Region, helping him with his writing. She felt much sympathy for him; he had a lot of good ideas and plans, but it was hard for him to speak English to people he didn't know well.

Her program of study in Ottawa involved rapid, intensive academic upgrading. She passed exams for four years of high school in less than two years and learned secretarial skills as well. Her study was primarily in language skills, social studies, and mathematics, but what she liked best was art. After working for a year in Pangnirtung as a typist in an administrator's office, she got a scholarship to study art in a small college in Montreal.

In Ottawa and Montreal, she met a number of native activists and her attitudes about northern development began to take shape through their influence. In the last year or two, she had become convinced that Inuit and Indian people had to help themselves and try to protect their rights. She knew that many Inuit resented the exploration for oil and the increase in jet traffic. She had known a woman in Cape Dorset who died of a heart attack after being frightened by a sonic boom, and she believed that the jets and other aircraft were driving away the caribou, and the oil from boats was killing the fish. She hoped these problems could be publicized by joining the COPE organization, which was active in the western Arctic.

In 1971, Ooleepeeka attended the initial meetings of *Inuit Tapirisat* (Eskimo Brotherhood), which became a national organization. By January of the following year, when I had returned to the United States, Inuit Tapirisat opened an office in Frobisher Bay to advise people on issues of employment, legal rights, and government policies. I was told that the woman who had organized for COPE in Frobisher Bay was both a national officer of Inuit Tapirisat and was appointed executive director for Baffin Island. I wrote to Ooleepeeka, asking for information about the organization and received a newspaper clipping of an interview with the executive director, which stated:

"Although her organization is ethnically-oriented, Mrs. W. dissociats it entirely from any thought of racism or militance. 'Discrimination is out of the question; we are a liaison between government and a native people. We intend to work with the government, not fight it.' "[12]

During a one-month return visit in the spring of 1974, I tried to contact Ooleepeeka, but heard that she was in Ottawa, working with Inuit Tapirisat on a special land claims project. Over the next few years, her picture appeared in ITC's publications as she continued to be active in various projects and to attend meetings all over the arctic and in southern Canada. Her training as an artist was put to good use in illustrations and cartoons for the ITC publications and various posters and other media developed to inform northerners of their legal and political rights.

Although in many ways Mina proved to be a contrast to Ooleepeeka, on first impression, she seemed the same kind of friendly, articulate young woman, modern in her choice of clothing, hair style, and mannerisms. She was one of many people who introduced themselves to me the first day I arrived in Pangnirtung in the late fall of 1969. At the bingo game that evening at the community house, I shook hands and exchanged introductions with numerous Inuit, but Mina especially stood out because of her clear English, her height, and her sensitive face. She told me that she was the local ticket agent for the airline, and we discussed how I should retrieve a sleeping bag that had not been loaded on the plane. She was tall, slender, and wore a man's nylon jacket over a lace-fringed blouse and stretch slacks. Her face was sensitive, moody, sometimes frowning as if she were anxious or perhaps could not see well.

Mina said she had been in Frobisher Bay two years ago and remembered seeing me at some of the dances. I did not remember her, but I had census data on her family among my records and the next day I pieced together some of her background. Mina had come to Frobisher from Lake Harbour in 1956 at the age of twelve, accompanying her father, his third wife, her older sister, married brother, and several stepsiblings. Both her mother and her first stepmother had died.

The family lived in a tent during their first year in Frobisher, and in the 1958 census Mina's father was listed as a garage worker for the Department of Northern Affairs. In 1957, her sister was in Cape Dorset and her brother lived in a campsite down the bay. Her parents adopted two small children, while her present stepmother's children by a former marriage remained in Lake Harbour.

Data from the 1963 census indicates further fracturing of the family. Mina's father committed suicide in 1960, and her stepmother died two years later. Her older brother settled in Frobisher Bay with a second wife, and Mina lived with this couple until 1968. Around 1960, Mina was referred by authorities to the Apex Hill Rehabilitation Centre because of drinking and

INSTRUMENTAL ACTIVITIES INVENTORY PICTURES. Four of the twelve Modified Instrumental Activities Inventory *images used by Ann McElroy to assess role aspirations of Inuit girls. Upper left to right: two of the most popular images of women's activities, seamstress in a crafts shop and store clerk. Lower left to right: two of the least popular ones, a woman making* bannock *(pan bread) in a tent, and a woman cleaning a seal skin with an* ulu *(woman's knife). (Drawings by Ann McElroy and Shiela Nicholson.)*

promiscuity.[13] At the Centre, she became literate in English and skilled in sewing and embroidery. Her only formal schooling was in Lake Harbour and in the south while hospitalized for tuberculosis for two years, and she had about a grade five level of skill in reading and mathematics. In 1962, Mina gave birth to an illegitimate child, given in adoption. In 1967, she married and had a baby. The couple returned to Pangnirtung to live with the husband's parents, and her sister-in-law legally adopted the baby.

Adoption is more frequent in Inuit society than in southern Canada and the United States. Nineteen percent of the children and unmarried young people under the age of twenty-five were listed as adopted in the 1967 Frobisher Bay census. Most of these children were given in adoption by unmarried mothers, by families with too many (or too closely spaced) children, or by women in poor health. It is unusual for a married couple to give their first child in adoption, as Mina and her husband did. Often infants are given in adoption to relatives or neighbors. The most frequent form of adoption is by a couple who can no longer have children of their own, usually because the woman is past menopause or has had a hysterectomy. In some cases, an elderly widow adopts a child to help her with housework and errands.

When I met Mina in 1969, she was living with nine other people in a small, three-bedroom house. She was employed by the airlines and had been a postal clerk previously; her husband, Jaco, was a mechanic. I visited her several times. The following section taken from field notes gives a sense of my first experience in her home.

Mina offered me tea and cookies and brought out a large box of photographs. Most of the pictures were of her brother's house in Frobisher, showing young people drinking beer, dancing, playing cards, holding guitars, and playing with children. Some scenes showed spontaneous horseplay and people clowning for the camera. Mina commented she really missed the good times in Frobisher. It was hard for her to bring friends into the house here, but she hadn't made many friends in Pangnirtung anyway. She said she really likes to dance, but now that she's married, not too many guys ask her to dance.

Mina asked if I liked music and showed me a stack of records, mostly country-and-western style by Johnny Cash, Elvis Presley, and Roger Miller. She had a few albums by the Beatles and the Monkees. I chose a Beatles album, and Mina put it on the record player. She danced a little, but seemed tense and self-conscious. Her husband's four-year-old sister picked up a record and began throwing it up in the air. Mina spoke sharply to her and grabbed the record. The child burst into tears. Jaco came out of the bedroom. He turned off the record player, muttering that it was too noisy to sleep and he was going out to play pool at the cafe. Mina shouted, "When are you coming back?" as he slammed the front door.

Mina looked unhappy, and I suggested going for a walk. She said she didn't feel like it, and then she asked if I would like to play checkers. We played five games. Then, she turned the board over and showed me how to play Snakes and Ladders. She began talking about her childhood in Frobisher Bay and all the boys she had dated. "We didn't go on real dates, you know. There wasn't any place to go, really. We just hung around the movie hall or the pool hall, or we'd go and get a hamburger at Joe's. Mmm, I really miss hamburgers and french fries, don't you? And sometimes the White guys would come down from the base, and they teased us a lot. When I was fourteen, I met a real nice White guy, and we wanted to get engaged. But my folks said I was too young and we couldn't get married. And then he went 'out' [south] and I really felt bad."

Mina's mother-in-law, Mary, came in carrying the baby in an amaut. She had been sewing at her daughter's house, and Mina urged me to look at the parka, which had arctic scenes finely embroidered across the back and sleeves. They began a heated conversation in Inuktitut. From what I could understand, Mary was making the coat for a teacher, and Mina was indignant that the teacher had offered only thirty-five dollars for the work. Mina was angry that Mary refused to press for more money.

Mina helped remove the baby from the amaut and held her for a few minutes while Mary pulled a pan containing raw seal meat from under the stove and ate a few slices. "She's wet," said Mina, and Mary took a disposable diaper from a box on the counter and changed the baby. Then she laid the baby on the couch and walked back to the stove. Does *una* (this one) like seal meat, she asked Mina. I understood her and said yes. Would it have to be cooked for the Kadlunak to eat it, she asked, again to Mina rather than directly to me. Mina answered softly, yes, probably. Mary responded *aahaluuna*, a phrase I had learned could signify mild exasperaton. She pulled a cast iron pan from the cupboard and measured out some lard. I felt embarrassed and protested, "that's allright. I don't mind raw seal." Mina laughed and said, "but *I* do! *Kuijana*—never mind. She's just teasing both of us."

Mina became a good friend during my stay in Pangnirtung. She was bored and welcomed my company. She taught me how to play the popular gambling game *paatiik*, as well as gin rummy and five hundred. She was an unconventional but enthusiastic Scrabble player, and when she quit her job, she spent many afternoons playing with a girlfriend. She helped me to learn to embroider and crochet, and we went to movies and bingo together often.

Considering the small size of the community, 586 people, with about fifty in Mina's age group, there were quite a few organized activities and classes available to help a young person keep busy. Mina participated in the home economics class organized by Adult Education personnel for school dropouts. But she had little interest in participating in church choir, the Anglican youth group, and various sports teams. She complained frequently of boredom and severe headaches. She was losing weight and afraid of developing active tuberculosis again, even though she continued to smoke cigarettes.

Mina's need for affection was strong and unsatisfied. Her husband's resentment of her dependence reinforced her generally negative self-image. I witnessed several brief arguments between them in their home and at the pool hall. The issue always seemed to be the conflict between his need for independence and her need for attention and companionship. She felt neglected; he felt restricted. She did not like liquor but was tempted to join him in drinking. The few times she did participate in drinking parties, however, quarrels and physical assaults resulted.

While Mina often spoke to me about difficulties with her husband and openly expressed fears that he might leave her, she never spoke about her children. She seemed to accept the adoption of her second baby by her in-laws without reservation or regret. Clearly, she had little attachment to the baby even though he lived in the same house. She said almost nothing about her deceased parents, but she often expressed unhappiness about being separated from her brother and his children.

Mina explained that she had quit her job because of her headaches and general poor health. A Euro-Canadian told me, however, that she had been fired because of erratic working habits and absenteeism. She held no other job while I was in the settlement.

I asked Mina to take a vocational interests inventory that I had been giving to school children to test some hypotheses about differences in male and female orientations. The test, a modified version of the Instrumental Activities Inventory developed by George and Louise Spindler,[14] involved sorting through twelve cards depicting jobs and domestic tasks being carried out by Inuit women (or by Inuit men, if the respondent is male). Mina chose "post office clerk" as her highest preference, but then changed her mind and said she preferred the "secretary" card. The only other card she chose in the free-choice situation was "housewife," showing a woman in a modern kitchen with two small children playing nearby. The nine cards she rejected included four traditional female roles, three modern roles (nurse, teacher, radio broadcaster), and two transitional occupations, store clerk and hospital cook.

Mina's choices on this quasi-projective test are similar to many of the seventy-six girls tested (all aged seventeen and under). Thirty-four percent chose as their highest preference a card in the modern category, 46 percent preferred the transitional category, and only 20 percent chose the contact-traditional category. In contrast, only 12 percent of the seventy-seven male subjects chose modern occupations, 68 percent transitional occupations, and 20 percent traditional occupations. In the unlimited choice situation (in which children could stack as many of the cards in their "like" pile as they wished), 32 percent of the boys chose contact-traditional roles, while only 21 percent of the girls included these cards.

The main pattern in girls' choices is that occupations were preferred over domestic roles. Only one girl tested chose the housewife card in the limited choice situation. The highest ranked occupations were store clerk, seamstress, cook, and secretary; the lowest ranking activities were traditional tasks such as animal-skin processor and "tentwife."

Boys also preferred wage employment, and highest ranked were store clerk, construction worker, and airplane mechanic. Traditional activities were intermediate: hunter ranked fourth, fisherman seventh, and carver eighth. Least preferred by the boys were modern professions: doctor, office clerk, and teacher.

The implication of these test results[15] is that young males and females in these communities have divergent orientations toward traditional Inuit roles. Hunting and fishing are still valued activities among boys; scraping fat off seal skins and making bread in a tent on a Coleman stove are not attractive activities for many girls. Further, while a number of girls can imagine themselves secretaries, nurses, or teachers, few boys aspire to male counterparts of these modern roles. Paralleling these test findings were differences in male and female employment patterns. More young women than young men were steadily employed in white-collar jobs. Considering the divergence in orientation, the high rate of marriage to southern Canadian men is not surprising. Schooling in the south, work as a secretary, teacher's aide, or interpreter, and then marriage to a teacher or administrator is the upward spiral pattern of more than a few Inuit women. This path was not open to Mina, with her limited schooling, record of drinking and open promiscuity, and poor health.

When I returned to Pangnirtung the following year, I was told that Mina and Jaco had moved back to Frobisher Bay. It was rumored that they had separated. When I saw Mina in Frobisher, she did not look well; her face was pale and she was thinner than I had ever seen her. She said things had gone badly for them that year, but they were living together again. Jaco was working on and off as a construction laborer, and she was not employed. They still did not have their own house and were living with her brother.

According to police records, Mina's husband had been arrested frequently that year. On one occasion, he was picked up shortly after midnight and charged with creating a disturbance in a public place. He was released the next afternoon and then arrested a few hours later for illegal possession of alcohol. Two weeks later, he was arrested two nights in a row, without charges pressed, for public intoxication. Four months later, he was arrested twice in three days, each time held overnight in protective custody and released the following day without charges.

Mina's sister-in-law followed a different pattern of drinking, with five arrests in six months: once in March, April, and June, and twice in July. She was sentenced to six days in jail in June for fighting and assault. Mina was not arrested at all during the six months covered by the data, and the community did not consider her a "problem drinker" in the way they regarded her husband and sister-in-law.

This pattern of frequent arrests, primarily for public drunkenness[16] in a "revolving door" process without effective treatment or legal action, was characteristic of many of the young people in Frobisher Bay. In a six-month period in 1971, 37 percent of all males and 20 percent of all females in the age group sixteen to twenty were arrested at least once for public intoxication and illegal possession of alcohol. Sixty-five percent (forty-three out of sixty-six individuals) of all males and 35 percent (fourteen out of forty) of all females in the age group twenty-one to twenty-five were arrested at least once. Ninety percent (twenty-six of twenty-nine) of the males and 96 (twenty-eight of twenty-nine) of the females in the age group twenty-six to thirty were arrested.[17] Thirty-seven percent of arrested females between the ages of sixteen and twenty-five were arrested more than once. The overall arrest frequency for individual females averaged two times in six months, with a range of one to seven times. Fifty-five percent of arrested males aged sixteen to twenty-five were arrested more than once, with an average of 2.5 arrests and a range of one to ten times.

Mina did not invite me to her house, and our conversation was brief. She seemed withdrawn and the easygoing relationship we had enjoyed in Pangnirtung no longer helped us find things to talk about. Mina was uncertain about future plans. They might return to Pangnirtung, but nothing was definite. It was hard to communicate with her; she displayed little interest in me, and she was reluctant to talk about herself. We ended up talking about the current movie in town. We finally said goodbye casually; I suspect with relief on both sides. It was the last time I encountered Mina.

Ooleepeeka's history exemplifies a pattern that many young Inuit women try to follow: schooling in the south, returning to the home settlement and finding a job, marriage (often to a Euro-Canadian who intends to remain in the North), and acceptance into Euro-Canadian society. At the same time, there is a retention of family ties, a reciprocity with kin, and a maintenance of identity as an Inuk. Ooleepeeka actually intensified her native identity through her activism. Thus, rather than assimilating to southern Canadian culture, Ooleepeeka's pattern is that of biculturation.[18]

Mina's history, personal characteristics, and life situation contrast sharply with Ooleepeeka. Her family migrated to Frobisher Bay when she was twelve, breaking off her ties with friends and relatives. The trauma of losing three mother figures and her father's suicide are reflected in her dependency on her husband and brother and her lack of involvement with her second child.

Mina's case illustrates a second pattern among young Inuit women, in which schooling has been sporadic, fracturing of the family through death and separation has occurred, and opportunities are blocked. Like Ooleepeeka, Mina is fluent in English, but with a grade five education she is not eligible for many jobs, and poor health and emotional instability have made it difficult for her to hold a job. She married late to a man who was still dependent on his parents and still involved in the young Inuit male pattern of heavy drinking and brawling, infrequent employment, and defiance of community norms through reckless behavior and daredevil feats of skill with snowmobiles, motorcycles, and motorboats. She finds this marriage unsatisfying, but she is reluctant to give it up. Despite the stress of her life, she does not abuse alcohol, but given her husband's and sister-in-law's patterns, she is at risk for alcoholism.

Although Mina was twenty-five years old, she was not at ease in an adult role and often expressed nostalgia for the "good times" of her adolescence —for the parties, dances, boyfriends, and freedom she had known. In many ways, there was still an adolescent quality in her preoccupation with games, records, movies, and clothes. Other than occasional jobs, Mina had few responsibilities. Considering that she had adopted out both infants, apparently she did not wish to be responsible for children, yet she was often extremely bored and frustrated with the emotional emptiness of her life. Without a stable parental figure to follow in her life, Mina seemed rootless and adrift, incapable of nurturing either an infant or herself.

Ooleepeeka's family has been remarkably stable in contrast to Mina's. It is clear that her father, who commands respect from both Euro-Canadians and Inuit and has maintained a balance between the old and new ways, has been a highly significant influence. He has been flexible in directing and advising his daughter, attempting to teach her respect for Inuktitut cultural elements, but also acknowledging the merits of opportunities in the Euro-Canadian system. The father opposed neither her advanced schooling in the south nor her marriage. The autonomy of Inuit women has always been relatively high in this traditionally hunting-gathering culture, and modernization has opened up more opportunities for women rather than shutting them out or oppressing them.[19]

Partly through favorable circumstances and flexible, supportive parental influence, and partly through her personal optimism and persistence, Ooleepeeka has adjusted well to modernization. She has developed certain traits, such as her manner of talking, which help Euro-Canadians to be at ease with her. Unlike many Inuit, especially older people, she is not emotionally insulated in dealing with Euro-Canadians, although she is capable of returning to the diffident, quiet style typical of her peers.

Ooleepeeka is able to talk about her feelings and problems and express hostility, almost an impossibility for most Inuit unless they are drunk or severely provoked. Her sense of anger is deflected, however, to abstract entities: the government, the school system, the economic and political forces that affect Inuit lives. Toward individual Euro-Canadians, she is tolerant, deferent, even nurturant. She believes it will be possible to rear her child in two cultural systems, and she depends on her mother to help in that rearing and to provide some of the continuity that she experienced in growing up. Her father also will provide a link with the past for the young child.

Emotionally, Mina was remarkably labile, changeable in mood. At times, she played the self-confident role that Ooleepeeka assumed easily—the talkative, warm, bubbly self-presentation that Inuit girls admired but were too shy and insulated to maintain. At other times, Mina was despondent, withdrawn, and sullen. Occasionally, she expressed negative, anxious feelings towards others and about herself, but more often the negativism was expressed in her frowns, hunched shoulders, and sensitive face that often seemed on the brink of tears.

Mina had little interest in participating in COPE or in Inuit Tapirisat, and she did not usually express negative ideas about the government or individual Euro-Canadians, although her resentment about the price of the parka was one exception. Her most positive attitudes were toward the pleasures and material goods that modernization and town living had brought. Her sense of cultural identity seemed amorphous rather than bicultural. She accepted her Inuit spouse and in-laws and she liked to embroider and gamble in the native style, but she also identified with movie stars, rock-and-roll groups, and other recreational aspects of North American culture. She preferred hamburgers and fries to seal meat. She found it difficult to hold down jobs but refused to contribute to the income of the household through crafts and piecework sewing. The pattern here is not one of strategic integration of old and new elements, as one sees in Ooleepeeka, but rather a mish-mash of impulses and reactions, without evidence of any plan or guiding rationale to Mina's choices.

The case studies of Ooleepeeka and Mina were chosen for this essay because they represent two contrasting orientations toward change. Ooleepeeka is responding with flexibility and emotional strength built upon a childhood of biculturation rather than assimilation. Ooleepeeka never expressed a sense of boredom. She carried out her incredibly busy life with relaxed energy. She could sit quietly with a friend and nurse her baby, and she could race around a baseball diamond. She interpreted with skill and patience; she was one of the best squaredancers in the village.

Ooleepeeka was both typical and prototypical of many Inuit women I met, but some were closer to Mina in attitude and behavior, individuals who were coping less well with culture change and were generally disaffected. It is possible that a person like Mina, weakened by tuberculosis and a number of parental losses, would be unhappy in any situation. Deprived of family continuity, adult responsibilities, and identification with a cohesive lifestyle, Mina truly fit the pattern of marginality that one often expects in a situation of rapid change. Time was an enemy to Mina, and she fought it by remaining adolescent and searching for entertainment and distraction. Without happy memories of the past, she could not expect a gratifying future, and without counseling or help from a parental figure, she is likely to continue drifting.

The Inuit of southern Baffin Island often use the word *uatshiaro*. It is not easily translated. Judging from many contexts, I would translate it as "time removed." The word refers both to the future and the distant past. It can also mean "in a little while" or "be patient, wait a bit, don't worry."

It is no accident that Inuit use a single term to express both the past and the future, as well as detachment from present concerns. This mindset is reflected in styles of adaptation and coping. Uatshiaro connotes continuity and cohesion. It provides a stable psychological base for many Inuit. Uatshiaro was a frequently used term in Ooleepeeka's home—the past, the future, patience, and optimism all linked together into a confidently positive adaptation to culture change. The pressures of change have been experienced by many generations now, but psychological continuity has also persisted to help individuals cope with these stressors. Among the many traits of Inuit, such as flexibility, patience, optimism, and selectivity, which have conduced to their adaptibility, the sense of timelessness is most critical. They have not lost the past, nor is the future an unknown, for Inuit feel a continuity between the generations and a strong link between past and future.

When one visits Frobisher Bay or Pangnirtung for the first time, it is difficult to see this continuity at first glance, and many visitors dismiss the Frobisher settlement as "not *real* Eskimos." One sees orderly rows of houses, children in sweatshirts and jeans, moviehouses, coffee shops, bingo games, and motorcycle riders. In many ways, this seems like any small Canadian town. But closer attention to small details reminds one that this is a distinctive culture—the sealskin frame or fish rack propped against a house, the muffled sputtering of snowmobiles or outboard motors at three in the morning, children playing hide-and-go-seek under the midnight sun in July, seven-year-old girls carrying siblings in amautit, young boys racing across rotten late-May ice floes to jig for fish, and old women sitting in early summer sunshine on lichen-covered rocks to sew a new canvas tent.

In a sense, the Inuit of southern Baffin Island have forgotten what the traditional culture was before contact with outsiders. The rapidity of change has been buffered by permeable cultural boundaries. Numerous British and Canadian traits were incorporated into the system in the early years of contact. If one suggests that any of these elements—the jigs and reels, the hymns and folk songs, the long cotton dresses, the mouth organs and hand-cranked sewing machines, were at one time Kadlunatitut, indignant or good-humored denials are invariably evoked. These elements represent the "old ways," adamantly claimed to be Inuktitut.

This process of incorporation continues, affirming the persistence and viability of a distinctive system of identity. The people of Pangnirtung organized their fishing and crafts cooperative in 1968. By 1971, they were identifying the cooperative system, as opposed to free enterprise, as Inukti-tut. The girls of Pangnirtung are not aware that the flowered, tassled boots they make and wear are of western Arctic origin. Inuit rock-and-roll bands gradually alter songs from popular recordings so much that the tunes are barely identifiable; these songs are considered Inuktitut. For most children, duffel parkas and rubber boots are "the old-time way," as are Coleman lanterns, wooden boats, telescopes, square dances, syllabic writing, bannock, tea, and many other traits.

In her *Culture and Commitment*,[20] Margaret Mead writes about traditional cultures: "contact with other peoples might not change this sense of time-lessness at all; the sense of difference reinforced the sense of one's own particular and ineradicable identity." Inuit parents emphasize a "sense of difference" to their children in a number of ways: partly by giving positive regard to their lifestyle, partly by making fun of the ways Euro-Canadians do things, and partly by categorizing as Inuktitut whatever Euro-Canadian elements they do like and wish to incorporate. All this buffers the impact of change. Mead further writes, "the perception of the new is rapidly engulfed by the style of the old . . . To destroy the memory of the past or preserve it in a form which merely reinforces the different present has been a continuous and highly functional adjustment by primitive peoples . . ."[21]

Through the life experiences of these two contemporary young women, we can see some of the factors underlying variation in response to modern-ization and change.[22] The differences between Ooleepeeka and Mina suggest that familial stability and continuity enable the individual to accept change and selectively modernize, thus increasing the chances of self-determination. Whether or not self-determination for the Inuit as a people becomes a reality depends as much on emotional resources for adaptation as it depends on political and economic decisions. We cannot leave psychological factors out of predictive analyses. Ooleepeeka and Mina will be grandmothers soon, and their pain, their triumphs, and their choices will form models for their children and their grandchildren. Inuit hold remarkable psychological resources, and despite criticisms and dire predictions of a "ruined culture," we can expect continued adaptation in future generations.

NOTES

1. The names of all people in these case studies have been changed, and certain identifying characteristics have been altered to safeguard their privacy.
2. For an account of this research see Ann McElroy, *Alternatives in Modernization: Styles and Strategies in the Acculturative Behavior of Baffin Island Inuit* (New Haven, Conn.: HRAFlex Books, ND 5–001 Ethnography Series, 1977).
3. See Ann McElroy, "The Politics of Inuit Alliance Movements in the Canadian Arctic," in ed. Ernest L. Schusky, *Political Organization of Native North Americans* (Washington, D.C.: University Press of America, 1980), pp. 243–82.
4. John J. Honigmann and Irma Honigmann, *Eskimo Townsmen* (Ottawa: Canadian Research Centre for Anthropology, University of St. Paul, 1965) and Nelson H. H. Graburn, *Eskimo Without Igloos* (Boston: Little, Brown, 1969) are excellent sources on this history.
5. Ann McElroy, "The Origins and Development of Inuit (Eskimo) Alliance Movements in the Eastern Arctic," in *Acts of the XL International Congress of Americanists* (Genoa) 2, pp. 603–11.
6. Franz Boas, *The Central Eskimo* (Lincoln, Neb.: University of Nebraska Press, 1964); and Asen Balikci, *The Netsilik Eskimo* (Garden City, N.Y.: The Natural History Press, 1970) are good ethnographic sources.
7. McElroy and Patricia K. Townsend, *Medical Anthropology in Ecological Perspective* (Boulder, Co.: Westview Press, 1985), pp. 16–28.
8. Richard Collinson, *The Three Voyages of Martin Frobisher* (New York: Burt Franklin, 1963).
9. William B. Kemp, "The Flow of Energy in a Hunting Society," *Scientific American* 225 no. 3, pp. 104–15.
10. Boas, *The Central Eskimo*, p. 17.
11. Minnie Aodla Freeman, *Life Among the Qallunaat* (Edmonton: Hurtig Publishers, 1978) is a highly recommended autobiography by an Inuit woman that describes the painful adjustment to life as a student in the South.
12. *The Eastern Arctic Star*, January 3, 1972, p.14.
13. See Honigmann and Honigmann, *Eskimo Townsmen*, for discussion of the Rehabilitation Centre in the Apex Hill neighborhood of Frobisher Bay.
14. George Spindler and Louise Spindler, "Researching the Perception of Cultural Alternatives: The Instrumental Activities Inventory" in ed. Melford E. Spiro, *Context and Meaning in Cultural Anthropology* (New York: The Free Press, 1965).
15. Ann McElroy, "The Assessment of Role Identity: Use of the Instrumental Activities Inventory in Studying Inuit Children," in ed. K. Ishwaran, *Childhood and Adolescence in Canada* (Toronto: McGraw-Hill Ryerson Ltd., 1979), pp. 54–71; Ann McElroy, "Canadian Arctic Modernization and Change in Female Inuit Role Identification," *American Ethnologist* 2 no. 4, pp. 662–86.

16. The majority of arrests of males under the age of twenty-five were for public intoxication (eighty-seven cases in six months), while most other offenses were violations of Euro-Canadian norms rather than injury to persons or property.

17. This high percentage is calculated on the basis of twenty-nine women in the age group twenty to thirty being listed in the government census. Women married to Euro-Canadians are not in the census; others may have been left out of the census. Eighty percent, or twenty-eight of thirty-five, would be a more realistic figure. It is important to remember that individuals who are arrested or detained are generally not stigmatized by their peers, and that the high figures represent the diligence of the police in preventing freezing deaths and road accidents of intoxicated people rather than alcoholism problems per se.

18. The notion of biculturation is taken from Steven Polgar, "Biculturation of Mesquakie Teenage Boys," *American Anthropologist* 62, pp. 217–35.

19. Ann McElroy, "The Negotiation of Sex-Role Identity in Eastern Arctic Culture Change," in eds. Ann McElroy and Carolyn J. Matthiasson, *Sex Roles in Changing Cultures, Occasional Papers* 1, State University of New York—Buffalo, 1979, pp. 49–60.

20. Margaret Mead, *Culture and Commitment* (Garden City, N.Y.: Natural History Press, 1970), p. 2.

21. Mead, *Culture and Commitment.*, pp. 16–17.

22. Also see George Spindler and Louise Spindler, "Male and Female Adaptations in Culture Change," *American Anthropologist* 60, pp. 217–33, and Norman A. Chance, "Acculturation, Self-Identification, and Personality Adjustment," *American Anthropologist* 67, pp. 372–93.

Gary C. Anderson is with the Department of History, Texas A&M University. He is a specialist in the ethnohistory of the Northern Plains, and is known for his books: *Kinsmen of Another Kind: Dakota-White Relations in the Upper Mississippi Valley, 1650–1862*; and, *Little Crow, Spokesman for the Sioux*.

Mary Black-Rogers is with the Royal Ontario Museum in Toronto. She is known for numerous studies of belief and value systems in the field of cognitive anthropology, focusing on Great Lakes Algonquians, particularly Northern and Southwestern Ojibwa. Her recent essays include: "Ojibwa Power Belief System," "Ojibwa Power Interactions: Creating Contexts for 'Respectful Talk,' " and "Ojibwa Taxonomy and Percept Ambiguity."

Jennifer S. H. Brown is in the Department of History, University of Winnipeg. She is known for research and writing on the northern fur trade and its involvements with native peoples and Métis, and other works concerning Northern Algonquian ethnohistory. Among her many writings are: *Strangers in Blood: Fur Trade and Company Families in Indian Country* and *The New Peoples: Being and Becoming Metis in North America* (co-edited with Jacqueline Peterson).

Geoffrey E. Buerger is with the Department of History, Rutgers University. He is working on a full-scale scholarly biography of Eleazer Williams and a historical monograph on the Deerfield massacre of 1704.

Colin C. Calloway is with the Department of History, University of Wyoming. He is particularly interested in British-Indian relations and frontier American renegades, and he is known for numerous essays and his book, *Crown and Calumet: British-Indian Relations, 1783–1815*.

Jerry E. Clark is an anthropologist and **Martha E. Webb** is an historian at Creighton University. Webb is a specialist in the history of science and medicine, while Clark is known for work on American Indian ethnohistory, particularly his book, *The Shawnee*, and essays on Potawatomi acculturation and Shawnee migration.

James A. Clifton an ethnohistorian and psychological anthropologist, is Scholar-In-Residence in Anthropology, Western Michigan University. His books include *The Prairie People, The Pokagons, A Place of Refuge for all Time*, and *The Invented Indian: Cultural Fictions and Government Policies*.

Thomas H. Johnson is at the University of Wisconsin—Stevens Point. He is an anthropologist-ethnohistorian, with special interests in medical anthropology and Indian health problems. Author of several essays concerning the

Wind River Shoshone, he is presently working on a book, *The Enos Family and Wind River Shoshone Society.*

Ann McElroy is with the Department of Anthropology, State University of New York, Buffalo. She is a specialist in psychological and medical anthropology, particularly maternal and child care, and has extensive field research experience in arctic Canada and among migrant workers. She is known for her *Alternatives in Modernization: Styles and Strategies in the Acculturative Behavior of Baffin Island Inuit, Sex Roles in Changing Cultures* (with Carolyn J. Matthiasson), *Medical Anthropology in Ecological Perspective* (with Patricia K. Townsend), and for many specialized essays and monographs.

James M. McClurken is with The Museum, Michigan State University. He is an anthropologically trained ethnohistorian, with special interests in Great Lakes area peoples, particularly social and economic adaptations to changing environments. He has participated in several Indian Treaty Rights federal court cases, is at work on a book, *We Wish to Be Civilized: Ottawa-American Political Contests on the Michigan Frontier,* and he has published several essays on these topics.

Jay Miller is an anthropologist associated with the Newberry Library and the University of Washington. He is known for his research among the Pueblo, Delaware, Salish, Tshimshian, and Numic peoples. He has published *The Tshimshian and Their Neighbors of the Northwest Coast* (with Carol Eastman), and numerous essays.

Donald B. Smith is with the Department of History, University of Calgary. He is a specialist in the history of relations between Indians and Anglo- and French Canadians. He is known for his books: *"Le Sauvage:" The Native People in Quebec, Long Lance: The True Story of an Impostor, "Sacred Feathers:" The Life of Kahkequonaby, or the Reverend Peter Jones,* and many biographical and historical essays.

Robert J. Stahl is with the Department of Anthropology, Northern State College, Aberdeen, South Dakota. His research has concerned the nineteenth- and twentieth-century Kiowa, the Native American Church, particularly among the Sioux, and American efforts to suppress this new religion. He is author of several essays reporting on his research.

Selected Bibliography

Erwin H. Ackernecht
1944. White Indians. *Bulletin of the History of Medicine* 15: 18–35.

Kevin Avruch
1987. The Emergence of Ethnicity in Israel: A Review Essay. *American Ethnologist* 14: 327–339.

James Axtell
1985. *The Invasion Within: The Contest of Cultures in Colonial North America.* New York: Oxford University Press.

E. Y. Babad, M. Birnbaum, and K. D. Benne
1983. *The Social Self: Group Influences on Personal Identity.* Beverley Hills, California: Sage Library of Social Research, vol. 144.

Homer G. Barnett
1941. Personal Conflicts and Cultural Change. *Social Forces* 20: 164–67.

Homer G. Barnett et al.
1954. Acculturation: An Exploratory Formulation. *American Anthropologist* 56: 972–1002.

F. Barth, ed.
1969. *Ethnic Groups and Boundaries: The Social Organization of Culture Difference.* London: Allen & Unwin.

Ralph W. Beals
1982. Fifty Years of Anthropology. In, B. J. Siegal, A. R. Beals, and S. T. Tyler, eds., *Annual Review of Anthropology,* vol. 11. Palo Alto, California: Annual Reviews, Inc.

Gerald Berreman
1981. *Social Inequality: Comparative and Developmental Approaches.* New York: Academic Press.

Brewton Berry
1963. *Almost White.* New York: Macmillan.

Phillip Bock
1988. *Rethinking Psychological Anthropology.* New York: W. H. Freeman.

David G. Bromley and James T. Richardson
1983. *The Brainwashing/Deprogramming Controversy: Sociological, Psychological, Legal and Historical Perspectives.* New York: Edward Mellen Press.

Edward M. Bruner
1957. Differential Culture Change: Report on the Interuniversity Summer Research Seminar, 1956. Items, Social Science Research Council, vol. 2, no. 1.

James A. Clifton
1975. Culture, Identity, and the Individual. In, P. Whitten and D. Hunter, eds., *The Study of Anthropology.* New York: Harper & Row.
1978a. Merchant, Soldier, Broker, Chief: A Corrected Obituary of Captain Billy Caldwell. *Journal of the Illinois State Historical Society* 71: 185–210.

1978b. Personal and Ethnic Identity on the Great Lakes Frontier: The Case of Billy Caldwell, Anglo-Canadian. *Ethnohistory* 78: 69–94.

1985. Leopold Pokagon: Transformational Leadership on the St. Joseph River Frontier. *Michigan History* 69: 16–23.

1987. Simon Pokagon's Sandbar. *Michigan History* 71: 12–17.

Abner Cohen
1969. *Custom and Politics in Urban Africa: A Study of Hausa Migrants in Yoruba Towns.* Berkeley: University of California Press.

1974. *Two-Dimensional Man: An Essay on the Anthropology of Power and Symbolism in Complex Society.* Berkeley: University of California Press.

Abner Cohen, ed.
1974. *Urban Ethnicity.* New York: Harper & Row.

Ronald Cohen
1978. Ethnicity: Problem and Focus in Anthropology. In, B. J. Siegal, A. R. Beals, and S. A. Tyler, eds., *Annual Review of Anthropology,* vol. 7. Palo Alto, California, Annual Reviews, Inc.

Elizabeth Colson
1968. Contemporary Tribes and the Development of Nationalism. In, June Helm, *Essays on the Problems of the Tribe.* pp. 201–206. Seattle: University of Washington Press.

Stephen E. Cornell
1988. *The Return of the Native: Native American Political Resurgence.* New York: Oxford University Press.

Vincent Crapazano
1984. Life-Histories: A Review Essay. *American Anthropologist* 86: 953–65.

Charles Crowe
1975. Indians and Blacks in White America. In, Charles M. Hudson, ed., *Four Centuries of Southern Indians,* pp. 148–170. Athens: University of Georgia Press.

Leo A. Despres
1975. *Ethnicity and Resource Competition in Plural Societies.* The Haugue: Mouton.

Geore De Vos and L. Romanucci-Eoss, eds.
1982. *Ethnic Identity, Cultural Continuities and Change.* Chicago: University of Chicago Press.

Virginia R. Dominguez
1986a. *White by Classification: Social Classification in Creole Louisiana.* New Brunswick: Rutgers University Press.

1986b. The Marketing of Heritage. *American Ethnologist* 13: 546–55.

Edward P. Dozier, G. E. Simpson, and J. M. Yinger
1957. The Integration of Americans of Indian Descent. *Annals of the American Academy of Political and Social Science* 311: 158–65.

Erik H. Erikson
1959. *Identity and the Life Cycle.* New York: International Universities Press.

1968. *Identity, Youth, and Crises.* New York: W. W. Norton.

1974. *Dimensions of a New Identity.* New York: W. W. Norton.

1975. *Life History and the Historical Moment.* New York: W. W. Norton.

John C. Ewers
  1962. Mothers of the Mixed-Bloods: The Marginal Woman in the History of the Upper Missouri. In, Ross Toole et al., eds., *Probing the American West. Papers from the Santa Fe Conference,* pp. 62–70. Santa Fe: Museum of New Mexico Press.

Stephen E. Feraca
  1987. *Why Don't They Give Them Guns: The Great American Indian Myth.* Unpublished manuscript.

Thomas K. Fitzgerald, ed.
  1974. Social and Cultural Identity: Problems of Persistence and Change. *Southern Anthropological Society Proceedings,* no. 8. Athens: University of Georgia Press.

Judith Friedlander
  1975. *Being Indian in Hueyapan: A Study of Forced Identity in Contemporary Mexico.* New York: St. Martin's Press.

Clifford Geertz
  1973. *The Interpretation of Cultures.* New York: Basic Books.
  1986. Making Experience: Authoring Selves. In, V. Turner and E.M. Bruner, eds., *The Anthropology of Experience,* pp. 373–80. Champaign: University of Illinois Press.

Erving Goffman
  1963. *Stigma: Notes on the Management of Spoiled Identity.* Englewood Cliffs, N.J.: Prentice-Hall.

Milton M. Goldberg
  1941. A Qualification of the Marginal Man Theory. *American Sociological Review* 6: 52–58.

Ward Goodenough
  1965. Rethinking Status and Role: Toward a General Model of the Cultural Organization of Social Relationships. In, M. Banton, ed., *The Relevance of Models for Social Anthropology.* New York: Praeger.

Arnold W. Green
  1947. A Re-examination of the Marginal Man Concept. *Social Forces* 26: 167–71.

Michael Green
  1987. *The Enigmatic Mary Muskgrove.* Paper read at the Annual Meetings of the Western History Association.

Gunnar Haaland
  1969. Economic Determinants in Ethnic Processes. In, F. Barth, ed., *Ethnic Group Boundaries: The Social Organization of Culture Difference,* pp. 53–73. London: Allen & Unwin.

Thomas Hagan
  1986. Full Blood, Mixed Blood, Generic, and Ersatz, the Persisting Problem of Indian Identity. *Arizona and the West* (Winter), 309–26.

A. I. Hallowell
  1963. American Indians, White and Black: The Phenomenon of Transculturation. *Current Anthropology* 4: 519–31.

J. Norman Heard
  1973. *White into Red: A Study of the Assimilation of White Persons Captured by Indians.* Mectochen, N.J.

June Helm, ed.
   1968. *Essays on the Problem of Tribe. Proceedings of the 1967 Annual Spring Meeting of the American Ethnological Society.* Seattle: University of Washington Press.

George L. Hicks and P. E. Leiss, eds.
   1977. *Ethnic Encounters: Identities and Contexts.* Duxbury Press.

Eric Hobsbawm and Terrence Ranger
   1983. *The Invention of Tradition.* Cambridge: Cambridge University Press.

John J. Honigman
   1976. *The Development of Anthropological Ideas.* Chicago: Dorsey Press.

Hugh Honour
   1975. *The New Golden Land: European Images of America From the Discovery to the Present Time.* New York: Pantheon Books.

George E. Hyde, ed.
   1983. *The Life of George Bent Written from His Letters.* Norman: University of Oklahoma Press.

Alan C. Kerckhoff and T. C. McCormick
   1955. Marginal Status and Marginal Personality. *Social Forces* 34: 48–55.

Charles F. Keyes, ed.
   1977. *Ethnic Change: Papers from a Seminar.* Seattle: University of Washington Press.

Arden R. King
   1974. A Stratification of Labyrinths: The Acquisition and Retention of Cultural Identity in Modern Culture. In, T. K. Fitzgerald, ed., *Social and Cultural Identity: Problems of Persistence and Change,* pp. 106–117. Athens: University of Georgia Press.

Arnold Krupat
   1983. The Indian Autobiography: Origins, Type, and Function. In, Brian Swann, ed., *Smoothing the Ground: Essays on Native American Oral Literature.* Berkeley: University of California Press.

L. L. Langness
   1965. *The Life History in Anthropological Science.* New York: Holt, Rinehart & Winston.

L. L. Langness and G. Frank
   1981. *Lives: An Anthropological Approach to Biography.* Novato, California: Chandler and Sharp.

Claude Levi-Strauss
   1962. *The Savage Mind.* Chicago: University of Chicago Press.

Margot Liberty, ed.
   1978. *American Indian Intellectuals.* St. Paul, Minnesota: West Publishing.

Robert Jay Lifton
   1961. *History and Human Survival.* New York: Random House.

Jocelyn S. Linnekin
   1983. Defining Tradition: Variations on the Hawaiian Identity. *American Ethnologist* 10: 241–52.

Ralph Linton, ed.
   1940. *Acculturation in Seven American Indian Tribes.* New York: Appleton-Century-Crofts.

Nancy O. Lurie
1971 (reissued 1988). The Contemporary Indian Scene. In, Eleanor B. Leacock and Nancy O. Lurie, eds., *North American Indians in Historical Perspective*, pp. 418–80. Prospect Heights, IL: Waveland Press.

Malcolm McFee
1968. The 150% Man: A Product of Blackfoot Acculturation. *American Anthropologist* 70: 1096–1107.

William H. McNeill
1985. *Polyethnicity and National Unity in World History.* Toronto: University of Toronto Press.

L. G. Moses and Raymond Wilson, eds.
1985. *Indian Lives: Essays on Nineteenth- and Twentieth-Century Native American Leaders.* Albuquerque: University of New Mexico Press.

Margarita B. Melville
1983. Ethnicity: An Analysis of its Dynamism and Variability Focusing on the Mexican/Anglo/Mexican American Interface. *American Ethnologist* 10: 272–89.

Robert F. Murphy
1964. Social Change and Acculturation. *Transactions of the New York Academy of Sciences,* ser. 2, vol. 26: 845–54.

Joane Nagel and Susan Olzak
1982. Ethnic Mobilization in Old and New States: An Extension of the Competition Model. *Social Problems* 30: 127–43.

Jay O'Brien
1986. Toward a Reconstitution of Ethnicity: Capitalist Expansion and Cultural Dynamics in Sudan. *American Anthropologist* 88: 898–907.

J. Anthony Parades
1974. The Emergence of Contemporary Eastern Creek Indian Identity. In, T.K. Fitzgerald, ed., *Social and Cultural Identity: Problems of Persistence and Change,* pp. 63–79. Athens: University of Georgia Press.

Robert E. Park
1967. Human Migration and the Marginal Man. In, Robert E. Park, *On Social Control and Collective Behavior.* Selected Papers. Ralph H. Turner, ed., pp. 194–206. Chicago: University of Chicago Press.

Jacqueline Peterson and Jennifer Brown, eds.
1984. *The New Peoples: Being and Becoming Metis in North America.* Lincoln: University of Nebraska Press.

Steven Polgar
1960. Biculturation of Mesquakie Teenage Boys. *American Anthropologist* 62: 217–235.

Frank W. Porter III, ed.
1986. *Strategies for Survival, American Indians in the Eastern United States.* Westport, Connecticut: Greenwood Press.

Anna P. Royce
1982. The Phenomenom of Ethnicity. *Science* 216: 48–49.

William McK. Runyan
  1982. *Life Histories and Psychobiography: Explorations in Theory and Method*. New York: Oxford University Press.

William J. Scheick
  1979. *The Half-Blood: A Cultural Symbol in 19th-Century American Fiction*. Lexington: University Press of Kentucky.

R. A. Schermerhorn
  1970. *Comparative Ethnic Relations*. New York: Random House.

H. L. Shapiro
  1942. The Mixed-Blood Indian. In, Oliver LaFarge, ed., *The Changing Indian*, pp. 19–27. Norman: University of Oklahoma Press.

Tamotsu Shibutani and K. M. Kwan
  1965. *Ethnic Stratification: A Comparative Approach*. London: MacMillan.

Donald B. Smith
  1971. Grey Owl. *Ontario History* 63: 161–176.
  1987. *Sacred Feathers: The Story of the Rev. Peter Jones (Kahkewaquonby) and the Mississauga Indians*. Lincoln: University of Nebraska Press.

M.G. Smith
  1983. Ethnicity and Sociobiology: A Review Essay. *American Ethnologist* 10: 364–67.

Edward H. Spicer, ed.
  1961. *Perspectives in American Indian Culture Change*. Chicago: University of Chicago Press.

Edward H. Spicer
  1971. Persistent Cultural Systems. *Science* 174: 795–800.

Melford E. Spiro
  1955. The Acculturation of American Ethnic Groups. *American Anthropologist* 57: 1240–1252.

Everett V. Stonequist
  1961. *The Marginal Man*. New York: Russell & Russell.

John R. Swanton
  1926. Notes on the Mental Assimilation of Races. *Journal of the Washington Academy of Sciences* 16: 493–502.

Ronald L. Trosper
  1981. American Indian Nationalism and Frontier Expansion. In, Keyes 1981, pp. 246–71.

Richard W. Trottier
  1981. Charters of Panethnic Identity: Indigenous American Indians and Immigrant Asian Americans. In, Keyes 1981, pp. 271–305.

Victor Turner and Edward M. Bruner, eds.
  1986. *The Anthropology of Experience*. Champaign: University of Illinois Press.

Lawrence C. Watson and M. B. Watson-Franke
  1985. *Interpreting Life Histories: An Anthropological Inquiry*. Rutgers University Press.

Anne Wortham
    1981. *The Other Side of Racism: A Philosophical Study of Black Race Consciousness.*
    Columbus: Ohio State University Press.

C. Young
    1976. *The Politics of Cultural Pluralism.* Madison: University of Wisconsin Press.

Index